HOOKED

ALSO BY LONNY SHAVELSON

A Chosen Death: The Dying Confront Assisted Suicide

Toxic Nation: The Fight to Save Our Communities from Chemical Contamination
(co-authored with Fred Setterberg)

I'm Not Crazy, I Just Lost My Glasses

Personal Ad Portraits

HOOKED

FIVE ADDICTS CHALLENGE OUR
MISGUIDED DRUG REHAB SYSTEM

LONNY SHAVELSON

 THE NEW PRESS, NEW YORK

Published in the United States by The New Press, New York, 2001
Distributed by W. W. Norton & Company, Inc., New York

"Down, Down, Down" written by Tom Waits.
Used by permission of Jalma Music. All rights reserved.

LIBRARY OF CONGRESS CATALOGING-IN-PUBLICATION DATA
Shavelson, Lonny.
    Hooked : Five addicts challenge our misguided drug rehab system / Lonny Shavelson.
        p. cm.
    ISBN 1-56584-684-2 (hc.)
    1. Narcotic addicts—rehabilitation—California—San Francisco—Case studies.   2. Narcotic addicts—
California—San Francisco—Biography.   3. Drug abuse—California—San Francisco—Case studies.   I. Title.
HV5833.S25 S53 2001
362.29'38'092279461—dc21
[B]   00–067556

The New Press was established in 1990 as a not-for-profit alternative to the large, commercial publishing
houses currently dominating the book publishing industry. The New Press operates in the public interest rather
than for private gain, and is committed to publishing, in innovative ways, works of educational, cultural, and
community value that are often deemed insufficiently profitable.

The New Press, 450 West 41st Street, 6th floor, New York, NY 10036
www.thenewpress.com

Printed in the United States of America

10 9 8 7 6 5 4 3 2 1

CONTENTS

ACKNOWLEDGMENTS

With my most heartfelt appreciation to Michael and Connie Pagsolingan, Darlene James, Darrell McAuley, and Crystal Holmes, who opened their lives to me and remain forever as friends. And in fond memory of Glenda Janis.

Warmest thanks to Fred Setterberg, who somehow manages to juggle being mentor, colleague, and close friend, all at the same time. And to Kim, for everything. My gratitude to those whose comments, editing, and support were crucial to the book's completion: Lisa Aliferis, Pete Bancroft, Deborah Bickel, Amy Espie, Susan Leibowitz, and Ann Van Steenberg.

This book could not have been written if so many people in the world of drug rehab had not willingly opened their doors to my prying. Their desire to explore and examine their work is what will make drug treatment the powerful tool that it can become. Cynthia Caporizzo, Colin Eaton, Jenna Glasscock, Fred Ponomarenko, Haroldo Torres, Jamie Tillotson, Judge Newton Lam, Judge Julie Tang, Ron Thomas, and the entire Drug Court team allowed me virtually unlimited access to their deliberations, and I thank them for being my teachers. At Target Cities, Tom Hagan and Wendy Goldberg provided remarkable access and insight, and Marillac Mayorga invited me to participate in the most difficult moments she shared with her clients. Tony Patchell and the Death Prevention Team showed me the streets, and kept me in awe of their work. At San Francisco's Department of Health Services, Dr. Larry Meredith opened the first doors for me, and Barbara Garcia and Eileen Shields kept them open for the duration. At the Haight Ashbury Free Clinic, Dr. Pablo Stewart and Suzi Kaplan provided never-ending insight. Outsiders had advised me I'd never get in the door to see the inside story at Walden House, a prediction proved entirely wrong when Debby Caruso, Dolores Alvarez, Sylvester Palmer, and the entire staff at 890 hayes welcomed me to The Family and placed virtually no restrictions on my work. For all of the structural and bureaucratic difficulties I found at Walden House, no individual working there showed anything but the strongest desire to help addicts improve their lives.

Finally, my sincere gratitude for their hard work and talents to my literary agent, Felicia Eth, and my editors at The New Press, Diane Wachtell and Lucas Smith.

PART I: TREATMENT ON DEMAND

MIKE, DARLENE, AND DARRELL

INTRODUCTION TO PART I: FROM CRAZINESS TO HOPE

MICHAEL PAGSOLINGAN, DRUG REHAB MORNING WALK FEBRUARY 1998

Thursday, August 29, 1996   Highway 101

Michael Pagsolingan barely notices the brilliant red sunset over the ocean as he barrels down Highway 101 heading south from San Francisco in his Dodge Ram pickup. But his intense cramps and profuse sweating from heroin withdrawal distract him from the pleasures of the drive. Easy to fix, he thinks, and reaches under the seat to pull out a packet of heroin.

Gripping the steering wheel in his left hand, Mike teases the packet open with his right and pours the white powder into a thin metal ashtray on the coffee-cup console he'd installed on the seat beside him. He flicks open his Zippo lighter and melts the heroin so he can suck it into his syringe.

He glances at the truck's side mirrors, checking more for the black-and-white of a police car than for traffic. Sliding into the slow lane, Mike eases his foot off the accelerator and watches the speedometer drop from seventy to fifty. He stretches his left arm out rigidly, clenching the steering wheel so tightly in his fist that the veins in his forearm swell like wiry bruises.

He tilts back, raising his legs off the seat to steer the pickup with his knees. Then he lets go of the steering wheel, tucks his arms across his chest, and skillfully drives the needle into a dusky blue vein in the flesh of his left arm. Mike wedges his knees even tighter against the steering wheel, looks down to check for the rush of blood into the syringe, then jams his thumb on the plunger to propel the thin brown liquid toward his brain.

His cramps ease immediately; he's used a good, strong dose. Then he blacks out.

The booming crash of grinding metal jolts Mike awake as his truck careens off the back of a Volvo, slams into a Toyota pickup alongside him, and then catapults through the exit railing and into a ditch. Emerging from his heroin haze at the edge of the freeway beside his totaled pickup, Mike discovers that he and the other two drivers are, miraculously, unharmed.

That was a stroke of luck, he thinks, leaning against his destroyed pickup, still basking in the warm glow from the drug.

And so, pushing his luck, Mike continues to shoot up with heroin. He lies to his girlfriend about being clean, steals from his father to buy dope, gets spotted with a needle in his arm by his young daughter, and generally does as much as possible to destroy his own life and those of everyone he comes in contact with.

"What was different about that day?" I ask when I meet Mike a year later. "What made you so desperate to get high that you didn't even pull the car over first."

He stares, as if not understanding the question.

"Different?" he says. "Nah, man, that was like a regular day. You know, the usual after-work kind of deal. Only thing different was maybe I used a little more dope, and I drank like a forty-ouncer of Olde English malt right before I hit the freeway. And did a little cocaine to balance that out. Oh, yeah, wait a minute! I had took three Klonopins, downer pills, just before the beer."

Mike pauses for a moment. "Hey, maybe you got something there," he continues, puzzling out his discovery. "It *was* a kind of different day. I usually don't do Klonopins if I'm going to shoot up with heroin on the freeway."

Saturday, January 17, 1998   Walden House

Mike adjusts his necktie and laughs at his transition from dope fiend to upright citizen as we cross the street from Walden House, his residential drug treatment program, to get a cup of coffee at the nearby Fillmore Grind. I'm three steps into the intersection, walking against the red light, when I realize he's no longer at my side. I turn and see Mike's six-foot-three frame gingerly balancing at the curb, his wide-eyed gaze darting in panic from me to the still-red signal light. I scamper back to the sidewalk.

"Look at me!" he exclaims, laughing and offering up a mock bow while still scratching at his needle-scarred arms. "I won't even jaywalk no more!"

The light changes to green and we hit the intersection, Mike chattering away about his progress in the program.

"Know what I've become?" he asks, jumping to the curb on the other side and turning to face me. "A rehab junkie! I'm a clinical monster!"

After twenty years of heroin and cocaine addiction, Mike's laugh, jaunty step, and ability to simply *talk* coherently beat down my cynical and intense pessimism about the power of a rehab program to turn his life around. If obeying a red light while crossing the street a block from his rehab program means Mike won't be shooting dope while driving after he graduates, then fear of jaywalking may be as good a measure of the benefits of drug rehab as any.

Or maybe Mike is just walking in lockstep to the rules of the program, nothing more than a period of temporary sanity that will rapidly fade away when he's back on the streets.

Over the next months, Mike remains a resolute rehab junkie. "I spotted Kevin selling crack outside the house," he proclaims at a house meeting, rat-finking on one of his 120 program Brothers and Sisters in the house at Walden. "And I own up to taking my own coffee permissions, and some snack permissions I shouldn't've done."

"Snack permissions?" I ask after the meeting.

"Yeah," says Mike seriously, confessing his sin. "I ate jelly beans in my room."

Six months later, Mike graduates with flying colors from the inpatient rehab program, moving from the watchful eyes of Walden House out to a Walden-supervised satellite apartment.

Friday, July 31, 1998   Walden, satellite housing

Mike throws himself onto the narrow bed in his first-floor room in the humble apartment above the noisy bus stop on Fillmore. Friday afternoon, three o'clock, he's left his plumbing job early, his back aching from a long week's work—a flare-up from disk surgery years ago, to which he attributes his initial addiction to heroin. The weekend looms like a hot desert waiting to be crossed. He'd been warned of the loneliness that hits after months in the mansionlike communal house of 120 recovering addicts, where his time had been absorbed by group meetings, shared meals, the trumpeting of past war stories and blustering forth of future hopes.

Alone now, he stares at the snapshots of his nine- and thirteen-year-old daughters pinned on the corkboard by his bedside. A knifelike desire to see them pains him more sharply than the taut muscles in his back. He imagines them hugging him, welcoming him home, but he knows that even months of rehab haven't yet earned him that trust. "One day at a time," he recites the mantra of recovery in his head. One . . . fucking . . . day . . . at a time.

Sinking back into the bed, he punches a button on the boom box on top of his bookcase and the gravelly voice of Tom Waits rumbles into the room.

he went down down down,
this boy went solid down

If only he could ease the anxious tension in his muscles, that gnawing pain in his back might ease up. And maybe his tormented loneliness with it.

The room faces west and at four o'clock the sun gains a rare victory over San Francisco's summer fog. But the bright sunlight flooding in irritates Mike's restless mind more than the heat soothes his tense body.

With the rumble of the bus below the window, he's up, out of the house, and scrunched down low into a seat rolling toward the Mission district when he spots Patricia striding toward Walden for the evening meeting. As she runs up the stairs, he sees the familiar slogan on the back of her T-shirt: "Walden House: There's No Hope In Dope."

"Shit," Mike mumbles to himself, sitting up again as the bus passes out of sight of the house, "if you got no hope, using dope is *not* the problem."

At 16th and Mission he swings down the steps and hits the pavement, spots his dealer across the street, and whistles softly, holding one finger in the air. "One bag, I need one, need one." Mike watches the man's eyes glance to the four street corners and then down the block. No cops. Then the dealer's head bobs rapidly, his own finger in the air. "Got one for you, get over here, move it man, got one for you."

"So I'm standing there by the BART station," Mike tells me later. "And it's clear to cross if I want to, and my guy's like, 'Come on, man!' And I'm not crossing! The fucking light's red and I will not jaywalk! Not even to score dope!" Mike is doubled over, giggling, remembering that day of his first relapse, the start of an extended, perilous dope run.

"The point is," he says seriously, bringing to his voice the characteristic street style of lilting emphasis and repetition. "The *point* is, that I was out there doing dope again. But I wasn't *me* no more. The fucking rehab program was in my head even when I was out scoring a fix! I can't hear the dope calling no more without rehab whispering right next to it."

From Warfare to Rehab

"Effective treatment," boasted federal drug czar General Barry McCaffrey to the U.S. Congress, "can end addiction." This pronouncement stood in stark contrast to our government's obsession with packing jails with junkies and lofting drug agents in armed helicopters over South American cocaine fields. Our nation's drug policy goals, announced McCaffrey, who heads the Office of National Drug Control Policy, "can only be accomplished with a significant expansion of capacity to treat the nation's drug users."

Nurtured along by this four-star general, the federal government has been bestowing upon drug rehab counselors near Boston crack houses a drug-battle status previously reserved for armed narcotics agents. This shifting battle plan toward rehab has been so surprising that the *New York Times* exclaimed in a front-page special report that "drug policy is taking another turn. Treatment is making a comeback."

But our national leaders are premature in their bold proclamations of victory by treating addicts. There remains a crucial question: Does treatment work?

I started researching this book wanting to believe that drug rehab can succeed. Yet with so many addicts heading from the streets to rehab, then back to the streets and drugs again, my declaration of hopefulness seemed foolish at best.

It was September of 1997 and San Francisco was embarking on a new era of "Treatment on Demand"—defined as "appropriate treatment within forty-eight hours for all addicts who say they're ready to kick drugs."

San Francisco was not alone in this new battle plan against the drug menace, a national shift in focus from arrests to rehab, trench warfare to treatment. Cities in Massachusetts, Arizona, New York, Maryland, and the federal anti-drug armada itself had been hyping drug treatment as their new combat strategy. General McCaffrey, the craftsman of the renowned and aggressive "left-hook" maneuver in the Gulf War, became our nation's drug czar in 1996—and has since slowly but surely drifted toward treatment. "The damage America may suffer if we provide inadequate drug treatment," he declared on September 1, 1998, "is a national tragedy."

If this rush to rehab is indeed going to ease our nation away from the disasters of addictions, we must first determine if treatment does indeed keep addicts off drugs. If, as the data seem to show, treatment programs don't actually keep junkies clean, this new push for rehab will simply become another dogma-based government strategy doomed to failure.

Rehab has to work for the hardest-core of the dope fiends—those who create the vast majority of troubles we've artificially lumped into a single set phrase: *the drug problem.* The U.S. Department of Justice has concluded that only a small percentage of the nation's drug abusers create "an extraordinary proportion of crime." Yet those most destructive addicts are the least likely to enter or be helped by rehab. This latest push toward treatment, then, may do no more than get the "better" addicts off drugs, leaving the hard-core troublemakers still disastrously addicted.

From 1979 to 1998, the number of drug users in the United States declined by 45 percent. But the percentage of robberies, murder, and mayhem attributable to drugs has spiraled incessantly upward (even as crime, in general, has declined). We are a nation of fewer drug addicts, yet our drug problem is accelerating. The relatively well-behaved addicts have sought or been brought to sobriety, while those who do the most harm have remained addicted, and destructive.

Those hard-core addicts (10 to 20 percent of users) have, depending on your point of view, either brought on the drug war, or are the tragic casualties of its battles. But if their frenzied addictions are indeed responses to lives often complicated by irresolute ghetto-poverty or psychological disturbances, then rehab programs that fail to address these underlying conditions will barely make a dent in our nation's drug disasters. That is why, when San Francisco initiated its new and idealistic Treatment on Demand policy, the newsletter of the rehab industry, *Alcoholism and Drug Abuse Weekly,* reported with less than unmitigated confidence, "The rest of the nation is now watching with a combination of envy and skepticism as San Francisco tries to become the national model for accessible . . . substance abuse treatment."

While Mike blamed his heroin addiction on the pain of prior back surgery, his counselors at Walden's rehab program knew that for him finally to kick drugs he'd have to delve deeper and confront a self-image of desperation and failure etched by years of foster care, child molestation, youth-authority incarceration, thieving, violence, and prison terms. Facing such a daunting history, how could any rehab program take Mike in at age thirty-seven and spit him out six months later with more than a reflexive phobia against jaywalking that kicks in while he's on the way to shake the hand of his drug dealer? Yet when Mike showed up at the door of the drug treatment intake center saying he'd had enough of crime, violence, and addiction, what else were they to do with him?

As an E.R. physician and journalist, armed with an OK from San Francisco's Department of Health, a tape recorder, and a camera, I submerged myself for two years in the worlds of hard-core addicts like Mike Pagsolingan, Darlene James, Darrell McAuley, Crystal Holmes, Glenda Janis, and dozens of others, following them as they jumped into rehab and bounced out the other end. When I came up for air myself a couple of years later, every preconceived idea I'd had about how drug rehab worked, or did not work, had been turned on its head.

There is a burgeoning movement in states across our nation to shuffle drug offenders from prison to treatment, and liberal bastions like San Francisco are staking millions of dollars on voluntary rehab programs. But my eye-opening experience in the world of the drug programs has shown that, before we shift hundreds of thousands of additional addicts into rehab, we must first treat the treatment system. While our policy makers are pushing drug treatment as if it were the panacea of the new millennium, few have actually peeked inside the programs to see what rehab is all about. They have not witnessed the battles between harm reduction advocates and the hard-core abstentionists. They have not seen the rehab programs heap abuses on addicts who have relapsed, the outright mistreatment of addicts who are also mentally ill, or the abandonment of lifelong addicts back to the streets after thirty to ninety days of treatment.

What can rehab really hope to accomplish, and how can it succeed? It was with these questions in mind that I ventured with the addicts from intake centers to Therapeutic Communities, from the mental health programs to the courts, from the streets to the programs and back again. My two years in the world of rehab illuminated both its wonders and, tragically, its present failings. Most important, I became convinced that many changes must and can be implemented to make drug treatment work.

The red crosswalk light at the corner of 16th and Mission caused Mike to pause for only a moment before he went after his dope. In that wink of time, however, a whisper of rehab had hummed softly in Mike's mind alongside the siren song of heroin. For Mike, not jaywalking was, of course, a minor achievement—followed by a major failure. But pay attention. It's a twisted and torturous road, I've learned, from craziness to hope.

Lonny Shavelson
Berkeley, California
October 2000

1:00 P.M. A revolving fan in one corner of the tiny treatment room at the Central Intake Unit blows stiflingly hot air at eleven nodding addicts slouched, eyes closed, in chairs along three walls, the fourth blocked by a blackboard and a vinyl table covered with discards of pizza boxes and paper plates, the meal that had enticed them to stop by. The deep, resonant tone of a Tibetan gong oozes from a boom box on the floor and breaks the thrumming, hypnotic noise of the fan. Nobody moves, afraid of dislodging the acupuncture needles dangling precariously from their ears.

On the street below, Darlene James furiously pedals her newly stolen mountain bike into the narrow space between a turning car and the curb. She flies into the air when the car hits the bike (her story), or as the bike hits the car (the driver's version). Before the police can get to the scene, she curses loudly at the man, wipes her bloodied knees with her hands, then limps back to the bike and continues pedaling up Mission to 1663.

W. Jumbé Allen, a tall, lanky African-American man, Doctor of Chinese Medicine, is easing another needle into an addict's ear when the door flies open and Darlene appears. Oblivious to the scene, sounds, and heat, she announces her presence and thrusts herself into a chair near the door. Stretching out one painful leg, she brushes against a strap from the dangling purse of the woman in the next chair. Darlene's cry pierces the room, "Let go of me!" She jumps from the seat and fumbles furiously at the door handle.

Jumbé eases from his chair and heads for Darlene, his lofty frame towering over hers as her bloodstained hands now pound at the door while her head twists about to face him. Jumbé squats beside Darlene, suddenly smaller than she is. She can barely hear his quiet voice.

"There's no one holding you. I promise. Look." He points to the chair.

"Let go of me," Darlene cries out again, but this time more softly, tears rolling down her cheeks. She glances apprehensively at Jumbé, still on his haunches next to her. "Tell her to let go of me. Please?"

Jumbé reaches his hand to Darlene's shoulder, gently guiding her back to the seat.

"I'll tell her, I will," he says.

She sits rigidly in the chair, then, looking around, begins to giggle. Jumbé's head tilts quizzically, and Darlene's gaze meets his.

"They've got needles in their ears!" she says, laughing.

He smiles. "Keeps the drug cravings down. Want to try?"

Her eyes widen in panic even as her mouth breaks into a teeth-gritting grin. "Well, like, thank you, no," she says in a precise Valley Girl imitation and, looking at the needles dangling from the ears of the woman next to her, adds in a course, stage whisper, "Not a fucking chance."

"Maybe tomorrow," says Jumbé, turning back toward the group, announcing, "OK, let's wrap it up."

One at a time the addicts move to the table and, using a small makeup mirror, pluck five needles from each ear and plink them gingerly into a tin bowl. The last one returns to his chair just as Marillac Mayorga, the group's counselor, walks in to start the day's meeting with the now acupuncture-relaxed junkies.

At the end of the group—Darlene's first day and mine as well—I write in my notebook:

DARLENE JAMES

Working against her: She's resistant, doubtful, probably psychotic, certainly hallucinating, homeless, angry, interrupts and is terrible at group process, has wandering thoughts and a severe drug habit—shoots methamphetamine. Black woman who's had five children taken away from her and trusts no one. Boyfriend, a fellow speed freak, about to get out of jail.

Working for her: She's here.

With well over a thousand addicts on drug treatment waiting lists every day, San Francisco maintained an even statistical keel with urban centers throughout the United States. Then, in November of 1996, the city's Board of Supervisors decided to sail ahead of the pack, announcing with classic San Francisco bravado a treatment plan that would become "a model for the country."

By the time Darlene has burst into the Central Intake Unit in September of 1997, Supervisors' Resolution 1055-96 for "Treatment on Demand" had rolled into action. To spread the word of its lofty goal of accessible drug treatment within forty-eight hours for any addict who wants it, the health department had scattered tantalizing flyers so thoroughly around town it seemed they'd been dropped from a helicopter and had blown to every street corner and alley by the blustery San Francisco winds.

Need help now? announced the flyers.

THE WAY TO TREATMENT AND RECOVERY TAKES ONLY ONE PHONE
  CALL
Easy Quick Access 1-800-750-2727
Troubled by what you did last night?
Troubled by your speed use? Troubled by your drug and alcohol use?
1-800-750-2727
An easy way to begin alcohol and drug treatment and recovery
Convenient and central locations . . . available in neighborhoods throughout the city
Our services are FREE!

In response to the health department's street outreach, Darlene and hundreds of the toughest-to-treat addicts hit intake units around San Francisco announcing they wanted off of cocaine, heroin, crack, alcohol, methamphetamine, angel dust, and many of the more exotic stimulants, depressants, supposed sex-enhancers, and other mysterious medicaments served up in San Francisco's not-so-unique drug stew.

But finding slots in treatment programs for all comers within forty-eight hours had been, of course, a mythological goal ordained by a cloistered Board of Supervisors. Down in the treatment trenches, the waiting time to get into programs was still counted in weeks and months, not days. Something had to be done with the addicts pounding at the doors, ready for rehab. To the rescue, a federally supported program called Target Cities—an early beneficiary of Washington's newfound attempt to drive the drug war toward rehab.

Below the bold banner headlines on the health department's come-one-come-all flyers, ran this qualifier: *And, if you have to wait for an opening in the treatment program that can best help you, Target Cities will enroll you immediately in its daily support groups.*

These daily federally funded Target Cities "pre-placement" groups became a melting pot of addicts of varying motivations waiting to be accepted into rehab programs. But potentially explosive delays—junkies are not famous for their waiting skills—were molded by the Target Cities staff into treatment strategies. While on hold for program slots the addicts were plied with pizza, acupunctured into relaxation, introduced to treatment concepts, and evaluated to see what type of rehab would best suit each one. As counselor Marillac Mayorga explained to each newly arrived client in her group: "Here, we try to get you ready for there."

By the time referrals are made to programs that range from outpatient drop-in methadone maintenance to intensive residential care, the Target Cities counselors know the addicts as individuals, with specific, stunningly different, and uniformly impossible-to-fill needs.

JUMBÉ ALLEN AND DARRELL MCAULEY

In the pre-placement group, Marillac tries to keep a hallucinatory Darlene from bouncing off the walls while, across the room, Mike dozes under the influence of heroin. Marillac moves toward Mike but is distracted when she catches, out of the corner of her eye, the shaking tremors of Darrell McAuley's hands.

"Are you OK?" she asks Darrell.

"Yeah, sure," Darrell's voice quivers from impending d.t.'s. He's had no alcohol for two days, after nineteen years of near-constant drinking. Marillac knows he's at the point of alcohol withdrawal where he's likely to have a seizure.

To add to her problems of the day, she has to introduce me to the group, a journalist wanting to hook up with addicts and follow them through rehab.

Marillac turns her attentions back to Mike, whose chin has drifted to his chest in a heroin nod. Suddenly his head jerks upward and he announces, "Yeah, that's right," in the pretext of participating in the group.

She touches his arm. "Michael, are you there?"

"Sure, yeah, sure," he says, surprised to see her.

"Listen, we're not going to refuse you services," the counselor tells him politely. "But please, do not come to group high. You're not paying attention anyway."

Marillac's comment is my first hint that, indeed, something new is up in rehab. For a drug treatment program *not* to kick out a user who continues to get high is rehab-world heresy, also known as coddling the junkie. Addicts come to get clean, reason the counselors; they can get stoned in the streets, not in group. Drug counselor training teaches that it's futile to offer therapy to a mind, like Mike's, still hazed in by heroin. Worse yet, Mike's nodding head and soft heroin-fog smile is a "memory trigger" to everyone else in the group trying to fight off their own drug cravings. "You got one guy in group coming in loaded," says Sylvester Palmer, one of the many counselors Mike will later encounter, "and it's like a cancer that's going to spread. We cut out that cancer to save the body." The traditional rule of rehab groups is straightforward: If you're using, you're out of here.

"That is the dumbest thing I've ever heard," proclaimed Dr. Pablo Stewart, a psychiatrist who specializes in addiction, to a meeting of hundreds of San Francisco drug counselors who'd gathered to learn the latest in rehab philosophy. "How can you treat an addict if he's not there? They come to treatment because they use dope. And you throw them out because they're using dope!" Dr. Stewart smiled at the uneasy laughter in the audience. "So can anybody here tell me of one other disease where the patient is supposed to be cured before he gets treated?"

Dr. Stewart's admonition notwithstanding, on my first day at Target Cities I wonder about the usefulness of having Mike there at all. In a cafe across the street after group, I ply him with coffee, searching for signs of intelligent life. Yet each time he begins to speak his eyes drift to a half-closed position and his chin leads his head downward. Then it jerks up as Mike starts another comment but, mid-sentence, his eyelids descend again and his head follows suit. I toss three quarters on the counter for his coffee, turn off my tape recorder, and give up on Mike before I even know him.

DARLENE JAMES

The next day, I'm back in the tiny, sweltering room as pre-group acupuncture begins. In chairs along the wall next to me, among the dozen addicts, I'm surprised to see that Mike, Darlene, and Darrell have all returned.

On the blackboard hanging on the wall, Marillac has written in colorful chalk letters the Alcoholics Anonymous mantra: *KEEP COMING BACK!* I look around the room at the bodies slouched in their blue plastic chairs, dozing off from either the heat of the room, the relaxation of the acupuncture, or the mind-numbing effects of hitting some dope just before group. Keep coming back? Necessary, I think, but certainly not sufficient. When the Tibetan gong sounds, everyone moves groggily forward to extract the needles and begin group.

Henrietta, a pink, hand-sized bean-bag hippopotamus, flies through the air straight at Mike. Darrell, finished with his daily "check-in" with the group, has tossed Henrietta Mike's way—it's his turn to check in. Mike's large hands, heavily callused from his work as a plumber, reach up and grab the hippo mid-flight. He awkwardly twists Henrietta's pink, floppy ears as he introduces himself.

"My name's Mike, and I'm a heroin addict," he begins uneasily, staring down at Henrietta. Her seams have been tattered by the torments of anxious addicts at innumerable daily check-ins.

"Hi, Mike!" the group calls out.

"Uh, yeah," he responds, looking at the blackboard to remember the questions he's supposed to address during check-in. *Why are you here?*

"I'm here to get placed in a—whatcha call it—drug house."

Mike looks crushed by the laughter that breaks out in the room.

"Yeah," Darrell calls out, giggling, "you mean, like a crack house!"

"Recovery program," Marillac offers quietly.

"Yeah, right, I'm here to get into a recovery program," he says, laughing now. "I'm done with drug houses."

"Thank you for staying awake today," says Marillac, her Nicaraguan accent lilting away any sarcasm Mike might read into her comment.

"Umm, yeah, you're welcome," he mutters, and tosses the pink hippo across the room as if it were burning a hole in his hands. Henrietta lands in Darlene's lap. She immediately renames her Henry, but declines to check in, shaking her head back and forth in quick, tiny motions.

"That's OK," says Marillac. "Just think about that one question: Why are you here? You can try again tomorrow."

Darlene heads for the door, tears rolling silently down her cheeks. Marillac, with a look of concern, steps in front of the exit.

"Darlene, we'd like you to stay," she says. "There's only fifteen minutes to go."

Darlene returns silently to her chair as Andrew, who now has Henrietta, begins his check in.

"My name is Andrew, and I'm—"

"Don't you ever fucking block my way again!" Darlene's wail pierces the room, her wide eyes staring menacingly at Marillac.

"I wasn't blocking your way," says the counselor softly. "You're free to leave any time you want."

"Then stay out of my face!" Darlene is sobbing loudly as she slams the door and disappears. An eerie silence trails behind her and descends on the room.

"No offense intended, Marillac," Darrell's quiet voice breaks the stillness, "but it was clear from here that you *were* blocking the door."

Marillac sighs and, looking at the ceiling, closes her eyes for a moment. Before she can open them again, the group rips into Darlene.

"Goddamn speed freaks shouldn't even be in here!" proclaims Alice, an alcoholic.

"They come in with a chip on their shoulder," chimes in Andrew, who mixes cocaine with his heroin to balance the downer effect with an upper.

"She even freaked out during acupuncture!" adds Terence for good measure. "She shouldn't be allowed in here while she's still doing speed. Messes up the whole group."

Marillac's eyes are wide open again, staring about the room.

"Look, you guys," she says, "there's only one thing wrong here. A human being who is suffering just walked out that door—and will probably never be back."

She glances around the silent room, frowning, worried.

"OK, let's call it a day," she says. "We'll try a fresh start tomorrow."

As the drug counselor reaches for her bag, the group bolts out the door.

"Hey, Lonny," I hear a voice call as I head down the stairs toward the Mission Street exit. Mike is right behind me.

"Sorry, man," he says, his heavy work boots pounding on the bare concrete steps. "I guess it wasn't too useful talking to me yesterday, huh?"

"Not to worry," I respond, "there'll be other chances."

"Hey, man, let's talk, buy me a cup of coffee, some cigarettes?"

"Can't today. Maybe tomorrow," I say, hitting the last step.

"Hey!" his voice echoes in the stairwell. "Today I'm straight, didn't shoot up this morning. Can't promise you nothin' 'bout tomorrow."

I pause, turning to see the expression that accompanied that comment—a soft, sincere smile. Except for the gap from his two missing lower teeth, Mike's handsome, rugged face could have been ripped straight from a Marlboro Man ad.

"I *would* like to talk with you," I say. "But Darlene told me yesterday where she camps out, in China Basin. I want to go see if she's all right."

"Yeah, man, that is one spooked-out chick! What's up with that?"

He holds open the glass door that leads to Mission Street and we step from the dingy hallway into the bright midday sun.

"Either she's shooting *way* too much speed and she's wigged out from that," Mike continues, his eyes blinking from the bright sunlight. "*Or,*" he booms out the emphasis as if he'd just uncovered the thought, "she's some crazy person—you know, a loony tune. Which do you think?"

"I don't know," I say slowly, "it's only our second day here. Let's talk tomorrow, OK?"

"Yeah, man, sure. Coffee and cigarettes? Buy me some lunch?"

"I'll see you tomorrow," I reply, and head for my car, puzzling over the essence of Mike's question about Darlene. If Darlene is paranoid and hallucinating because she's mentally ill—a loony tune, as Mike put it—she'll need intense mental health treatment, not just a counselor telling her to get off drugs. But methamphetamine—speed—can so hype up your brain chemistry that a hallucinatory paranoia storms in, creating delusions and voices as if you *were* psychotic.

If Darlene's hallucinations come from an underlying mental illness and not the speed she shoots up every day, then she's walked through the wrong treatment door, not only making her own therapy ineffective but interfering with that of the others in the group. Drug counselors have a hard enough time with drug abusers who *aren't* psychotic; they want the shrinks and psychologists to deal with the mentally ill. But if Darlene's craziness does come from shooting speed, then drug treatment is exactly what she needs.

I'm heading for China Basin, and the first of dozens of conversations and adventures I'm to have with Darlene over the next year. It's not until well into the year, however, that I finally realize that this chicken-versus-egg question—which came first, the paranoid hallucinations or the drug use—has no relevance in helping Darlene through the agony of her disordered thoughts. Rather, the rehab programs' obsessions with distinguishing true mental illness from drug-induced hallucinations reflect their own desire to compartmentalize and classify clients rather than treat them as whole—albeit hallucinatory and addicted— human beings.

Over the next year I watch Darlene, already trapped in her own disorganized thoughts, become even more ensnared by ours.

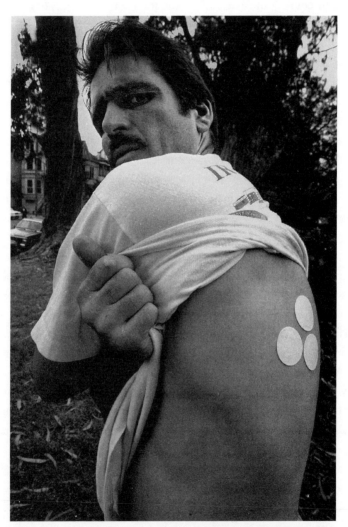

MIKE, WEARING MEDICATED PATCHES TO DECREASE HEROIN WITHDRAWAL SYMPTOMS

While Darlene James appeared unlikely to find help in dealing with her addiction, Mike Pagsolingan seemed undeserving of help with his.

Here's how Mike qualified for funds from the new rehab services: He quit his job as a plumber, racked up two felony convictions, smacked his first wife in the face when she caught him stealing from her purse to buy cocaine, then broke into his girlfriend's ATM account to get money for heroin. Next, he showed up stoned for Marillac's group at the federally funded Target Cities' Central Intake Unit.

The government had already spent tens of thousands of dollars on Mike—in his younger days at the Youth Authority after a bungled teenage attempt at armed robbery. When he outgrew the juvenile system and continued to rack up felonies, thousands of more dollars were consumed by courts, public defenders, and for a couple of years of room, board, and guards to watch over him in jail. Now, under new rehab policies, the government was floating even more money Mike's way.

At first blush, Mike Pagsolingan is not the kind of guy you'd want to reach out to with a helping hand. If you extended a hand to Darlene, she'd be more likely to run in fear than to take your outstretched palm. And Darrell's hand seems too sweaty and tremulous from alcohol withdrawal to grasp anything for a while. Mike, Darlene, and Darrell make unappealing choices for poster children to convince the public or policy makers to turn tax dollars toward treatment funds.

Yet addicts like these three—the most resistant, demanding, often unlikable, and arguably the least deserving of treatment services—are precisely the type of difficult junkie that rehab programs must succeed with if they are to make a dent in the crime, violence, and craziness that comprise *the drug problem*. The number of illegal drug users in the United States declined from twenty-five million in 1979 to fourteen million in 1998 (the most hard-core four million consume two-thirds of the drugs). Yet the number of drug-related hospital emergencies increased by 60 percent during that same period, and drug-associated deaths quadrupled. A 1997 study showed that 50 to 75 percent of all criminals apprehended in twenty-three cities across the United States had positive drug tests. And according to White House estimates, "the social costs of drug use continue to climb, reaching $110 billion in 1995, a sixty-four percent increase since 1990."

While we've driven addiction rates down, we have not reduced the disasters brought down on our heads by the addicts. Effective treatment programs must welcome, even seek out, the most demanding, disgusting, inarticulate, manipulative, crazy, and uncooperative drug addicts. And somehow help them to change.

In the group at Target Cities' Central Intake Unit, Mike, Darlene, and Darrell seemed the least likely to make it to clean and sober. Yet they were the most crucial for the program to help.

Soon after the city's Board of Supervisors passed Resolution 1055-96, for Treatment on Demand, I made an appointment to speak with Dr. Larry Meredith, the charismatic chief of San Francisco's Substance Abuse Services and a prime mover in the freshly invigorated rehab movement.

Dr. Meredith is a tall, thin, gray-bearded man who is as comfortable walking the ivy paths of academia as he is hanging out with addicts in alleys, or with San Francisco's politically empowered elite in their hallowed halls of government. Meredith brought together drug researchers, the city legislature, addicts, and the rehab community, initiating the grand scheme for Treatment on Demand—rehab for all addicts who seek it, within forty-eight hours.

"Let me tell you where I'm coming from with this," begins Meredith, pulling up a chair alongside the large, polished-wood conference table that fills his office, which long ago surrendered all visible surfaces to mountains of papers and reports. "I'm proposing that San Francisco be a laboratory for this whole idea that treating drug addiction works."

Meredith's tone is more Sunday preacher than health bureaucrat, scientist, or social innovator. "If we can diminish drug use," he exclaims, "we'll save on jails, homelessness, child abuse, foster care—you name it. And the fact is," insists the drug chief, "treatment works! And with a high return on every dollar you invest."

But a 1994 RAND study for the Office of National Drug Control Policy, I point out to Meredith, concluded that only a small fraction of heavy cocaine and heroin users achieved long-term abstinence from drugs after treatment. A similar federal analysis found that eight of every ten cocaine users relapsed within three to five years of treatment. A March 1996 report, the Treatment Protocol Effectiveness Study, evaluated, among other programs, drug rehab Therapeutic Communities. "Fewer than one in six [participants]," the report noted, "complete the one- to two-year course of treatment." That same investigation, reviewing methadone detoxification, found that "patients show a rate of relapse greater than ninety percent." And in a summary published in 1997 in the *American Journal of Drug and Alcohol Abuse,* Dr. George De Leon and colleagues wrote that "dropout is the rule in all treatment modalities . . . [and] most admissions to programs do not stay long enough to receive treatment benefits."

Meredith merely smiles as I recite this discouraging litany of drug treatment failures. Then he reaches to a pile on the table and pulls out a heavily underlined booklet, *Evaluating Recovery Services: The California Drug and Alcohol Treatment Assessment.* Buried in the densely packed graphs and analyses is the data behind Meredith's cry for treatment. For every dollar spent on rehab, says the study, seven are saved down the line.

While Meredith still holds the booklet in his hands, I point out the sections that show how ineffective the programs were in keeping addicts off drugs: Half the treated cocaine users continued to get high, three of four junkies still shot heroin, and two of three treated alcoholics kept on drinking. And yet, Meredith shows me, in spite of such discouraging rates of drug abstention brought forth by rehab, the addicts who'd been through treatment programs were committing two-thirds fewer crimes. While the majority were still using drugs after rehab, their quantity of drug use and crimes had plummeted: drug sales offenses, decreased by 61 percent; use of weapons or physical force, down 71 percent; number of months involved in criminal activity, slashed 77 percent.

If we judge rehab programs only by their ability to keep addicts off drugs, they fail miserably. But examine the details of how the addicts change their lives by going through treatment, and a spectacular success emerges. Meredith leafs through the pages of the California research booklet, to the conclusion stating that "the cost of treating approximately 150,000 participants . . . was $209 million, while the benefits received during treatment and in the first-year afterwards were worth approximately $1.5 billion in savings to tax paying citizens, due mostly to reductions in crime."

"But is there any research," I ask Meredith, "that has evaluated an open-door policy like your proposed Treatment on Demand, where millions of scarce health dollars will be spent to treat every addict whose only demonstrated ability to do rehab is to call an 800 number on the phone? Has a system with such a continuously open door ever been evaluated?"

Meredith shakes his head. No.

"Every department in this city," he stresses, sailing smoothly on, "faces the drug problem—Social Services, Housing, Employment, Criminal Justice, Job Safety, Homeless Services. Yet each one cops out on the issue: 'You fix their addiction,' they tell me, 'then we'll find them housing'; or, 'You fix their addiction, then we'll find them jobs.' Drugs cost this city $1.7 billion annually in lost revenues—" He stops as his secretary pokes her head in the room to say he's well overdue for his next appointment.

Meredith heads down the hall to the elevator, past a nearly billboard-sized placard leaning against the wall—a leftover from a presentation to the city's Board of Supervisors that won the drug chief his cherished Treatment on Demand bill.

He points to the heading of the chart:

COST OF DRUGS TO THE COMMUNITY

"It adds up to $1.7 billion," he proclaims again. "Annually!"

I glance down the list.

Public assistance/Homeless services
Foster care
ER/Psychiatric care
Police/Court/Jail
Public safety
Quality of life
Injury and illness

Crime and violence
Loss of earnings
Decreased tourism
Family disintegration

Then, down the right side of the board:

COMMUNITY'S RETURN ON TREATMENT INVESTMENT

Lower ER/Psychiatric use
Reduced use of public assistance
Fewer homeless
Hospitality and tourism industry increased revenue
Taxes paid through employment
Safe and healthy neighborhoods
Reduced theft and victim losses
Improved business environment
Family preservation
Improved quality of life

We continue down the hall to the elevator and Meredith shakes my hand, in a rush to get to his next meeting.

"This push for more rehab looks good on paper," I say. "Mind if I dig around to see how it plays out in the streets?"

"I'll make some calls for you," replies Meredith. "I'd like to know more about that myself."

2: THE STREETS

DARLENE JAMES

"Just go over the Third Street bridge into China Basin," Darlene told me when I'd asked about the homeless encampment where she lives. "There's this long fenced-in parking lot? That's where I keep my house."

The black steel drawbridge at Third Street spans a canal that separates China Basin from the San Francisco mainland, isolating the tiny peninsula from everyday traffic. Abandoned warehouses and factories line the shore. I spot the homeless encampment as I swing left just over the bridge, and pull up beside a long chicken-wire fence that seems to block all access to the lot.

The wind blows strong and cold off the water, and the San Francisco fog adds an eerie quality to the just-before-sunset light as I find the round hole cut in the bottom at one end of the long fence. I squeeze through to walk on the cracked concrete of the abandoned parking lot that runs along the canal. Abandoned, that is, by whoever owns it; the parking lot is now an expansive, yet unofficial, homeless housing development. I tighten the collar of my coat against the wind and walk past lodgings that range from a pristine alpine mountaineering tent to a tattered yellow sheet of plastic stretched between a shopping cart and the wire fence, suspended over a soggy mattress. Loose flaps dangling from dozens of tents and tarps make slapping noises in the wind. The scene of the fog-shrouded waterside encampment seems even more eerie because not a single human being is in sight.

As I walk along, uneasily gazing about for signs of Darlene, the heads of men and women pop out from each tent-cave to check out the stranger.

"He's OK," Darlene announces as she comes up from behind me carrying a bucket of water from the canal, a beautiful German shepherd prancing by her side. Heads vanish back into their tents and the encampment again appears strangely deserted. It's as if the two of us, and the dog, are standing alone in a hastily constructed postapocalyptic city whose inhabitants were then wiped out by some second cosmic catastrophe. That second catastrophe, I will learn, is methamphetamine.

Darlene is laughing. "I didn't think no government agent was going to *visit*," she exclaims. "I just thought you wanted to know where I lived."

The dog is licking furiously at my hand, and I squat to pet it.

"That's Bruce," she says.

"He's friendly," I reply. "Guess I don't smell like a government agent."

"*Bruce* is a *she*," Darlene corrects me, "and if you're not a government agent, what are you doing here?"

"If I am a government agent, why are you laughing and talking to me?"

She skips away, Bruce running at her side, to where a line of shopping carts along the fence is surrounded by an elaborate outfitting of poles, tarps, and blankets to form a multi-roomed cave. Within seconds, she's gone and I'm standing alone in the wind outside her place.

"The door's open," a squeaky, singsong child's voice calls from inside. I duck under a flap and see only Darlene, stretched out luxuriously on a quilt-covered mattress, surrounded by neatly filled bookshelves, a boom box hooked up to a car battery, and a low-slung bedside table topped with an alarm clock, ashtrays, notepads, a Walkman with headset, and a rack of cassette tapes.

"This is *my* house," the voice of the little girl again, clearly coming from Darlene.

"What's that voice mean?" I ask.

"It just comes out sometimes," she says, frowning, back to her usual husky tone.

I sit on a small wooden stool at the foot of her mattress, my back against a plywood board that forms one wall of her cave.

"You seem much less worried than at group," I note.

"That's 'cause this is *my* house," she says straight out. "And *that*," she waves her hand dismissively in the direction of the world on the other side of the canal, "is *their* house."

Darlene reaches to the bedside table and grabs the Walkman, placing padded earphones over her head, adjusting them on her ears, then rotates the volume control to high. Even a few feet away I can hear the throbbing pulse of a Madonna song and can imagine how it must be pounding through her head.

"Sometimes," announces Darlene, her finger waving in time to the music, "I'm OK in their house. Other times, like at group today, I'm not."

"What happened today?" I ask, but her head is bobbing to the music, my voice losing out to Madonna's.

"Darlene," I say, tapping her knee, "a little loud?"

"Has to be," she replies, "keeps the noises down."

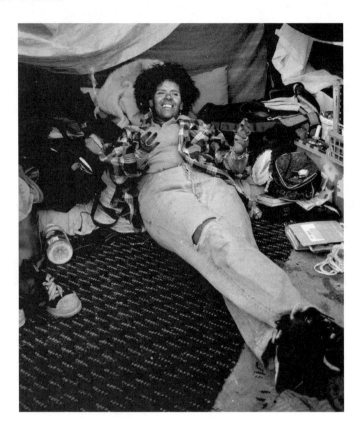

"What noises?"

"Never mind," she says. "Sometimes I say what I'm thinking instead of just thinking it." She pulls the headset off, then stands.

"Can you drive me across the bridge to get some dog food? Bruce is hungry. I can come back on my airplane." She points to the mountain bike just inside the tent flap.

"Nice bike," I say, ducking out of the tent and into the wind, noticing in the growing darkness that there are two more mountain bikes chained to the fence.

"Change that," I say. "Nice, umm, three bikes."

"That's my work," says Darlene. "Can we go now?"

She wheels the bicycle toward the hole in the fence, but stops for a moment at the tent nearest the opening.

"Hey, Red!" she calls out. *"Red!"* A flap swings open and a man appears in the aperture, about forty, wearing a white T-shirt as his only protection against the cold. He holds the flap open with one long, heavily tattooed arm. His other arm hangs at his side, a syringe dangling by its needle pokes into the fleshy side of his elbow below a red-bandanna tourniquet.

"I've got a guy wants this airplane," Darlene tells him. "So I'll have some money for the package when I come back."

Red nods silently and drops the flap, his ethereal image disappearing into the tent.

"Package?" I ask, as we tuck her bike into the back of my car.

"Speed," she says, "crystal meth. I sell airplanes to get money to buy speed, then sell the speed to buy, you know, things. Just 'cause I'm in some drug program don't mean I can't make a living!"

Darlene laughs, then adds: "But that don't mean I use the stuff. I ain't doing that no more. So don't go telling at group that I'm still doing drugs!"

"Wouldn't think of it," I say, turning on the engine and heading with Darlene and her airplane back over the Third Street bridge.

"You know, you never did get to answer that check-in question at group."

"Which one's that?" she asks, distractedly looking down the dark alleys as we drive off the city side of the bridge.

"The question on the blackboard, 'Why are you here?' "

"Why am I where?"

"In group, drug rehab."

Darlene rolls down her window, cold air blowing into the car.

"I'm here," she proclaims, turning back toward me from her search out the window, "to be better today than I was yesterday."

"Yesterday?"

"Well, not really yesterday, but, you know, *yesterday.* When I was running down the street screaming and butt-naked and they took me to the hospital for a week and William said he got really scared? But he's in jail now, so I went to the drug program so I wouldn't scare him like that again when he gets out. But then that bitch blocked my way today, so I don't know."

She rotates suddenly, thrusting her head and torso out the window, yelling, "Hey, Billy, wait, now you hold up there!"

All I see is darkness and fog down an alley, but Darlene has opened the door and flipped the passenger seat forward to pull out her bike.

"I thought we were getting food for Bruce?" I ask.

"Got work to do first."

She slams the door closed, then her face is at the window. "See you in group tomorrow?"

"You'll be there?" I ask.

" 'Course I'll be there! What did you think?" Then she jumps on her bike and pedals down the alley.

I reach across to close the window against the cold fog blowing in. Pulling out from the curb, I glance back across the bridge at the dim glow coming from candles in the makeshift tents across the canal.

If I lived where and how Darlene does—I draw up the image in my mind—I'd probably do a lot of speed, too. And I'd most likely start hallucinating. And I'd never know whether it was the speed that was driving me crazy, or if the harsh reality of homelessness had driven me so crazy that I shot speed.

Either way, if I could somehow, by sheer force of willpower, pull myself together, I'd show up at Target Cities' Central Intake Unit, and keep coming back.

I head from China Basin into the city, wondering whether Darlene will indeed be back in group the next day. And if she does keep coming back, can she, Marillac, Jumbé, and the addicts in the group all reach beyond their fears to create some functioning, therapeutic whole?

What's the goal with Darlene, anyway? I wonder. Getting off speed will only minimally improve her life if she stays on the far side of the China Basin canal. To continue living there, she may even *need* to shoot speed.

If Darlene's clear-line separation between *my house* and *their house* comes from the delusions of a psychotic mind, can drug rehab counselors really cross into her house, and bring her out to theirs?

I wonder who is most afraid—Darlene of us, or we of her?

There's a clanging of bells and the flashing of red lights behind me. I glance in the mirror and see the black-steel drawbridge over the China Basin canal as it splits in two, rising into the night sky. I stop to watch the powerful motors lift tons of hard steel and roadway, then lower them again to form a jagged, cold seam between the two shores.

W. JUMBÉ ALLEN AND DARLENE

"The way I see it," Marillac tells me the next day, "Darlene is not appropriate for our group." We're standing in the hallway, waiting for the addicts to return from a smoke break between acupuncture and the daily "pre-placement" session with those still waiting to get into programs.

"I don't know if Darlene's weird behavior is because she's on drugs," continues Marillac, "or due to her own internal chemical imbalance. Or maybe it's because her kids were taken away, or she's being abused, maybe being raped out where she lives. There can be so many things going on with her that just to think about it is scary."

She glances down at the clipboard in her hands. "Four new clients have signed into my group today," she sighs. "And we're trying to find a residential program for Mike. He's reachable now, but if we don't get him off the streets soon, he'll be gone, so we're checking openings at Walden House. And Darrell's being evaluated at Acceptance Place, because he's already been at Walden House and split. He says he needs a program that's just for gay men, so let's hope Acceptance Place *accepts* him."

Marillac glances at her watch and hustles down the hall to escort everyone back from the smoke break. "I just can't give Darlene the attention she needs," the counselor tells me softly as we get within hearing distance of the waiting addicts. "So even though she needs more adjustment time and may not be ready for a full program, we've got to get her out of here. We're sending her to a program called STOP. I'll tell her after group today." Marillac's voice is down to almost a whisper. "You know what I think, Lonny? That there is no cure for Darlene. But we'll try what we can."

Darlene passes by with the others, offering Marillac a straightforward "Hello, how are you today?" Then she calmly takes her seat next to Darrell, who cuts an almost comical figure, an air of refinement from his bush of elegantly thick black hair offset by his sweaty T-shirt and frayed shorts.

Darlene appears as a changed woman, wearing a crisp white blouse and a pair of new jeans. Her neck is adorned with gold and silver chains. Glistening bangle bracelets click on her wrists when she moves her arms. And from each ear dangles a small crystal earring that catches the sunlight streaming through the room. As Darlene turns her head back and forth, rainbows of color dance on the sides of her face. She's carrying a notebook and a felt-tip pen and sits with legs crossed and the pad in her lap, as if she's the group secretary ready to take notes. She looks around, sees Henrietta the Hippo on the nearby table, and reaches out for her.

"I'd like to apologize for yesterday," Darlene says, opening the conversation.

"That's OK," says Darrell, who has spent years in rehab groups and follows all the rules, except the part about not drinking. "But you should start by checking in," he instructs Darlene, pointing to the blackboard.

"My name is Darlene," she begins haltingly, "and I shoot methamphetamine."

"Hi, Darlene!"

"What I'm feeling today is confusion. I need to work on not being so aggressive and blunt. But being aggressive and blunt has helped me a whole lot, so maybe what I need to do is still be aggressive and blunt, but less angry?"

She looks around the room, as if expecting an answer. "Yeah," she continues, her voice speeding up to fill the silence. "I need to work on my anger. So I'll try to understand what you people are saying to me—but one at a time, don't come at me all at once. OK?"

"Thank you Darlene," says Marillac. "That is much better today."

"Really?" the voice of the little girl pops out. "Am I really better today than I was yesterday?"

While Darlene grins with pleasure, Marillac eases Henrietta from her hands and tosses the hippo to Mike.

"My name's Mike, and I'm a heroin addict."

"Hi, Mike!"

"I'm feeling . . ." He pauses, looking at a list posted on the wall entitled *Words to Describe Feelings.* "Yeah, I'm feeling optimistic. *And* apprehensive. And, um, excited. And worried." He rumples his brow into a thoughtful frown. "Hey, I'm a fucking walking contradiction, huh?"

Darlene responds, laughing, her arms thrown into the air, bangle bracelets clanging together. "Yeah, me too! I'm filled with those"—she laughs again—"contrashditions! Yeah, I got those, too, you see—"

"Darlene," Darrell breaks in, "it's Mike's check-in time. And I haven't had my chance either."

"But Marillac said I was better today! So I—"

"It's OK," says Mike, "I'm pretty much done. I got to get going anyways, I'm supposed to be at some interview to get into Walden House."

He tosses Henrietta to Darrell and stands, brushing dirt and mud from the clothes he hasn't changed for days. Mike's girlfriend hasn't let him in the house since she got her bank card back from him.

"Good luck, Mike," says Darrell.

"Yeah, thanks," replies Mike, heading for the door. "If I don't get off the streets soon, I'm a dead man."

With the lofty goal of getting as many addicts into treatment as soon as possible supported by everyone from federal drug czar General Barry McCaffrey and local drug chief Dr. Larry Meredith, down to Marillac and the Target Cities' staff—Mike, Darlene, and Darrell's goal of moving quickly into treatment programs seems reachable. But almost no one who'd planned this new rapid route to treatment had imagined that the most significant obstacle to getting quick help for addicts would come from the rehab programs themselves.

When Mike walked out the door of Marillac's group clutching in his hand a referral slip for residential treatment at Walden House, he had no idea that Walden was philosophically opposed to the most basic principles of accelerated access to treatment.

In fact, San Francisco's plan to move addicts quickly from the streets into rehab had run into resistance from both on high and down low. When Larry Meredith was designing Treatment on Demand he'd called David Mactas, then director of the federal Center for Substance Abuse Treatment, and boasted that San Francisco was "going to eliminate waiting lists." Mactas's response was cool, recalled Meredith. The federal executive told the San Francisco drug chief that waiting lists are not such a bad thing since they act as a "motivational screen"—eliminating addicts who are unlikely to succeed at treatment, those not even motivated enough to tolerate a few weeks' wait.

"That belief is based on all this b.s.," asserted Meredith in a later interview. "Who says the addicts aren't motivated? My wife asked me last night if I'd called my mother, and I said no. It's not that I'm not motivated, but the timing wasn't right. I'm a great believer in timing. When an addict says he's ready, it's like aikido or jujitsu, you move *with* the energy that's there—not against it."

Meredith's poetic philosophy was not shared by Mactas in Washington, nor by many on the front lines of drug treatment in his own city. Dolores Alvarez was program director at Walden House when Mike had his intake interview, her office down a polished-wood hallway in an elegant Victorian mansion—now home to 120 recovering addicts in the heart of San Francisco's Fillmore District. Reading through the flyer that had announced the city's Treatment on Demand program—*THE WAY TO TREATMENT AND RECOVERY TAKES ONLY ONE PHONE CALL*—Alvarez shrugged. "We make them go through some tough hoops to get into this program," she said, "so they won't throw it away so easily. We make them work for it."

At 2:00, Mike is on time for his Walden intake appointment.

"Hey," he asks the secretary while waiting to be interviewed, "can I step outside for a smoke?"

"If you can't restrain yourself," she replies, "might as well leave now."

At 4:30, Mike is still waiting. "I was like in nicotine withdrawal," he tells me later. "But I was sure it was some kind of test, so I stuck to my chair. They got me in just before 5:00."

At the end of the interview with intake manager Steve Maddox, Mike reaches out to shake his hand. "I'm ready, man. Where do I go next?"

Maddox hands him a slip of paper with two numbers carefully inscribed: a phone number and Mike's secret code for the program's waiting list. His personal contact at Walden is to be a message machine. Maddox instructs Mike to leave his code number on the tape every day, to demonstrate his interest in Walden.

"Sure, man, I can do that," says Mike. "How long will it be before I'm in?"

"We can't tell you that," replies Maddox.

"I mean days, or weeks?" asks Mike, staring at the slip of paper.

"Just keep calling every day," says Maddox, leading Mike to the door. "That way we'll know you're still interested. If the machine's message has your number on it one day, that's your day to come in."

Walden officials call it "the demonstration period," an intentional treatment obstacle meant to screen out the weak, unmotivated, or those just looking for "three hots and a cot"—bed and board. These barriers to therapy, the very antithesis of Treatment on Demand, are the subject of contentious debate in the world of rehab.

Most often, it's a crisis that propels a junkie toward treatment: job loss, injury, an arrest, an overdose, or simply running out of money and scams to get more dope. Tom Hagan, Clinical Coordinator at Target Cities, calls those moments of crisis "windows of opportunity"—the time interval to get addicts into a program before they're lost to the streets again. Addiction researchers have found that longer waits are "associated with a decreased interest in entering treatment and with significant increases in legal involvement, incarceration, family separation, and rates of death." One study, aptly entitled "Hello, May We Help You?" demonstrated that 60 percent of addicts who called for help and were offered an appointment that same day showed up; wait longer, only 38 percent appeared.

Mike lumbers down the stairs after his Walden intake interview, out into the streets at dusk, only a block from the city's heroin-trade center at 16th and Mission. He stops to light a cigarette and notices the card with his personal code number still held tight in his hand. Taking a long draw on his cigarette, Mike thinks about Walden's insistence that he demonstrate that he's sufficiently motivated to get into their program. The fact that he'd already shown up every day for the fed's Target Cities' groups, and rushed from there daily to the local Haight Ashbury Clinic to get medications to decrease his drug cravings, did not mean much to Walden. His motivation for rehab had to be proved by Walden's regulations, not those of other agencies.

"These treatment people are real nice," Mike tells me. "But their rules are bustin' my ass. I guess they get tired of people checking into programs and then out again. But if I wasn't already on drugs, this runaround would drive me to using them."

Mike takes a drag on his cigarette, looking about him in the streets of the Mission. "What more do they want me to do to prove I'm ready?" says Mike in frustration. "I'm tired of hurting people I love, ripping them off to get drugs. Look, I can't keep trying to argue my way into programs. I thought they *wanted* me off dope. They're losing me, man."

Not lost to Mayor Willie Brown were the political gains from blessing drug treatment plans.

On October 14, during the same hour that Mike is being interviewed at Walden intake, Mayor Brown announces in his State of the City address that "the most progressive city in the nation" has reached, among a multitude of achievements, Treatment on Demand for drug addiction. Yet while Brown claims "national precedent" for his city, those on the front lines with the addicts speak out angrily in protest.

"Saying that we've achieved Treatment on Demand," rehab counselors tell the press, "is not reality." On that day, they announce, there are over a thousand addicts on waiting lists. The wait for one of Walden House's slots—information kept secret from Mike during his intake interview—is running three to five weeks.

Just after Brown ends his speech, a dispirited Mike walks from Walden's interview office out into the Mission district. By nightfall, he and an old street friend are holed up in a dirty room nearby, fresh balloons of heroin at their sides as they search their arms and necks for bulging veins.

Mike's drug use has been low for a few weeks, his tolerance to heroin changing daily. But he's bought his usual number of bags and is melting the white heroin powder to liquid in the flame of his favorite Zippo lighter, then sucking it into a syringe. Proud of his veins—"I got the best ropes, man"—Mike doesn't need to tie off with a tourniquet. He finds a bulging blood vessel and punctures it with the needle, feels the hot rush of the heroin. Then everything goes black.

Mike barely feels the bucketful of ice his friend throws down the front of his pants to keep him awake and breathing until the ambulance arrives. Nor does he hear the sirens, or see his friend running down the stairs as the paramedics storm up to his room. And he has no awareness of the paramedics injecting Narcan—a heroin antidote—into his vein. The first sounds Mike hears as he comes groggily back to consciousness are the paramedics' voices, hovering over him as they load him into the ambulance.

"This guy was about dead."

The use of calculated demonstration periods to screen out unmotivated addicts is not the only reason drug users like Mike confront long waits before gaining access to treatment beds. The other is financial. Rehabilitation from heroin, like using the drug, is expensive. It costs $55 a day to keep an addict in Walden House, $10,000 for a six-month program.

But it's not cheap to have junkies like Mike *out* of treatment either. "I figured it out," he says. "I spent fifty-eight thousand dollars on dope last year."

Mike's felony convictions came before California's "Three Strikes" law was passed. But his next crime will count as a third strike, mandating a twenty-five-year sentence, with an outlay of $25,000 each year for his incarceration. No matter where the government keeps Mike, he's a costly citizen.

For the time being, though, waiting to get into Walden, his habit is down to $105 per week. So keeping Mike on the streets during a demonstration period might have been cost-effective—except for the overdose. By the time he's released from the emergency room as the sun rises on the morning after his OD, ambulance and hospital costs to San Francisco add up to $1,540. The cost of the few hours in the hospital to treat one overdose equaled thirty days of residential drug treatment.

And Mike is one of the fortunate ones. There were 200 deaths from heroin overdoses in San Francisco alone that year. The year before, 1996, 70,500 heroin addicts were brought to emergency rooms across the United States—each visit costing as much as a month of drug rehab.

Every day in San Francisco 1,000 to 1,400 addicts asking for help are kept on waiting lists instead of in applicable treatment programs. The number for California as a whole is

8,000. And for each person waiting, no one knows how many have given up, don't even bother trying to get in, or perish from overdoses. UCLA's Drug Abuse Research Center claims that three to four addicts want treatment for every available slot.

In 1997, while Treatment on Demand was struggling to get off the ground in San Francisco, Baltimore's Mayor Kurt Schmoke was initiating his own exemplar for drug treatment. Yet even with his best efforts, 59,800 Baltimore addicts had access to only 5,700 rehab slots.

In New York City, 60 percent of those paroled from prison who abuse drugs and do not get into treatment programs are back in jail within just three months. In October of 1997, the same month that Mike overdosed in San Francisco, New York Mayor Rudolph Giuliani proposed an ambitious $80 million plan for New York to "lead America in massive reductions in drug abuse." The majority of the funds, he hoped, would come from state and federal sources.

In spite of their boisterous proclamations in support of rehab, however, the feds have been less than forthcoming with funds for New York, or any other city. Four months after Mike's overdose, San Francisco was still scrounging about to fill a $14 million shortfall from the $20 million it needed even to approach Treatment on Demand. That week, General Barry McCaffrey, director of the White House Office of National Drug Control Policy, announced at a press conference, "If you don't like the $36 billion a year incarceration tab, we've got to take some funds and focus in on the addicted with drug treatment programs."

McCaffrey directed $72 million in block grants (from an $18 billion budget) for the states to "get at the treatment requirement." Yet San Francisco alone estimates its costs at $20 million, while Baltimore's is $32 million.

Money for national and international police actions has always vastly outpaced funds to treat addicts at home, and will continue to do so. The drug war budget Congress approved to "reduce drug use to half its present level by 2007" contained a hefty 52 percent expansion in funding. Yet drug treatment programs received only a 17 percent increase.

With the release of the new-millennium budget, McCaffrey himself proclaimed that the feds had "put their money where their mouth was and invested up front in prevention and treatment." But San Francisco, Baltimore, and New York remained insufficiently funded to approach the rehab goals lauded by their mayors and backed, in theory, by Washington.

As a result, addicts like Mike, even if they can prove their motivation by running a gauntlet of demonstration periods—and survive—continue to wait on the streets for treatment beds yet to be funded.

Community Health Outreach Workers (CHOWs), hired when Treatment on Demand started up in San Francisco, try to reach addicts when the perfect opportunity has arrived to get them into rehab—just as they hit the proverbial bottom. "If an addict's in the hospi-

tal," says Larry Meredith, "we should have someone right there to say, look pal, we've got something for you; hang on, we'll take you right over to rehab." Meredith seemed lost in fantasy for a moment. "Of course"—he smiled to cover his frustration—"some people might think that's coddling the addicts."

In the emergency room recovering from his overdose, Mike is in no danger of being coddled. If a CHOW is there in the hospital, he doesn't find his way to Mike. It's still dark in the early morning when Mike is released, on foot in the streets of the Mission.

Wandering alone in his filthy clothes, hungry and out of money, Mike finds a watermelon in front of a grocery store, breaks it open, and eats breakfast, wondering where he can go next. He finds an empty doorway and curls up to sleep. At noon, though, Mike stumbles into 1663 Mission, on time for Marillac's group at Target Cities.

"That darkness was taking my soul with it," Mike tells Marillac when she gasps, seeing his bedraggled presence in the hallway. "I thought I was dead," he tells her, near tears.

Marillac puts an arm around Mike. "We're glad you came back," she says softly, "this is where you should be. That's the most hopeful sign, Mike—for an addict to start using again and still show up for group. I've got high hopes for you."

Target Cities' staff swings into action. Mike's window of opportunity is wide open, but they know it might not stay that way for long. By 4:00 that afternoon, they've found him a residential detox bed at a program called Ozanam.

"This guy was motivated enough to come back to us after an OD," coordinator Tom Hagan tells me while waiting for the van to pick up Mike. "So we're moving fast. Imagine telling someone in Mike's condition we'll have something in a few weeks? This is a great example of what the new system is all about."

In the van on the way to Ozanam Mike sits with head in hands, until he learns the driver is an ex-addict, now one and a half years clean and sober. Soon they're trading war stories, Mike leaning forward, laughing as if he were in a cab on his way to a dinner date rather than en route to a detox center that's been described in group as "hard-core, man, hard-core."

"Hell," Mike tells the driver, "Ozanam's not as good as Walden House, but I've got me a rehab bed!"

They pull up at a dusky windowless building that resembles a factory more than a shelter. Mike grabs a final smoke, bummed off a man sitting on the sidewalk by Ozanam's gray metal door, then rings the bell and disappears inside.

The next day, he's back on the streets, making it over to Mission Street just in time to meet me and Darrell hanging out in front of Target Cities.

"Man, you shoulda *seen* that place!" he tells us, laughing. "Jail mattresses on the floor, wrapped in plastic. You keep your clothes on in case something bites you and you gotta run!" Mike is giggling, giddy from the experience, racking up another war story for his junkie annals.

"The food at Ozanam!" he cries out. "Leftovers from the Donner Party! Some old wino must have died and they cooked him up. In the morning you shower off the lice, then they mop over the mattresses. The water in the bucket gets so dirty the last mattresses are washed in black water."

Mike shakes his head, smiling again. "That's one place I ain't going back to," he says, and Darrell, who during years of alcohol and crack addiction has learned the ropes of every drug program in San Francisco, takes over.

"I'll give you the number for Lifeboat Lodge," he tells Mike. Darrell pulls a pencil stub from behind his ear and a piece of paper from his pocket, putting them in Mike's hand while also pulling two cigarettes from the pack Mike's holding.

"Lifeboat's a *much* nicer place to stay than Ozanam," says Darrell, lighting Mike's cigarette and then his own. They're like two visiting businessmen meeting on the street and discussing the better hotels of the city. "Call at 8:00 A.M. to get one of Target Cities' reserved beds at Lifeboat," Darrell advises Mike. "There's little dividers separating the sleeping sections, and a room with a TV, and—"

"Nah, man"—Mike is laughing, interrupting him—"I ain't never done no shelter thing, don't want to start now. I called my cousin, told him I really need help from the family now. I can stay at his place while I wait for Walden."

Not missing a step in his role as street rehab counselor, Darrell reminds Mike that he needs to call Walden and "keep demonstrating" or he'll be waiting at his cousin's forever.

We walk him to the phone booth on the corner and Mike calls Walden's message machine, carefully reciting his personal code to demonstrate he's still interested in their program. "My number's not up yet," he tells us as the bus pulls up and he swings through the door, heading to his cousin's.

"You have to keep trying," Darrell shouts out to him, "it took me weeks, but I got in!" Mike's gone before Darrell can add that, yes, he'd once gotten into Walden, but then had split the program on a crack cocaine binge. He turns to me, still cherishing his street counselor role. "Those demonstration calls are a bitch," concludes Darrell.

But the reasons for Mike's long wait to get into rehab go far beyond entry-restricting demonstration periods, or local and federal financial shortcomings that limit the number of available beds. Mike played a personal role, as well.

During his Walden intake conference, interviewer Steve Maddox had watched the tightly constricted pupils of Mike's eyes, and noted the slur to his voice.

"Based on his condition that day," Maddox tells me later, "I'd personally have denied Mike space at Walden. I mean, he came to his intake interview high! I didn't think he'd make it through demonstration, let alone the whole therapy."

Then Maddox hesitates, a moment of reflection on the uncertainties of predicting who will or will not get off drugs.

"I've been wrong so often," he continues. "Many who I thought would make it never did. And many I thought wouldn't—they've made it through."

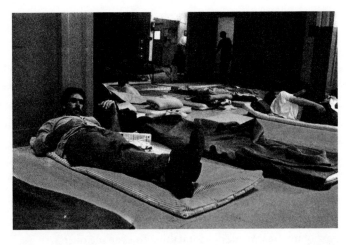

OZANAM

3: NOBODY *VOLUNTEERS* FOR DRUG TREATMENT

DARRELL MCAULEY

If the theme of the burgeoning national drive toward rehab was to assist the most difficult addicts in getting off drugs, Act One foreshadowed doom. On stage, an increasingly frustrated Mike slammed down the phone each day when he called the Walden answering machine to demonstrate his continued interest and, week after week, found that his number was not yet up. Darlene, bearing an improved wardrobe and mannerisms with each daily appearance at the Target Cities groups, lashed out in fury when advised that she was "inappropriate" for the sessions and had been referred out to a program for "clients with mental problems." Darrell, holed up in a homeless shelter waiting for an opening at Acceptance Place, noted on an intake questionnaire that he had once, briefly, taken Prozac. His acceptance into the program was put off until he could have an extensive psychiatric evaluation. "I don't get it," complained Darrell. "Shouldn't seeing a shrink be something they offer as *part* of my treatment, not something to keep me out?"

Watching Mike, Darlene, and Darrell in those first few weeks made Treatment on Demand seem like it was running bizarrely backwards, with junkies fighting to get into rehab while the programs struggled to keep them out. The burden of proof of worthiness, readiness, or sheer ability to undertake treatment was falling on the addicts—an impossible scenario.

I did not yet understand that the fierce power of an addict's obsession with drugs is matched, when the timing is right, by an equally vigorous drive to be free of them.

Over the next year, Darrell McAuley would become my muse, caretaker, and guide—as much philosopher as performer—as the Treatment on Demand show played itself out. A veteran of drug treatment groups in Vermont, North Carolina, Massachusetts, Oregon, and California, and literally thousands of Alcoholics Anonymous meetings (and dozens of Narcotics Anonymous meetings), Darrell has lost his dog in a drunken haze, split open his head after falling out a window, been hospitalized for myriad other stupor-induced traumas, had seizures from delirium tremens—and has continued to drink heavily and smoke crack through it all.

From the moment he started drugs and alcohol at age ten to his wizened thirty-one years when he showed up at Target Cities, Darrell had been sober for three years. Seven weeks before he arrived at Target Cities he'd blown out of Walden House, lured back to the streets by an offer of free beer and crack cocaine after five months in Walden's intensive residential rehab program. Then he was punched in the face by the same man who gave him the crack, and was too ashamed to go back to Walden. Instead, he hit a protracted binge of booze and passed out in an all-night movie theater, all his money stolen. So he headed to Target Cities, apologized for having left Walden, and again requested rehab.

Darrell himself seems hard-pressed to say why he became such an incorrigible drunk and dope fiend. "I don't think I do drugs because I have some diagnosable mental illness," he tells me after Target Cities group one day. "I'm not like majorly depressed, I'm not bipolar, I'm not schizophrenic, I'm not agoraphobic or phobophobic. I'm just an alcoholic who has never been in touch with his feelings, or has drowned out whatever feelings he has with alcohol and drugs. And what a place to be! What is a person who can't be in touch with his feelings? He's nothing.

"I really didn't even have a bad childhood," adds Darrell, almost wistfully, as if having been beaten, sexually molested, or crazy might ease him into a more comfortably plausible explanation.

Darrell tends to downplay his own problematic history, growing up gay in rural Vermont, becoming so self-conscious he developed a blustery and bilious attitude that, combined with his drinking, has won him few friends. Darrell's self-description is that of a loner, not so different from the rest of us that you'd give him up for a drunken goner. Yet that's what he became, in spite of years of the best repeated rehab.

"From the day I picked up a bottle, in seventh grade," he explains simply, "it was—euphoria! I thought, 'This is great! I could do this for the rest of my life.' And that's the only explanation I have."

"Nobody *volunteers* for drug treatment," Darrell tells me as we walk through the seedy Tenderloin district, heading for Lifeboat Lodge. As he'd advised Mike to do, he's laid claim to a bed in the homeless shelter while he demonstrates his interest and waits to hear from Acceptance Place.

"Of course we'd rather be out here getting high," he continues, working his way through the crack and heroin dealers who congregate near the shelter. Whispered voices touting, "Bennies, base, nose candy; you need it, I got it," flutter through the air as we pass by.

"We've been *forced* into rehab," emphasizes Darrell.

"I sure haven't seen anyone forcing Darlene or Mike into treatment," I reply. "Or you, for that matter."

"Listen," says Darrell as he winds his way through the open-air drug market, "I drove back here from Seattle a year ago, and I was so desperate for a drink that I double-parked my car, left the keys in it, and ran into a liquor store. By the time I came out, my car was stolen, and all my belongings with it. It was raining, I was wearing a pair of shoes with no socks, shorts with no underwear, and a T-shirt. That's all I had left."

He stops, his voice cracking. "And I had left Beatrice in the car. Haven't seen her since."

"Beatrice?"

"People who don't have dogs," replies Darrell, "don't understand how hard it is for me to deal with losing Beatrice. All of a sudden, she pops into my head, a hot day, Beatrice running at my side, panting, staring up at me. And I feel like I need to bawl. But I've held back my tears until my throat hurts so much my Adam's apple is sticking out—because I'm afraid to be alone and crying, afraid that if I do I'll start drinking again."

We're at the door to the homeless shelter and Darrell wants to get away from the temptations of the street. He's been addicted, at various times, to marijuana, alcohol, crack, an assortment of hallucinogens, lottery tickets, and, he insists, the peanut butter and milk chocolate cupcakes called Funny Bones.

"We're all forced into treatment because of what's happened to us," says Darrell, heading into the shelter. "It's because of what we've done to ourselves and everybody we care about. Look at Mike—he used to be a plumber, married, children, nice house. Now he's not allowed to see his kids, sleeps on the floor at his cousin's, no more money for dope. And Darlene, sixteen years homeless, on speed, hallucinating. Can you imagine? And me, after I lost Beatrice I kept on drinking and fell down some stairs, broke my collarbone and bruised every other bone in my body. All these policemen came and I was in four-point restraints and carted off to the hospital. *That* is how I started looking for treatment this time. It's not like we've suddenly chosen rehab! It's that we've hit the mother of all bottoms. Only place lower is the grave. And when we're between the morgue and the programs, most of us—not all—will head for the programs."

Darrell smiles sardonically, holding open the door to the shelter before moving in to search out an empty cot, scrunching up his face at the acrid smell of beer, vomit, and urine floating up from the nearby gutter.

"Sure, it seems like the programs are fighting to keep us out," he advises me, nodding good-bye. "But remember, we're fighting just as hard to get in."

I stand alone on the corner by the homeless shelter, my head shaking "no" to each offer of crack, meth, heroin, and weed that passes my way. To hear it from Darrell, the disasters brought on by drink and drugs finally generate an agony intense enough to propel an addict toward clean and sober. But from all I had heard from the counselors and drug experts, it was personal agony that had driven most addicts to drugs in the first place.

"What should I pay attention to when I talk to your clients?" I had asked Marillac when she'd agreed to let me sit in on her pre-placement group at Target Cities.

She smiled, as if the question were too simple. "No matter what our clients tell you," said the rehab counselor, "all the street-tough stories, the dope stories, all the fun tales of copping and getting high and being crazy—forget about that. Addiction is not about chemicals, and it stops being fun faster than they can shoot their first dose. What it *is* about is pain. Mike and Darlene and Darrell—I don't know them so well yet, but I promise you one thing. The drugs are not what brought on their problems. They *started* drugs to cover up their suffering. And they're here now because the dope no longer covers that pain. So if anybody in my group tells you they use heroin, or cocaine, or speed, or whatever because it makes them feel good, you tell them they're lying. The drugs make them feel *less bad*. And when that stops working, they show up here."

Abandoned by his biological mother, Mike was adopted into a devoted, extended family of Filipino immigrants, bound together by having survived the torturous Bataan Death March in the Philippines during the Second World War, and a protracted pilgrimage to San Francisco. So Mike's tall, burly looks belie his adopted *Pagsolingan* surname. Even today he favors eating in San Francisco's Filipino restaurants, the waitresses staring in wide-eyed surprise when the six-foot-two white man orders *dinuguan*—pork blood stew—in perfect Tagalog.

"If you knew the loving family my brother and I were adopted into," says his sister, Michelle, "the good Catholic house we were raised in—you'd never believe Michael could become some drugged-out criminal."

Michelle's description of the loving Pagsolingan family of her early childhood years rings with truth. After that, for good reason, her memory blurs. But her brother's is crystal clear.

"I remember a can opener flying at my dad," says Mike. "I was five, and I'm holding on to my mom's leg, crying, telling her to stop. But she just kept at it. Then my father started sobbing, and he picked me up and hugged me. After my mom disappeared, my dad tried to keep us with him."

Mike recites this part of his story with a flat, apathetic tone, as if speaking of someone else. Then a tenderness enriches his voice.

"My dad loved us, man, and we'd have done anything for him. He was a good father, trying to hold it all together, but we got took away by social services because he was gambling too much, had collectors chasing him."

Mike can't remember much about the many foster homes he and his sister bounced in and out of, beginning when he was seven. Except for one. "White room, brown-framed bed, mattress, no sheets, no covers," he recites the details. "That's in the neighbor's house, not our foster home. The neighbor's bedroom."

His voice is subdued, almost inaudible.

"It wasn't so much that the guy molested me," he intones, "but that for like three years I knew he was doing it to Michelle, too. And I didn't *stop* him. So I got all this shame about that, man, and then I think, wait a minute—I was eight years old, what was I going to do?" He stares down at his hands, and adds, "Don't matter when it happened, I see that room every day."

By the time Mike told me this story I had interviewed dozens of addicts in treatment programs across the city. Almost half told similar stories of being sexually molested in childhood. I heard it so often that, each time, I went back to check my notes from the others. I decided it must be some quirk, a statistical fluke or something about the way I'd been focusing my questions during the interviews.

I checked it out with Darrell. "Even though other physical and verbal childhood abuse is more common," he told me, "sex molestation comes up so often in rehab because of how intense it is. You lose all trust in the world, I guess. Those who were molested as kids just can't figure out where to put that, so many turn to drink or drugs, or *something* to numb out the memories."

Nonetheless, after reviewing my notes, I remained incredulous. The rate of childhood sexual molestation, I thought, could not be as high as I'd been hearing.

On December 2, 1998, the *Journal of the American Medical Association* published an astounding report that collected data from 166 studies on the sexual abuse of boys. The report, by Drs. William Holmes and Gail Slap of the University of Pennsylvania, found that "The perpetrators tend to be [heterosexual] males who are known but frequently unrelated to the victims. The abuse typically occurs outside the home, is repeated and involves penetration." An interview with Dr. Holmes confirmed my sense that, when addicts in rehab "run their stories" to each other, a surprisingly large number start off with childhood molestation. "By the sixth grade," said Dr. Holmes, "the rates of using alcohol, cocaine, marijuana, and intravenous drugs are up to twenty-five to fifty times higher for boys who have been sexually abused than for boys who have not."

Studies of girls had long before shown that some 60 percent who enter drug rehab have experienced incest and molestation as children. Seventy percent of the addicted women had been raped or molested *prior* to their substance abuse.

The significance of such high rates of sexual abuse for both men and women in drug rehab programs is profound. "Remembering and reexperiencing feelings associated with sexual trauma," notes the *Journal of Counseling and Development,* "is a major precipitant of relapse."

Mike and Michelle left foster care to rejoin their father, and a new mom, when Mike was twelve. "My dad's friends would say, 'Oh, so this is your son,' " recalls Mike. "And my dad would tell them, 'Yeah, we adopted him. His name is Michael, he's emotionally disturbed.' He'd include that when he introduced me," says Mike, "like right after I got back to him from foster care. I'm still trying to figure that out, man. I mean, I had a temper, acting out, whacking kids around and stuff. But 'emotionally disturbed'? What was with that?"

Soon after leaving foster care, Mike, with his new friends, learned to fake brawls in front of mom-and-pop grocery stores. When the owners came out to break up the fights, Mike would run in and steal beer for them all. By fourteen, he was living in Huckleberry House, a home for juvenile offenders.

"It just progressed from there," says Mike. "I don't know if I blame it on my childhood, or peer pressure or what—it just happened. Reds, Quaaludes, Valiums, like when I was fifteen and sixteen. Then 714s and Roarers and Black Beauties. And for my seventeenth birthday, my girlfriend gave me a gram of coke."

I ask Mike if he thought being molested had any relation to his drug use.

"I don't know, man," he says. "There were so many things, how can anybody figure a question like that? I'll tell you one thing, though. A couple of years back I start getting these freaky dreams, the guy raping me, the white room, all that. And then I get this view of my dad, sitting on the blue couch with his head in his hands, and he's crying."

We're in the kitchen at his cousin's house, and I see as he's sipping coffee that Mike's hands are squeezing the porcelain cup so hard his knuckles are white.

"Stop the story there if you want," I say.

"No, man, let's do it," he replies, swiping his blue denim shirtsleeve across his eyes. "I spent four hundred fifty-seven bucks on dope one day after the dreams started, and I used it all in like six hours. So I came home and went straight to my wife's purse for money to get more. She tried to stop me, and I socked her in the face. And then I realized what I'd done and ran outside and hung myself from a tree with my belt."

Mike hears my gasp and responds with his oft-repeated expression when he needs to pause and break the tension in our conversations, a long, drawn-out, "Fuuuck."

"The goddamn branch broke," he continues. "Can you believe it? My wife runs out to the garden, and I'm lying in the dirt with this belt around my neck, tied to a broken tree branch! And all I'm thinking is, 'Don't let my daughters see this, please, God, don't let them see.'"

"I screwed up with my girls so many times," Mike tells me. "I'll never forget the look on Jessica's face when she walked in and I had a needle in my arm. She was nine years old."

Mike never physically or sexually abused his own children, but quickly admits the significance of having neglected them. "In my entire time with my kids," he says, "there was only eighteen months when I wasn't doing drugs."

While it may or may not be true, in Mike's particular case, that his own abuse as a child was "responsible" for his drug addiction, there is no doubt of the self-perpetuating cycle by which children who are abused, neglected, and later addicted often become parents who abuse or neglect their own children.

Joseph Califano, Jr., U.S. Secretary of Health, Education and Welfare during the Carter administration, now heads the National Center on Addiction and Substance Abuse at Columbia University. In January of 1999, the center concluded a two-year study of the relationship between parental drug addiction and child abuse.

"Substance abuse causes or exacerbates seven out of ten cases of child abuse or neglect," the study reports, also concluding that "children whose parents abuse drugs and alcohol are almost three times likelier to be abused and more than four times likelier to be neglected than children of parents who are not substance abusers."

From 1986 to 1997, those same years in which the number of drug addicts in the United States was reduced by nearly half, the numbers of abused and neglected children, according to the center's study, increased from 1.4 million to more than 3 million—again demonstrating that we are a nation of fewer drug users with an ever-increasing drug problem.

"Our report," announced Califano, "exposes how alcohol, crack cocaine, methamphetamine, heroin, and marijuana are fueling this population explosion of battered and neglected children."

The report, however, stopped short of addressing the tightly bound linkage of mental illness, poverty, lack of education, and ghettoized living to both drug use and child abuse. To claim that child abuse is *caused* by drug addiction without emphasizing other conditions that led both to the abuse *and* the addiction, is to drive us further toward the simplistic conclusion that it is drugs, and drugs only, that create our problems. Dr. Alan Leshner, Director of the National Institutes of Drug Abuse, notes that "Determining the exact relationship between child abuse and drug abuse is exceedingly difficult, given the role that variables such as poverty, family dysfunction, and the level of social support for victims . . . play."

But these social factors do not seem to be reflected in our current approaches to drug rehab. From 1994 to 1997, in-home social services provided by child welfare agencies to families with children at risk of abuse—from all causes—were cut by 58 percent. The report by Califano's center found that only 5.8 percent of addiction-treatment providers thought they could rapidly place addicted parents at risk of abusing their children into residential treatment programs. And residential rehab programs that allow parents to stay in residence *with* their children are the most scarce of any programs in the country, often forcing addicted parents who want rehab to choose between treatment and putting their kids in foster care.

The lack of adequate rehab for parents addicted to drugs begins with pregnancy. In Rocky Mount, Virginia, Britta Smith, pregnant and addicted to crack cocaine, went through the phone book calling every treatment program listed, only to learn that none accepted pregnant women on Medicaid. When Smith continued to smoke crack, the Commonwealth of Virginia filed charges against her for fetal endangerment. "These women beg for treatment," said Lynn Paltrow, an ACLU attorney who helped defend Smith against the charges, "and they're turned away. Then they're arrested for not seeking the treatment that's not available."

Rehab for pregnant addicts, if done well, can break the cycle of addiction and child abuse. Dr. John McCarthy, an addiction specialist in Sacramento, California, runs a program in which 88 percent of mothers addicted to heroin are treated and able to "successfully parent their children." "However," notes Dr. McCarthy, "these recovery rates can be achieved only by combining medical/obstetrical care, psychiatric care, and drug treatment." Most addicted women, he quickly adds, do not have access to these services. That lack, says Dr. McCarthy, creates "increased vulnerability to drug use among a generation of parents whose children suffer when they suffer."

None of this, of course, is to argue that parental substance abuse is not a major factor to be considered in protecting children from harm. But to treat substance abuse as an issue isolated from psychological and social roots is an invitation to continued disasters—passed from this generation on to the next.

Mike's childhood molestations had put him at severe risk for later drug abuse. And his child abuse, drug use, and suicidal depressions made it likely that he'd later neglect his own children, putting them at greater jeopardy of suffering the same disasters for which he is now desperately seeking treatment.

"I'm sorry man, it's all so fucking weird," says Mike, wiping at his tears after telling me about his suicide attempt by hanging. We'd been alone at his cousin's house, but it's dusk now and his cousin and young nephews are due back for dinner any minute. And Mike hasn't yet made his daily demonstration call to the Walden answering machine.

"I hated myself for what I had become, and for what I did," he says. "I mean, that was my daughters' mother that I hit, the woman I loved. And she's out there in the yard with me on the ground, saying she still loves me, come in, it'll be OK. But I was scared of what would happen if I went back, that I might hurt her or the girls. So I left."

Years later, separated from his wife and in another relationship, with Connie Slattery, Mike tried to stop using heroin.

He describes Connie as "an angel," a woman who's "got all her ducks lined up—in a row, man!" Connie is straight, says Mike, she doesn't do drugs. "When we met, I was straight too," he adds, "straight out of jail. For burglary."

"I really needed what Connie had," Mike tells me. "Normalcy." Desperate to maintain their relationship, he tried to stop shooting heroin.

"Man, I was like ten days clean," he recalls, "and I'm getting these pictures in my head, same as in the dreams, but they're hitting me now when I'm awake. White room, the bed, the guy on me, everything. And I start shaking all over, sweating. I can't sleep at night because these pictures are coming at me. And Connie's laying next to me really worried. I mean, I'm like this when I'm *not* doing drugs."

With Connie's encouragement, Mike found his way to a psychiatrist out in San Francisco's Sunset district.

"I tell this shrink lady about these memories coming up," he recalls. "She says, 'Of course you're having flashbacks, it's 'cause you quit using dope! Your mind's clear enough to remember things now.' So she diagnoses me with that PTSD thing. Post-traumatic stress disorder. Tells me I need really intensive therapy, man, got to deal with all those memories."

Mike laughs, shaking his head back and forth, quietly setting his coffee cup down on the kitchen counter.

"Then she tells me she can't be my shrink and work with me on those memories until I'm like two months clean, not using dope. Can't do therapy with no dope fiend who's still getting high, she says. It don't work. Come back when I'm clean."

He blows air over his chipped lower teeth, a whistling noise accompanying his long, sighed "Fuuuck."

"So at first I'm like buying it, you know, what she says kind of makes sense. But then I'm thinking, now what do I do? I'm having these flashbacks that are so real they scare me half out of my skin, and I go to this shrink and spill my guts, let her know all my secrets. I just finish telling her I don't get that crap in my head when I'm using heroin, and she tells me to come back when I've been off the dope for two months. I'm bawling like a little bitch when she tells me that."

"After a major trauma, like sexual assault," says Dr. Pablo Stewart, an expert on the relationship between drug use and mental and emotional illness, "our brains do a wonderful thing, they shut down, numb out. But it doesn't last forever, which leads to intrusive thoughts, nightmares, daymares, flashbacks that dominate every inch of their being. So what do people do with those intrusive thoughts? They numb them out again. How? Alcohol and drugs. Drugs and alcohol are not as bad as the intrusive thoughts. Until you give them something better, *expect* them to drink or shoot dope."

Mike sits at the kitchen counter in his cousin's house.

"I lasted two days after seeing the shrink before I did my big hit," he says. "Six rockets, loaded syringes."

His right hand points to his left forearm, then his thumb and index finger squeeze in rapid, pincerlike movements. *"Wshh, wshh, wshh,"* he hisses. "I hit one right after the other, man. And I would have done six more if I had 'em. I was going for that final high, the big one. Woke up two days later, laying in a pile of my own shit in some hotel room. Couldn't believe I was still alive."

We sit silently as the room dims, near sunset, and neither of us moves to turn the light on. I ask, trying to orient myself, "What year was all that?"

Mike stares, then says softly. "This year, man. Three months ago."

The front door bursts open and his nephews come barreling into the house, baseball mitts on, pleading with their uncle to come out and throw some balls with them while there's still some light. They charge out the door and he turns to me, first laughing at the antics of the boys, then turning somber again.

"Scares the hell out of me just to be here," says Mike. "Because I'm beginning to realize, for the first time, man, I have to learn how to live all over. Like from the very beginning."

He picks up his cousin's phone and dials Walden's answering machine, listening to the list of numbers for those accepted into the program that day, none of which is his. He waits for the beep and recites, "This is Mike. Number twenty-one. Still here, still waiting."

"Hey, man," he tells me, "thanks for coming by," and heads toward the door and the shouting voices of his nephews.

"I mean, look what we've been talking about today, huh? I ain't even *in* rehab yet and all this stuff's coming up. I tell you, though, I miss my girls like nothing in this world. Whatever Walden wants me to do in that program so I'm able to be with my girls again, I'm going to do it."

Mike grins his Marlboro Man smile.

"But if Walden ever gets to my damn number," he says, "that program's going to have one piece of work cut out."

The sunrise barely dents the chill of the morning wind blowing off the waters of China Basin and into Darlene's improvised tent. She thrusts her feet deep into the end of her sleeping bag, pulls the top over her head, and tugs her large brown teddy bear even tighter against her chest. Darlene squeezes her eyes shut against the light pouring through the thin plastic tarp suspended over her. Then she sits bolt-upright, one arm swinging out of the sleeping bag while the other tries to wrap the bag around her for warmth, the loosed arm searching for the small clock near the pile of cassette tapes at her side.

She squints at the clock, sees the hands pointing to two-thirty. Wide-awake now, and puzzled, she holds the timepiece to her ear. There's no humming noise. The AA batteries she'd "borrowed" to be certain she'd wake up on time had died.

Darlene is up in a flash, pulling a thick but fog-moist gray sweater over her head against the cold. Throwing open the lid of the metal shipping trunk at the foot of her sleeping bag, she drags a skirt out from the densely packed clothes. She'd washed the skirt the day before, a dollar's worth of quarters at the Laundromat, and now, although thoroughly wrinkled, it's at least clean. Darlene squirms her two-hundred-plus pounds into the skirt, rummages for a shirt that might match the red-flowered print, and extracts a tight black velvet tank top. Too cold to even think of changing from sweater to tank top, she shoves it into her backpack and heads out to get a shower. For her first meeting at STOP, the drug program she'd been referred to by Target Cities, she would at least show up in better clothes than her usual torn-at-the-knees jeans, and with her hair not sticking out a foot from her head in an untamed Afro.

The STOP group meeting is at 10:00, and when Darlene runs from her tent and across the parking-lot homeless encampment to the water, carrying a bucket back for her dog, Bruce, she notices her long shadow cast by the low-slung sun and sighs with relief.

Pulling Bruce from where the dog is still asleep alongside Darlene's sleeping bag, she ties her to the fence and rummages in the shopping cart next to the makeshift tent, finding a bag of dog food and pouring out a bowl. Then Darlene unlocks one of her two airplanes chained to the fence, slings her backpack over her shoulder, heads for the hole in the wire, and squeezes herself and the bicycle through. She jumps on and pedals furiously across the Third Street bridge—into *their* world.

Darlene careens her airplane into the courtyard where the homeless wait for breakfast and showers at Martin de Porres. The food line is long this morning and she opts for a hot shower first. She places her backpack safely within arm's reach while she bathes and then stuffs her wet hair tightly into a blue wool cap. Warmer now, she pulls out the black velvet tank top from her backpack and finishes dressing. Slinging on her metal bangle bracelets, then taking silver necklaces and earrings from the front of her pack, she checks out her image in the single steamy mirror above the sink. Darlene has gained some ten pounds since she stopped shooting speed over a week ago, and the tank top clings to her too-exposed cleavage. She decides that a second shirt on top will bring her appearance up to program par. Heading out to the box of donated clothes in the open plaza, she finds a red-plaid front-button woodsman's shirt and pulls it on, the front hanging loosely open. Then, sitting on the ground while a crowd of homeless mill about her, Darlene carefully brushes on two layers of purple fingernail polish.

From there to the breakfast line, where for the first time she finds someone with a watch: 9:45. She wolfs down a serving of oatmeal, shaking her head when friends in the crowd come by to talk about where some good methamphetamine might be found that day.

"I don't do speed no more," says Darlene repeatedly, pushing food into her mouth as she tries to ignore their sarcastic replies. She hides her hurt feelings when they walk away from her, saying, "Yeah, wait until William's out of jail, then we'll see."

Darlene shakes off a chill, running her hand along the goose bumps lining her skin.

"I can't even think about William," she'd told me days before. "Since he's been in jail, if I think about him everything gets mixed up. Like I hear the word 'Jackson' all of a sudden."

Darlene had put her hand next to her ear, tapping her fingers together to mimic chattering lips, her way of letting me know when she's referring to the noises in her head. "I don't even know who Jackson is," she said. "I *like* to think about William, but I can't because that other noise fucks it all up. My mind's just too damn loud!"

She rises from the bench at Martin de Porres, takes her bowl and silverware to be washed, shouts good-bye to her friends, and grabs her airplane for the ride over to her first group meeting at STOP.

"We've recommended STOP to Darlene for a number of reasons," says Target Cities clinical coordinator Tom Hagan. "STOP is specifically for people who abuse stimulants like speed and crack. And the STOP staff are skilled in working with psychotic clients, drug-induced or not. STOP is an intensive day-treatment program, a few hours or more per day, five to seven days a week. And we've been able to place people there quickly." In an ideal world, Tom tells me, Darlene would be sent to a live-in, rather than a daytime-only treatment program. But Darlene, as is true for most long-term homeless, would not even consider the idea of such a restricted life.

Tom casually omits one other reason for sending Darlene to STOP: she's been driving the Target Cities' staff to distraction. Darlene has remained untrusting of Marillac, the group counselor, and has fixed her attentions on her individual placement counselor, Kathy Meyers. An African-American woman who has known hardships equal to Darlene's, Kathy became her advocate, friend, and counselor.

"Some people believe in spirits and some don't," Darlene says, trying to explain the difference she sees between Marillac and Kathy. "It's like—you need to look into the sky sometimes, and Marillac doesn't and Kathy does. OK? Kathy's up *there* with me," says Darlene, pointing vaguely skyward.

"Often, I just listen to Darlene, without asking her to do anything," says Kathy, sitting in her tiny office at Target Cities where she keeps the lights dimmed to near-darkness and her computer pushed to the back of her cluttered desk as if to hide all seeming pretense. "I listen, and I make no demands of her, so that if nothing else Darlene feels there's this one place she can be heard. My door is open for that even though my job is to place her in a program, not be her long-term counselor. She's formed a connection, and she feels safe and wanted here. That's all I'm asking so far."

At Target Cities staff meetings, though, Kathy has taken some heat for her close, time-consuming attachment to Darlene. Talking to me now in her office, her voice trails off; there are three other clients waiting to see her and she's trying to explain the staff's decision to get Darlene moved quickly out to STOP. Kathy won't say if she agrees with the move or not.

"Darlene is such a challenge," she says, waving at the door to let her next client know she'll be right there, "and we're so close to winning her over. But the whole staff has talked about it, and I can't be her therapist, with her dropping in every time she's upset. We're simply not set up for that here. She needs a structured program, so I've talked to Darlene about STOP as the place that can actually *help* her."

On my way to Marillac's group I run into Darlene, slice of pizza in hand, in the waiting room. She gets up and gives me a tight hug, trying to smile but barely hiding her tears.

"I thought you were at STOP today, first day there," I say, backing up for a better look at this strange apparition in red-flowered dress, black velvet too-tight tank top, and red-plaid cotton shirt.

"I got there five minutes late," she says, "maybe ten," sitting down again to munch at her pizza. "The lady at STOP told me to go away, says I have to learn to be on time if I'm going to be in their group. And I went through the war zone to get there!"

"What war zone?"

"*The* war zone," she replies. "Everybody's like racing back and forth trying to get to work, stores, school, and I'm flying my airplane through traffic. *That* war zone. So I get to the STOP place five minutes late and—" Darlene starts crying, throwing her pizza on the table. "And that bitch tells me to come back tomorrow, on time. She says, 'We have our rules, and you have to follow them like everybody else.' Well, I'm *not* like everybody else!"

"Maybe you can try again tomorrow?" I offer. "What did you tell her?"

Darlene wipes at her eyes, then giggles. "I told her to kiss my big black ass!"

"Uh-oh." I try to hold back, but begin laughing with her.

"So I guess I can't try again tomorrow, huh?" she asks.

"I don't know," I reply. "It's probably not the worst thing they've ever heard. Not a great start, though."

Mike comes bounding through the door, still waiting for Walden, still coming every day to Target Cities.

"Hey, Darlene, bring that pizza inside and eat with us," he says, rushing to be on time for Marillac's group.

"I went in there already," says Darlene. "Marillac says I'm supposed to be at STOP, so I can't be in group here no more. She gave me a piece of pizza, though. I'm waiting to talk to Kathy."

I ask Darlene to meet me after group, and head inside the room with Mike.

"How come she didn't get into STOP?" he asks.

"Didn't get there on time."

"You kidding me?" Mike stops in his tracks. "I thought that's a group for like homeless crazy people who are strung out on drugs? Far as I can tell, Darlene's only got two times: daytime and nighttime. Jeez, give her a break! It's amazing she showed up at all."

In group, on the empty chair where Darlene usually sits, there is a single purple rose. "It's a Sterling," she tells me later, "the best-smelling rose in the whole wide world! I gave one to Marillac, and put the other on my seat when she told me I couldn't be in the group no more."

Acronyms and definitions galore have been created by health professionals to describe people like Darlene: *MICA,* mentally ill chemical abusers; *MISA,* mentally ill substance abusers; *CAMI,* chemical abusers with mental illness; *SAMI,* substance abusers with mental illness; or, most commonly used, *dual diagnosis,* referring to someone with one diagnosis of a mental illness and a second of a substance abuse disorder. In rehab circles, these clients are referred to as *double trouble,* while the U.S. Department of Health Services notes that "a preferred definition is *mentally ill chemically affected [person].*"

Not surprisingly, the framers of Treatment on Demand had foreseen the dilemma of the Darlenes—how to deal with the MICAs, MISAs, CAMIs, and SAMIs that would crowd the doors of the treatment centers once they were thrown wide open. "The system must not allow for difficult clients who can be served, to be turned away because they are difficult to serve," wrote the Treatment on Demand Planning Council, a community advisory board to Larry Meredith and the health department. "Optimally," they added, "services should adjust to the needs of the clients, rather than attempting to mold clients to be appropriate for the services."

The trademark of dual diagnosis clients like Darlene is *disorder.* Their hallucinatory and delusionally disordered thinking is exacerbated by disordered and impulsive drug use, which saturates their lives and thought processes with even more disorder. So rehab programs for dually diagnosed clients argue, of course, that their task is to impose order on such disordered lives. Chaos would reign if they didn't establish, and strictly enforce, rules. Groups would be disrupted by clients barging in late, dominating the conversation, interrupting, cursing, yelling, threatening violence or carrying out their threats. The rehab programs cannot be as disorderly as the clients they are trying to treat.

Yet insisting that Darlene be on time to her first treatment meeting for dually diagnosed clients is like ordering swimming students to float on their first day of class. Some will bob safely, and that part of their education can be skipped. Others will drown, making further instruction difficult.

Darlene was referred to STOP because she was tormented and overwhelmed by her disordered thinking. She was sent away because her thinking was too disordered to get her there on time.

"You focus on only one thing when a dual diagnosis patient arrives," says psychiatrist Pablo Stewart. "How do we get her to come see us again? After that, we can start working out the details, step by step. But if we push too hard and she won't come back, where does that get anybody?" Dr. Stewart summarizes the dilemma succinctly: "You can't do any treatment," he says, "unless you've got a patient."

But you can't do any treatment unless you've got a program. In a fine balancing act, programs' needs for sanity are weighed against the insane lives of their clients. Poor judgment calls are inevitable. It's easy to look back and say that Darlene should have been invited to stay even though she'd arrived late, that she first be engaged in treatment and *then* requested to come on time. But such armchair psychology is a luxury denied to rehab counselors working on the front lines with some of the most difficult clients.

Any effective drug rehab system must stretch and mold itself to accommodate the seemingly inappropriate needs and behaviors of people who abuse speed and act crazy, since meth and mental illness are particularly common partners. In San Francisco, says the Treatment on Demand Planning Council, "fifty percent of clients reporting speed as a primary problem are considered to have psychiatric problems." Speed—a drug that hypes up the mind like a thousand cups of coffee—truly does make people crazy; and crazy people often use speed.

Methamphetamine (known in the streets as crank, meth, ice, speed, or crystal) is not unique to urban drug centers like San Francisco. In Pismo Beach, a small coastal town far from the urbanity of both San Francisco and Los Angeles, 85 percent of drug-related arrests in 1998 netted a suspect under the influence of methamphetamine. While 90 percent of the nation's speed is produced in California, there's an extensive national methamphetamine distribution network that makes Federal Express seem inefficient. In 1998 *Time* called meth the "powdery plague on America's heartland," reporting on the "Midwest crank belt, from Oregon to Iowa, where the drug is known as the poor man's cocaine in towns that barely had cocaine in the first place."

The pernicious combination of speed and mental illness has filled rehab programs around the country with hallucinatory, dually diagnosed addicts who make Darlene seem easy to work with. But you don't have to be on speed to enter the tormented world of those with dual diagnoses. The federal Substance Abuse and Mental Health Services Administration, in a 1997 summary of research on all dual diagnosis clients, found that "fifty-one percent of those with a mental disorder have at least one addictive disorder." Viewed from the addiction instead of the mental health side, the numbers are equally disturbing. "Between forty-one and sixty-five percent of those with an addictive disorder (to drugs other than alcohol) also have at least one mental disorder," states the federal agency. Thirty-seven percent of alcoholics have a second psychological disorder.

Given these data intricately interconnecting substance abuse and mental illness, Marillac's counseling room at Target Cities, filled with alcoholics, heroin junkies, speed freaks, and crackheads, becomes as much mental health clinic as drug rehab center. Dr. Stewart goes as far as to argue that most cities would do better combining their mental health departments and substance abuse services under one roof.

Currently, that is far from the case.

At a meeting of hundreds of drug rehab counselors in San Francisco, Dr. Stewart did a quick experiment.

"All the mental health counselors in the room," he announced, "raise your hands." About half lifted their arms up high.

"How many of you have substance abuse counselors working directly with your organizations?" asked the psychiatrist. Three-quarters of the hands dropped, accompanied by an audible sigh from the audience.

"OK," said Dr. Stewart, "all the substance abuse counselors raise your hands." Half again.

"And how many of you have mental health counselors working directly in your organizations?" Again, three-fourths of the hands dropped down.

"Now," said Dr. Stewart, "let's have some fun. How many are here from the criminal justice system?" About twenty hands reached for the sky.

"And how many of you have either mental health *or* substance abuse counselors working directly in your organization?" Only two hands stayed up.

"All you mental health folks, and all you substance abuse folks," exclaimed the psychiatrist, "will you *please* start working with each other—because most of the time, you're dealing with the same clients!"

In one sense, Darlene's referral to STOP reflected her good fortune. It's rare that someone with combined mental illness and addiction makes it to one of the scarce and scattered dual diagnosis rehab programs like STOP. More commonly, dually diagnosed clients arrive randomly at either the Department of Mental Health or Community Substance Abuse Services, under their own power or guided in by the police. If they enter the door at Mental Health, they become a client with a mental illness who happens to use drugs. If they make their entry at Substance Abuse Services, and the drug counselor correctly diagnoses the mental disorder, they become drug addicts who are also dealing with a mental illness.

In an overburdened system, clients are bounced like Ping-Pong balls between the two agencies. "I can't treat your psychosis and hallucinations," mental health counselors tell their dual diagnosis clients, "until you're off drugs. You need to go to Substance Abuse Services first." And the drug abuse counselors tell *their* dual diagnosis clients, "I can't get you to stay off drugs until you're not psychotic and hallucinating." They refer them to mental health services.

In fact, Mike had first heard about Target Cities from the psychiatrist who correctly diagnosed his post-traumatic stress disorder, but then was told that his mental illness couldn't be treated until he was off drugs. His first response was to shoot up with six rockets in a row and nearly die. Only after that did he arrive at Target Cities for drug treatment, and get referred to Walden—where his PTSD was promptly forgotten in their efforts to keep him off heroin.

Darrell expresses a cynical suspicion about the dual diagnosis dilemma, saying it's too easy for addicts and alcoholics to ask for, and receive, mental illness labels.

"Hell, I could be on lithium, Prozac, you name it, from the way I've behaved on booze and drugs over the years," he says. "If I had wanted to claim depression or being manic or something to get more government benefits, I could have convinced them of that. But appearing to be crazy, that's just part of the cycle of using drugs and then getting sober over and over again. Alcoholism can *look* like depression, and coming off alcohol makes you look like you're hyper and crazy. We may act like we're mentally ill, but we're basically just addicted."

Yet when he delves back over the many and varied AA groups he's attended over the years, Darrell quickly concedes the linkage of mental illness and substance abuse disorders. "I would say it's about fifty-fifty," he says. "Some people are just babbling, can't even get out a coherent sentence. Others are so depressed they just sit in the corners, crying, not saying a word. And hardly any are getting real psychiatric care."

Darrell waited for weeks at the homeless shelter in the heart of the Tenderloin's drug market while Acceptance Place tried to figure out what to do with the fact that he'd once, briefly, been prescribed Prozac, a medication for depression. Since one-third of alcoholics have a history of major depression, it is astounding that such a program did not have counselors capable of evaluating and treating both problems. Finally, after an evaluation by an outside psychiatrist, Acceptance Place let him in.

But Acceptance Place is in no way unique. The Substance Abuse and Mental Health Services Administration reports that, for the ten million U.S. citizens with dual diagnoses, "The number who are receiving care by clinicians trained to treat them in an integrated and effective manner is generally agreed by experts to be very small. . . . Every survey . . . has indicated that most members of this population receive inadequate, ineffective, or no treatment services. The cost to the individuals, their families, and the nation is enormous."

So while Darlene's first day at STOP provided a precarious beginning, she had at least not been sliced in two between mental health and substance abuse services. And she'd had the further good fortune to have Kathy and Target Cities to run back to, albeit with tail between her legs.

Tom Hagan, hearing that Darlene has bounced back to Target Cities after telling the STOP counselor to kiss her ass, listens carefully and then leans back in his office chair.

"God knows Darlene is frustrating," he says. "She gets on people's nerves, and she's a good example of one of the more difficult people to keep engaged in treatment. But interestingly enough, that's one of the things Kathy's been able to do—keep Darlene engaged, and coming back. So even though at this point some of my staff are saying, 'Get her out of here,' from my point of view we just keep up what we've been doing. And Kathy," he adds, "loves the challenge of challenging the programs, advocating for her clients. She'll get Darlene another shot at STOP."

"I do this job because I really do care," says Kathy. "And Darlene senses that I'm not just going through the motions with her or anybody else who walks through this door." She calls STOP and arranges for Darlene to have another chance.

I drive out to China Basin to find Darlene and tell her she can try STOP again the next day. If that doesn't work out, Kathy's lining up another program called Genesis, for homeless, dually diagnosed clients.

As I make the sharp left turn just over the Third Street bridge into China Basin, Darlene flies by on her airplane, hitting the brakes and turning around when she sees my car.

"I don't think you want to hang with me right now," she says, out of breath from riding so fast.

"Can't think of why not," I reply.

"Because I just did a hit," she laughs, "first time in ten days. And Darlene James is not here on Planet Earth!"

She's shouting and laughing at the same time, a high, shrill, bewitching voice that I had not yet heard.

"I thought you didn't do speed anymore?" I ask.

"See over there," says Darlene, pointing to the parking-lot homeless encampment, to Red's tent near the hole in the fence. "There's a whole bunch of people there, bigger than the Target Cities group, bigger than this whole fucking city! And I'm the only one not doing speed and there's a lot of energy coming at me from them."

Her voice has quieted. She's leaning her bike against the car, and she begins to cry. "Nobody understands that," she says quietly.

"I'll try if you want," I say.

"I'll deal with the purple roses later," replies Darlene.

"What?"

"Nothing."

"I lost you."

"Yeah, I lost me too. You and Darrell and Mike and Kathy, and even Marillac, have become a part of me now, but I'm not going to die because you dumped me. I'm not."

Darlene spins her airplane around and begins circling the car, once, twice, three times, and then pedals furiously over the Third Street bridge and out of sight.

WALDEN HOUSE

Eight weeks after he'd first shown up at Target Cities asking for help with his drug addiction, Mike receives a call from Walden telling him to get over there, bags packed.

"They called *me,*" he says with breathless exhilaration. "I hadn't even phoned their machine yet today! I'm excited, man, in a really positive mind," he exclaims, bubbling over. "I've been straight all this time hanging out at my cousin's—now I get to be in the program and stay that way."

Moments later, his elation quiets. "You know, now that I'm going to Walden," he says, "I don't need them so much. I mean, those paramedics saved my life, then to the emergency room and back out on the streets. I nearly died while I was waiting for Walden. It's made it harder for everybody, and fuckin' dangerous, too."

Then Mike grins. "Don't get me wrong, man, I ain't trying to be ungrateful, and I'm going in with high hopes. But I can't help thinking it's just sheer luck that I'm alive and still wanting treatment."

In the imposing Kings Hall on the third floor of the palatial building at 890 Hayes Street, now called Walden House, crystal chandeliers hang from a lofty, arched ceiling. Designed for a high-society family, the mansion was converted to a Catholic monastery in 1893. After the 1906 earthquake, when the city's asylum for the insane collapsed and the surviving inmates ran free, the nuns rounded up the "demented running wild about the city" and held them in the convent under lock and key. Today the mansion houses 120 junkies trying to stay off drugs, and all past incarnations of the building seem still at play.

On his first day, Mike walks The Boulevard—the mansion's long hallway—his Big Brother introducing him to the Walden Family members as they stroll by. "Welcome home, Mike!" each Walden Brother and Sister repeats, energetically grasping his hand.

For the next three hours Mike does Walden's initiation monad: He sits in the hallway just inside the mansion's ornate double front doors, his body rigid in a hard wood chair, head contemplatively bowed, silent. Any eye contact with those passing him in the bustling hallway is strictly forbidden. If he speaks, he's out the door.

At first, Mike meditates only on the Walden rules he'd just learned. "Damn," he thinks, "I can't talk to anybody outside the house for two weeks."

But three hours is a long time for Mike to sit still, and doing the monad has its intended effect.

"I got to thinking about the wrongs I'd done to people I love," he says later. "I remembered when my daughter Jessica walked in and I had the needle in my arm. And my dad, I'd do anything for my dad, but all's I could remember while I'm sitting in that chair was stealing from him to get dope. So here I am doing this monad thing, and I keep seeing that look on my dad's face when he found out I'd been robbing him."

Mike walks up the stairs to the dorm room. "What an asshole I've been," he thinks. "I'm in the right place. This is where assholes wind up."

Upstairs in the dorm, Mike is assigned to read his "ABCs," the Walden House rulebook. "WE ARE EXPLORERS. WELCOME!" it starts out. "At Walden House you will completely re-examine your life. . . . Remember, it is a program and in order to make it work you need to learn the program way of doing things."

Mike reads through the list of Clinical Tools used by The Family: *One-to-Ones, Running Your Story, Pull-ups, Learning Experiences. Haircuts* are public reprimands from the staff. "You are told," instructs the manual, "THIS IS A HAIRCUT. . . . Assume the Haircut posture. . . . Once the Haircut is over, your response is 'Thank You.' You then leave in a respectful manner."

Therapeutic Communities like Walden have a reputation for parroting militaristic models of behavior modification. Mike had heard about it on the junkie grapevine: "Walden believes addicts have this character defect," he sums it up. "Like the Marine Corps, they tear you apart so they can build you up again. It's like you're some tooth covered with plaque; they got to scrape it off."

In Therapeutic Communities across the country, such "scraping" techniques—applied to some 100,000 addicts a year—include everything from *doing a monad,* where clients "sit quietly and think about one's life," to announcing addicts' errors in *The Program* by hanging signs around their necks, or by organizing a *House Meeting* where *The Family,* en masse, screams in-your-face curses at a member who has disobeyed the rules.

The National Institute of Drug Abuse describes the work of a Therapeutic Community as ". . . an organized effort to resocialize the client . . . with clear norms regarding personal responsibility and behavior which form the core of treatment. Learning, accepting and internalizing these norms is accomplished through a highly structured treatment process that requires active participation by the client in a context of confrontation."

Mike, when he's first permitted to talk to "outsiders," ponders his own definition of Walden's Therapeutic Community: "I can't decide if this place is some kind of a cult," he says.

Within hours of my first visit with Mike after his two-week Walden orientation (read: "isolation") period, he takes me up to the luxurious Kings Hall where I'm to be introduced to the entire Family.

As we enter the hall I feel Mike's hand on my shoulder, guiding me along to make sure I walk the perimeter of the formidable chamber and don't disrespectfully step toward the center of the polished wood floor. We sit next to each other in two of the plastic stackable chairs that line the paneled walls. I cross my legs while waiting for the rest of The Family to march in and find their seats, but Mike nudges me lightly with his elbow, his chin jerking quickly up and down to draw my attention to his example of the proper way to sit—feet flat on the floor, back erect, head bowed, waiting.

I assume the position.

"Good evening, Family," barks Mike, rising, when all are seated.

"Good evening, Mike," a chorus of 120 voices echoes back.

"Thank you, Family," his voice booms across the chamber. "I want to introduce my friend Lonny. He's a reporter who's going to be around a bunch."

Mike nods to me and sits again. I rise, taking my cue.

"Good evening, Family," I begin, too softly.

"Good evening, Lonny," they bellow back.

While I'm explaining that the Walden higher-ups have graciously allowed me to observe The Program, and I indeed will be "around a bunch," my mind is racing with the question that will occupy my mind, and Mike's, for the duration: After his prolonged wait for treatment, has Mike now arrived at a finely tuned but nonetheless pop psychology–oriented and questionably effective cult? Or is this Therapeutic Community a bona fide therapy whose confrontational methods of "resocialization" can actually lead flawed addicts back to constructive lives?

My introductory Family Meeting adjourns, and The Family of addicts files quietly out along the perimeter of the huge hall. I follow Mike out to The Boulevard and can't help but admire how healthy he looks and how contented he seems, only two weeks into The Program. Then the onslaught begins.

"Welcome home, Lonny!" dozens of hands pat me on the back, then reach out to shake my own. The Walden Brothers and Sisters ask questions about the work I'm doing, wonder when they'll get a chance to *run their story* for me. They're smiling, laughing, joking as if they'd known me for years.

And it works. I can remember no time in my life when I've felt more warmly and sincerely welcomed by any group of people. I've been there barely three hours, I hate being in crowds—and Walden feels like home.

As I leave for my real home that night, each and every person I pass on The Boulevard greets me by name. "Hey, Lonny, see you back soon. Glad you're here."

"Hey, man, thanks for coming," says Mike, giving me a warm hug before he retreats down The Boulevard to rejoin The Family.

I find myself smiling as I head to my car, looking back at the glowing lights coming from the impressive mansion on the corner of Hayes and Fillmore. From the outside, no one in the world could guess what was going on inside that fantasy castle of 120 hard-core junkies living together in the roles of smiling, amiably gracious Brothers and Sisters.

A great chunk of the new rehab plans across the country, I realize, is focused on getting addicts into programs that are, in large part, similar to Walden. But what, I think, does getting addicts to say please and thank you, to sit straight and smile on command while theatrically engaged in a bizarre enactment of military regimentation and family love—what does all that have to do with keeping them off drugs?

MIKE AND THE FAMILY RECITE THE WALDEN CREED AFTER A MEETING IN KINGS HALL

"You've got your lives back," announces Sylvester Palmer to the dozen addicts gathered in a circle for the meeting of his *caseload*—the small groups assigned to each rehab counselor at Walden. "You're clean and sober," he pauses while the group applauds loudly, then adds, reminding them, "at least for today."

Mike sits erect, listening attentively, the heroin nod he'd manifested at group in Target Cities now long gone.

"So here's the deal," continues Sylvester, "the Walden Way. You all aren't the kind of folks who play by the rules. You do things your own way—and that's how you got here. So at Walden, you can't act like no junkies and speed freaks no more. 'Cause if you don't *act* like junkies, you won't use no junk.'"

In his own way, Sylvester had summed up the fundamental behavior modification approach used by Therapeutic Communities to treat addiction. An addict's shooting up with drugs, stripped to its barest essentials, is a behavior to be stopped. The addict is an immature family member in need of "self-control and discipline." The focus is on managing conduct, while the myriad psychological causes that may have led to the addiction fall to second place.

"In the Therapeutic Community," notes drug treatment historian William White in his book, *Slaying the Dragon*, "the grown addict is pictured as an infant: immature, irresponsible, stupid, impulsive and incapable of empathy with others. Treatment is conceptualized as a process of emotional maturation achieved through heightened self-awareness and self-discipline."

Dr. George De Leon, who directs the Center for Therapeutic Community Research, says that a Therapeutic Community's fundamental goal is to impart to the client a "View of Right Living." "In general," notes Dr. De Leon, "sobriety is a prerequisite for learning to live right, but right living is required to maintain sobriety."

Walden House subscribes to those basic Therapeutic Community principles. "In many ways what happens at Walden House," says its orientation manual, "is a reparenting process. It's like growing up all over again, only this time you rid yourself of the negative or bad habits you've developed. . . . From here on in, you will be responsible for your actions. So think before you act, and start playing by the rules."

"Therapeutic Community works for addicts who've lost the structure in their lives, or never had any," says Sylvester to Mike and the rest of his caseload gathered in a staid wood-paneled meeting room at Walden. Sylvester, an ex-convict and ex-addict, is himself a Therapeutic Community graduate, now Mike's assigned counselor.

"You got meals here, housing, work to do, a daily schedule," he continues. "And rules, rules, rules. Sure, some of you, maybe all of you, can just fake your way through The Program. Hell, we even encourage that. *Fake it till you make it*—you follow Walden's rules for six months, nine months, and you're going to leave here knowing how to control your urges."

In his first weeks, Mike is surprised at Walden's scarce focus on drugs and addiction, but rather on changing the behavior patterns that typify the daily activities of most hard-core addicts.

"There's been hardly any speeches about drugs," he says, taking a smoke break by the metal railing on Walden's long back porch. "They're giving me groups on things like anger management. You know, like if someone gets in your face and it ain't going nowhere? Instead of punchin' 'em out, you go, 'Hey, it's OK, you're right, man. I'm outta here!'"

Mike laughs, saying he hasn't yet had the chance to test that particular technique. "Or maybe someone in The Family tells me, 'Hey, Mike, you're talking too loud in the cafeteria, man, we can't even think.' I say, 'Hey, thank you so much for the pull-up. So nice for letting me know.' "

Few experts doubt that, at least while the addict stays in *The Community,* such intense structure and rules do impart effective training in impulse control. "A considerable number of clients never have acquired conventional lifestyles," writes Dr. De Leon. "Mainstream values are either missing or unpursued. . . . Their Therapeutic Community experience can be termed *habilitation*—the development of a socially productive, conventional lifestyle for the first time in their lives." Dr. De Leon's choice of words begs the question, though: Can an addict acquire a conventional lifestyle in such an unconventional place as Walden? And if so, will the changes be maintained in the outside world, far from the taut embrace of The Family?

After two weeks of enforced isolation from any contact with the outside world, Mike makes his first phone call—to speak to his daughters at his ex-wife's house. But Walden's strictly enforced regulations say that another Family member of more senior status has to *buddy* a client through that first phone call and, essentially, eavesdrop on the conversation.

"Look," his ex-wife tells Mike on the phone, his phone buddy Roy standing right by his side, "I'm not letting you talk to the girls. Just because you're in some program doesn't mean I'm going to let you hurt them again."

Mike can hear Jessica and Michelle's voices in the background. "Mommy, we want to talk to Daddy."

"Listen, please," he says, trying to maintain his calm. "They *want* to talk to me."

"Not a chance," she replies, and hangs up.

Mike slams down the phone and heads for the large double front doors of Walden, telling Roy he's going to get his kids. But his phone buddy stands his ground, gently nudging Mike toward the counseling office.

"I'm out of here, Floyd," Mike tells the counselor on duty, "going to pick up my kids, bring 'em to Connie's so's we'll all be together, the way it should be."

Floyd stands up at his desk, one of the few people around as tall as Mike. "OK," he says calmly. "And then what?"

The question stuns Mike. "Thinking of my kids," he tells me later, "I get this churning in my gut. But that was the first time I felt that gut pain and didn't run off reacting to it. Sure, I might have taken my girls and got 'em over to Connie's," he continues, but smiles. "*And then what?*"

Mike answers what is now his own repeated question. "And *then,*" he pauses, "I would have lost visitation rights by grabbing 'em like that, been bummed out and gone to my guy and hit a bag of heroin. If Floyd hadn't stopped me with that question, I'd have been out there on the dope again."

Mike sums up the intangibles of Walden's resocialization process: "What I've got," he says, "is these silly phrases spinning 'round my mind. *Stick and stay. Trust the process. One day at a time.* And mostly, when I get some weird fucking impulse in my head, I ask myself, *And then what?* It sounds unbelievable, man," says Mike, "but I ain't never asked that question before. Far back as I can remember, I just did whatever popped into my head."

Mike strolls The Boulevard, singing out Walden clichés while everyone laughs, calling him a *clinical monster.*

"But the real thing," he continues, "is I'm beginning to see my kids' viewpoint. Their dad's been a junkie for years, so what if he's in some program? I got to earn their trust. I keep thinking, I'm with The Program now, everything's hunky-dory again. But I can't get complacent, man. There's still plenty of ways I can screw up."

What Walden and other Therapeutic Communities do achieve for their clients, most agree, is "program sobriety": while within the boundaries of The Family, they stay clean. When tormenting thoughts, doubts, or cravings fly into an addict's mind, over a hundred Brothers and Sisters are there to respond, to offer a *pull-up,* to *run their stories,* to engage in a *one-to-one,* to remind them to *trust the process* and to *live one day at a time.* And during each of those one-day-at-a-times there is barely a free moment for intrusive thoughts to distract and torture an addict who, at Walden, is jolted awake at 6:30 A.M. and moves rapidly through room inspection, breakfast, the morning Family Walk in the park, the *tighten ups* that leave the mansion sparkling clean, on to meditation group, stress-reduction group, lunch, anger-control group, caseload meeting, dinner, evening meeting, *TCI* (Therapeutic Community Interaction), and the final tighten up, until the overhead speakers boom throughout the mansion, "Good evening, Family, it is now personal hygiene time," followed by Family Bedtime at 11:00 P.M.

For those who don't follow the rules and regimentation to the T, the consequences are clear. The walls of The Boulevard are lined with benches that resemble long church pews, invariably filled with Brothers and Sisters, heads bowed, who'd shown up late for meals or meetings, used inappropriate language, hadn't shown proper respect to staff, or had perpetrated a host of other infractions. "The bench is a tool for re-focusing," says the Walden manual. Silence is enforced, and "once you are on the bench, no matter how you got there, you can only be taken off by a staff member."

Mike's first breach of the rules is to remain in the bathroom brushing his teeth for five minutes after personal hygiene time has ended. For this, he receives a *learning experience*. At the Family Meeting the next night, he stands at attention in front of the Walden Family and barks out, "Good evening, Family. My name is Michael Pagsolingan. On December fifteenth I received a learning experience. I received a learning experience for brushing my teeth beyond personal hygiene time. My learning experience consists of announcing at three evening meetings: Family, what did I do wrong? I did not follow the personal hygiene rule. Due date, December eighteenth. It has not yet been fulfilled. Thank you, Family."

The recitation is precise, and memorized; for each pause or word missed, mispronounced, or slurred, another day is added for the Learning Experience to again be recited. For some residents weeks go by before they get it right, letter perfect, three times in a row.

"Learning Experiences are given as a learning tool and not as a punishment," states the Walden manual. "This type of Learning Experience not only helps him or her to remember a norm, it helps reinforce the norm within the community. . . . Failure to complete a Learning Experience could result in a *contract,* being placed on *the chair,* or even being asked to leave program."

Yet for all the regimentation, rules, and regulations, it is an intangible sense of community that seems to be Walden's most effective tool. "The primary therapist and teacher in the Therapeutic Community," notes Dr. De Leon, "is the community itself."

Michael Wallace is Mike Pagsolingan's *bunkie* at Walden, sleeping in the top bunk in their tiny fourth-floor dorm room. Wallace acknowledges he came to Walden only to avoid a jail sentence for petty theft, and leading the police on a high-speed chase across the city.

"They wanted to give me six years," Wallace tells Mike at dinner one night, ticking off prior felony counts: reckless endangerment, auto theft, assault with a deadly weapon on a police officer. "That was the high-speed chase," he notes. "Technically, you don't have to actually hit them."

Wallace, a small man of twenty-seven with a soft blond beard under his lower lip, leans back in his chair in the cafeteria while Mike lowers his fork and tries to visualize his placid roommate leading the police on a wild chase across town.

"The D.A. told me"—Wallace continues his war story—" 'no ifs or buts, you're going to prison.' " But Wallace's parole officer recommended a year's time, served at Walden, and the judge bought it. "My parole officer and Walden really went to bat for me," Wallace tells Mike as the two clear the cafeteria table of their dinner plates and head up the winding stairs of the mansion to the nightly Family Meeting. "They gave me another chance."

Then Wallace tells the truth. "I used Walden to get out of jail so I could split and go to South America," he tells Mike. "I had no intention of hanging out for any drug treatment."

The therapeutic tool that finally made Wallace *get with the program* is not listed in the Walden manual. "It was bowling," he tells Mike as they ascend to the meeting. "Who'd believe I could enjoy bowling," exclaims Wallace, "unless I was totally stoned. But five of us from the house went together, and I had a blast! Just being with people, laughing. For so long I'd gotten pleasure from twisted things, ripping people off so I could get high. And here I was, bowling, having a great time—and it wasn't detrimental to anyone."

Wallace breaks into a grin. "I guess it is kind of dorky to have my breakthrough from bowling," he says. "But just living in a community of one hundred twenty dope fiends trying to get well has surprising effects."

Wallace and Mike file into Kings Hall, carefully walking the perimeter to the chairs along the walls, then sitting erect, feet flat on the floor, waiting for the meeting to begin.

"I would never have made it to South America anyway," he whispers to Mike. "I would have written bad checks to pay for a fake passport and, while waiting, done some dope. Couple of months, I'd be back in jail. That's just reality for me. So I'm staying right here with The Family."

The imposing street facade of the mansion at 890 Hayes Street yields up one solitary hint of the origins of Walden's therapeutic mixture of cultlike Family camaraderie and militaristic behavior modification. At the foot of the long staircase that leads to the ostentatious double-doored entryway past which resides The Family is a simple wooden plaque that reads "Today is the first day of the rest of your life."

There is no citation, but if credit were to be given where credit is due, it would read: Charles Dederich, founder of Synanon. While the plaque marks the physical entrance to Walden, Dederich and Synanon mark—many would say mar—the philosophical underpinnings of all Therapeutic Communities across the country.

At the big old floppy hotel on a Santa Monica beach where Synanon grew to strength in the fifties and sixties, few would have guessed that Dederich and his communal flower-children followers were sowing the seeds for an empire of drug rehab programs. "Synanon," wrote ex-member Phill Jackson in a memorial article when Dederich died in 1997, "was one of those funny things happening when dear old dad and mom frolicked in Elysian Park, dressed in bellbottoms, leather, and feathers (or, likely enough, in nothing at all . . .) while the fragrance of Patchouli and home-brewed dope filled the Summer air. It was, in short, groovy."

Dederich hadn't started Synanon intending to be groovy, but rather to be a "big man" and "make history" with a new and innovative way to treat alcoholics. He might well have achieved unqualified acclaim as the founder of the techniques that today treat 100,000 addicts annually in Therapeutic Communities, if he and Synanon had not detoured along the way through utopian commune, religious cult, and, finally, attempted murder.

On warm nights in Ocean Park, California, in the mid-fifties, Dederich and some fellow alcoholics would gather three times a week to experiment with group interactions that were soon to be called *The Game*—a rule-ridden therapeutic encounter that used ridicule and abuse to break through the denial that, in theory, kept alcoholics drinking. By 1958 Dederich had founded a "therapeutic commune" called Synanon, The Game had continued to evolve in complexity, and addicts had joined in with the alcoholics.

"The prime engine of Synanon was 'The Game,' " recalls Jackson, describing it as "a therapy group that included mostly clones of Attila the Hun," and as "emotional surgery without anesthetic." Yet Jackson remains convinced, if not enamored, of its efficacy. "The Game," he remembers, "caught so many addicts and drunks by the scruffs of their nasty necks and flung them into a process that eventually led most of them back into the wide world as functional and productive citizens. The Game . . . caught me, hooked me, scared the shit out of me, and taught me some home truths and survival skills that have served me well to this day. . . . It was a harsh, illiberal, insulting, and degrading system, and dammit, it worked and worked well."

The Game had an elaborate set of rules and roles that governed every aspect of Synanon's personal and communal life, including *pull-ups, confrontations,* and time on *The Bench* for errant Family members. "It was Marine Corps Boot Camp for civilians," recalls Jackson. "[Residents] swept floors, washed dishes, scrubbed toilets, and suffered insult and verbal assault in The Game. Contact with the outside world was forbidden for some extended period until the new resident had achieved control over self and had earned respect."

In short, as intricate as Synanon and The Game were, you could transport an assemblage of late-nineties Walden Family members back in a time machine to Synanon in the fifties and sixties, and they'd feel right at home.

By 1964 there were 500 recovering addicts living in Synanon, and its evolving philosophy of communal living began to attract hippies, dropouts, and flower children looking for alternative lifestyles. "Squares," writes drug historian William White of the nonaddicts who joined Synanon, "were drawn to the emotional intensity, brutal honesty, and social cohesion of the Synanon 'game' and the Synanon community."

But as Synanon grew to a celebrated social phenomenon for rehabilitation of addicts and personal growth for squares, so grew the accusations that The Game was more brainwashing than it was therapy. Dederich had a simple answer, claiming that the brains that arrived at Synanon were very much in need of washing.

By 1977 Synanon had grown to a $13.7 million enterprise, and accusations of cultlike oppression by Synanon leaders were spreading like wildfire. For Dederich, though, even The Game was no longer an adequate tool of control. "New levels of member coercion," writes White, "included mandatory daily aerobics, a prohibition of sugar, mandatory diets, the shearing of the hair of all members, pressure for women to get abortions, and mandatory vasectomies for all men who had been in the Synanon community for more than five years."

Soon, Dederich had his own security force, armed with a $60,000 cache of weapons. On October 11, 1978, Paul Morantz, a lawyer who had sued Synanon, reached into the mailbox outside his house and was greeted by the snapping fangs of a four-and-a-half-foot rattlesnake. Morantz survived, and the trail of evidence led back to Synanon. When the police found Dederich, he was in a drunken haze. They carted him off to jail on a stretcher, under the bright lights of TV news cameras. The founder of The Game and the harsh punitive tactics of the Therapeutic Community pled no contest to a charge of conspiracy to commit murder—and received five years' probation.

That particular war story in the history of drug rehab might well have stopped right there. But during the years of Dederich's increasing paranoia and tyrannical leadership, other Synanon leaders had spread like army ants about the country to establish their own Therapeutic Communities based on the initial principles of The Game. John Maher founded Delancey Street in San Francisco; David Deitch, Daytop Village in New York; Naya Arbiter, Amity in Tucson. By 1975, when Dederich was spinning out of control, 500 Synanon spin-off communities had set up shop. Many joined together to establish the Therapeutic Communities of America—among them, Walden House.

The Game itself, described by historian White as "a synergy of leaderless group therapy, confrontational theater, verbal riot, group confessional, and improvisational comedy," officially closed down with the demise of Synanon in 1991. Dederich died, at age eighty-three, in 1997.

But to this day, long-separated from Synanon, Therapeutic Communities like Walden face a difficult contradiction: While struggling to shake off Dederich's dangerous cult imprint, they tightly embrace the treatment principles he originated. This paradox leaves the door wide open for critics, who are quick to cite continued use of Synanon-like methodology to buttress their claims that today's Therapeutic Communities are cultlike brainwashing programs that keep addicts under control in "program sobriety" while under the rule of The Family, with little effect on "street sobriety" when they get out.

Therapeutic Community leaders respond that they have evolved past Synanon, and most have diminished the intensity of the confrontations used in newer versions of The Game. "You can't terrify people into change," notes Arbiter. "Addicts already think the worst about themselves, so putting dunce hats on them and making them do ridiculous, repetitive chores just reinforces their low self-image. Instead, we try to pour love and respect into each other and keep creating community in larger and larger circles. Amity is really a place of the spirit, not of schedules."

Walden House's present Chief Executive Officer, ex–Synanon member Alfonso Acampora, is "responsible for many of the clinical tools used today," notes the *Walden House*

Journal. "He modified the harsher Synanon . . . methods to get rid of the shaming and de-humanizing aspects, without losing the best of what was then known as attack therapy."

Yet those still interested in seeing The Game at work today need only step into Walden's Kings Hall on any night when a House Meeting is called—and The Family decides whether an errant Family member will be allowed to stay.

At 6:00 P.M., as if on cue, Mike and every Walden resident start up the long, winding steps to Kings Hall. Even Ron, sick with flu, trods along in slippers and bathrobe. The procession ascends in silence, all eyes solemnly lowered. Marlin, the counselor for the night, has called a House Meeting to decide if Paul—who'd split, used drugs, and then asked to come back—could return to The Family. For the past three days, he's been held in The Chair, doing a prolonged monad: "The Chair represents being back at the beginning, before you were accepted into the family," says the Walden manual. "On The Chair a person has one foot in the program, and one foot out the door. . . . The person on The Chair is on a *Reflection* while physically on The Chair, in their room, while going to the bathroom, etc."

Kings Hall is arranged like a theater in the round. Circular rows of seats surround a clearing in which sits an aged hardwood chair, placed in opposition to Marlin's padded staff armchair. The residents file in and take their places, backs straight and chins tucked down until Marlin shouts, "Focus up," and all heads rise at once.

"A House Meeting," announces the counselor, "is not about abusing the guy, it's to see if he should come back into The Family. One person gives focus at a time—and give him a chance to answer." Marlin surveys the room for each nod.

"Bring him in."

Paul's taut neck muscles reveal his tension as he reads the list of his transgressions. "I used drugs," he recites. "I had sex with one of the Sisters, and when I split," Paul looks up from the page, "I took her with—" His words are drowned in the first cry for blood.

"Paul," the shout echoes off the walls, "you ain't learned *nothin'*! What you doin' here?"

"You weren't with The Program," another outcry. "Get real—or get the fuck out!"

"Let him answer," barks Marlin, but the next accusation is flying before Paul catches a breath.

"Did you know Arthur?"

Stunned silence.

"He was my bunkie here," murmurs Paul.

"Do you know he's dead? Overdosed."

Paul spins toward the speaker. "Wasn't me who dragged him down."

A woman rises slowly. "Nobody said you did, Paul," her soft voice nearly disappearing in the high-ceilinged room. "But show us some *feeling*. Why are you here?"

"Because I love Walden," intones Paul. "And 'cause I ain't doin' no more drugs!"

Kings Hall fills with deafening whoops, whistles, and catcalls.

"Listen to *that* junkie."

"Ain't no dope fiend can't see through your bullshit! Get your ass out of here!"

"If you ain't using drugs no more, what you need Walden for? You just a scumbag using this Family!"

"You're a dope fiend with an attitude—you ain't part of this house!"

Marlin is on his feet, yelling, "Focus up!" The room quiets to whispers, all nodding to each other, the jury's mind made up.

"Paul, I'm going to help you out here," says Marlin, settling back into his chair. " 'Cause if The Family votes now ain't nobody going to support you being back here. You keep justifying, you keep rationalizing, thinking, thinking, thinking. That's been your bullshit m.o. since you got here, and we're going to change that, right now, or you can die out there in the streets."

Paul stares at Marlin, then spits out, "I can't prove nothing to you," and rises to head for the door.

"Get your ass in that chair," barks Marlin. "You got two minutes, one last chance to save your life." He turns to the gathered audience. "Nobody asks no more questions. Let Paul say why he should be in this Family. He's got two minutes."

The counselor looks at his watch and Paul shoots him a puzzled look, then sits down. For the first minute, he says nothing, staring at the floor. With no one shouting at him, nothing to respond to in anger, Kings Hall looms large, a desolate expanse. Paul is trembling before he finally speaks.

"If I'm back on the streets," his head is still bowed, voice almost lost, "I'll be dead." It takes another minute for him to continue, but Marlin has stopped watching the time.

Paul leans forward in his wooden seat, elbows on knees, face toward the floor.

"This Family's the only chance I got." His crying makes it difficult to catch each word.

"I could stay at my mom's"—Paul's nails dig into his palms—"but I can't face my sisters 'cause I didn't stop my father when he beat them."

It's the first time Paul, after months of Walden groups, has mentioned his family. He rocks forward, head now tilted upward, looking about the room.

"I need your help." His eyes widen. "I can't be alone no more."

Paul swipes at his tears, bringing his sobs under control. "You keep asking why I mess up?" He stands slowly, sweating in the silence. "I'm a fucked-up dope fiend. What do you want me to say?"

Marlin nods, and two designated Family members take Paul by the elbows and escort him from the room so The Family can vote.

"*You* are the Therapeutic Community," Marlin tells The Family. "Paul's history doesn't speak well for his chances of success here. So it's a big investment of your energy—all of you—if you let him back. Any comments before you vote?"

Hands shoot up around the room.

"I'll support Paul, 'cause he's sick and needs my support."

"I'll support him, and I'll ride his ass while he's here!"

"At least if he's in here screwing up, we got a chance to do something about it."

"Maybe this time," says one final voice before the vote, "he'll make it through."

The escorts march Paul back in, to face Marlin slouched in his padded chair across the empty space in the circle of addicts.

"Do you believe in a higher power?" asks the counselor.

Paul's tone is again arrogant, defensive. " 'Course I do," he blurts out.

"Well then," replies Marlin, "He's with you today. This Family is giving you another chance."

A hundred junkies jam around Paul, slapping his back, and the chant of "Welcome home!" fills Kings Hall.

Mike and his bunkie lay awake in their beds at two that morning, whispering in the dark.

"Recovery's like heroin," murmurs Wallace. "The more you do it, the more of a habit you get. Maybe Paul will make it."

"All I'm going to think about"—Mike's voice floats into the darkness—"is today. Today I am not hurting myself. Today I'm not hurting my kids, Connie, my family. That's worth something, man."

Wallace hears Mike's voice cracking, and slides to the floor by his roommate's lower bunk.

"I'd love to be out in the world," says Mike, turning to the wall to hide his tears, "and not be using dope and stealing. But I can't do it by myself. I need The Family now."

The next morning, I speak with Walden director Dolores Alvarez. Mike's counselor, Sylvester, joins us in a seat by her large wooden desk in the office at the mansion. Dolores smiles mischievously when she hears that The Family voted to bring Paul back into the house.

"It *always* goes that way," she explains. "These aren't the old Therapeutic Community days. We're a kinder, gentler program now."

"We don't do that confrontational stuff no more," agrees Sylvester. "That's the old days."

"If that House Meeting wasn't confrontational," I note, "I'm glad I wasn't there for the old days."

Dolores laughs. "The House Meeting is a setup, like a theater to blow up the picture, make it bigger than life so they recognize their behavior. The Family comes up with the same answer each time at a House Meeting."

Her eyes crinkle upward. "After all," she concludes, "what's the alternative?"

———

The alternative to the still-present tactics of confrontation and insults in Therapeutic Communities, critics say, is not to abuse addicts as part of their therapy—not even in a kinder and gentler fashion.

Darrell, recalling his own four months in Walden, agrees with Dolores's description of the House Meeting as a form of theater. But he sees the acting as directed more by the clients than by the counselors and staff.

"Walden's attack stuff becomes this weird little *game* for the clients," says Darrell, unaware of the word's Synanon significance. "When you're in that hot seat, they *want* you to cry, to break down, to admit something really dramatic or horrendous in front of the whole Family. So you learn to come up with something because you know that's what it takes to stop the abuse. You confess to something, *anything!* You use the right words, and you cry. You give them what they want, so they'll back off."

Darrell doesn't blame Walden's attack methods for his relapse after four months in the program. "I mean, we're addicts—we've been scamming all our lives!" He laughs. "So you can't blame Walden if we keep scamming in there."

Darrell does say that Walden's harsh confrontations kept him from even considering a return for more treatment after he relapsed. "I fucked up, a real bad relapse," he admits of his setback after being clean and sober with The Family. "But I wasn't about to go back and face a House Meeting in order to start again. Personally, I'll admit my own mistakes," says Darrell. "But I'd rather have them ease it out of me than beat it out of me."

The question of the efficacy of such attack therapy becomes especially important for women in recovery programs.

Dr. Mindy Thompson-Fullilove, assistant professor of clinical psychology at Columbia University, has studied the effects of Therapeutic Community techniques on women, many of whom entered rehab to *escape* abusive relationships.

"We're dealing with incest, rape, domestic violence, homelessness, stillbirth," lists Thompson-Fullilove in an interview for an article, "Sobering Truths." "This is their reality. This is their day-to-day life."

Thompson-Fullilove's concerns about the Therapeutic Community are shared by many other treatment providers. "Particularly for women who do have an abuse history, treatment in a Therapeutic Community seems to be a repeat experience of abuse," notes Dr. Wendy Chavkin, of the Chemical Dependency Institute at New York's Beth Israel Medical Center. And at Veritas, a Manhattan program for women, coordinator Lynette Choice observes, "The old Therapeutic Community model is really predicated on the idea that the person has a false sense of superego that needs to be stripped away. What I see coming through these doors are very fragile egos that have been stripped away of everything. I can't strip egos that aren't there. These women have heard too often they're not worth anything in society. The biggest work is to focus on the worth they bring to life."

Back at Walden, Dolores shrugs off such criticisms. When I interview her the day after

Paul's House Meeting, she's just come from her morning room inspection—during which she'd dumped drawers full of clothing on the floor in the women's dorm because "they weren't neat enough."

"Couldn't such actions," I ask her, "like getting angry and throwing stuff around, remind some of the women of abusive treatment by their husbands, families, or even their pimps?"

"Jeez," sighs Dolores, whose reputation among the women in the house is indeed more of kindness than of hard-core abuse. "I was trying to make a statement to the whole Family, what's acceptable and what isn't acceptable. And if feelings came up in response to me throwing drawers or whatever I did with their clothes, then that gives them a chance to deal with those feelings in group later. That's good—it brings it right up front."

"But it is true," I note, "that more women than men split from Walden."

Dolores glances at Sylvester for confirmation, then responds. "You've got to remember, women have most of the responsibility for their children, so the children take them out, draw them out of here. It's also easier for women to get money—through prostitution—to go out and do drugs. So, women leave Walden more often than the men do."

Yet the National Institutes of Health pins the high rate at which women leave Therapeutic Communities on the programs themselves: "Female attrition may be accounted for," says the federal institute, "by the observation that Therapeutic Communities generally are characterized by a male-dominated orientation with little provision for the special needs of women."

Sylvester rises to leave; he has to deal with three Family members who came late to group that morning. He shakes my hand warmly and concludes, as if summing up the contradictions faced by present-day Therapeutic Communities: "Walden works for women and it works for men—because we provide a warm, nurturing environment for our clients. I mean, sure we have this tough-love thing going. But you've been around here for a while now, you see the warmth from this Family. It's that warmth, the sensitivity, man, it's like—there's no pressure. I really mean that. Multimillion-dollar mansion, all this hugging going on, roof over your head, good food, counselors to care about you, lots of people around. So making it through here ain't no big trick—get up, have breakfast, make your bed, clean some dishes, sit in a few groups. This place can be *too* warm and fuzzy. We got to balance that out."

I head out of the office with Sylvester to the Family Meeting where he's going to contend with the three who came late to group.

"Don't forget," Dolores reminds me on the way out, "we're providing structure to people who've had no structure. And we're providing resources for a person to change. We've got therapists, GED instructors, women's groups, men's groups, anger groups, caseload, job training. Just by interacting so intensely with the others here, they find out who they really are." Dolores wraps it up, unintentionally, with a fundamental Synanon precept. "I mean, it's The Family that's the treatment here!"

MORNING MEDITATION

Sylvester and I leave the office just as the overhead speakers ring out, "Good morning, Family! There is a Family Meeting in Kings Hall. Now. Repeat, all Family Members report to Kings Hall immediately."

When The Family has taken its place in the chairs along the walls, Sylvester asks the three who were late at morning group to step to the center of the room.

"This is a Haircut," he announces, and they assume the Haircut Position.

"Whose program is this?" Sylvester booms out the question.

"Our program, Sylvester!" they bellow back.

"So if you're not going to work your program, come on time to groups," says Sylvester, "we can arrange for you to be out of here. Is that what you want?"

"No, Sylvester!"

"All right then, you've lost all weekend privileges and will remain in the house for three weeks."

"Thank you, Sylvester!" They shout the only acceptable response to a Haircut, turning and filing silently out of Kings Hall with the others.

Mike catches up with me on the staircase down to The Boulevard. An experienced plumber, he's been assigned to work in the house maintenance crew. As we stroll The Boulevard he's stopped by both Family members and staff, asking if he can fix this stuck window, that leaky faucet, another of the old, cranky steam heaters. Pad in hand, he keeps a list of chores and each day receives thanks from his Brothers and Sisters for the work he's done.

"Yesterday," he says, "I threw my back out lifting that damn heater in the hallway."

Mike reminds me that it was the pain from his original back surgery that led him to switch from cocaine and embark on his ever-spiraling heroin habit. "So I asked for a *lay-in*," he says, Walden's permission to take a break and rest.

We've gone down to the maintenance supply room in the basement of the mansion, Mike picking through some washers to fix a faucet before he's due at anger management group.

"So I'm up in my bed on the lay-in yesterday," he says, "and I'm thinking, fuuuck, I feel like I'm sleazing. I'm missing out on the groups downstairs, man. So I realize, hey, this Family has really got to me. I mean, a couple of months ago I would have been, 'Hey, cool, I got a chance to lay in bed! Hey, where's my TV, where's that remote control!' " He laughs, finding the washer he needs.

"I been thinking back to my time waiting to get into Walden," he says, "when I overdosed. Then laying on that stinky mattress in Ozanam. Everything was coming down at once, man. I thought I was through, I'm going to be a dope fiend the rest of my life, man, that's it."

Mike dabs grease on the faucet to seal the washer, then turns the water full force and soaps down his hands, spanking clean.

"I nearly died getting here," he says. "But this place is just what I need. I got my support group, my peers, my Little Brothers and my Big Brothers, and they give me the goods on how to get through the program. I listen to every word Sylvester says, and now I'm my caseload's rep to The Family."

Mike dries his hands and strolls off to anger management group—the model Walden resident.

As I'm heading down The Boulevard to leave for the day I run into Sylvester again, and mention how Mike seems to be thriving in the program. He laughs, shaking his head.

"Let me tell you something about a Therapeutic Community," he says. "A guy like Mike, he knows how to work The Program. He listens, he's articulate, he's thoughtful, he knows how to carry himself in The Community, he don't get angry at folks, he has no hygiene problem or anything—so Mike doesn't get much bad focus thrown at him. He gets to watch a lot of other people get focus, thinks he's learning from their mistakes instead of barreling on and making his own. Hell, the worst thing I think he's done so far is brush his teeth for too long. So I don't know what's up with Mike yet. He hasn't been tested."

"How will he be tested?" I ask. We've reached the end of The Boulevard, the foyer before the ornamental double doors of the house entrance. Near the frosted-glass windows etched with long graceful lilies are four residents on The Chair, heads bowed.

"I don't know how Mike will be tested," says Sylvester thoughtfully. "In the old days, we used to create an issue, you know, get in his face and accuse him of something, set him up for a fall so's he could learn how to pick himself up again."

"How long ago were the old days?"

"Couple of years," says Sylvester, almost wistfully.

"But today," he continues, "we have to wait guys like Mike out, can't do that old stuff to test him. He might find out he's got HIV, or there's some police warrant still out for him, or he'll mess up with one of the Sisters in here, or his girlfriend waiting out there'll go out on him. Something's going to happen to test Mike, I'll guarantee you that. Something always happens."

I head toward the door as Sylvester sums up. "I'm an old junkie myself, and an ex-con to boot, and I'll tell you one thing. You may think Mike's doing just fine, but he ain't come out with nothin' yet that tells me why he was doing dope and messing up his relationships and his life to the point where he nearly killed himself. And if all he does at Walden is fix faucets and go to groups and doesn't get to what's really bugging him, he might just as well be out on those streets as in here with this Family. So far, Mike's just not getting into any trouble. Nothing really deep about that, and nothing that'll keep him off drugs once he's out of here. This place is no more than a long picnic, if that's all he wants it to be."

Sylvester pulls at the heavy front door and holds it open for me. "You reporters and out-siders keep coming in here," he says, "asking about abuse and confrontation, House Meet-ings and Synanon and shit. Well, you just hang around and watch Mike, and you take it from an old addict like me—if he don't get pushed any harder, or push himself harder, that boy's going to be out there with a needle in his arm faster than you can turn around. You think we're being too confrontational? I think we need to get in his face even more."

Sylvester shakes my hand as I leave. "But them was the old days," he smiles, heading back into Walden.

Sitting at home that night, taking notes from the day with The Family, I glance through Mike's story about the last time he'd been off heroin, when the flashbacks of his childhood rape had reared up to torment him. "White room, brown-framed bed, mattress, no sheets, no covers," he'd said. "I got all this shame about that, man." When he'd hit the needle again, said Mike, it had been to chase away those nightmares.

Now, at Walden, off drugs once more, it is the obsessive fervor of his daily interactions with The Family that keeps Mike's flashbacks at bay, numbing them out just as the heroin did before.

Distracting addicts from their inner torments creates an illusion of healing, so that Mike and his Brothers and Sisters appear more emotionally stable while at Walden. But busy schedules, rigorous rules, and all of the techniques of behavior modification go only so far toward bringing about the inner changes that addicts need to *stay* off drugs.

"That confrontational stuff really does keep you in line," explains Darrell. "It's so much easier not having to think for yourself, to just follow the rules and look good. But then that's it. You have to stay in that environment forever if you want to keep sober!"

Dolores and Sylvester acknowledge that Mike must delve deeper into the effects of his emotionally tormented past if he is finally to leave drugs behind. Yet there is only one trained psychotherapist on Walden's staff for the 120 addicted Family members. Mike gets to see her once a week, in a group with a dozen other Brothers and Sisters. He informed her of his post-traumatic stress disorder brought on by years of childhood sexual abuse, and she promised to refer him to a specialty group outside of Walden. But then, overwhelmed by the sheer number of clients she was following, she never made the referral. Mike continued to work only with rehab counselors trained in a provocative and aggressive style of behavior modification.

Can Mike break through the shame about his repeated childhood rapes, and his humiliation about so much of his life since then, by being "pushed even harder," as Sylvester suggests? Or do the methods of the Therapeutic Community encourage him to take fewer risks, to close tightly into himself so that he draws little *focus* from The Family, to avoid, instead of take on, the most central issues that plague him?

"I've only been at Walden a little while," says Mike. "Maybe I'll learn to take the heat, 'cause it ain't no good being here if I don't change who I am. This Family thing, the Brotherhood, Sisterhood idea—that works for me. I feel that. And I'm watching what others do and trying to learn. But, man, I don't know if I can get used to this attack stuff."

Maybe tougher love and more confrontation will push Mike into facing the emotional torment that has drawn him to drugs. Or, possibly, he needs the safety of a kinder program, and more therapeutic expertise, before he can expose the deepest of his wounds and make real progress toward a lasting sobriety.

Either way, one day Mike will walk down The Boulevard and out of Walden where, instead of The Family greeting him every night, he'll be met once again by his ghosts.

With the first torrential winter rain, the China Basin homeless encampment springs to life. Darlene and her speed-freak friends, in curiously formal procession, march across the Third Street bridge hauling home newly found plastic tarps and wooden warehouse pallets—supplies to winterize their dwellings. They work en masse to hoist their already soaked homes and clothing onto the pallets, rising barely up over the ever-growing stream of brown water that surges down the sloping, cracked slab of concrete to the canal.

The encampment buzzes with industry. Spurred on by the shouted proclamations of two self-selected queen bees, workers dart from pallet to pallet with an ever-accelerating level of

frenetic energy—fed by the sweet honey of methamphetamine. China Basin's homeless encampment is, for the moment, a Quaker barn raising on speed.

During an early-morning pause in the squall I drive over the bridge, watching the surreal
parade, wondering how Darlene is weathering the storm. During the month since she'd arrived at Target Cities she's become increasingly coherent, and has continued to drop in and
visit with her counselor, Kathy. Although she still shoots speed, her frequency and dosage
have dramatically decreased. Kathy has become ever more hopeful that the now calmer (albeit still hallucinatory) Darlene will finally make it through an intake interview and into an
outpatient drug rehab program, Genesis, that works specifically with dually diagnosed
homeless addicts.

"Basically, I've mellowed out," Darlene told me when I last saw her, a week before this
first winter storm. "I shot up with meth like only once this week, instead of twice every day.
And my noise is quieter."

But Darlene's anger had flared again, thinking of her still endless hunt for rehab. "You
see," she exclaimed, "it was me, myself, and I who got better—*without* their groups! But
pretty soon, Kathy says, somebody'll let me in."

"Let me ask you something," I had wondered, hesitant to spoil a good thing. "If you're
making so much progress on your own, what do you need the rehab groups for?"

Darlene laughed at my heresy, munching on a piece of chocolate chip cookie, California Fancy, that she'd found "still-wrapped and fresh" in a Safeway Dumpster. "I need
the groups for *support*," she said, slipping easily into her newly learned rehab jargon.
"I need *their* support, I need *your* support, I need *Kathy's* support, I mean, just talking to
you now is, you know—*support*! Anyway, groups are what Kathy says I need to stay
clean."

Darlene offered me a piece of the cookie and, when I declined, frowned and fed the rest
to Bruce. We'd been sitting by the opening to her makeshift tent on that then-sunny day,
and she pointed about her in the parking lot.

"Who else am I going to talk to?" she asked, pursing her lips and waving around the
scene. "Everybody around here's way up there on crank," she said, using China Basin's favored expression for methamphetamine. "And I'm fighting to come back down. So I've
been trying not to trip out on all *their* trips, just stay away from them. Now none of them
wants to talk to me no more, and if I don't get into some group I'll get even crazier than I
am now! So I've been cleaning up my place, organizing things, you know, trying to keep occupied. And I've been walking a lot."

Darlene had indeed been intentionally spending more time away from Red and the others in China Basin, and that alone had mellowed her out some, distanced her from the
street-contagion of crank and craziness.

But her walking a lot was less than intentional. Someone had stolen Darlene's last airplane, and she hadn't yet headed to her favorite spot at the bike rack outside of Gold's Gym

to get another one. "Stealing's a sin," she said, and then giggled. "See, I really *want* another airplane. But Kathy doesn't want me to lie to her, so I can't do my airplane business 'cause she'd just freak on me. So for now I'm walking." She shook her head in disbelief. "Freaks *me* out, though."

Darlene's lifestyle changes did seem to be moving, slowly, in a hopeful direction. But Kathy knew it was only a matter of time before Darlene would again be seized up by the daily routine in the China Basin speed hub. Darlene's response to the harshness of the streets and the pressure of her peers had been, throughout sixteen years of homelessness, to shoot meth. As the rains set in, early this year, Darlene's newly found rehab resolve seemed unlikely to weather the winter.

I park my car, then duck through the hole in the fence and scan the scene. But there is no sign of Darlene. Then I see Bruce, gleefully splashing in muddy puddles with a half dozen other dogs. At the farthest corner of the lot I spot an isolated long, wooden pallet on which a huge mound of drenched clothes and a folded-over sopping-wet mattress are heaped under a stretched-out blue plastic tarp. On top of the sheeting, like a prince on a throne, is Darlene's white stuffed Snoopy dog. Walking slowly over, I call out her name. A tearful and bedraggled figure peers warily from behind the pile of clothes.

With a wan smile and head hanging down, Darlene walks to my side, leans her head on my shoulder, and, without a word, raises sad eyes toward mine. Then she lifts her arm and places it fondly around my shoulder. Cold water drips from the sleeve of her soaking-wet brown sweater, down my neck. She breaks out in a high-pitched laugh at her trick.

"Nobody's allowed in here if they're dry!" cackles Darlene.

"You're drowning me!" I protest, pulling away as she dances a pirouette before moving in with a deep hug that drains even more water onto me from her sweater.

"I *squish*," she exclaims in her little girl's voice. Then, seriously, "But I'm OK. Really."

"I was worried," I tell her. "How come you're not joining the party?" I nod over to the raucous gathering at the other end of the encampment, where they've now hooked up a boom box and a throbbing punk-rock bass rhythm fortifies the construction frenzy.

"It's not the same here no more," she says quietly, reaching up for her soaking-wet Snoopy on top of the blue tarp. She holds the dog at arm's length in front of her and dances to the music, swaying slowly at first, then spinning in circles.

"There's nobody here for me now," she starts, head nodding to the rhythm of the music. "Everything's changed."

Darlene's voice speeds up and her dance gets quicker, in dizzying Whirling Dervish circles, as she cries out in singsong to her stuffed-animal dance partner.

"Darlene ain't the same
the dope ain't the same
the peoples ain't the same

they are whacked out
drugged out
crazied out
shot through
cranked up—"

She stops spinning suddenly but, still swaying from a dizzying drunkenness, falls to the wet ground, hugging Snoopy protectively to her chest.

"So I guess we stay by our lonesomes now," she tells the dog, stroking its head.

Darlene sits stock-still for a while. Then she gets up, carefully places Snoopy back on his throne on the tarp, and turns to me.

"Help me get set up?" she asks softly. And we set to work.

The report that came back to Kathy from the Genesis program after Darlene interviewed there that week of the first rain was straightforward and simple. They will take Darlene into their group for homeless dually diagnosed addicts if, and only if, she quits shooting speed and takes antipsychotic medications to stop her from hearing voices.

"Genesis won't take me, not unless I take government drugs," Darlene explains as I drive her to an appointment with Kathy and Tom Hagan at Target Cities, to talk about her options.

"The Genesis lady said I'm not on the same *level* they're on," she continues, suddenly rolling down the window and yelling across traffic at the top of her lungs as a bike messenger flashes by—"Yeeeow! Neat Cannondale! Watch out, or that airplane's *mine!*"

She rolls the window back up, laughing. "Sorry, I get a little distracted still. See, Genesis says the voices and my being so hyper will interfere with my *progress.*" She adds a sarcastically haughty British accent to *progress.* "So I told them I can do four things at once but they said no thank you, the programs they have can't handle certain people."

"Certain people?" I ask, as we pull up at Target Cities and climb the stairs to meet Kathy.

"Yeah," says Darlene. "Like Mike, he's in that Walden program now; and Darrell's got into that Acceptance thing. And I'm not as nutty as I used to be, but I guess I'm still too nutty for even the nutty people's programs. So it's just me still left out."

"What about your voices lately? How's the noise when you're doing less speed?"

Darlene turns in frustration just as we reach the reception desk in the Target Cities waiting room. "*Genesis* needs to deal with the noise part, OK?" she exclaims. "Like you and me deal with my noise, like me and Kathy deal with my noise! Like *I've* dealt with my noise far back as I can remember. It's like, something pops into my head, and I answer it, and we continue on from there. OK? If Genesis can't deal with that, it's not my problem, it's theirs! I'm like hardly doing any drugs, and now they want to put me on *their* drugs, 'cause they don't like those other communications to get through to me 'cause it scares them. Well, I'm scared, too. I'm scared of those government drugs, you know what I'm saying? But unless I take government drugs, Genesis won't help me out with my drug problem."

Kathy walks in, having heard Darlene's voice from her office, some twenty feet from the waiting room. Darlene gives her counselor a warm embrace, and they head inside.

"Kathy, I came here to get *off* drugs," I hear Darlene start the conversation, "not be put on them. I was scared, but I didn't freak out at the Genesis interview, I promise! Can't you find someplace that can deal with me on my level?"

Kathy closes her door, and I head over to talk to Tom Hagan, Target Cities' clinical co-ordinator, who will meet with Darlene after Kathy.

"What's your news before I talk with her?" Tom asks, settling back into his chair. "This isn't going to be easy."

"One summary," I respond. "She says Genesis told her she's on a different level than they're on. And Darlene agrees. She just thinks Genesis should start at her level, not she at theirs."

"What's she been reading?" Tom laughs, and I get his message immediately. Throughout the nation the new push for rehab has been joined by a controversial policy, to the dismay of the feds, named harm reduction. And Darlene had just about recited the lyrics to its theme song.

"We have three words to define what harm reduction expects from an addict," says Dan Bigg of the Chicago Recovery Alliance. "Any positive change."

Bigg's program, a grassroots hodgepodge of services intended to make addicts' lives better—in whatever way possible—is nationally notorious as the place where the principles of harm reduction are effectively and fanatically put to work. The plan is straightforward: Short of getting junkies to stop using drugs, there's much that can be done to reduce the amount of harm they do to themselves and to the rest of society. If you won't stop doing dope, say the harm reductionists with a seemingly infinite logic, we'll help you use less drugs, spread less disease, have less violent lives, steal from fewer people, become somewhat less crazy, and even, possibly, a bit happier. We'll offer all sorts of help, they say—*and* you can still do dope.

In harm reduction circles, the first commandment is, *Meet the clients where they're at.* As Darlene had put it: Genesis is more capable of starting the rehab work at her level of functioning than she is at theirs.

"A harm reduction approach to drug treatment," says a leading textbook, *Substance Abuse,* "provides a spectrum of services that collectively meet the different needs of individual drug users. The services are offered in response to the needs and wishes of drug users, instead of demanding that users conform to rigid treatment program requirements."

In Darlene's case, a program that encompasses harm reduction principles would welcome her with open arms, offering up congratulations for doing less speed, for calming down, getting her voices to scream a bit more quietly at her—even for such a nebulous success as moving her tent-cave thirty feet from the others in the China Basin encampment.

In a journal article about harm reduction techniques for clients with dual diagnoses, Dr. Kate B. Carey notes that even "twenty-four hours of abstinence may constitute a reasonable initial goal. Noticeable changes in pattern, such as interruptions of using days with brief strings of sober days may represent significant progress. . . . The effort should be recognized, and labeled a success, so that the client may feel an enhanced sense of self efficacy and control over substance abuse. Feelings of personal efficacy are central to many psychological models of change. The harm reduction philosophy . . . provides more opportunities for successful experiences and tries to avoid unrealistic goals that set clients up for failure."

Progress comes in incremental steps, say the harm reductionists, with drug-free living a far-off and often unachievable (although not undesirable) goal. So if an addicted, homeless, hallucinatory speed freak is not ready to stop shooting speed, not willing to or capable of coming on time to every group, not able to stop yelling out or acting out, or if she won't take "government medications" to stop her voices—well, there's still much that can be done.

If the harm reduction movement had left it right there, at an almost inarguably logical and reasonable position, the drug treatment world would not have divided into two armed, deeply entrenched encampments that to this day continue to fire bullets of contempt at each others' rehab philosophies. And Darlene would not, unknowingly, be caught in their crossfire.

Lobbing grenades at the harm reduction camp are the soldiers of abstention who believe, with a commonsense logic that equals that of harm reduction, that the only way to deal with drug abuse is to stop using drugs. Halfway measures, they argue, do not work and only push addicts even deeper into a denial that says, "I can use drugs, and I'll be OK." The abstentionists claim that any attempt at merely reducing the harm of drug use simply encourages addicts to stay addicted. From Alcoholics Anonymous and the spin-off Narcotics Anonymous groups, on through Walden House and into the very vernacular of common household, government, and business language, the abstentionist approach is summarized in two words: *zero tolerance.*

Even rehab counselors who have come to embrace harm reduction principles still see the valid points of the abstentionists. "I came to this harm reduction idea kicking and screaming," says Imani Woods, a now converted harm reduction advocate in Seattle. "I was like, right, you give an addict options and you know what they'll choose? They're going to get high! But then I came face-to-face with the facts—sobriety ain't for everybody. As a public health worker, I had to ask myself the simple question: What about those for whom abstinence doesn't work?"

Woods lists the diseases her rehab clients had picked up while she'd still drilled the rule of "only abstention counts" into them: abscesses, blood and heart valve infections, hepatitis, AIDS. Many had died. "So I learned how to teach people how to better manage their drug use," says Woods. "That was a big one for me."

Darrell, however, finally bedded down at Acceptance Place and beginning the hard work of his own recovery, scoffs at the very idea of harm reduction. "That's an addict's dream!" he exclaims. "We'll figure out a hundred new ways to abuse a system like that! Addicts are great scammers, years of practice. Tell us you'll help us out and we can still use dope and drink? Where do I sign up?"

Having recovered and relapsed more times than even he cares to admit, Darrell disdains any rehab program that does not insist on perfect abstinence. "I am abstinent, or I am drunk," he concludes. "There's nothing in between."

The rehab world would seem ample enough to contain, even welcome, different and well-reasoned philosophies. But as is often the case, differences lead to dogma, and both the harm reductionists and the abstentionists share the blame for carrying their reasoning and rehab practices to such extremes that the only possible outcome was war.

In Oakland, just across the bay from San Francisco, the national Harm Reduction Coalition distributes an instruction book called *Getting Off Right: A Safety Manual for Injection Drug Users,* with chapter titles including "Preparing Your Shot," "Inserting Your Needle," and "Some Tips for Getting Veins Up." Although their intent is to make shooting drugs safer for those who, in spite of all efforts, continue to inject drugs, it's easy to see how such a manual raises the hackles of rehab counselors who are struggling to convince their clients that all drug use is a form of slow suicide.

"Preparing for and planning your injection drug use," notes the Harm Reduction Coalition's injection manual, "is one of the most important things you can do to achieve your desired results. . . . Before getting high, you should assess the safety of your setting and evaluate your state of mind . . ."

At Walden House, any addict who admits to a state of mind that includes getting high safely would be hauled straight to Kings Hall to be confronted by The Family, in no uncertain terms, at a House Meeting. Mike had watched while Walden dragged Paul through his House Meeting after he'd split, used drugs, and then asked to come back. And nobody had screamed in Paul's face, "Hey, you damn junkie, glad you shot up safely while you were out there!"

In fact, among the distinctive Walden vocabulary learned by every Family indoctrinee, from *haircuts* to *monads,* the expression *harm reduction* never rears its ugly head. I ask Mike, months after he's well ensconced in The Family, what he thinks about harm reduction. "What's that?" he replies, adding that he'd occasionally heard the expression around the mansion, and had guessed what it meant. "It's like an insurance policy, right?" he says. "You know, if we use drugs and get hurt, Walden might be sued or something, so they carry this special harm reduction insurance to decrease their risk; it's a low-liability insurance plan."

Yet Walden would be the first to acknowledge that there are those, like Paul, who leave their programs and head to the streets to do dangerous drugs in hazardous ways—only to later return and be accepted back into The Family for another try at rehab. In their own way, Walden is deviating from zero tolerance and toying with a bit of harm reduction, so that addicts who relapse don't return to The Family with abscess-laden arms, an HIV infection—or dead from an overdose. "You can't treat a dead addict," is another harm reduction motto, and it would seem hard to quibble.

Yet quibble they do. In written testimony to the U.S. Senate, General Barry McCaffrey describes harm reductionists as ". . . a carefully camouflaged, exorbitantly funded, well-heeled elitist group whose ultimate goal is to legalize drug use in the United States," through "a slick misinformation campaign" that "perpetrates a fraud on the American people." And in a *New York Times* op-ed piece, McCaffrey adds, "At best, harm reduction is a halfway measure, a halfhearted approach that would accept defeat."

Back in San Francisco, Dr. Marsha Rosenbaum, the director of the West Coast branch of the harm reduction mecca called the Lindesmith Center, responds, "We just don't accept those war metaphors. At least *we* keep people in treatment even if they're not completely abstinent. At least they're still alive and in the programs!"

Then Dr. Rosenbaum draws forth an expression reminiscent of the best of wars: "We, of course, think we have reason, compassion, and humanity on our side."

Watching all this from the sidelines is Professor Mark Kleiman, long-term drug rehab researcher at the University of California, Los Angeles. "There is colossal bad faith on both sides of the harm reduction issue," he tells me. "It's become impossible to have a sensible discussion about the details of which drug policies might actually work."

Caught in the harm reduction–versus–abstention bickering, Tom Hagan waits for Kathy to finish talking to Darlene about why Genesis will not accept her into their program unless she first takes medications to stop the voices that have been part of her life for as far back as Darlene's memory can take her.

"Darlene is a great example of where a harm reduction approach might do wonders," says Tom before she comes in to talk with him. "Harm reduction would say, 'Do what Darlene needs initially. Get her engaged in treatment. Offer her something before you demand something from her.' "

Tom sighs when I ask why that's not the approach Genesis is taking.

"The fundamental harm reduction principle of *meet the clients where they're at,*" he replies, "has been lost in all this arguing among the programs. At times, I'm almost afraid to bring it up."

But before Tom, Kathy, and Genesis might even discuss *meeting Darlene where she's at,* they have to discover just where "at" is for her—why Darlene is so terrorized by any mention of taking "government drugs."

When she'd run butt-naked through the streets in her worst speed-induced hallucinatory nightmare, weeks before first coming to Target Cities, Darlene had been dragged by the police to the county hospital psychiatric ward, where she'd been involuntarily committed and put on increasingly powerful doses of an antipsychotic medication named Haldol. When she was released, they gave her a bottle of baby-blue pills (which Darlene calls "the strongest the government makes"), with a strict warning that if she didn't take the Haldol those voices that had driven her naked into the streets would soon return to haunt her.

But Haldol, the Model T of medications that can eliminate hallucinations, had long ago been replaced by modern and improved antipsychotic drugs that do not cause Haldol's disabling sedation, described by Darlene as "like being sucked into some spiderweb." In a presumed cost-saving measure, the county hospital had prescribed the older, more toxic but less expensive pills.

Yet Darlene had continued taking the Haldol, intensely frightened that "the next time I go up *there,* with the bad voices, I'll never come down again." On Haldol, she had stopped hallucinating. She was also barely able to move.

"I was so slowed down," Darlene remembers, "it was like being dead. So I shot a whole bunch of meth just so's I could get up and walk again. Then the voices came back." In effect, on Haldol, Darlene had increased her speed use.

In Darlene's pharmacological summation: "Speed brings me *waaay* up here." She stands on tippy-toes, hands as high to the sky as she can reach. "And those government drugs bring me *waaay* down here." She does a deep knee bend before creakily struggling to stand again. "I can't figure which is more scary," she concludes.

And while Darlene is being considered for the program at Genesis, no one has yet figured out that the "government medication" she'd once been on had been Haldol. So they don't tell her about better pills, and Darlene feels trapped between being, as she describes it, a "government zombie" or a "China Basin crazy." At this point, the latter feels more comfortable.

Having finished talking with Kathy, Darlene is knocking on Tom Hagan's door. Before he opens it, Tom tells me, "Genesis is right in some ways, you know. This isn't just about harm reduction. Darlene really does need to be on medications to calm her down before she'll get any benefit from the groups, or have a chance in hell at actually staying clean. While she's still out-of-control hallucinating and shooting *any* speed," he concludes, "her chances of responding to rehab are about zero."

I nod, just before he turns the handle on the door, and ask, "And Darlene's chances of coming into the program, following all their rules, and taking medications right away?"

Tom smiles wanly. "Also about zero," he says. "Wish us luck!"

I wait for Darlene in the same cafe where, months before, I had sat with Mike. On her way home, Kathy spots me through the window and pokes her head in. "It's good, all good," she says hurriedly, then flashes a smile and thumb's-up sign and is off to catch her bus.

Ten minutes later, Darlene blows in with the energy of a hurricane. "Take me for pancakes," she laughs. "I'm starving! And don't ask no more questions! I need food!"

I'm buying, but it drives Darlene nuts to see me plunk down more than two dollars for a meal—the price of one croissant at the cafe—so we head for her favorite greasy spoon on 6th, off Mission. I've learned not to push Darlene for details before she's ready, so we sit silently, except when she rolls down the passenger window to yell at guys flying by on airplanes.

The menu, scrawled in Magic Marker, is taped on the walls over the oily surfaces of the Formica tables in the Bowery-style cafeteria, teeming day and night with people who dress in one of two styles: the grime of the streets, or the gold necklaces and shiny athletic suits of the street dealers. The place is steaming hot and overcrowded, the guests are loud and demanding, and the scene is carefully presided over by an elderly Chinese man and his two elfin daughters, who might be over eighteen.

Darlene merely waves her hand at the menu above her and the younger of the two women scribbles on a pad the Chinese equivalent of "pancakes, hamburger patty, bacon, french fries, biscuits and honey, extra butter and syrup, $1.99." And for me, also without asking, "pancakes, no butter." We've become Grand Restaurant regulars by now, greeted each time we enter with a warm smile, great service, and no wonderment at all when I tether Darlene to a microphone and record our conversation as we wolf down pancakes and, in Darlene's case, some extra calories to carry her to the unknown time of her next meal.

Within minutes, as always at the Grand, a fight accompanies our food.

"I ain't payin' till I get fed!" a tall, scraggly-bearded man staggers to his feet at the table just behind us. I can smell the alcohol on his breath from five feet away as he bends to scowl in the face of the waitress. She budges not an inch and says only, "You pay before food comes." Standard Grand policy.

"Yo! Brother," a voice booms out from one of the gold-chained customers. "The lady's asking you nice." The drunken man, wobbling, mumbling to himself, barely notices the outcry. "You heard me," the other slides his chair back from the table. "I *said,*" he advises the drunken man, "get the *fuck* out the door!"

The second waitress slips between the two men's tables, while her sister repeats softly,

"No trouble, no trouble," and artfully maneuvers the tall man toward the exit. Then she wipes off his table and invites the next waiting customer to be seated.

Darlene, not missing a bite, informs me, "The tall guy ain't only drunk, he's mentally ill. And that other dude with the chains, he's like *high,* but he's not crazy."

"Congratulations," I reply. "An instant answer to the dual diagnosis dilemma. And the two waitresses?"

Darlene giggles. "They," she says, "are way out there cool!"

But within moments Darlene is frowning, poking at her food.

"One of them married the white boy," she murmurs, her eyes welling up with tears. "Ain't that nice? Yes! But then they got a divorce. No, the kids don't know yet."

I wait until she looks up at me, then move one hand to the side of my ear, tapping my fingers together in our signal for when she's conversing with someone that only she can hear. She sees my sign and slowly nods, wiping at her tears, then digs back into her pancakes.

"That was in *my realm,*" Darlene tells me, our other code expression. "You see, I didn't know until today that I'd hurt my spirit that bad, did so much damage."

Puzzled, I ask, "You still in your realm?"

"No, shithead," she says. "I'm back. I thought you wanted to know what happened with Kathy and Tom? What they told me."

"I have been curious," I reply, watching Darlene's sly grin as she toys with me.

"What they told me is what's going to keep me clean," she continues, dripping an entire packet of honey onto one of her biscuits and taking it all in one bite. "It was about, you know, the damage to my spirit. I mean, I knew all that damage stuff before Kathy and Tom told me, but I didn't *really,* like, know it? Actually, I didn't see it until this very minute!"

Darlene points to the door through which the tall, mumbling man had just disappeared. "See, I can't be like *that,*" she says. "So I told Kathy and Tom—I ain't shooting no more crank. And I'll take their government drugs."

"Do me a favor?" I ask, and she stares at me, waiting. "Could you ask Darlene to come back? I think I'm talking to somebody else."

Darlene giggles, pleased that she'd surprised me.

"I *am* going to take their pills," she affirms, "and I ain't doing no more speed, no more nothing! Well, maybe a little marijuana, but that don't count. And I can't eat all this, either," she laughs, pushing away her still-half-full plate. "I'm up to like two hundred twenty pounds because I've been doing less crank. And if I *really* go off the Jenny Crank diet—methaaaamphetamines!—I'll be so fat Genesis will need *two* chairs for me!"

"Exactly what did Tom and Kathy tell you?" I ask, still a bit stunned by her turnaround.

"Lots," says Darlene, enjoying the game of cat and mouse. She hands over a piece of paper, a referral to a drop-in psychiatric clinic where she can get her government drugs without charge.

"Drop me over there before you go home?" she asks, pushing away from the table. "I need to start on my pills."

"What Darlene and I did," Tom Hagan says when I swing by at 5:30 P.M. after dropping her off at the Westside Mental Health Clinic, "was a dance. That's really the truth of the matter. A lot of listening, a lot of acknowledging of where she's coming from—at least what I could make of where she's coming from. She's still really way out there."

Tom pauses to respond to a knock on his door from one of the Target Cities intake counselors. "We've got a client crisis," the counselor tells him. "We're going to need your help." Tom apologizes for cutting our conversation short.

"So Darlene had her say with me, and I just listened," he says as he leaves the office. "But then I talked to her about how she's become stuck. She's describing all this stuff in her life that's just not working anymore for her, and I said we simply can't help out while she's still flying high on speed and talking to people nobody else can hear."

Tom heads down the long hallway toward the shouting voices of a counselor and client in a conference room. "In the end," he concludes, "I told Darlene I didn't want to have a debate with her, that I've had lots of experience with clients who hear voices on speed, and that these medications have been helpful. I asked her to try them."

"Actually"—he laughs as we near the shouting—"I was sure I'd blown it with Darlene. I mean, harm reduction theory out the goddamn window! I wanted her to do what *we* wanted her to do, and I pushed for it."

Tom pauses, trying himself to understand what had happened with Darlene.

"You put twenty counselors in a room," he says, "and you get twenty different definitions of what harm reduction is. It's hard enough to work with addicts without all this squabbling. What we need is flexibility, because neither side is right. You do harm reduction for some, insist on abstinence for others. This isn't a battle between the two groups, it's a fight to work with the addicts. We need all the tools we can get."

"So what made you switch over with Darlene today?" I ask. "You could have asked Genesis to accept her into the program with congratulations for doing less speed, and tackled the psychiatric-medication issue later."

"I was surprised, too," says Tom. "I mean, I'm a harm reduction fanatic! But at times, not pushing strictly for abstinence is like betting against a client's success. For Darlene, halfway measures seemed kind of a nonsolution. So I risked losing her, insisting on what she really needs to do to get better. And she took the bait. But you know what I really thought she'd tell me?"

I picture Darlene in my mind and hazard a guess. "Kiss my big black ass?"

"You got it." Tom laughs. "And it was a close call. But let's not get carried away. We're not about to watch Darlene go riding off into some clean and sober sunset very soon. I'll promise you that."

There is no visible sunset in San Francisco for weeks, as El Niño settles in and the skies pour forth the fiercest, most torrential winter downpours since 1862. "It's an astounding year," observes William Mork, California's climatologist, "unlikely we'd see anything like it in our lifetime."

As torrents of water, mud, and misery flood the city, drug rehab becomes the least of the Health Department's concerns. Even program administrators like Tom are drafted to pace the streets and try to persuade the most resistant homeless to head for emergency shelters. Tom finds himself climbing down muddy embankments to hidden homeless encampments, guided by the city's new Homeless Death Prevention Team, to beg soggy denizens of the streets to move indoors. The city opens an enormous emergency shelter in a hangar-sized warehouse at Mission Rock, a mere three blocks from Darlene's tent in China Basin. And in perhaps the most extreme example of harm reduction at work, the sacrosanct "No drugs, No violence, No threats of violence" policy enforced at all city-run shelters is modified to an unwritten, "Just step outside to do your dope, we'll let you right back in."

But in her own isolated corner in the China Basin encampment, Darlene will not budge. "I don't do shelters," she says simply. "I'll stay here and drown before I'll sleep in some big old room with hundreds of people. I'm a private person. There's no room for all my stuff in there, and people'll steal it anyways. But if they offered me an apartment," she says with no hint of sarcasm, "I'd think about it."

Yet while the winter's El Niño transforms San Francisco into an ominously dark urban rain forest, my summertime pessimism about the chances of success for drug rehab turn strangely optimistic.

Darrell is tucked safely in at Acceptance Place, with twelve other gay men in a stucco home in a tranquil residential neighborhood just above the Mission district. "I still feel lonely here," he tells me, "but that's just my own thing. I mean, I'm barely sober after how many years now? I don't know how to relate to people when I'm not drunk or high. It feels so awkward!"

Acceptance Place is a "social model" rehabilitation house, practicing a milder form of Walden's militaristic behavior modification. The house maintains a strict schedule of group therapy, AA and NA meetings, communal meals, morning walks, counseling sessions, journal writings. Everyone is expected to find a job and to contribute both work and money to the program. And while there are face-to-face confrontations in the groups, Acceptance Place's style and tone are a Boy Scout jamboree compared to Walden's Marine Corps–like basic training, a tone enhanced by having twelve addicts in the house instead of Walden's 120.

"Walden's great for some people," says Darrell, "but Acceptance is working out better for me. I'm still afraid to get to know people, though, kind of lost even with this small a group. So I'm on this emotional roller coaster. But that's the same thing that happens every time I get sober. I've got to work through all these feelings that I've numbed out for so long."

Darrell pauses, as if hearing my silent skepticism about the words I've now heard from so many addicts: *But this time is different.* "It *does* feel different this time," he intuitively responds. "I suppose if I really understood how to describe to you just *what* is different, I'd be healthy and wouldn't need to be here. So I'm working on it."

The nation's newly invigorated drug rehab efforts, although with some delay, have found Darrell a place that fits him well.

My visits to Mike at Walden continue as an adventuresome voyage to a far-off land, filled with exotic rules and rituals, their mysterious meanings to be deciphered only over time. As I become an honorary member of The Family, I find myself satisfied with letting my questions and doubts be answered by the newly learned platitudes that now rattle in my head: *Trust the process,* I say to myself as I wonder if putting someone on the bench for snacking in his room is really "therapeutic." And I murmur *Gratitude is having one good friend* each time I hang out on The Boulevard and share a *one-to-one* with a Walden Brother or Sister.

I know the whole thing is a setup, an imitation family united by a contrived culture. But I'm willing, for the time being, to *wait it out*, to *take it one day at a time*, to agree that *we've only just begun.* Mostly, watching the hammering rains that continue to flood the streets outside, I hear over and over on The Boulevard, *Gratitude is having a nice warm bed.*

In spite of my reservations about cultlike abuses at Walden, I've come to appreciate its eccentric blend of tough love and tickle-your-funny-bone. On Thanksgiving day, Sylvester gathers The Family in Kings Hall. Those with relatives nearby are to be allowed home for dinner, and he's laying down the rules.

"If there is wine on that Thanksgiving table," announces the tall, muscular ex-addict, "you get right back here—because you cannot be around alcohol while in this program."

He waits for the barked chorus of "Thank you, Sylvester" that indicates he's been heard, and understood.

"So I don't want to hear about no cocaine-stuffed turkey bird," he continues without a hint of a smile, "that jumped off the table and was running around the room. And you just hung out with it!"

Even Sylvester's brow-furrowed stare doesn't stop the roar of laughter and high fives that break out among The Family, shattering the strict formality of a Kings Hall meeting.

"So you have a good Thanksgiving," smiles Sylvester. "Stay on track, and by this time next year you'll be home again, cooking up your own turkey."

"Thank you, Sylvester," booms the chorus of voices, and he dismisses them for Tighten Up, the nightly bustle of cleaning that keeps Walden so highly polished that the original mansion owners would consider it primed for the next grand ball.

I chat with Mike as he heads off to clean the toilets in the upstairs dorm bathroom. Rummaging about, he finds an extra bucket and sponge and, laughing, says, "If I got to do it, you got to do it." Mike's mood reeks a contagious optimism. I grab the sponge and we get down to work.

"I took three of these last night," Darlene tells me, holding out the small white pharmaceutical bottle of Zyprexa, a new antipsychotic medication that causes none of the drowsiness of Haldol. I look at the label: *Take one tablet before bedtime.*

"Three?" I ask, pointing to the listed dosage.

"Yeah, I know," laughs Darlene. "I'm taking some extras, getting ready for my interview at Genesis."

Before I can comment she's up and, pulling a sweater over her head, out of the tent. "Today's the fifteenth," she tells me. "I've got a surprise for you, but I need a ride."

On the first and fifteenth of each month, Darlene picks up a $163 welfare check. Lunch at the Grand Restaurant today, she tells me, is on her. But first we head for the Mission district to get her check and cash it in.

"The surprise," Darlene says excitedly on the way over, "is that I'm getting married. I want you to store my wedding dress where it'll stay dry."

"I thought William was still in jail?" I ask, driving past heroin central at 16th and Mission, out toward 24th where the welfare checks come in. As on every first and fifteenth of the month, the streets are mobbed, fresh cash flowing.

"William *is* still in jail," says Darlene, watching the scene out the window. "But he's getting out in like a month and we're getting married this summer—on the ferry boat on the Fourth of July. Wait till you see my dress! The only thing William's going to like better than me in that dress is me out of that dress. I've put down fifteen bucks on layaway out of every welfare check, and today all $360 for the dress is paid up."

"Our government dollars at work," I note, in wonderment.

Darlene glances annoyingly at me. "That's fifteen government bucks less," she explains self-righteously, "spent on methamphetamine."

She cries out for me to stop the car and jumps out as I pull to the curb. Within minutes she's back, counting through a wad of twenties and ones. Darlene separates out fifteen dollars, tucks the rest in her bra, and directs me three blocks down to a clothing store. The display window seems filled as much with gaudy stage costumes as with clothes.

The store is humming with welfare payday shoppers. The woman behind the counter, frowning when she sees Darlene, wordlessly reaches back and pulls down a paper-covered dress from the rack. She takes Darlene's fifteen dollars and hands her the package, making a final mark on the layaway form.

When Darlene appears from the dressing room, every single shopper in the packed store does a double take. Her size twelve, slinky, silver-sequined, sky-blue velvet wedding gown, with deep black fishnet décolletage, is stretched tight as skin over Darlene's ample body. She's put her muddy boots back on, and her Afro is squished in various directions from when she'd pulled the dress over her head. She flings her arms up, swivels her hips Hollywood-star fashion, and beams out a grin that would melt the coldest of hearts. Blushing in front of the stares of every customer in the store, I embrace Darlene while she cries the tears of a new bride.

"Should I change before we go to the Grand for lunch," she asks, "or wear it there?"

"Maybe you should change," I suggest. "Just to keep it clean and dry."

She disappears into the dressing room. While waiting, I realize for the first time that day that Darlene has been talking only to me—not a word with her hidden voices.

"How's your noise today?" I ask as we drive. "You seem different on the Zyprexa."

"Truth?" she asks, and I nod.

"It's still there," she says softly. "I mean, I hear the voices, but they're kind of in the background more? It's like, now I can answer one question from them and talk to you at the same time." Darlene giggles. "See, I did it just now, so fast you didn't even notice."

But as I slow the car, looking for a parking space in front of the Grand, she bolts out the door, falls, and gets up in the middle of the street, screaming obscenities at a woman who'd just flashed by on a bicycle.

"You fucking killed his baby!" shrieks Darlene as brakes squeal and a driver swerves, narrowly missing her. "Goddamn, come back here, you fucking murderer!" she cries as the bicyclist disappears in the distance. Then she stomps over to the curb and, ignoring me, into the Grand.

"That was in your realm?" I ask, worried, as I catch up to her and grab a chair at our table.

"I'm not always crazy, you know," says Darlene, still glaring and nodding in the direction of the bicyclist. "That bitch Suzie got pregnant from Wayne and had an abortion. Damn baby killer. You know what I'd do to have that baby?"

We sit silently for a while, Darlene slowly calming down. I've asked before about her five children, taken from her by child protective services. But that's all I know. "There are places you aren't going with me, that are over the edge," she'd told me the first time I'd inquired about her children. "Don't ask about my kids, because I'll just go off on you."

Darlene barely touches her pancakes, fries, or biscuits and honey. "I can't even *think* about Suzie having that abortion," she says. "My mom had them tie my tubes after I had Sean. So women who can still *have* babies got no right to kill them." She pushes her plate away.

"Damn, I'm not always some nutcase," she explains, searching my face. "Just sad sometimes. Can I go home now?"

A brief burst of sunshine hits Darlene's corner of the China Basin homeless encampment. We chat while she hangs out wet clothes on the fence to dry, then she pulls out her bottle of Zyprexa and swallows yet another pill. "I'm preparing for my appointment with Genesis tomorrow," she explains, foraging through her trunk of damp clothes to pick an outfit for the interview. "There's still some noise," she tells me, "and sometimes I go so far back I collide with myself. I can't be doing that during no interview tomorrow."

She folds back a flap of plastic that covers the entrance to her tent. Still dry under the flap is a Sierra Club calendar, this month's photo a lush field of brilliant yellow mustard extending to a bright blue horizon. Darlene hands me the calendar, pointing to dates she's crossed off with a thick black *X*, counting each one out loud.

"That's thirty-four days without no meth," she announces, carefully folding the calendar back into its protected space.

"But now I'm addicted to these government pills," says Darlene. "My noise is down, and now most of the time I can just brush it off."

"You've had those voices for years. Are you happier without them?"

Darlene is confused by the question.

"No," she replies after a long pause. "Certain people make me happier."

"Who?"

"Kathy. And you. And maybe the people at Genesis will. See my noises don't bother *me*, they bother all of you. *You're* the ones who are happier when I have less noise."

"You're right, you know," I say. "I liked you when you still had a lot of noise—but it's sure nicer talking to you now that you don't."

"Yeah, I guess I'm nicer talking to me, too," laughs Darlene. "But I got work to do today, so you've got to go." She's standing over me now, hands on hips, glowering down until I rise, puzzled, to leave.

Then she's laughing again, frantically rummaging through the duffel bag in her tent, finally producing a rusted old jack from a '91 Volvo and holding it proudly, reverentially, to the sky.

"Oh, no!" I say, recognizing her "equalizer." The jack, intended to lift a two-thousand-pound car, fits perfectly between the bars of a Kryptonite bicycle lock. Two twists of the jack handle and the lock bursts open. Seconds later, Darlene has a new airplane.

"Don't you say a fucking word," she warns me. "I can't do no meth, I'm taking government pills, I got to go to government groups—so don't go bitching about me getting a new airplane!"

"OK," I surrender. "I'm outta here."

"And don't go telling Kathy, neither," Darlene yells as I crawl through the fence to the other side of the encampment. "She's already pissed off 'cause I smoked a joint the other day. She hears about my new airplane, she'll call off this whole Genesis thing."

Darlene is breathless when she calls my home office number the next evening from a phone at the Caltrans station, the nearest telephone to her house.

"I think I did it!" she yells above the clatter of trains pulling in and out.

"Did what?"

"Genesis! The lady was real nice at the interview, because she'd heard about me and wasn't expecting what came through that door when I got there. I mean, I was cool! I took an extra pill before I went and told her straight out, I am not no wing nut, I am not no loony tune, and I ain't no bat in no belfry!"

"That must have done it," I answer, laughing. "What'd she say?"

"She said she'd call Kathy, get me set up for groups there."

"Congratulations!" I yell over the noise.

"What? I can't hear you. Goddamn trains. Bye."

Hanging next to me in my office, safe and dry, is Darlene's sky-blue, sequined, size-twelve, federally funded wedding dress—in itself not a problem, except it means that William, absent during her recent "rehab," is about to leave jail (assault and battery on another homeless man during a jealous rage over Darlene) and enter her life again. And Darlene still lives thirty feet from the epicenter of the methamphetamine capital of the United States, has lived in the streets for sixteen of her thirty-two years, has lost all five of her kids and still breaks into a fury even thinking about that, swings from topic to topic as if on a motorized seesaw, smokes marijuana when she's not shooting speed, and, when the mood hits, heads for a brief visit to a nearby gym with a Volvo car jack and comes back with, on average, a $1,200 sports bike (her taste in airplanes, it seems, is more sophisticated than her taste in wedding dresses). The thirty-four "drug-free" days she's carefully marked off on the Sierra Club calendar below the brilliant mustard field is certainly an impressive display, but it's no more than a jagged approximation of any truly amphetamine-free reality.

Darlene's fundamental core of existence has merely gone from hell to hellish. Does it make any real difference to Darlene or anyone else if the flames of her hell have declined from char to scorch?

"I'm one for harm reduction," Kathy had told me when she'd arranged Darlene's "Phase Two" interview at Genesis. "I'd prefer to see Darlene trying to get her mind back together, in whatever way she can. If she can reduce her drug use, that's fine. I just need to see some progress and I'll hang in there with her. We don't have to go all the way, but if there's *no* progress we're all just wasting our time."

And yet, what harms are being reduced with Darlene? Does the previous owner of her new bicycle agree that, through all this effort on the part of multiple agencies, she's been rendered less harmful? Have thousands of sorely needed health dollars (and thousands more to come) been spent so that Darlene, still sleeping in China Basin with Bruce and waiting for her boyfriend to get out of jail, could now become slightly less terrorized than on that day when she'd first arrived at Target Cities? What are the long-range chances of success, however defined, with this hallucinatory speed shooter who first ran away from home at age six and started using drugs when she was ten?

"In twenty-five years of substance abuse and mental health work," Tom Hagan had told me, "the one thing I've learned is that making forecasts is risky at best. I could reel off a list of folks who I wouldn't have bet anything on their making it, and now they've got six, ten, fifteen years of recovery under their belts. But I'll tell you one thing that's certain, nobody gets to clean and sober along some straight road. So if you look at any *one* point in time during someone's rehab, you can be convinced they'll stay clean forever, or they'll be out in the streets shooting up tomorrow. I've been wrong so many times I've just stopped guessing, and give everyone their best shot at it."

With that, Tom hit on the core conflict behind all the blather and bluster dividing the entire rehab community over harm reduction: the complete lack of ability to predict who will succeed and who cannot.

"*Nobody* can tell which patients will make it to stable abstinence," emphasizes Dr. Pablo Stewart, who claims he initially meets all clients where they're at, *and* pushes each one as hard as he can toward pure abstinence. "What gets me all fired up about this harm reduction debate," says the psychiatrist, "is that the harm reduction folks are writing people off, thinking the best they can get to is some lesser form of drug use. They're writing off the mentally ill, they're writing off the homeless, they're writing off ethnic minorities, they're writing off the poor. Well, especially for the homeless, especially for the mentally ill—we should try everything we can to get them sober! The problem is not that the homeless and mentally ill or anybody else can't get to clean and sober, it's that we're not giving them the kind of services they need to get there. So what's harm reduction say? Accept halfway solutions, it's the best we can do. Nothing could be further from the truth. You might start with some harm reduction to first get them engaged, but then you also provide them with their best shot at true sobriety."

Sitting in my office after Darlene's phone call from the train station, I pull out my photograph of her from that first day she'd arrived at Target Cities. I stare at the image of a woman with arms folded tightly against her chest, lips pursed shut, and sheer terror in her eyes. Then I think of the Darlene I'd spent the day with yesterday, still crazy, still Darlene, yet so much calmer, less hallucinatory, more focused, connected, and communicative. And tomorrow morning, she's on her way to Genesis.

But at seven that morning, the city's bulldozers, without warning, rip apart the China Basin camp. The mayor has launched his citywide strategy to keep the homeless moving.

Darlene awakens in panic, then frantically dumps in a shopping cart the few belongings she can save. She calls and I drive over the Third Street bridge to witness the devastation. Within an hour, the encampment is reduced to rubble.

I can't help keeping Tom's words in mind. "Nobody arrives at clean and sober traveling a straight road." The bulldozers, I hope against all reason, are merely digging potholes that Darlene will slip into, and back out of, as she continues her crooked road up from hell.

The San Francisco Board of Supervisors' Health, Family and Environment Committee members sit at a high polished-wood dais in their distinguished hearing chamber at City Hall. They've taken on a studied appearance—court justices who've removed their black robes and rolled up their sleeves to manifest a more laid-back style to the overflow crowd of officials delivering reports and, as always, seeking a bigger slice of the city's financial pie. On schedule for public report at 11:00 A.M. are Dr. Larry Meredith, the originator of Treatment on Demand and a leader of the national move toward drug rehab, and the Department of Health's Substance Abuse Services team. But the supervisors' laid-back style is matched by their bureaucratically glacial meanderings and, at 1:30 P.M., Dr. Meredith and a good part of the city's Department of Health managers are still waiting in the long hallway outside of chambers for their turn with "the Supes."

Although we've been in touch, I haven't seen Meredith personally since our first meeting in his office months ago. He spots me in the crowded hallway and, looking restlessly at his watch, now showing 1:45, notes, "Well, you can see how efficiently things work for Treatment on Demand here at the top. How's it looking down in the streets?"

"About the same." I smile, restless myself because I had told Darlene I'd meet her at 2:00 in front of City Hall, to take her to get some dry blankets from the Homeless Death Prevention Project nearby. It's been three rainy weeks since the bulldozers tore down the China Basin encampment, and she's moved five times since then in search of a place where the police won't chase her away each morning.

"We've been trying to site three new residential facilities, get the treatment waiting list down," Dr. Meredith tells me, looking around the crowded hallway, "but you can see how fast things move in this city. What we need to get Treatment on Demand off the ground," he notes, "is somebody who knows nothing at all about drug rehab, but who's one hell of an efficient bureaucrat."

There's a rumbling at the far end of the hallway and the sea of waiting officialdom slowly parts. Coming at us down the passageway is Darlene. She pulls up alongside Dr. Meredith, hoists her low-cut sweater up to cover at least part of her cleavage, pulls her wool cap down tighter over her head, and shouts, "Damn, Lonny, I thought you were meeting me outside!"

"Darlene," I say, turning to face Larry Meredith, and praying for harm reduction, "this is Dr. Meredith. He's in charge of all those programs you tried to get into. Larry, this is Darlene."

Tall, thin, and gracious in mannerism, Meredith shifts the manila folders under his gray-suited arm and extends his hand to shake Darlene's.

"Which rehab programs did you try for?" he inquires.

"You're like, *the* boss?" she asks, unreservedly looking him up and down and then, without skipping a beat, "I been to Target Cities, STOP, Westside Mental Health, *and* to Genesis."

"And where are you now?" asks Meredith.

"In the streets," replies Darlene, "shooting speed."

Meredith is silent for a moment, and Darlene rushes to fill in the space. "Show him the pictures," she says, turning to me. I had told Darlene I'd bring her copies of the photos from the day the bulldozers had knocked down her house.

Pulling the images from my bag, I briefly outline to Meredith Darlene's trajectory from diminished drug use, to taking antipsychotic meds, to her acceptance into Genesis and, on the day she was to start in rehab, the destruction of her home. Lost in a hallucinatory speed frenzy while she'd run ahead of the bulldozers, Darlene never did make it to Genesis that day, or any day after.

"Since then," Darlene quietly sums up, showing Meredith one of the photos, "I haven't been doing too well. Can you get me a place to live? I mean, if I had a housing thing, I might get it together again. I keep getting chased and having to move everything I own, and I can't do that without shooting no speed, which you guys keep telling me I'm not supposed to be using."

Meredith, as if discussing a proposal from one of his health department deputies, nods thoughtfully, brow furrowed, and I watch with no small delight as the drug chief and Darlene engage in a discussion about housing and drug issues.

"The problem we're having," explains Meredith earnestly to Darlene, "is that our drug counselors weren't trained to help with the specifics of housing issues. So we're working—" he ruffles through the papers in one of his folders—"to get some federal Housing and Urban Development funds to get some trained housing counselors in the drug rehab offices."

"So when do I get housing?" asks Darlene.

"It's expensive, and it takes time to develop resources," replies Meredith. "But we're working on it."

"Then how come you tore down the house I had?"

There's a sigh of relief in the packed hallway as the announcement comes through that the supervisors' committee is now ready to hear the report from Community Substance Abuse Services. But Meredith stays with Darlene an additional moment before joining his coworkers.

"Darlene," he says sincerely, "I'm really sorry they did that to your house. But it wasn't the health department or drug rehab people that did it. It was a totally different part of the government." He looks inquiringly my way.

"Highway department," I tell him. "But they didn't give the required warning before they broke up the encampment. Nobody from homeless services knew until it was all over."

"We only got one government," says Darlene, "don't you guys talk to each other?"

"We try," says Meredith, turning to head into the meeting. "We have to expand the rehab system in ways that integrate with the lifestyles of the drug users. We're stacking the odds against successful treatment the way we do things now, I know that. We'd love it if the people who knock down the homeless camps would notify the health department first, but it's just not happening. It was good talking with you," Meredith concludes, heading through the door into the supervisors' meeting. "Let me know if there's anything I can do to help out."

"How about some dry blankets?" says Darlene. But we're standing in an empty hallway.

If harm reduction is the big brother of drug rehab, then "integration of services" is his young sidekick. They're lost without each other.

"If we are going to make a difference with substance abuse problems," Larry Meredith had told me during our first interview, when idealism had overrun pragmatics, "then we have to realize that drug abuse is related to housing is related to health care is related to joblessness is related to poverty. You can't deal with any one of those without dealing with all of them. So what we're hoping to do is use drug abuse, the social issue of the day, to reframe this whole city so that we work together." Meredith trailed off, way ahead of himself and the realities of the day.

"I guess it's kind of a sixties holistic notion," he laughed, "but you know, you stay around long enough and things come back again. When you look at the multiple problems that individuals have now, in particular the co-occurring epidemics of substance abuse, homelessness, mental health problems, and HIV, they are simply not separable. We've become stuck in this crazy corner, and the only place to move is toward integrating services."

"Each rehab client is also a consumer in many different bureaucratic fiefdoms," says Michael Siever, co-chair of the Treatment on Demand Planning Council, the watchdog of the city's enhanced rehab programs. "And each fiefdom doesn't communicate with each other. So when we started Treatment on Demand it was *essential* that there be integration of services. That was our key theme in making rehab work."

The problem, of course, is that there is a separate and independent government agency for every social service listed by Meredith, and then some. So reality hit hard and fast. When public health specialist Charlie Morimoto was first hired to help initiate Treatment on Demand, he was given the curious title "Integration Specialist," and assigned the task of unifying the Department of Mental Health and Community Substance Abuse Services. "You wouldn't believe the resistance I ran into right off," says Morimoto. "There wasn't a chance in hell of getting mental health and substance abuse services together. The turf war between those two agencies makes the drug war seem simple." Morimoto's title was soon changed to "Director of Planning and Operations."

"We soon learned that it's easier to just focus on creating new treatment slots," recalls Morimoto's colleague Siever, "than to tackle the kind of government attitude changes that are really needed."

While true integration of services is a pie-in-the-sky dream, coordination and communication between government departments need not be. Darlene might have been sustained in her upward spiral toward sanity and sobriety had the police department, which supervised the highway department's destruction of the homeless encampment, merely advised the health department that the bulldozers were on the way. Housing and substance abuse counselors could have hit the camps before, or along with, the tractors and men wearing hard hats. If that didn't work, and Darlene had still, understandably, freaked out, hit the speed again, and stopped taking her medications—at least Kathy and Tom would have known what was going on. They could have switched into harm reduction mode to get

Darlene safely through the setback, kept her engaged in the system until she was again able to move ahead.

As it was, after her house was bulldozed, Darlene simply didn't show up at Genesis. And no one at that program or at Target Cities knew what had happened, or where she was. After months of hard work that had finally hinted at bearing fruit, Darlene simply dropped off the rehab map.

I drive Darlene, dry blankets in hand, to her newest temporary outpost in a muddy fenced-in lot behind the Bladium, an ice-hockey rink about three blocks past the Third Street bridge into China Basin. She grimaces as she reaches to open the door, her hand puffy and swollen from an abscess forming where she'd missed a vein and injected speed just under her skin.

"You going to be OK?" I ask.

Darlene is silent, withdrawn. Her noise is back in full force.

I offer to phone the city's homeless outreach team, let them know where she is. They can check in a few days to see how she's doing, bring some more blankets out in their van, a nurse to look at her abscess.

Darlene glares back at me. "That's a government van," she says, pulling open the car door and grabbing the blankets. "Last time I let government people know where I was, when I signed up for Genesis and took those pills, they came out and bulldozed my house. See, all those little pieces of government talk to each other, they're all in cahoots."

She slams the car door closed. I drive off, wishing she were right—that those little pieces of government did talk to each other.

On the morning of December 31, The Boulevard bustles with activity as The Family prepares for Walden's New Year's Eve bash. The decorations committee has mobilized in Kings Hall and garlands of brightly colored balloons and long, curlicued crepe paper–streamers dangle from the ornate ballroom chandeliers. The music committee has already revved up the sound system, sliding monitor levers on high to throw the bass into a booming hyperdrive. So when the Recovery Rap band starts rehearsals for that night's dance, the mansion vibrates as if hit by a series of earthquakes.

New Year's Eve at Walden, as in the rest of San Francisco, rages with enthusiastic traditions and boisterous celebrations of new beginnings. But there is a one-of-a-kind New Year's ritual unique to Walden, initiated with the rising of the sun on this last day of December: the entire Family is locked in the house.

"You got to remember," says counselor Marlin Mayorga, "we're living in a house full of dope fiends. Things can go wrong, real wrong."

All passes are canceled, although Family members who have achieved O.S.—own strength—are allowed to venture some fifty feet out the door, as far as the corner mom-and-pop grocery to retrieve smokes or snacks. For the rest, there's football, videos, TV, board games, special meals, and the usual Walden one-to-ones and group meetings. But treading on the streets of San Francisco as New Year's Eve approaches is strictly forbidden. For those craving excitement, the clean and sober dance in Kings Hall as midnight draws near will have to do.

Locking down the entire Family may seem overly cautious, even for Walden House. But if Walden's counselors had their preferences, the house lockdown would start at Thanksgiving, continue straight on through Christmas, run across the New Year, and then continue for a week or so into January for good measure. In Walden, just as outside, the holiday season is laden with celebration and merriment, and tremendous anxiety and tension. Pour that stress into a houseload of recovering addicts, mix well, and the resulting explosion blows a number of them out to the streets in a frantic search for their dealers.

In one counselor's caseload, "The Believers," five of fifteen members were lost to relapses between Thanksgiving and the December 31st lockdown. Other counselors' caseloads, "The Bomb Squad" and "The Soldiers," suffered similar losses.

"We've had so many *splitees* there's empty beds all around the house," says Mike as I join The Family in their morning preparations for the New Year's Eve festivities. "But for every dope fiend that splits this place," he adds, "there's like ten waiting out there to get in. I've got two new Little Brothers just assigned to me."

Mike escorts his Little Brothers—one of whom is six-foot-four—down The Boulevard, making introductions. Exclamations of "Welcome home!" merge with shouts of "Happy New Year!"

Walden's season-of-cheer losses include more than splitees who've vanished to the streets. Those sticking with the program have also been hit hard by the holidays. The whole Family seems to have caught the jitters.

"Things are way too loose around here," announces Marlin at the morning Kings Hall meeting. The ex-addict and ex–gang banger slouches deep down into the cushioned staff lounge chair, surveying the entire Family sitting erect in their own rigid seats.

"I seen one of you running down The Boulevard yesterday," announces Marlin. "You heard me—running on The Boulevard! And not one person from this Family *pulled him up*, gave him a *learning experience*. I had to do the *pull-up* myself, and that ain't right."

Marlin is up now, circling the room, stopping for a moment to catch the eye of each silent Family member.

"This house is so loose," he announces, "even *bans* are breaking down."

The angrier Marlin gets, the more quietly he speaks, so the Family in the huge hall has to strain forward to hear him. He stops in front of Gloria, whose gaze moves quickly down from his. She stares at her shoes.

"Stand up and explain to this Family what a ban is," commands the counselor. "Because you're on a ban with Darnel, but you and nobody else in this room seems to understand what that means."

Gloria rises slowly. "People get put on a ban," she says in a gravelly voice , "when they are not allowed to communicate with each other, in any way."

She sits down, task completed.

"Stand again, Gloria," instructs Marlin, " 'cause you're on your way to *the bench*. I seen you and Darnel on The Boulevard this morning, smiling and passing hand signals."

Gloria begins to speak, but Marlin waves her down. "Your time to say something was this morning, when you could have said, like, 'Thank you,' to whichever Brother or Sister had given you a pull-up, pointed out your mistake."

Marlin pauses, looks around the room, then addresses the entire Family, his head bobbing in emphasis.

"But Gloria didn't have no chance to say 'Thank you,' did she? 'Cause nobody from this Family gave her no pull-up! If there was enough room, I'd put this whole Family on the bench!"

A week before New Year, his seventh week at Walden, Mike had awakened "feeling really fine, like I got my whole life ahead and it's all roses from here. I mean, I'm like buoyant!" He knocked on the door to Dolores's office. "Just thought I'd say hello," he told Walden's director, "tell you how good I'm feeling."

"Nice to see you so happy," replied Dolores. "But watch out."

"Watch out for what?" Mike said, laughing. "Watch out for being happy?"

Dolores smiled with him, but then shook her head.

"You get too happy, Mike, and you forget where you've been before this. *And,* you forget that you're not yet where you want to be. So don't go getting careless on me, now."

The next day I looked for Mike, and found him on the bench.

"Promise me you won't laugh?" he began his explanation. " 'Cause if staff sees, they'll think I'm not taking this seriously."

I nodded.

"See that banister over there?" Mike's lips twitched as he struggled to stifle a smile. "I was feeling so good yesterday and I saw that shiny, long, curved wood banister."

He paused, unable to hide his grin, checking around to make sure no one could see.

"Wheeee!" Mike continued, laughing. "I put my butt on that banister, legs straight out in the air, and went sliding down. Two flights, full speed ahead! But I had some grease on my shoes from the plumbing I'd been doing so when I hit the floor I slid across the whole damn Boulevard, fell on my ass when I hit the wall."

He reached into his back pants pocket to show me a tattered copy of five typewritten sheets, titled, "Unwritten Rules."

"They're making me read all these, over and over," said Mike. He flipped the pages to rule number 74: "No leaning or sitting on banisters."

The carefully typed pamphlet of Walden's unwritten rules includes, "No wearing sunglasses in the facility"; "No putting your feet or legs on chairs without medical orders"; and "No Dijon mustard." Dijon, it turns out, contains alcohol.

When Mike had flown off the banister and across The Boulevard, a dozen Brothers and Sisters had watched in awe. Although the house may have been loose and out of control, as Marlin noted, they all *supported* Mike. In Walden-speak, *support* means ratting to the staff about any member's deviant behavior, to support that person's sobriety. In Mike's case, The Family's support landed him on the bench with a fresh copy of 117 unwritten rules to memorize.

Sylvester took Mike off the bench that afternoon, assigning him to wash greasy pots in the kitchen each day. And at every evening Family Meeting for the next week, Mike must stand at attention and recite: "On December twenty-sixth I received a learning experience. My learning experience is to wash pots and pans to remind me of my lack of awareness of house rules. This learning experience is not yet completed. Thank you, Family!"

"I don't get it," Mike tells me as we wait for the start of a Family Meeting and he rehearses for an error-free recitation of his learning experience. "I've been doing real good, man," he says. "I been following the program, barely been thinking about dope! I mean, I got some drug cravings, but I'm feeling real strong against them. But nobody's saying, 'Hey, good work, Mike!' It's like, I'm being punished for feeling so good."

I talk with Darrell about how robust Mike seems, and how suspicious Walden is of his boisterous contentment. We're slouched into an overstuffed sofa in the cozy living room at Acceptance Place, talking over tinny music that blasts from a large-screen TV under which four men sprawl on the carpet. They're held spellbound by a video of *Fatal Attraction*.

"Mike's on a pink cloud," says Darrell. "That's what AA calls it. You feel so good when you first get clean and sober that you start rejoicing. But watch out for pink clouds," he continues, "because when you're flying that high and you're so self-assured, the slightest setback knocks you on your ass. And addicts take shortcuts to feel good again. What's the best shortcut? Getting high! When Mike falls from his pink cloud and starts dealing with his issues he's going to want something stronger than flying off a banister to make him feel better. And the staff knows that. They've all been there."

Darrell leans toward me and cups a hand near his mouth, as if whispering a secret. "I mean, look what was just in my mind."

I turn toward him, puzzled.

"Sitting here all cozy, watching videos," he explains, "I had this sudden thought. It would be *so nice* to have a warm little setup with me, some crack in my pipe, and just float away. I mean, I can *feel* it!"

Darrell signals for us to move to the couch at the far corner of the room, away from any chance of being overheard by the others, even with the video blasting.

"Just this morning," he continues, "I was on my way to my new job in that chic chic cafe. I had money in my pocket and I had this impulsive thought of calling in sick to work. So my boss would think I was at home, and Acceptance Place would think I was at work. Then I could go have a couple of drinks."

"What'd you do?"

"I just kept on walking," Darrell replies, "and kept on fantasizing. Then I got to work, and I went in."

"How often do cravings like that come up?"

"Oh, not often." Darrell laughs. "Once a day, once an hour, once a minute. Right now. And I promise you, Mike's got those same cravings. He's just hiding them in his pink cloud. So Walden may seem paranoid in how they're treating him, but it's just past Christmas, heading for New Year's. Who do you think is winning, the drug cravings or the programs? Next time you're at Walden, look at the blackboard by the door and count up the names of the splitees posted there. Walden's doing everything they can to keep from writing 'Michael P' on that board with the rest of those who've headed for the streets."

"Doesn't Acceptance have a similar list?" I ask. "Aren't you afraid you'll be on it?"

"Of course," says Darrell. "They're falling like flies here, too. Everybody's on edge from the holidays; the place is jammed with junkies fighting off drug cravings. But me? I'm not going to be stupid and leave a warm bed and a place to live through the holidays. Why would I do that?"

The intangible intensity of drug cravings, their power and ability to grab addicts by the scruff of their necks and toss them from the best of programs, shapes the dilemma of drug rehab. Walden is filled with men and women who've suffered egregiously from their drug use and, almost without exception, come to rehab with a feverish yearning to stay off drugs. Each is surrounded by 120 fellow residents-in-recovery, encouraging their progress toward sobriety. And each is guided by a staff of ex-addicts who are experienced and knowledgeable role models, mentors who *have* made it.

Yet some 80 percent of the addicts who enter Therapeutic Communities for their first visit don't stay the year to graduation; most are gone within thirty days. On the blackboard in Walden's front hall between the entrance foyer and The Boulevard is the week's tally. Splitees: 11.

As I walk The Boulevard at Walden it seems impossible to grasp why such a group of motivated and willing subjects would find it so hard to simply *stick and stay* with the program.

Yet the call of drug cravings often howls louder in many addicts' minds than all the rehab voices in the Walden mansion combined. In a never-ending cycle, Family members split the program, new Little Brothers and Sisters come in and float up on their pink clouds of new-found sobriety, then their own cravings come on strong and they descend to earth and head for the streets. New Little Brothers and Sisters take their places.

Sylvester gathers Mike and the rest of his caseload about him, clipboard in hand.

"I just did the paperwork on Bea and the others in my caseload who've split," he tells them. "So I want you to hear me out. Bea just phoned me and she said, 'Sly, I can't make it out here. I'm wet and cold and there ain't nobody left to take me in. I need to come back to The Family.' "

Sylvester looks down at his clipboard, then at each of his nine remaining clients. "I told Bea the only thing I could," he says. "Go over to our intake office, and get on the waiting list with everybody else."

"Fuuuck," whistles Mike through his teeth.

"You got it." Sylvester nods. "So you think about how wet and stormy it is out there. And then remember that Arthur Hudson split this program and was dead in a chair with a needle in his arm for three days before they found him, his body all stiff! Ain't too long ago he was in this house with you all. So somebody tell me, which of you am I going to fill out one of these splitee forms on next?"

Sylvester waits, as if expecting an answer.

"I've driven rich cars, stayed in penthouses," says the tall, muscular man, leaning back in his cushioned staff chair. "But the end of *my* journey was in the street, living behind a Dumpster. So I been there. I know where it's at. And you all been there, too. But now you're sitting in this mansion, quiet and nice, back from your meal of grits, sausage, pancakes, and eggs, served right up to you. You're safe, got friends and staff who care about you, a view of San Francisco out your window. Man, that is God watching out for you! So who's going to explain to me how some hit of dope got to be so powerful in this world it can take you out, just like that?"

"The first time I did heroin, it was the greatest thing on earth!" says Mike, heading to the kitchen for his daily greasy pot washing. "That first hit, man, it was like some weight lifted off my whole life. It's hard to describe. Doing heroin was like—a euphoria!"

Mike swings the kitchen door open, then turns and laughs. "Hey, what is 'euphoria' anyway? I mean, I hear everybody say it, but I never found out what it means. All I know, man, is it's the best feeling I ever had."

Whatever euphoria may be, humans have made incredible efforts to achieve it and, later, to describe it. Remains of the first humanly cultivated opium poppies (the source of morphine, from which heroin is derived) are found in archaeological diggings from the Neolithic period, some 9,000 years ago. Which means that people were striving to grow opium, and presumably use it, when they'd just barely learned to make tools from stone. And the first true agricultural society, the Sumerians, sowed and harvested fields of opium poppies around 5,500 years ago. In the oldest-known written language, they named them "joy plants."

Later, descriptive language became more refined. Homer, in the *Odyssey*, spoke of a "wondrous substance" possessed by the daughter of Zeus. "Those who drank of the mixture did not shed a tear all day long, even if their mother or father had died, even if a brother or beloved son was killed before their own eyes by the weapons of the enemy." In the modern literary history of opium, in San Francisco, Lenny Bruce described taking it as "like kissing God."

Our species' obsession with the power of opium predates Walden by at least 9,000 years. And opium's modern-day spinoff, heroin, is merely one of a variety of drugs that can bring an addict to Walden.

"The first time I did cocaine," Mike tells me, "was in '81, when I worked as a warehouseman. I became more productive, in work, and in sex. Hell, my whole life became more productive."

If opium is the drug of euphoric relaxation (the Roman god of sleep is depicted as a young boy carrying poppies), cocaine is the drug of euphoric stimulation. And the human-cocaine bond has an ancient history that reads like that of heroin, but from the other side of the world.

Between 3,000 and 5,000 years ago in South America's soaring Andes, natives migrated across arduous altitudes while chewing coca leaves (the source of cocaine). The drug that mixed with their saliva not only energized their lofty expeditions, it suppressed their appetites so that they could trek even farther without eating. Today, their descendants still measure walking distances in units of the *cocada*—the high-altitude range you can hike with the aid of one cheekful of coca leaf.

At lower altitudes and in later times, the stimulant effects of cocaine were lauded by Pope Leo XIII, Sigmund Freud, and the Coca-Cola company, which, until 1903, used cocaine instead of caffeine to stimulate sales and to "restore wasted energy to both Mind and Body." Cocaine also energized pharmaceutical companies, with Parke-Davis offering a cocaine-based elixir that would "make the coward brave, the silent eloquent." (Opium, at the time, was used in Mrs. Winslow's Soothing Syrup as a teething remedy for babies, along with Grove's Baby Bowel formula to calm the infant's other end. And the Bayer Company, which in 1898 was the first to synthesize a drug so remarkable it required a heroic name, Heroin, marketed it as being "highly effective against coughs," which, among other things, it was.)

"Every human culture in every age of history has used one or more psychoactive substances," write Dr. Andrew Weil and Winifred Rosen in their book, *From Chocolate to Morphine*. The one exception that Weil and Rosen could find were the Alaskan Inuits. Leafy plants rich in mind-altering chemicals, it seems, never grew naturally on frozen tundra, nor was it hot enough for alcohol to ferment. So the Inuits remained clean and sober. But as soon as modern transportation and marketing brought distilled beverages to their doorsteps, the Inuits joined the rest of our intoxicated world.

Considering findings from the archaeology of ancient civilizations and the pharmacology of modern times, the human quest for euphoria seems universal. "The desire to alter consciousness periodically," writes Dr. Weil, in his book *The Natural Mind,* "is an innate, normal drive analogous to hunger or the sex drive."

But if Stone Age opium gatherers or coca-chewing Andean natives had become as blissfully high and intensely hooked as Mike and his Walden rehab cohorts, civilization would never have progressed to the point of building cities like San Francisco. Somehow, in the more than 9,000 years of humans chewing and imbibing intoxicants, the drug problem remained mostly at bay for the first 8,800 or so. There was no need for a Walden House in the Andean peaks to help early coca-leaf chewers get off drugs and back to their migrations. And Stone Age recovery programs would have searched high and low to find opium addicts in need of rehabilitation so they could develop tools and agriculture.

The reason is simple: dosage.

In the high Andes, a peasant bearing a full load of wood on his back might trek all day chewing up some two ounces of coca leaves. During that twenty-four hours, his brain would be hit by less than a half-gram of cocaine—the amount Mike often snorted in one single, rapidly inhaled, purified and concentrated dose.

Chew as he might, for as long as he could, the Andean trekker did not get high on cocaine, nor addicted to it. A. L. Spedding, an anthropologist who has studied Bolivian coca leaf chewers, says the effect of cocaine at Andean dosages is like that of a strong cup of coffee. Mike compares San Francisco's street cocaine to coffee as well. "It's like a quadruple double espresso," he says, "mainlined into your arm."

"I consider it most significant," writes Dr. Weil about the Andean coca chewers, "that these Indians use drugs in natural forms. . . . By contrast, most of the drugs in use in our society . . . are highly refined, often synthetic chemicals."

Scientists first extracted pure chemical cocaine from coca leaves in the late 1800s. A soaringly popular tonic and beverage industry soon followed, with Coca-Cola leading the way. When disastrous addictions developed, the government banned such use of the drug, but the cat was out of the bag. Ever more pure and potent forms of cocaine, from powder to crack, have hit our streets every day since.

Although opium addiction has been with us since the Middle Ages, until recently only the very affluent could afford the drug. "The peasantry," writes Martin Booth in his book

Opium, A History, "were kept blissfully ignorant of opium's enslavement by way of their poverty." Today, Mike is rarely more than a few blocks from a ten-dollar bag of opium refined to heroin, and a high so intense it makes the effect of opium in prior centuries seem like the rush from a chocolate bar.

The hypodermic syringe was invented in 1853, soon after morphine was chemically purified from the opium plant. Both discoveries came just in time for the American Civil War, at which time injecting morphine to get a rapid and intense effect led to so much addiction that doctors named it "Soldiers' Disease." Today, when Mike buys his ten-dollar bag of morphine-derived heroin, he can cough up another dollar for a plastic syringe and needle.

Our brains contain a highly evolved network of neurological wires that connect to a nerve complex aptly called by scientists "the pleasure center." That cerebral focal point of euphoria is stimulated by sex, a good meal, a delightful thought, a view of the most wondrous mountains or of your first-born child. But nothing hits and stimulates our brains' pleasure centers with a more rapid and intense rush of sheer, inexplicable euphoria than a concentrated dose of heroin or cocaine.

Over tens of thousands of generations, in response to a universal craving for euphoria and relief from anguish, human beings have been bound in a biological relationship to plants containing low concentrations of intoxicating chemicals. But now, modern chemical wizardry offers Mike and the entire Walden Family the ability to achieve a historically inconceivable high from those very same intoxicating plant chemicals, concentrated a thousandfold, shot straight to their brains.

Yet we don't all need to be locked up in Walden as New Year's approaches. No one knows precisely what draws a person to heroin or cocaine in the first place (nor to damaging excesses of food, sex, or the viewing of wondrous mountains). Neither is it known why some who try drugs become addicted, and others don't. But once the addiction takes hold, for whatever reason, an addict hears only one internal message about dope: *get more.* It is that perpetual, unyielding drive to *get more* that eventually destroys their lives—and drives some of them, in sheer terror, to Walden. And that same drive to *get more* compels many of those addicts in rehab to head for the streets again, where, for ten dollars, they can attain history's greatest euphoria. Or they can stay at Walden, for the clean and sober dance.

On the morning of January 1, Walden's drug rehab Family sweeps up the detritus of the prior night's in-house festivities. The names of those found missing, the newest splitees, are scrawled in chalk on the blackboard at the entrance to The Boulevard.

Mike is up early this New Year's Day, washing floors with the cleanup team.

Darrell heads out the door of Acceptance Place, to grab a bus downtown for a long day's work serving up pastries, lattes, and espressos in the cafe on the first floor of San Francisco's luxurious Nordstrom building. It's the biggest shopping day of the year, and the entire city is indulging.

In a concrete cave just above Highway 280, Darlene sleeps off a night of drinking, wild dancing, stealing purses, and shooting speed.

After the city bulldozed her house on October 17, Darlene vanished into the insanity of the streets, El Niño, methamphetamine, and her own internal noises.

But on the night before Christmas, my phone rang and I heard a familiar voice.

"Hiiii, Merry Christmas and all that. I've missed you," said a surprisingly cheerful Darlene, without introduction. "You've been driving me nuts—you, and Kathy, and Tom, your voices all keep shouting, 'Call me, call me, call me!' "

"I'm glad you listened," I said. "I've been worried about you."

"I'm hanging in there," replied Darlene. "William's out of jail, and we're keeping dry. We found a new mansion to live in. It's really pretty, like living in a garden. Please, please, come visit me?"

"I've tried to find you, been asking all around."

"Really?" It was her little girl's voice.

Darlene explained how to find her new house, at the top of an overgrown, steep incline of a hill that buttresses the eight lanes of Highway 280 as it courses along San Francisco's eastern shore.

"You climb the fence at 18th Street where that walkway goes over the freeway," she explained. "Then find the path through the plants and step *over* not under the safety wire by the road, so you don't slide down. Go way uphill to these caves in the concrete wall over the freeway. That's my new mansion! We call 'em the Opera Boxes 'cause you can watch the cars from there but they can't see you too good. But be careful when you come," added Darlene. "There's a long drop, and a whole bunch of traffic."

I stayed silent for a moment, trying to visualize my next adventure with Darlene, precariously perched by her mansion on a cliff above rush hour.

"Oh, one more thing," she said, just before hanging up. "You guys from Target Cities are like stuck in my brain, and William's going nuts about it. And he's got this temper problem? Love you. Bye."

I check in with Kathy at the Target Cities' offices before heading out to find the Opera Boxes. Darlene had phoned her, too, but Kathy'd had only a moment to talk with her between clients.

"I don't think there's much more I can offer Darlene," the federally funded drug intake counselor tells me. "I mean, she disappears for months, then suddenly calls. I know the city bulldozed her house, but what can I do with that? I'm her placement counselor, so I can try to get her into drug programs. But I can't be her secretary, appointment manager, and housing agent—although Lord knows she needs all three to ever make it into a program."

I tell Kathy I'll be heading out to find Darlene.

"Wait a minute," she says thoughtfully, never giving up. "Because she was once hospitalized on the psychiatric ward, Darlene's been clustered. That means she has a case manager in the mental health system. It's required. So instead of dicking around with these little drug groups we've tried to send her to, she should get over to her case manager at mental health. Hell, if the drug groups couldn't deal with her, well, cross 'em out! Tell Darlene to go to the people who've got the funds and power to really make some changes—mental health. It's a long shot, but if Darlene asks specifically for her case manager we might luck out and get her in the system. She does have options, they're just not here with me. I do drug programs. Her case manager can deal with housing, counseling, medications, all of it."

I ask Kathy who her mental health case manager is. Darlene has never mentioned she has one.

"She probably doesn't know," replies Kathy. "Case managers carry some two hundred clients, and almost never actually *meet* them. But if Darlene asks for and gets to see her case manager, and then gets back to me, I can ask the case manager to move things along for us. Tell Darlene to go over to Westside Mental Health, where she got her pills for Genesis that last time. Then I'll see what I can do."

I head out to start my search for the Opera Boxes, but Kathy calls out as I reach the door of her dark, tiny office. "When you see Darlene," she says softly, "give her a big hug for me."

It's not difficult to find the right section along the high barbed-wire fence at the highway overpass. A hinged gate leads to a steep dirt incline that climbs up alongside the freeway, clearly marked with a red-lettered highway department sign: DANGER! DO NOT ENTER. A coil of barbed wire atop the fence highlights the warning, and a bulky padlock on the gate enforces it. By the time I'm over to the other side there's a large tear in the seat of my jeans from the barbed wire.

The path climbs steeply uphill through thick underbrush, with a cable strung ineffectually about two feet off the ground in hopes of preventing a trespasser from sliding down the hill. The ground vibrates from speeding trucks and cars as I climb up some thirty feet toward a ten-foot-high concrete retaining wall built to keep rockslides off the highway.

Spaced regularly in the concrete barrier are dome-topped cavelike indentations, each about five feet deep. In the fourth cave sits a shoulder-height igloo-shaped structure made of thick black tar paper pasted together at odd angles. Looking up from the freeway through the dense foliage on the hill, it's invisible.

Suddenly Bruce is barking and a tiny slot flips open on a wall of the tar-paper igloo. Two unfamiliar steel-gray eyes peer from the dark inside, then disappear.

"Give us a minute," Darlene calls out.

Moments later, a panel on the tent pushes out and a man with a long blond ponytail appears, one hand pulling at a scraggly beard that extends from chin to his chest, the other grabbing to pull up the zipper of his pants.

"I guess you're William," I say, extending my hand. "Welcome home."

He looks down, scuffing at the dirt and overgrown foliage with his large, steel-tipped boots.

"You better be able to prove you're a reporter," says William with the rapid-fire speech and darting eyes of a meth user. "You've been hanging around Darlene," he adds, "and I say you're a cop."

William squats to look at the photo-ID tag hanging from my camera bag, marked, "San Francisco Police Department: Press Pass." He lifts it up. On the back is a scrawled signature. Typed under it, "Chief of Police."

Then he laughs, and reaches his hand out to shake mine, his head bobbing like a pigeon's. "No undercover would be stupid enough to carry that ID around," he says. "Not in sight, anyways."

He turns to the tent, not releasing my hand.

"He's legit," announces William. "You can come out."

"No hard feelings," he says, still squeezing my hand, unyielding. "I'm suspicious of guys being around my girlfriend while I was in jail. Get my message?"

Darlene seems in a trance, moving slowly through the flap of the tent, wearing large-framed sunglasses in spite of the dim fog and the beginning of yet another of this winter's interminable rains. She stands facing the tent, not even glancing our way. Her lips move in a bare murmur of incomprehensible words.

William spots a leak in the tar paper on top of the igloo and jumps to it like a valiant Boy Scout in the woods, pulling wire and rope together, twisting them about with his pocket knife, all the while chattering amiably about his recent time in jail. Within minutes, he has energetically reconstructed the roof, watertight.

Darlene remains stock-still, staring blankly ahead, mumbling. In William's presence, it's as if she's vanished.

Then, as quickly as he had appeared, William grabs a bicycle leaning on a nearby tree and takes off down the path toward the fence. Darlene watches his retreating form and calls out, "Love you, William," but the constant roar of the freeway drowns her voice. He pulls open the padlock, swings the gate forward, and disappears.

I move closer to hear what Darlene is saying over the howl of cars and trucks below. Finally, I make it out, the same question, over and over: "Did I do something wrong?"

For the first time since I arrived she looks straight at me, repeating the question, tears rolling out from under her sunglasses. I reach up and gently lift them from her face, staring at her bruised, black-and-blue eyes.

"I have these spells," says Darlene, taking the sunglasses and sliding them back on, covering the bruises. She's standing in the drizzling rain, trembling in the cold, her voice hoarse from crying.

"See, I fall on the floor and have like these seizures and hit myself with my hands, get all banged up," she says. "Can we go get pancakes?"

"Not if you're coming back here so William can hit you again," I say.

"That's none of your business!" shouts Darlene. "I'm having these seizures, just like before my last nervous breakdown when I got took to the hospital. And that freaks William out because I hurt myself."

"Next time he might do worse than punch you."

"See! William was right! He told me that as soon as you saw my face you'd accuse him of doing it. But that's not it. Something evil takes over my spirit and makes *me* do it."

"Can we go someplace where it's dry?" I ask.

"Pancakes," asserts Darlene, heading down the path toward the fence above the freeway. "Is God a vengeful God?" she asks. "Even with someone who's not evil?"

"You mean," I decode, " 'Can Darlene get hurt even if she didn't do anything wrong?' "

"But I didn't *do* anything wrong."

She swings the gate open and holds it for me to pass through, giggling at the long rip in the seat of my jeans.

"I didn't know you guys had cut the lock," I explain.

"You know what?" she laughs. "You'd die if you had to live out here like we do! Wouldn't survive a day. So stop worrying so much about me, or William. We can take care of our own asses. You take care of yours."

At the Grand Restaurant, Darlene barely touches her pancakes, fries, or double cheeseburger.

"We can take what's left back to William," she says, and then her tears well up, and she pulls a paper napkin from the dispenser on the table to hide her face.

"I waited six months for my snuggums to come back from jail." The words break through her sobs. "I gave him perfect vision, and now he won't even walk down memory lane with me. I have my evil self and my regular self, but they're all one now. So there's no *me* no more."

I move my right hand to my ear and tap my fingers together.

"Your realm?" I ask.

"William's been gone for such a long time, and now he's back," says Darlene, trying to return to a realm we both understand. "I could be what he wants me to be," she says, "but I don't *know* what he wants me to be! And that's so sad it tears me apart. All we do is shoot meth and more meth, and we never even talk to each other no more. And all my noises are back. I can't keep *my* life together and *his* life together and the whole *world* together with all this noise shouting at me."

The smaller Chinese waitress sees that Darlene has stopped eating. She pauses silently by her chair, puts her hand warmly on Darlene's shoulder, then leaves a Styrofoam container on the table.

"Can you take me to that mental clinic, where Kathy wants me to go?" asks Darlene, stuffing food for William into the container. "I want some of those pills that quiet my head noises."

At the Westside Mental Health Clinic, a low, squat building with brightly painted murals adorning its stucco walls, the uniformed guard in the front hallway recognizes Darlene immediately and, with a warm smile, greets her by name.

"Your hair's gorgeous!" exclaims Darlene as the guard laughs and shakes her head to free up exquisite, waist-long cornrows, then hands Darlene a clipboard so she can sign up for a drop-in visit.

" 'Course my hair's beautiful," says the woman. "It's grown a foot since you been here last! You ought to be visiting us more often, Darlene! What you need today?"

"More pills."

"I'll set you up with the counselors," says the guard. She leaves her desk to unlock the door to the clinic waiting room. Taking Darlene's hand gently in hers, chatting warmly, the guard escorts her in.

For an institution responsible for the long-term care of multitudes of San Francisco's mentally ill, the staff of the Westside Mental Health Clinic has somehow created an atmosphere that feels more like your friendly neighborhood bank than a government psychiatric clinic.

A large, counter-style reception desk overlooks a waiting room filled with well-padded blue vinyl chairs. The room is immaculately clean, its linoleum floor freshly polished. Framed, brightly colored posters adorn the walls alongside bulletin boards filled with flyers and referral information for HIV care, battered women's shelters, clinics for sexually transmitted diseases, child care services, and more.

The staff, men and women dressed mostly in respectful business suits, moves up and down a long fluorescent-lit hallway. Closing doors quietly behind them, they stroll in and out of patient consultation rooms and flow, one at a time and in groups, through a large wooden door labeled "17" by the reception desk just off the entrance to the long hallway.

So much heavy staff traffic moves continuously in and out of door 17 it seems there must be an entire skyscraper of an office building behind it, a mysteriously concealed "Central Control Agency, Mental Health." Beyond that door, I guess from what Kathy told me, are the mental health clients' case managers.

Darlene takes a seat across from a pencil-thin man wearing a dirt-stained jogging suit, staring fixedly at a point on the wall just below a TV set tuned to a news channel. He's holding a soda cup from McDonald's, sucking the straw and making slurping noises, although the cup has long ago been sucked dry of all liquid.

"This is the clinic the hospital sent me to after my running-naked breakdown," Darlene tells me.

"*Common* breakdown," observes the man across from her, moving his stare from the wall to gaze briefly at Darlene. "I confess. I identify," he says, then returns to his staring.

"The hospital sent me here so's I'd keep taking that Haldol stuff," Darlene continues. "But the next time, when Target Cities and Genesis sent me back here, I got those Zyprexa pills that I took bunches at a time and they quieted my head. Those are what I want now."

Darlene watches the suited-up counselors disappearing through and reappearing from door 17. "I bet they got a file like a phone book on me in there," she says. "I been here so much even that guard knows my case."

"And your case manager?" I ask. "Behind that door, too?"

"Who's that?" asks Darlene. "Never heard of no case manager."

Door 17 opens yet again and a young, redheaded woman heads for the counter, checks the list, and calls Darlene's name.

"That's me!" she jumps up.

"Ever been here before?" asks the woman.

"Hundreds of times," Darlene says, laughing.

"Wait a minute, then," says the woman, still not identifying herself, and vanishes again through door 17.

Case management is designed "to create a 'no wrong door' approach to services," writes Dr. Nelba Chavez, administrator of the federal Substance Abuse and Mental Health Services Administration. Wherever in the system clients with serious mental illnesses show up, at whatever door, they're assigned an individual case manager to guide them along. For mental health patients, already befuddled by their own internal voices and dialogues, case managers have been declared essential as advocates and guides to services deemed crucial to their clients' survival.

The U.S. Department of Health further defines the goal of case management for mental health patients: "Case managers see to it that clients do not get 'lost in the system.' "

The very concept of case management—having a single advocate whose sole function is to supervise and steer a mentally ill person through the myriad and diverse pathways of a complex mental health establishment—might well have been designed with Darlene in mind.

"Without case management," says the Substance Abuse and Mental Health Services Administration, "many severely ill patients would decompensate, need to be hospitalized, or become homeless." Of course, by the time Darlene is sent by Kathy in search of her mental health case manager, she has already decompensated, been hospitalized, and has long been homeless. But it's never too late to start.

Case managers, according to the journal *Hospital and Community Psychiatry*, "link patients with direct services, monitor patients' progress through a variety of milieus, educate patients about psychiatric and substance abuse disorders, reiterate treatment recommendations, and coordinate treatment planning across programs."

And when a case manager, in the true role of patient advocate, shuttles an at times bewildered mentally ill patient through a maze of individual bureaucracies that deal with medical care, psychiatric care, pharmacies, food stamps, housing aid, vocational training, and even transportation to appointments, it's not merely a helpful practice. It's the law. The federal Public Health Service Act *requires* that any mental health agency that receives federal funds provide case management services to patients with mental illnesses.

But the same does not hold true for substance abuse patients. "A comparable [case management] requirement," states the Substance Abuse and Mental Health Services Administration, "is not built into the Federal mandate for alcohol and other drug abuse treatment services," since those agencies "usually do not have enough social service staff to handle the case management functions." This is why Darlene finds herself again referred by Kathy, a federal substance abuse counselor, back to mental health services, where Kathy knows Darlene must have a case manager.

"I don't believe in bouncing clients like Ping-Pong balls between substance abuse and mental health," Kathy tells me. "But mental health *has* to provide her with case management. And substance abuse services—which means me—is just not set up for that. Sure the politics frustrates me. So I keep my focus on the client, not the politics. A mental health case manager can get Darlene on the right medications, help her with food, transportation, disability income. I can't get near those services! But if her case manager works with all that, maybe Darlene will start showing up here again and I can finally help her with a drug program."

Kathy shrugs. "Darlene needs more than me as some friend she can drop in on and talk to. She needs care, real care! God, I have to do *something* for her. And if that means bouncing her back to mental health, let's go for it!"

Darlene stares at door 17 at Westside Mental Health, wondering where the young redheaded woman has disappeared to, who she is, and when she might return.

"All I need is some of those pills," she tells me, "then I can get out of this place." Her eyes roll sarcastically toward door 17. "It's getting spooky seeing all those people disappear like that."

I tell Darlene that Kathy thinks this time she might get more help than just a bottle of pills to quiet her voices. If she asks to see her case manager, there is a whole range of programs and services that might open up—from food stamps to disability checks to medications, health care, housing referrals, even dry blankets to help her through the rains of El Niño.

"Pills is what they give me," Darlene replies simply.

Then she giggles, and her fantasy begins.

"If I do have one of them case-manager-whatever persons," she laughs, "know what she's got back there for me?" Darlene's eyes twinkle, staring at door 17. "She's got me a brand-new Cannondale bicycle! My dream mother of an airplane! And the reason it's taking so long to see me is 'cause that case manager lady's getting me some Shimano gearshifts for the hills!"

Darlene stands at her seat, her wrist arcing through a twisting motion at a make-believe gear lever. I fear she's about to shoot across the waiting room on her imaginary bicycle. But she sits down, quiet again.

"Or maybe just a new teddy bear for me to cuddle at night?" she says softly. "Can my case manager get me that? William doesn't cuddle with me no more."

A man of about fifty shuffles up to the reception counter, sliding his feet along the floor instead of lifting them as he walks, his head tilted down as he says in slow, deliberate words, "Need Dr. Roberts." He turns back to the waiting room to find a seat and nearly stumbles as his pants, too round about the waist and too long at his ankles, trap his legs.

"That's so sad," says Darlene, watching him. "See, that's not from doing dope, that's being sick. It makes me want to cry."

Twenty minutes later, door 17 swings open and the young woman with red hair stands over Darlene, looking through a thick yellow file folder.

"Darlene James," she says, still not identifying herself. "What can we do for you today?"

"Noise pills," replies Darlene. "See my noises come from doing speed, but they're here even without speed now. And that's the truth! And if I could get rid of my need to tell the truth I could probably make the noises go away myself. But I always tell the truth, because that's just who I am. So do I have to keep waiting anymore?"

The young woman searches through Darlene's chart. "I see you've been to Target Cities—methamphetamine, right?"

She flips to the front-page summary sheet.

"Kathy Meyers at Target Cities," says the young woman. "Let me check." And she heads back through door 17.

Darlene is all smiles. "Yeah!" she cheers. "Kathy must have called, to get my case manager to see me!"

Stretching her arms straight out in front of her, Darlene pretends to rev up the gears on her new bike again.

"Do you know who the redheaded woman is?" she asks.

I shake my head. No.

"The Emerald City gatekeeper!" Darlene cries out. "If she lets you in, you get to see the Wizard!"

She revs the gears again.

"Past that door," Darlene whispers gleefully to me, watching to be sure she's not letting the others in the room in on her secret, "is the long, green land filled with Munchkins and flowers and—"

She puts on the tiniest little girl's voice, "Please, please, I have to see the Wizard! He's the *only* one who can help me!"

She's up, laughing now, pretending to dance with Toto and the Scarecrow, heading to the reception desk and beginning to sing out, "But I *have* to see the Wizard! See, Kathy says I've got this case manager—"

Door 17 swings open and a bespectacled woman of about fifty with salt-and-pepper hair, bearing a warm smile, accompanies the young redheaded woman to Darlene's side. Darlene stops her dance, tilts her head sideways and stares, wide-eyed, expectant.

"I'm the therapist who supervises the interns," says the woman. She points to her younger colleague. "And this is my intern you've been talking to."

The therapist, who is not Darlene's case manager, points down the long fluorescent hallway. "Let's see if I can help you out," she says. "There's a room down here."

"Not through there?" asks Darlene, pointing to door 17, eyes glowing.

The woman laughs. "No, not in there," she says. "There's an interview room right down this hall."

Darlene offers a literal curtsy and, winking at me, nearly skips down the hallway to an empty square cubicle of a room in which sit three straight-backed plastic chairs, and nothing else.

The three women disappear inside.

I'm staring at the TV news with the man still making slurping noises from the empty McDonald's cup when the waiting room seems to explode.

"Goddamn, Lonny, will you tell them?" Darlene cries out, a foot from my head.

I look up and see the therapist and the younger woman scurrying up behind her.

"Tell them what?" I ask.

"There seems to be some confusion," says the supervising therapist, leafing through Darlene's chart as if in explanation. "When Darlene was here last, she was sent by Target Cities. We started her on medications and Target Cities was supposed to be placing her in a drug program. But there's no record that she's ever been to the drug program, or even back to Target Cities."

"It's Target Cities what just sent me here to you!" screams Darlene.

"Exactly," says the therapist, her voice calm. "See, you do understand. You're supposed to be getting your services there, at Target Cities. We don't know what plan they have for you, and we don't want to interfere without checking with them first."

"Then fucking call Kathy!" growls Darlene.

"Thank you, Darlene," says the therapist. "That's just what we need to do. Excuse us for a moment." They turn and disappear through door 17.

"I did like I promised," Darlene turns to me. "I asked to see my case manager but they just kept asking me the same questions over and over, like, 'Have you ever been in jail?' and 'What drugs do I do?' and 'Where do I live?' And I kept answering until finally it was too much and I told her I've answered every one of them questions every damn time I've been here and they should just read my fucking chart! So they look at my chart and it says I'm supposed to be at Genesis. So I told them I ain't at Genesis because they bulldozed my house and—"

Darlene stops suddenly and throws herself into the blue vinyl waiting-room chair closest to door 17, tears rolling slowly down her face from under the sunglasses she hasn't removed the entire time she's been here.

Thirty minutes later, the younger woman pushes through door 17.

"I'm sorry this is so difficult, Darlene," she begins, squatting at her side. "It's just that it's not clear to us who has the right to be treating you. You've been to so many places and programs, and we can't just step in and interfere with what they're already doing, like at Genesis. See, we try to coordinate services here, so you don't get lost."

Darlene, calm now, asks, "Did you talk to Kathy?"

"We did," says the woman. "And she said you're here because you haven't been showing up over there."

Darlene knits her eyebrows in confusion and then, ever so slowly, starts to giggle.

"How can it be," she says to the woman, her words breaking through the laughter, "that even when you make sense you don't make no sense?"

The young woman smiles, rising from her squat next to Darlene.

"Well, I think we've got it straightened out now," she says, reaching out to shake Darlene's hand. "Can you come back and see us in a week or two? We need permission from the other programs to treat you."

Darlene shrinks back in her seat.

"Permission?" she says softly, puzzling through the word. "Like, you mean from whichever part of the government owns me?"

"Well, it's really not like that. We're just trying to get your care organized properly."

"Well, that's OK," says Darlene, putting on her best Valley Girl–imitation accent. "Please give me a call when you find out who my owner is. Or maybe, don't call me, I'll call you."

The woman holds out her hand to Darlene. "We'll see you again, then?"

"But of course," says Darlene politely, and she watches the young woman head back through door 17. Then she walks toward the exit from the Westside Mental Health Center.

"See you later, Darlene," calls out the guard with the long, graceful cornrows. "Now don't be so scarce before your next visit, OK?"

We reach the street outside the clinic, and Darlene squints into the fog and drizzle as if trying to orient herself.

"I wish that guard lady with the beautiful hair had been the Emerald City gatekeeper instead of that redheaded lady," she announces. " 'Cause I bet that cornrow lady could have got me in to see the Wizard."

"Case manager, Darlene," I correct. "Not the Wizard."

Darlene skips down the street to the car. "Take me back to the Opera Boxes," she says. "It's going to pour rain any minute, and I got to get home to William."

The drizzle is increasing, and ominous, billowing storm clouds are blowing in from the Pacific.

"See"—Darlene laughs out—"at the end of the long, green land filled with Munchkins and flowers is a great big old sky of smoke and clouds. And there's this voice, like that therapist lady's? But that voice is all you hear and you never get to see no government Wizard because there ain't no Wizard—just some face up in the clouds that don't do nothing."

Had one person at the Westside Mental Health Center—preferably her mysteriously absent case manager—said to Darlene, "You're here with us, welcome, wait, how can we help you?"—might that have gained the trust that would have encouraged her to come back? The answer is unknown, since Darlene never returned.

The two therapists, who are not case managers, were right in calling Target Cities to coordinate Darlene's care with Substance Abuse Services. But there is no reason not to have attempted to engage Darlene that day. Had they offered her anything more than "Can you come back and see us in a week or two?" it might have signaled to Darlene that, should she return, she would get more than yet another runaround. Or, had they actually introduced Darlene to her case manager, Darlene might have been helped to find dry blankets, offered aid with transportation to return again, set up with food stamps or other services, received assistance in negotiating the system so she could receive those "noise pills" she had come for in the first place. As it happened, though, Darlene left with nothing—not even a reason to think of coming back.

The absence of any case management for Darlene is indicative of the seeming lack of *any management* that could impose order on the myriad substance abuse programs and services that have proliferated since the mantra of rehab took hold across the country.

"I've had hundreds of clients as lost to services as Darlene is," Kathy told me. "And not just those who were hallucinating!"

"One problem with the rehab industry," says Darrell, still tucked away at Acceptance Place, "is they get so focused on the drugs that they forget about the rest of the stuff. Like, don't drink and you'll be OK. Don't shoot up and you'll be OK. But we've been shooting dope or drinking because we're not OK! We need help with a lot more than getting off drugs!"

Each organization that treats addicts grapples every day with the therapeutic reality that drug rehab involves much more than rehabilitation from drugs. In 1998, the Substance Abuse and Mental Health Services Agency became so attuned to the need for case management for *all* addicts in treatment—not just those with mental illnesses—that they published a treatise of "best practice guidelines" entitled "Comprehensive Case Management for Substance Abuse Treatment."

"Many in publicly funded treatment programs," states the federal agency, "do not have a high school diploma. Some are homeless, and those who have been incarcerated may face significant barriers in accessing safe and affordable housing. Many substance abuse clients have alienated their families and friends or have peer affiliations only with other substance abusers. Women in treatment have often been victims of domestic violence, including sexual abuse; some women in treatment may be living with an abuser."

"Case management is needed," concluded the agency that oversees substance abuse care, "because, in most jurisdictions, services are fragmented and inadequate to meet the needs of the substance-abusing population. . . . The strongest rationale for case management may be that it consolidates to a single point responsibility for clients who receive services from multiple agencies."

Yet among the forty individually run rehab agencies in San Francisco, a city where addicts have access to 135 different drug programs of all shapes and sizes, there is no effective case management to guide those clients through the rehab maze.

In fact, Target Cities, the central intake unit referring clients out to the various city programs, pursued no follow-up to ascertain what had happened to Darrell or Mike while they were in those programs, or after they left. The staff had no idea if its rehab referrals for the two had led to success or disaster, or whether those clients were in need of additional aid. Only because Darlene had stopped by Westside Mental Health did the city have any knowledge that she was still alive.

No case manager or organization ever said to Darrell, Darlene, or Mike, simply, "If you need help with other services, or if you run into troubles with drugs again, we are still here for you. We're the ones you call."

Clients being treated for substance abuse "need to re-create their lives," notes Dr. Camille Barry, acting director of the Center for Substance Abuse Treatment. "They need to find new housing, jobs—some means of productively using the hours that were spent seeking and using drugs. Thus, education and job skills, housing assistance and other aid are essential if the patient is to break old ties and start a life free of drugs."

A case manager is an escort to those essential services required to sustain sobriety—the most effective insurance that government treatment dollars will actually lead addicts toward better lives.

The 1999 annual report by the White House Office of National Drug Control Policy, headed by General McCaffrey, is elegantly bound in a glossy red, white, and blue cover bearing the seal of the President of the United States. Presented formally to Congress as a yearly evaluation of the efficacy of our National Drug Control Strategy, the 219-page document does mention the term *case management*—once, in a footnoted reference.

In August of 1998 the four-star general who formulates our national drug policy traveled to the Mexican border to see how our efforts at drug interdiction were faring. "You've got eight hundred people working at these border crossings," the general announced in dismay. "And nobody's in charge!"

Standing at the border in San Antonio, General McCaffrey summed up the need for military case management at the international crossing. "Nothing in life works without coordination," he declared, complaining of "lack of central coordination" in our efforts to block drugs at the border. Then he immediately produced a plan, the Border Coordination Initiative, to implement "coherent, coordinated efforts" to link together some fifty state and federal drug-interdiction agencies.

One can only wonder what McCaffrey might have demanded had he ever visited San Francisco's Westside Mental Health Center with Darlene, and stared in awe at door number 17.

9: RELAPSE PREVENTION

At the stroke of midnight in Kings Hall on New Year's Eve, Walden's Recovery Rap band breaks into the world's most appalling version of "Auld Lang Syne." But it is drowned out by a riotous New Year's cheer that bursts forth from The Family. Mike turns from his dance partner and is swept into one embrace after the next as Brothers and Sisters howlingly congratulate one another and prance in celebration across the mansion's polished floor to bring in the New Year.

"Next year's the best year!" shouts Gloria as she embraces Mike, twirls him about, then spins off to her next hug.

"We're still here! We made it!" His roomie Michael Wallace throws his arms around Mike who, barely recovered from Gloria's twirl, nearly falls over.

At the instant that Wallace releases him, Mike is clasped again.

"Today is . . ." shouts Jonathan, hugging Mike. The pair, laughing, join in on a jubilant two-part harmony, ". . . the first day of the rest of your life!"

By the tenth embrace, Mike seems a bit stunned. By the fifteenth or so, he's sobbing. He walks slowly across Kings Hall toward a chair in the corner far from the joyous crowd, swiping at his eyes with the sleeve of his shirt.

"I'm thinking about my daughters," he says softly when he sits down. "I wish they could know, man, that their daddy's starting this new life. Nineteen ninety-seven is gone. I mean, it's still there, I got to deal with what I did. But now I'm moving forward, too, and when all these Brothers and Sisters started hugging me like that . . ."

His voice cracks and he wipes at his eyes again. "I realized right there," he says, "that I can do this. It's like the first time that I know—I'm going to make it."

Mike closes his eyes, his head nodding up and down, fist clenched in his lap. "I can do this," he repeats, and starts a slow determined chant, quietly under his breath. "I can do this, for me. I can do this, for my daughters. I can do this, for Connie."

He looks up and glances around Kings Hall, where the crowd has now settled into quiet conversations and soft, emotional embraces.

"Damn, I miss Connie," says Mike of his girlfriend, shaking his head.

Each Family member had been given the chance to invite one significant outsider to Walden's clean and sober New Year's dance. On December 26, however, the day to apply at the office for permission to bring a guest in, Mike had been confined to the bench in penalty for his celebratory but illegal slide down the mansion's long wooden banister. Restricted to the bench, he'd missed his chance to do the paperwork so that Connie could join him on this New Year's Eve.

And because Mike was only six weeks into the program, Sylvester turned down his request to go *out on a clinical* with Connie on another night. Instead, Mike received a pass for dinner and a movie with her. But denial of permission for a clinical meant that sex was prohibited.

Now, an hour into the New Year, Mike watches the couples in Kings Hall cuddling up for a last embrace before all guests have to leave. He is painfully aware of Connie's absence. While The Family provides intense emotional support, romance between Family members is forbidden. If Brothers or Sisters develop even a hint of sexual desire they are to *own it* immediately to a counselor, who then declares that the two involved must *give each other fifty feet* at all times. If one is seen within fifty feet of the other, the next step is to put them on a *ban*—no visual contact, no writing, no communication at all. If they break the ban, they're out of Walden.

The prohibition against sex between Family members ranks at the top of the list of program sins. Walden's *Cardinal Rules* are easily, and repeatedly, recited: "No sex, no violence, no threats of violence, no drug or alcohol use of any kind." Sex with a Family member is seen as incest and anyone caught is immediately *spotted*—removed from the house on the spot.

"We're not saying that sex is a bad thing," explains Sylvester. "It's just that we're living on top of each other here, and if there's sex in this house there's a big potential for a Brother or Sister to be emotionally hurt. That, or jealousy in The Family, can take the whole house down."

Sex outside of The Family is permitted, but not in the mansion and only when the counseling staff has decided that a Family member is stable enough to handle the emotional consequences likely to crop up when that client is allowed out on a clinical. Until that time, celibacy is the rule.

Shortly after 1:00 A.M., all outside guests have gone. Mike and Michael Wallace help sweep up the debris in Kings Hall from the New Year's dance, then head to their dorm. Mike, still moping about Connie's absence, asks Wallace to read Psalm Six from the Bible with him.

"When I was staying at my cousin's house waiting to get into Walden," says Mike, "I got to glancing through the Bible and Psalm Six caught me up. I been using it for strength when I'm down, and I want to share it with one of the Sisters, Lara Webb, in the morning. She's been having a hard time in the house, man, and I think it'll help her out."

"*O Lord do not rebuke me in your anger,*" Mike reads out loud from the Bible he keeps by his bedside. "*Or discipline me in your wrath, Be gracious to me O Lord, for I am languishing . . .*"

The next morning, he recites the entirety of Psalm Six to Lara Webb. Then he turns himself in to staff for having feelings of lust. But not, as the counselors had long suspected, for Lara Webb.

"I came within six-and-a-half inches of breaking the Cardinal Rule about sex," Mike tells Floyd, the counselor for the day.

"OK, you gotta say with who," responds Floyd, waiting to hear Lara Webb's name.

"Samantha Matthews," says Mike.

Floyd looks at him with brow furrowed. "She's a graduate," he says. "She's not even in the house anymore."

"She came back to pick up her stuff," replies Mike. "And she's technically still my Sister 'cause that's how I knew her. She saw me in the basement doing my laundry and she comes up and says, 'Hey, Mike, it's cold down here, I'm going to the boiler room to warm up.' I mean, that was a blatant invitation!"

Floyd nods his head, waiting Mike out.

"We didn't do nothing!" Mike insists, staring at the counselor. "She went into the boiler room and I'm like, OK, I'm getting out of here. So I left right away and talked to my Big Brother, and now I'm telling you. But I have to *own my own,* man. I was in lust with a Sister! It was that close! So I'm supporting myself—I gotta be put on a ban with Samantha."

When Mike had flown down the banister to The Boulevard, all who had witnessed it had *supported* him. By telling the staff that Mike had broken a house rule, they were supporting his sobriety. As Mike describes it: "Out there I called it rat-finking on me. In here, they call it supporting me."

"We are each our Brothers' and Sisters' keeper," says Dolores, the house director. "So there's no such thing as snitching anymore. With everybody looking out for one another, more people are going to make it. At Walden, we support each other."

But those clients who are *running a good program* don't wait to be supported to staff by a Brother or Sister when they break a rule. "It's better to support yourself," says Mike. "You know, confess before they turn you in."

So Mike supports himself to Floyd, and in the process supports Samantha Matthews for coming on to him in the basement. He volunteers to be placed on a ban with Samantha. Then he supports himself to Sylvester, and to his co-counselor, Horace; and then to some half dozen of his Brothers and a number of his Sisters on The Boulevard; and he supports himself again at *check-in* for his caseload meeting. Then Mike asks Maria, a caseload Sister, if she'll call Connie and explain what had happened with Samantha. He doesn't want Connie to be upset when she visits and sees Mike's name alongside Samantha's, prominently displayed on Walden's entryway blackboard under the bold letters, *On a Ban*.

Then Mike supports himself to Samantha, before the ban kicks in, to let her know that he had supported her to staff.

"Man, she got pretty pissed off," he says, "that I told all these people about her. But then she tells me, 'Hey, I respect what you did, Mike. You're here for your program and you stuck with it.' "

Maria calls Mike's girlfriend, Connie, to tell her that the incident with Samantha shouldn't upset her, but instead should allow her to trust Mike all the more because he was honest with The Family about what had happened—or did not happen.

"You can come to me whenever you need to," Maria tells Mike when she hangs up the phone. "Because when you talk out your problems, you take away their power over you."

For Maria, and for the majority of Mike's Brothers and Sisters, and the staff, the Samantha episode reinforces what they already believe: Mike is running the perfect program.

Still, Sylvester is worried. "Ain't no better con artist than a junkie," he says. "I know. I been there."

It's only a small hop from *running a good program* to *working the program*—strategically manipulating the complex Therapeutic Community rules to your advantage. A cynical eye might view Mike's reaction to Samantha's sexual come-on as a strategic response, working the program to his own benefit. By supporting himself and asking for the ban, Mike is prohibited from being near Samantha—not much of a sacrifice since she no longer lives in the house. And in the process of supporting himself repeatedly, he becomes closer to Maria and gains the respect of the staff and Walden's Sisters (and some of the Brothers). And his girlfriend outside Walden receives a good report from inside the program. Also, Mike has distracted the counselors from their worries about him and Lara Webb.

Sylvester pulls me aside. "Your guy is TC smart," he says, using the shorthand for Therapeutic Community. "He knows that if he follows the rules he don't get no heat put on him. But all I'm seeing is that he's not getting into trouble. Nothing really deep there. I'm going to wait him out. Something is up, and Mike ain't talking about it."

By the end of his second month at Walden, Mike has fixed most of the worn-out pipes and faucets in the house, and repaired its ancient heating system. In this coldest of San Francisco winters the antiquated, rusty radiators that now whistle with steam and warm the mansion seem to be singing the praise of this tall, handsome plumber who has so quickly endeared himself to The Family.

Mike is on his way to winning Walden's Stepper of the Month award. Sylvester, though, is watching quietly, waiting him out.

From Walden's four Cardinal Rules, to forty-four pages of written house rules, to five pages containing 117 "unwritten" rules, one might almost mistake Walden for an Emily Post finishing school (Unwritten rule #47: No slouching in your seat during group) rather than an agency focused on keeping hard-core addicts off drugs. Of course, long lists of rules are essential to maintain safety and sanity whenever any 120 people are housed under one roof. But Walden's unwritten rules extend beyond its walls and include directives prohibiting littering, jaywalking, even "No buying merchandise from street vendors who don't have a permit to sell." Among 117 unwritten rules in the rehab program, drugs or alcohol are mentioned only twice: "No associating with people who use drugs or alcohol," and, "No using Dijon mustard, mouthwash, or cough syrup that contains alcohol." The 115 other rules focus on proper behavior, not substance abuse.

"At Walden House," says an introductory manual read by all Family members, "there are many rules designed to help us develop the self-control and discipline necessary to lead a more positive, productive life."

The linkage between such rule-oriented behavior modification therapy and drug rehabilitation is based on the straightforward reasoning that *any* deviation from self-control and discipline places an addict straight on the path back to drugs. An entire new field of drug rehabilitation called "relapse prevention" supports that reasoning.

The main tenet of relapse prevention is that relapse actually occurs well in advance of an addict's return to drugs. "The relapse process," states the Substance Abuse and Mental Health Services Administration, "is marked by predictable and identifiable warning signs that begin long before the return to use or collapse occurs."

In virtually all drug programs today, relapse prevention courses teach specific skills that help clients spot relapse warning signs—red lights flashing before the crash. At Walden, relapse warning signs are tightly intertwined with the extensive house rules.

"This Family is heading for a train wreck!" bellows Sylvester at the morning Kings Hall meeting on February 16. "People have been taking permissions. Starts out with a guy getting staff's OK for a peanut-butter-jelly sandwich. Then he gets to the kitchen and eats two sandwiches, gives himself permission to deviate from the plan. Next thing you know he's got himself some soup, then a whole meal—gone from wanting a sandwich to stealing. And stealing's how he used to get drug money. So you see where he's heading? It sounds picky, but that's how relapse starts, little picky things."

Sylvester is pacing the polished floor at Kings Hall, checking around him to be sure The Family is listening up.

"You're supposed to have no more than fifteen dollars in your pocket at any time," Sylvester continues. "That's in the rules. So here's Sharon, on The Boulevard yesterday, holding twenty dollars. And she tells me it's OK, she's holding ten of hers and ten for somebody else. Well, tomorrow she'll be holding thirty, and she'll think that's OK, too. And when she's up to fifty it'll be burning a hole in her pocket 'cause she knows that's enough for a good run of heroin. Then she's out that door and it's the end of her recovery—and maybe her entire life."

Before a recovering addict does drugs again, says relapse prevention specialist Terence Gorski in his book *Staying Sober,* there are "attitudes and behaviors that lead to active addictive using." Those attitudes and behaviors, *stinking thinking,* are the reason behind Walden's all-consuming rules. In a relapse prevention model an extra peanut butter and jelly sandwich is not an inanimate object, but a vivid reflection of an attitude. So relapse prevention teaches addicts a connect-the-dots reasoning: You broke a rule to get food; you eat compulsively when you're lonely; you've used cocaine in the past to fight off loneliness; that sandwich shows you're at risk of relapse. In an ideal relapse prevention world, a learned and preplanned action would follow: Put the sandwich down and call someone to talk about how lonely you feel.

"Big trouble five miles ahead! Big trouble one mile ahead. Turn back!" says Roland Dumontet, a Walden relapse prevention counselor who tends toward the highway metaphors that run rampant in relapse prevention circles. "You should realize that you're heading down your old road again," says Dumontet, "in time to hit the brakes."

But at times this hypertuned focus on the deeper significance of even the most innocent-appearing behaviors leads to a vigilance that can distract as well as educate.

Alice Malcolm, a recovering alcohol and cocaine addict and a Walden splitee, says she'll never again go back to any Therapeutic Community. "I wound up thinking so much about their rules," she says, "that I didn't have the energy or time to pay attention to my recovery. I can't tell you how distracting that place became! It's hard to believe anybody finds time to work on their own issues while they're trying to deal with hundreds of regulations over every part of your life."

Mike trots down The Boulevard so as not to be late for his morning caseload meeting, and screeches to a halt. On the floor by the bench is a piece of paper.

"See how loose this house is getting!" says Mike. "How many people have walked by and not picked that paper up? There's so many I can't even support them all to staff."

Then Mike shakes his head. "It don't matter," he says. "They'll be doing dope soon anyways, can't even control themselves enough to keep the house clean."

He squats to pick up the paper and throw it in the nearby trash, in sight of the open office door through which the staff observes proceedings on The Boulevard.

That night Walden House empties out as every Brother and Sister who has received his or her *own strength* strides down the street to the Fillmore Center for a clean and sober dance. It's a benefit for a woman who needs a kidney transplant, five dollars at the door "for those who have it." Steve Maddox, Walden's intake evaluator, is in charge at the ticket table.

Packed into the crowd at the entrance to the building, Mike passes in front of Steve. He turns his right pants pocket inside out and lets the only dollar in his pocket fall into the waiting donation basket. Steve nods his thanks for the donation. A moment later Mike is lost in the crowd, dancing up a storm.

Barely visible in the gyrating frenzy of more than one hundred clean and sober addicts, a photographer sets up a six-foot-tall Valentine's heart backdrop in a far corner of the packed dance hall—five dollars for a Polaroid, proceeds to the kidney transplant recipient. First in line is Mike with a Walden Sister. The photographer cries out for the couple to smile, the flash pops suddenly, and Mike digs into his left pants pocket, peels off one five-dollar bill from the twenty dollars he's carrying, and then turns—right into the scowling face of Steve Maddox.

"You lied to me," shouts Steve over the blaring music, not noticing as Mike's Walden Sister scurries out of sight.

"Man, I'm sorry—" Mike begins, but Steve cuts him short.

"I don't want to hear it," he says, leading Mike to the front door and out into the foggy night. "Get back to the house and sit with yourself," says Steve. "And think about what you did to that woman who needs a kidney, showing me you had only a buck in your pocket, cheating on the donation."

Most of The Family is still at the dance, so when Mike hits the mansion its halls are silent. He walks down The Boulevard and puts himself on the bench, where he doubles over, his fist rolled into his belly.

"Damn!" Mike exhales through clenched teeth. "Shame! Right in my gut. What did I do? Junkie scamming! I thought I had a good program going."

The next morning Sylvester assigns Mike to write a thousand-word essay, *Why honesty can save my life.*

"If I am not honest," he writes, "people will see me as a liar even when I'm telling the truth. And then everybody'll shut me out, and then when I'm in trouble and need them they'll say, 'Mike's just throwing bones, looking for attention.' So then I'm all alone, and next thing I'll do is pick up a couple of bags of dope and a needle."

Tucked into that essay is one of Mike's most painful truths: "Alone" is the most frightening word he knows. But the essay on honesty is written, turned in, and then ignored. Mike again focuses all his energy on running the perfect program, following the rules. He picks up every last piece of loose paper on the floor of The Boulevard, fixes every leaking faucet from attic to basement, follows each and every house rule and then some. But what Mike doesn't follow is the fundamental rule of relapse prevention: Hook up every unusual behavior to an inner mood that drives that behavior, and learn from it.

"So then I'm all alone," Mike wrote in his essay, and his next thought was about picking up some dope and a needle. Instead of delving more deeply into why being alone so intensely frightens him that he'd head back to drugs, Mike hones in on picking up scraps of paper on The Boulevard. And the staff is glad to see that he's back on track.

Weeks later, when Mike leafs through his notebook to show me his essay on honesty, a small, square photograph falls to the floor.

"Damn," he says, handing it to me. "Forgot I still had that."

In the Polaroid photo from the dance, Mike smiles grandly in front of the big red Valentine's heart. Next to him, laughing, her arm draped around his waist, is Lara Webb.

It does little good for addicts in recovery to recognize their scamming, cheating, stinking thinking and behaviors that tell them they're on the path to relapse—unless they have a support system, a group of trustworthy confidants to help lead them back from the precipice of relapse to the narrow road of clean living and sobriety.

"Our clients have got to put their emotions out there," says Walden counselor Hansel Cancel, "let their pride down, disclose things that are painful, feelings they don't want to admit they've ever even had. They've got to hook up with Brothers and Sisters who they can talk to about their worst fears, people who'll help them through it. If not, I mean, these are junkies—when they're in trouble and hurting, if they don't have a support system to provide help, they'll get it from drugs."

Mike finishes his daily plumbing work and heads to the afternoon *touch-base* where his Brothers and Sisters in Sylvester's caseload gather to discuss their activities and feelings of the day. He is dead-out exhausted. Walden's wake-up call is at 6:30 every morning and Mike rarely goes to bed before 1:00 A.M.—staying awake and working until he knows he'll collapse immediately into sleep. In this way, he's learned to avoid lying in bed awake and alone with his racing thoughts, fears, and memories.

Now, at caseload, Mike joins the others in a circle of chairs in a wood-paneled room just off The Boulevard. Darcy leads off with the first check-in.

"I'm scared as hell about my kids," she says, her hands folded in her lap to control their trembling. "I'm here at Walden, so I can't tell if my husband's getting near my kids at home. I'm afraid he's doing it to them, just like he raped me. And I can't bear to think about it because that's what happened to me when I was my kids' age."

Darcy struggles to hold back her tears, then goes on. "So I had nightmares all last night, hardly sleeping, and when I get this exhausted is when I think most about doing dope. But I got through today without using, and I want to thank you all for being here with me."

The entire caseload breaks into applause, congratulating Darcy for bearing through another day without numbing out on drugs.

One by one, Mike's Brothers and Sisters take their turns. Mike is last.

"After each touch-base with you all," he says, "you know, talking about being afraid to sleep, kid molestation and all that, I really feel my bond getting stronger with each of you."

But Mike says nothing about his own memories of being repeatedly raped as a child, nor of his intense and persistent shame at having failed to prevent his sister Michelle from suffering the same ordeal while they lived together in a foster home. He remains silent, too, about his still-present nightmares—waking in a sweat, crying out in the night from his tortured dreams.

In his caseload's touch-base, Mike listens well but speaks little.

"Addicts have a way of taking on appearances that everything is OK," his caseload Brother James Henderson tells me. "They think, hey, I'm in treatment, I have arrived! But mostly, they act like they're OK because they're too petrified to say what's really going on for them. So Mike knows how to carry a conversation just right; he has a lot of humor and he commands respect because of his size and because he's such a gentleman. But you never get much below the surface with him, so you wonder what's really going on, what pieces are missing?"

Fears of Walden's techniques of confrontation and punishment also contribute to Mike's withdrawing into himself, not raising his hand for help as he starts to drown. He says nothing in his touch-base group, to his counselors, or to any Brother and Sister about how his intensely frightening loneliness has led him to *deviate* with Connie, the two curling up in bed at her apartment every time Mike gets permission to leave Walden to have dinner with her, without permission for a clinical.

"I know I'm deviating from the rules when I'm with Connie," he tells me. "But it's like, when my mind ain't occupied by working or by listening to other folks talking, these weird thoughts come into my head, real scary shit. And it feels better when I'm holding on to Connie. So I know I'm deviating by being in bed with her when all I got from Walden was permission for dinner. But if I tell anybody about sleeping with Connie they'll support me to staff and then Sylvester's going to freak out on me because I deviated from the plan. Then he won't even let me out for dinner no more. And it ain't like I'm really doing something wrong by sleeping with my girlfriend. So I'm keeping quiet about it."

Most significant, though, Mike's fear of informing anyone in The Family that he's sleeping with Connie also prevents him from talking to his Brothers, Sisters, or counselors about *why* his fear of loneliness has driven him to deviate from the rules so he can be with Connie. He becomes so distracted with hiding his behavior, he spends little time thinking or talking about his reasons for doing it.

And it's not only fear of punishment from Walden that keeps Mike from speaking openly to his peers. It is also his shame.

"I really admire the Brothers and Sisters in my caseload who hold up their hands," says Mike, "ask for help, deal with their issues, spill their guts. So I watch them, learn from their growth. But, man, I just can't do it like they do. Damn, I got all these feelings inside, those memories, all this weird flashback stuff. And I feel like I'm pathetic for having that still, like I'm weak or something. So I keep my mouth shut 'cause I'm ashamed."

Mike's quiet reserve about his own tortured feelings is not an unusual reaction among Family members.

"It's human nature to take the easiest route," says James Henderson. "It's a rare individual that comes in here and says, 'Hey, I want to tear myself down, make myself feel even shittier than I already do.' And Walden's style is to confront you, attack you to pull even more emotions out. So people like Mike and me who've been in jail, juvenile halls, institutions—we've learned to look good, stay quiet, don't draw attention to ourselves because we don't want to take the heat."

But by not drawing attention to themselves, not exposing their most intense personal fears, Mike and James also shun the self-exploration and understanding of personal issues that form the crucial insights they will need to maintain their sobriety.

"Self-confrontation is necessary," notes relapse prevention expert Terence Gorski, adding that if addicts are to remain sober they must confront feelings they are intensely afraid of dealing with. Gorski also emphasizes that an atmosphere of confrontation— "attacking the person's character and tearing down self-respect"—can cause more harm than good. "Relapse-prone [addicts] are often in severe pain," observes Gorski. "They are holding on to their defenses for dear life . . . Attacking these defenses creates high levels of stress. High stress causes confusion, emotional overreaction or emotional numbness, or memory problems. As a result, harsh confrontation often makes the relapse-prone person worse."

From the days of Synanon to present-day Walden, such intense confrontation has been the hallmark of treatment in Therapeutic Communities across the country. So while the Walden staff clearly understands the need to help clients like Mike open up emotionally, many of Walden's techniques intended to expose his emotions actually have the opposite effect.

"I know it's *me* who I'm cheating by not talking about my stuff," says Mike. "I know I got to start raising my hand more when I'm having a hard time inside. But, man, you open up feelings around here and it's like you're some insect under a magnifying glass with a hundred and twenty junkies and staff staring down at you, some of them thinking they should squash you just enough so you get up and come out stronger. Don't get me wrong, I mean, some of this Family are great folks! So if I'm keeping to myself that's my fault, not theirs. But I've been keeping my stuff inside for thirty-seven years, and yelling at me doesn't encourage me to start spilling my guts now."

Mike sums up his own relapse prevention plan.

"I'm going to hang in here at Walden," he says, "learn from watching other people grow. I ain't opening up about everything inside me 'cause there's some people I just can't trust with my shame about what I done in my life. But I'm doing OK, things are going good. I ain't using drugs, and that's what it's about. Right?"

Walden House might agree with Mike's basic premise that relapse prevention is about not using drugs, but not with his plan for how to get there. "Relapse is a problem of loss, and it's a problem of isolation," says Walden relapse prevention specialist Roland Dumontet. "As long as the client is isolated and cut off from The Family, he's cut off from support, cut off from people that can give him another view of what's happening. And that's when he gets into trouble."

On May 25, six months after he arrived at Walden, Mike advances to *pre-re,* the last phase of treatment before reentry into the community. "I'll finally get weekend passes," he says, "and I get to hang out in the pre-re lounge and watch videos." He stretches his hand straight in front of him and pumps his thumb up and down. "Man, talk about cravings!" he laughs. "I've been in remote-control withdrawal for six months now! I need a TV fix."

Before he's allowed to join his fellow Elders in Walden's pre-re lounge (outfitted with telephone, TV, soft couches, and a desk with computer for writing résumés), Mike is required to have a job, an essential element in his forthcoming reintegration into the world outside of Walden. But he contemplates his first job offer with mixed feelings.

"My mentor here in the house is going to hook me up with his friend who owns a plumbing company," says Mike. "But, man, I don't know. It's the job that Arthur Hudson had."

He utters Arthur Hudson's name in a soft, reverent tone. Arthur has become a larger-than-life Walden icon.

"Remember," Sylvester reminds his caseload whenever he gets the chance, as if they could forget, "that Arthur split this program and was dead in a chair with a needle in his arm for three days before they found him, his body all stiff! Ain't too long ago he was in this house with you all."

"I don't know," Mike tells me, thinking of the plumbing job he's been offered. "I mean, it's a good job, and I still got my tools stored down at my dad's house. I can make some bucks, start saving some money for when I'm out of Walden and back in the world again." He shakes his head. "I'll take the job, I guess. But it gives me the creeps thinking this was Arthur's job and then he, you know, just stopped showing up."

Mike walks down the long staircase to The Boulevard trying to get the image of Arthur Hudson out of his mind, heading for the counselors' office to talk with Sylvester about his pre-re planning, getting ready for his final months of rehab after he moves to a Walden-run satellite apartment.

"There's things I'm going to miss about this house," he tells me, laughing suddenly as he slides his hand along the staircase banister. "And I'm scared about being away from The Family. You know, the Brothers and Sisters keep my head from going off into dangerous places. In here, when my thoughts go weird on me, I got like a hundred and twenty people I can pull over and say, 'Hey, how're you doing, let's go have a cigarette, get some coffee.' It takes my mind off stuff."

Mike reaches The Boulevard and walks past four Family members confined to the bench, in silence, for a variety of house offenses. He knocks on the staff door, waiting for Sylvester to answer.

"I got to remember when I get out there alone in the satellite apartment," Mike says, "that I can always come back here, find someone to talk to."

The door opens and Sylvester catches his last words.

"You need somebody to talk to?" says Mike's counselor sternly. "Better start with me. We're moving you back to the dorms."

"Aww, man, I got me a nice suite with just four guys on the third floor now," says Mike. "I'm getting ready to go out of the house to a satellite apartment, and you got me moving backwards! What'd I do that you're sending me back to the dorms?"

"How come you don't know if you did something or not?" asks Sylvester, leaning on the door to the counselors' office, his tongue twirling a toothpick as he watches Mike. "You're supposed to *know* when you do something, and support yourself."

"Man, are you playing with me?" asks Mike. "I got no idea what you're talking about."

Sylvester stares, waiting. Then he laughs and swings the door open for Mike to pass through.

"Just checking, just checking," he says, turning and sitting in his reclining chair behind a paper-covered desk, motioning for Mike to sit nearby.

"We decided to move you to the dorms 'cause a bunch of new Little Brothers have arrived and they need somebody to look up to, show 'em the ropes. Staff picked you as their program mentor."

"Do I get something to say about it?" asks Mike.

"I don't know," says Sylvester, rocking forward in his chair. "You ain't had a whole lot to say to me about much of anything recently. You got something to say about this?"

"I guess not," responds Mike. "Damn! Why did you fuck with me like that? You just tried to trap me!"

" 'Cause you're running the perfect program," says Sylvester. "That's why we picked you as mentor, right? You're all ready to be out of this house, but before you go you can set an example for the Little Brothers that just got here. Teach 'em the rules."

Mike and Sylvester begin to lay out plans for his leaving the Walden mansion for the satellite apartment he'll share with two other addicts in recovery who are already there. The focus of their conversation is on the support network Mike is supposed to set up for himself outside of the mansion—places to go, people to talk to so that he doesn't become isolated and return to his old patterns that, in the past, have included drugs.

Relapse prevention classes teach two techniques to get through the transition from the highly structured in-house program to more independent living outside: Build up a support system in the community, and stay away from *triggers*.

In the days and weeks before leaving for satellite housing, Mike has been testing his triggers.

On Walden's back porch on the day Sylvester moves him back to the dorms, Mike takes a smoke break with his caseload Brother Clifford Martin. He reaches into his pocket, takes out a gold Zippo lighter, and flicks the flame to light Cliff's cigarette.

"Damn!" says Cliff. "I thought you don't use that Zippo no more?"

"I'm testing myself," says Mike, holding the lighter to his own cigarette. "If I'm going to be out of the house soon, I got to be sure I can handle my triggers without going off the deep end."

The Zippo is the lighter Mike used exclusively, for years, to cook his heroin before shooting up. He's kept it out of sight since the day he'd arrived at Walden, until now.

"I miss the routine around the dope as much as I miss the dope," Mike tells Cliff, rolling the Zippo back and forth in his right hand. "I had my special spoon and this Zippo to cook up the powder, nice and brown, melted down, and a little piece of cotton to suck it from the spoon through the needle so it's filtered real thin. You set the cooking works out just so, get it all ready. It's like this religious ritual."

Mike takes a long haul on his cigarette, then he and Cliff fall silent.

Mike's Zippo is a trigger, nothing more than an object that brings on a memory of his past drug use. Triggers have a potency that can send addicts with the most resilient recovery programs spinning straight back to their dealers.

In a number of experiments, scientists who study drug addiction used highly advanced PET scanners to take pictures of the electrical activity of addicts' brains. Immediately after an injection of cocaine or heroin, the images from the scanners showed hyperexcited nerve endings firing like lightning in the intoxicating pleasure centers of their brains. For those addicts in recovery, who'd been clean and sober for months, the scientists played a video that showed needles puncturing veins, or heroin being cooked up in a spoon. Their pleasure centers lit up on the scans exactly as if they had injected the drugs. And at the very moment when their nerves were pulsing with light on the scans, the addicts in recovery told the scientists they were having intense drug cravings, or that they felt high. The memory *triggers* of shooting dope approached the potency of the drugs themselves.

"Man, put that Zippo down and stop talking spoon talk!" Cliff laughingly pushes Mike away. "Last time I had a craving like the one I'm getting listening to you now, I supported myself to Sylvester."

"Yeah?" asks Mike, incredulous. "What'd he say?"

"I was like trembling," says Cliff, "telling Sylvester I'd had this fantasy of shooting up, and that I actually felt high! I mean, I was stoned! Sylvester just laughed, says it happens to all of us. The problem ain't the cravings, it's what you do about them."

Mike snaps the Zippo closed and slides it into his pocket.

"What you've got to do when something triggers you and the craving for dope hits real strong," says Cliff, "is get hold of somebody you trust. Then you say, 'Hey, man, I'm about to do something really stupid—help me out.' A craving's kind of like a wave—if you can ride over it, it passes."

It was easy enough for Mike to slip his Zippo out of view. But for every physical trigger like the Zippo or his special spoon, there are emotional triggers much harder to tuck away. Of the three most common triggers that can bring an addict to relapse, say the researchers, physical objects like Mike's Zippo are the least powerful, and the easiest to avoid. Even seeing drugs themselves, or people using dope, ranks second. At the top of the list of the potent relapse triggers that can suck an addict back to drugs is exasperating, emotional stress.

"Increased stress," states Gorski in *Staying Sober*, "leads to a state of free-floating anxiety and compulsion. The person feels compelled to do something, anything, to relieve the anxiety . . ." Addicts know from past experience and conditioning that when stress and anxiety hit hard, drugs will ease their minds, provide a short-term reprieve from the torment of their thoughts.

For Mike, isolation is a potent trigger, to which his response has always been to hit the needle. The scientists who've studied cravings and triggers report that this will continue for years to come.

At Walden, consumed and distracted by the program's busy schedule and the boisterous company of his Brothers and Sisters, Mike's loneliness, flashbacks, and terrors have been held at bay. But when those emotions return they will trigger cravings that only the most stalwart might resist. When that happens, if Mike hasn't lined up a support system of confidants prepared and trained to talk him through it, he's likely to find his dealer instead.

Relapse researchers have found that drug users in recovery are exquisitely sensitive to the emotional triggers dignified by the acronym HALT: Hungry, Angry, Lonely, Tired. When these feelings hit, say relapse prevention specialists G. Alan Marlatt and Dennis C. Daley in the textbook *Substance Abuse*, "The client should then determine how and when to ask for support or help." To achieve this, Marlatt and Daley emphasize that recovering addicts must plan in advance to deal with relapse, even to the point of rehearsing what to do when the cravings come on—as they invariably will.

"Rehearsal [for relapse] . . . helps increase confidence as well as clarify thoughts and feelings regarding reaching out for help," write the two relapse prevention experts. "Many clients, for example, feel guilty or shameful and question whether or not they deserve support from others. . . . Asking for support is very difficult to accept."

Marlatt and Daley recommend that addicts in recovery carry emergency relapse prevention cards with them at all times, "with instructions to read and follow" and the phone numbers of the people in their support system who can pull the addicts out of the irrational tailspin brought on by an emotional or physical trigger.

"This is a great class!" proclaims Mike, coming out of Walden's Friday 3:00 relapse prevention group. "We got all these new things to think about—external and internal triggers that connect us to the times we did dope. And man, my personal list of internal triggers runs a mile high! Guilt, shame, dishonesty, loneliness, thinking about my kids, my sister, being abused, even just having too much time on my hands. All that can put me, *bang,* in relapse mode. And that's when I'm supposed to raise my hand, talk to somebody about what's up, ask for help."

Mike is suddenly quiet.

"Man, if I talked to somebody every time I got into one of those trigger feelings, I'd spend my whole life talking, talking, talking, every damn minute! I got to figure this relapse prevention out, or I'm going to wind up on the spoon again. And I'm out of Walden and into satellite housing in like two weeks!"

He walks down The Boulevard, passing by the weight room where the Brothers and Sisters work out—both their bodies and their frustrations. He goes in, lays back on the incline bench, and starts pumping iron.

"I ain't worried, man," he says, at first breathing slow and easy, then starting to puff hard, sweat staining his T-shirt. "See, I've had drug cravings and I've played out the tape in my head, to see where they'll go."

Mike puts the weights down, lying flat on the bench, panting.

"Last week," he says, "I was laying right here on this bench, my heart racing and I'm sweating, and it feels just like I'd done some cocaine and heroin, right in the vein! It was that heart-pounding and sweating thing that triggered it. Whew, I was high! So I ran the tape in my mind, the needle going in, the pounding in my head, sweating, floating away on the rush from the dope."

Mike stops, sits up on the exercise bench, and stares forward.

"And I get to the end of the tape I'm playing in my head," he says, "and it's a fucking overdose! I mean, whenever I get a trigger now I play out the tape like I was shooting up. And every time it ends at that same place. I'm dead. Overdosed. Arthur Hudson sitting there and nobody finding me until I'm rotted and stinking. So when I get a craving, I just play out the tape. Just now, even describing it to you, it's like I'm feeling high, a hot little rush coming on. But then I wind up dead. So I ain't going there. I ain't going where Arthur went 'cause I can play that tape in my head and it'll keep me off the dope. Now *that* is some strong relapse prevention, better than talking to anybody—that picture of me dead with a needle in my arm."

July 5, the day before Mike is to move from the mansion to his satellite apartment, is Lara Webb's birthday.

By now, their affectionate toying with each other (as Mike calls it, "like Brother and Sister stuff") has strongly reinforced suspicions in the house that the two are *contracted up*— an item. To quell the rumors, which Mike insists are false, he's volunteered to be on a ban from Lara. So during her birthday celebration in Kings Hall the day before Mike is to leave for satellite, he stands at the opposite end of the huge ballroom from where Lara blows out her birthday candles. And as The Family breaks into Walden's raucous, foot-stomping version of "Happy Birthday," Mike stands tall with his mouth tightly shut—lest anyone suspect he is communicating with Lara and violating their ban.

Suspicions about Mike and the women at Walden started almost as soon as he'd walked in the door that past November. All Little Brothers and Sisters during their two-week orientation phase are not allowed to make outside calls, nor to talk with anyone of the opposite sex in the house except during group meetings. But during Mike's first week, he was sitting at attention with a dozen Sisters and Brothers waiting for a treatment session to start. Floyd, the session's counselor, was late, and Mike began chatting with the Sister sitting next to him. When Floyd arrived, he read Mike the riot act.

"Floyd just tore into me," says Mike, who recalls sitting with his head hanging down throughout the counselor's harangue. "Then I told him, 'Hey, Floyd, thanks for the pull-up! But I'm just a stupid dope fiend here to learn to control my impulses. You got to hold me back from the women.' "

The counselor had stared at Mike, then cracked up.

"You'll do OK," he said, laughing. "You can be a stupid dope fiend around this house, but not a womanizer."

The label stuck. Articulate, thoughtful, kind, and hardworking, Mike soon proved he was not a stupid dope fiend. But he had a much harder time shaking off the womanizer label.

Now, seven months later, after Lara's birthday party winds down in Kings Hall, Mike heads to the dorm to gather his clothes in preparation for moving out of Walden the next day.

"I've been *taking focus* from the staff about the way I talk with the women ever since I been here," he tells me, sorting his clothes so he can wash them in the morning before leaving. "I keep saying, what are you talking about with this womanizing stuff, they're my Sisters! And the staff goes, 'Yeah, right.' "

Mike stuffs his dirty clothes into a sack, pulling it tight. "But really," he says, "they *are* my Sisters. And I ain't been coming on to them, especially not to Lara."

After his months at Walden, Mike slips easily into therapyspeak. "I think the male staff is projecting their own feelings on to me," he concludes. "It's like, if they were as friendly as I am with the ladies, that'd mean they were coming on to them. So they think that's what I'm doing. So I asked some of the Sisters, in front of Sylvester, 'Am I flirting with you guys?' And they say, 'Oh, no, you're like our Big Brother, that's all.' "

Mike pushes his laundry bag under his bunk and sits down. It's 11:00 P.M., too early to even think of sleeping. It had taken only a few moments to pack: his clothes, a few books (his Bible, neatly bookmarked at Psalm Six), and a crystal pendant he'd received in honor of being elected Head of Core, the group of eight clients who act as Walden's program advisers.

Mike places his Head of Core crystal pendant carefully alongside his laundry bag so as not to forget it in the morning. "I'm real proud of that," he tells me. "Gives me hope!"

He pauses, sitting on the edge of the bed and staring down at his hands, freshly callused from his new job refurbishing the plumbing in renovated, low-rent housing projects.

"I been thinking about being away from The Family," he says slowly. "Even at satellite with two other guys in the apartment, I'm still scared, man."

He gets up and we leave the dorm, not wanting the conversation to waken the Little Brothers he's mentoring.

"So what'll I do with this loneliness stuff when I'm out of the house," says Mike, pacing in the hallway. "Where's all the Brothers and Sisters, man? Just being by myself in the new apartment after work, I'll be sitting there alone late at night, flipping the remote on the TV, trying to distract my thoughts."

Mike laughs, playing out the fantasy, running the tape in his head. "And what's on the TV? Sports, and a fuckin' beer commercial! So I'm all alone in the apartment, thinking about that warm glow from the beer—"

He stops.

"Damn!" he laughs. "It's like I've relapsed before I even get to flip the channel!"

Mike looks at his watch, approaching midnight.

"I'm going to get some sleep, before I go off the deep end here," he says. "I'm already feeling lonely, and I ain't even out of the house yet. All the Brothers are asleep, and it's one of the Sisters who's doing the night watch. I can't talk to her this late at night," he says, " 'cause everybody would think I was trying to get with her."

"Tell me what it is about being lonely," I ask, "that worries you so much?"

Mike begins pacing again, chewing over the question as if it were something new to him.

"It's that place where it's just me and my thoughts," he says finally. "You know, like that fantasy thing about being high I got when I was lifting weights? Or late at night, when I see that white room with the bare bed and the guy who did me as a kid? I been OK with that stuff inside here at Walden, but that's the real world I'm leaving for in the morning. What's going to happen if I get pissed at my boss or he gets pissed at me and I start feeling shitty? What if things between Connie and me get messed up? I mean, Connie and me were doing great before Walden, but when she'd leave for work and I was alone in the house before I went to my own work, it was like, damn, I'm uncomfortable! I don't like being by myself 'cause of those thoughts I get in my head. Guilt, shame, those are the two biggies for me. You know, from being violated when I was a kid, and 'cause of how I ain't done so well being a dad to my girls. All kinds of garbage comes into my head. It's that 'woe is me' thing—that's the big one. And what have I done every time that's popped up in the past? Dope!"

Mike holds open the door to the dorm, about to go in.

"Aww, hell," he says, "I'm just getting scared, sitting on my pity pot. I'll get over it. I know I'm stronger now, these ain't those old times. I'm doing OK again, have been for seven months. And I been playing out this loneliness stuff enough times in my head as part of relapse prevention that I'll recognize it when it comes up. And then I'll know what to do."

Mike laughs and, nodding his head, recites the relapse prevention creed: "Pick up the phone, not the drugs."

Before he goes off to bed, he tries one more joke to lighten his mood.

Holding an imaginary phone handset to his ear, Mike cries out, "I'm relapsing, man, pick up the phone! What do you mean, leave a message at the beep?"

At 7:00 the next morning, Mike bounds down to the basement laundry room, switches his clothes from washing machine to dryer, and heads back up the stairs to the counselors' office off The Boulevard for his exit interview with Sylvester. Within moments, he's back on The Boulevard.

"I thought there'd be this big long good-bye," Mike tells me. "You know, Sylvester giving me some good recovery thoughts to chew on, to take with me to satellite and all that. So he asks, 'Got your bags packed, Mike?' I say, 'Yeah.' And then I'm waitin' for the speech. But Sylvester says, 'OK, you're outta here.' That was it, man, the whole thing!"

Mike laughs and runs down the stairs to pick up his laundry. Hefting the bag with all his belongings on his shoulder, he heads out the door from Walden's basement to the street, passing baskets of dried and folded clothes, one labeled "Lara Webb."

"Aww, damn," he mumbles and, putting his bag down, grabs a piece of paper from the nearby bulletin board and scribbles quickly, glancing around the empty room to be sure no one's watching. Then he wraps the hastily written note around his Head of Core crystal pendant, tucks it in the basket with Lara's clothes, and rushes out the door.

Walden maintains apartments for reentry-phase clients in virtually every neighborhood around San Francisco. But Mike has lucked out. Five Hundred Fillmore Street is just three blocks uphill from the mansion.

He trudges up the hill lugging his bags of clothing and books, opens the iron-grated gate at the locked front door of the apartment building, and then immediately holds his nose against the smell of mildew coming from the frayed hallway carpeting. Up one flight of stairs, the door to apartment 101 on the right is already open and Gomez, one of his two roommates from Walden, greets Mike.

Gomez works as a disc jockey at night, and his sound system is set up now in the tiny living room so he can spin disks and rehearse. Mike can barely hear himself think as he strides down the hall past a kitchen that reeks of old spaghetti and burnt coffee grounds, into the first bedroom on the right. He dumps his clothes in one of the two low-slung single beds, noticing his roommate's clothing scattered about the other bed and the floor.

"Damn," mutters Mike, turning toward me. "I been thinking about inviting my two girls over and cooking them dinner one night soon, showing 'em their daddy's out of the program and doing OK. This place better get cleaned up quick. Couple of weeks out of Walden and these guys have become pigs again!"

It's July in San Francisco, and the morning fog has cleared. Mike is sweating from carrying his bags up the hill and into the heat of the closed room. He pulls open his bedroom window just in time to hear the roar of a city bus pull out right below his first-floor window. Then he heads to the other bedroom, pulls open that window as well, and looks down. From the alleyway below, tucked between two worn-brick buildings in this low-income neighborhood, the distinct sweet odor of crack cocaine floats up to him.

"Aww, no," says Mike, laughing. "What'd they do, pick this apartment as some kind of trigger test?" He shuts the window, choosing the heat over the odor, and heads back to his room.

Mike pulls open the closet door next to his bed. On the floor is a disarray of dirty clothes, pictures, tattered sheets of paper. He turns around just as Gomez comes through the bedroom door.

"That's Hudson's stuff," says Gomez over the blare of the music.

"Arthur Hudson?" Mike stares at him.

Gomez leans over to look into the closet, then bends to start cleaning some of his own clothes off the floor of the room, throwing them onto his bed across from Mike's.

"Yeah," he calls over his shoulder. "You got Arthur Hudson's old bunk and closet. Ain't none of the other guys who's been here since then have wanted to clean out his stuff from in there."

Mike slumps on his bed. His elation as he'd bounded from the mansion early that morning has quickly ebbed. He reaches into the closet and pulls out a crumpled photograph of Arthur Hudson and his kids.

"Aww, damn," says Mike, his eyes welling up with tears. He turns the photo over, reads a date and a scribbled note on the back. "Daddy, we miss you. Things are going good in school and with Auntie Barbara. She says you'll be home soon."

Mike scoops up the clothes, photos, and letters into a box and sticks them on the top shelf of the closet. "It's like they've put me into some bad movie here or something," he says. He wipes at his eyes and then decides to head back to Walden and grab a box lunch before he goes off to work. He strides back down the hill from the satellite apartment, through the ornate front doors of the mansion, and immediately runs into Gretchen, one of the counselors.

"Back so soon?" she asks.

"Yeah," laughs Mike, "I missed you guys. Gotta grab a box lunch before I go off to work, haven't had time to set up cooking at satellite."

Mike moves to go around Gretchen, in a rush to be on time for his job, but she steps in front of him.

"Glad you stopped back, Mike," she says, " 'cause you're going right down that Boulevard to sit on the bench."

"What?"

"Lara Webb supported your lucky ass," says Gretchen, "about that pendant you left in her laundry, and the note. You may be all filled up with yourself, big man out at satellite, perfect program and all that, but you're still part of Walden and you broke a ban! So you're on the bench, on self-reflection until Sylvester can get with you."

"But I got to get to work, they're waiting for me at my job!"

"Your job," exclaims Gretchen, loudly enough so everyone on The Boulevard can hear, "is to work on your recovery! Far as I've heard, we've got a House Meeting planned for you. Going to finally figure out what the hell's been going on, how long you been lying to us, and whether you can stay with this Family or if you're out of here."

After his day on the bench Mike is back at the satellite apartment that evening, forbidden to leave or even turn on the TV. Gomez is off at his job spinning disco discs. Mike's other roommate works the night shift at a hotel. Mike is alone, sitting silently on the couch when I get there.

"It was just this quick impulse to give Lara something for her birthday," he tells me, trying to puzzle together the past twenty-four hours that seem like weeks since he'd left the mansion.

"Damn, what did I just say?" he exclaims. "That's just it, man, I acted on impulse. I mean, what are we supposed to learn in this program? If I couldn't control the impulse to leave that note and pendant for Lara, I won't be able to control the impulse not to do dope. It's the same thing, man, that's what we've been taught—you gotta think before you act. What else is relapse prevention about? Aaah, man, I've really blown it. They're going to fry my ass for this one! I broke a ban, like *the* biggest rule!"

Mike rolls into a ball on the living room couch, rocking back and forth.

"What did you write in the note to Lara?" I ask.

He looks up, then smiles.

"Three words."

"What three words?"

"It's like a code, you know? I just wrote down, '*Three words,*' then I wrapped the paper around the pendant."

He stares at me, eyebrows raised, waiting for me to guess.

"I love you?"

"Bingo!"

"Damn!"

We sit quietly for a while, both wondering what Walden's reaction might be.

"OK," I say. "So you violated the ban. Bad idea, no doubt. But what's the real crime here? How much can they punish you for this? What's the point?"

"Breaking a ban is a felony offense," Mike recites the Walden rule softly. "They can do whatever they want with me."

"And meanwhile?"

"Meanwhile, I got to report in at the house every morning, then go out to my job, then back to sit in the chair at Walden until bedtime every night, when I can go back to satellite to sleep. I do that every day until they bring me in front of a House Meeting."

"*The* House Meeting?"

"Yeah," says Mike, staring at his hands and nodding slowly. "The whole bit in Kings Hall, with me in the center and a hundred and twenty junkies surrounding me, giving me all the heat they can pour on my ass and me trying to explain myself. Then they vote me in or out of the program."

"What're you going to tell them?"

"I don't know yet," says Mike. "But they're going to want to hear a lot more than about some love note to Lara Webb."

He rolls over on the couch, tucking his arms behind his head, pulling forcefully downward until his neck seems to double over.

"This is getting me sick," he says, "just thinking about what I did, blowing my program so quick. And what's going to happen because of it. My gut's doing flip-flops, man."

He gets up from the couch and heads for his still unmade bed in the back room.

"I'd better get some sleep," he says. "Got to be up early for work tomorrow."

I head for the door, leaving Mike for his first night alone at the satellite apartment.

When Mike shows up at the mansion the next morning to report in before going to his plumbing work, Sylvester tells him the job is off.

"You'll be sitting on the Chair all day," he says to a stunned Mike. "But that's a good thing, man. We're helping you with your program."

Sylvester leads Mike, still dressed in his stained work clothes, to the armless hardwood chair by Walden's ornate front hallway where all the Brothers and Sisters pass in and out of the house. Mike sits, his body rigid.

"The Chair," says the Walden manual, "represents being back at the beginning, before you were accepted into The Family. . . . A person may be placed on the Chair for committing a major offense. Anytime you are placed on the Chair, there is a chance you will be asked to leave Walden House. You are placed on the Chair to think about your behavior. Why did you do what you did?"

The manual also instructs The Family on how to deal with a Brother or Sister on the Chair. "When a person is on the Chair you cannot speak to or recognize them in any way. They got themselves there through their actions, and for any personal growth to take place they must be held accountable. The person on the Chair is on a Reflection . . . This reflection stays in place until the person's status in the program is determined."

By the rules, Mike, sitting on the Chair day and night in the front hall, is ostracized, spiritually shunned (even eye contact is forbidden) while the ebb and flow of The Family's daily events surge around him.

Mike takes up his place, like a seated sculpture in the hallway.

"OK, I got to get ready," he repeats to himself. "They'll kick me out of here and all I got to do is concentrate on one thing—I ain't going to use. I'll get a hotel room to live in, go to work. But I ain't going to use, that's the bottom line. I ain't going to use. I will not use."

The tall double front doors to Walden open and close and the faces and voices of Mike's Brothers and Sisters pass by, laughing about their day, talking about plans, heading to groups and meetings.

With the cool breeze of nightfall and the door repeatedly swinging open to let Family members in for the evening, Mike, still in his short-sleeved work shirt, begins to shiver. Horace, the counselor for the night, brings him a white, hospital-style blanket and Mike bends forward and pulls it over his torso and head—a ghostly apparition camped out in the hallway.

For dinner, he receives a plate of mashed potatoes and okra. Horace sees what Mike is eating and gives him permission to run to the cafeteria and make a peanut butter and jelly sandwich. He's got five minutes to return to the Chair.

"Your guy's finally being tested," Sylvester tells me, leaning back behind his desk in the counselor's office. "Look what he was doing, leaving secret notes. That's the behavior you do when you shoot dope—sneaking, lying, hiding. Addictive thinking. That ain't the thought process of a guy in recovery. See, Mike's journey's a lot like mine—he's been on shelter floors, been down and out, so he's got spiritual stuff inside, suffering that makes him want to get clean. Mike *wants* to do the right thing, but there's emotional issues he hasn't resolved. And now we've got us a tool to find out what's up with him. So we'll hold a House Meeting, pour on feedback from his peers, see if he can take the heat, make some changes."

At 8:00 P.M. on his second full day in the Chair, Mike is suddenly moved as much by reflex as by thought. He sits bolt-upright, flexes his stiff muscles, and heads for the front door. But at the moment he rises from the Chair a hand touches his shoulder and he hears soft, whispered words, Maria's voice. "Mike, please, don't go." He sits back down.

"That touch on my shoulder, it was like some miracle," he recalls later. "I sat back in the

Chair and thought about my girls, my family, Connie. If I'd have walked out that door, man, that'd be it. I'd show up at home and they'd say, 'What you doing, Mike?' I split the program, I'd tell 'em, and they'd look at me, 'What'd you learn in there, anyway?' Then I'm asking my own self, sitting in that damn Chair—fuck, what did I learn?"

In spite of the blanket, Mike begins shivering again.

"I got to finish this program, no matter what," he tells himself. "It's good that I blew it now, not later when I was out in the world and thinking I had it down, not watching my impulses. I know where that could have led. It's good that I'm in this chair. This ain't for the girls and Connie no more. I got to finish what I started here, for me."

On the third day, at 6:00 P.M., a Brother and Sister arrive at each side of Mike's Chair and tell him to stand for his House Meeting. Solemnly escorted on both sides, he ascends the long staircase to Kings Hall where he will be seated in the circle at the center of the entire Family. As Mike slowly climbs the stairs, Charles Perky, the tall, stick-thin, acne-scarred counselor who will be in charge of the House Meeting, prepares to address The Family.

Kings Hall is again specially arranged like a theater in the round. Seats for 120 Brothers and Sisters circle the center arena where Charles's low-slung cushioned staff chair faces a second rigid wooden seat, awaiting Mike.

I watch as the entire Family *assumes the position,* on *reflection,* heads bowed, feet planted firmly on the floor, hands flat on their knees. Their silence echoes from the walls of the chamber. Harsh shadows from their seated bodies are thrown to the floor by the light of the overhead crystal chandeliers.

"Focus up," Charles barks out suddenly and all heads rise in unison.

"This House Meeting is about your brother Michael P. I want all twelve of his Brothers and Sisters from Sylvester's caseload to move to that center row we've set up, near Mike's place. You all will start the focus."

Feet and chairs shuffle as Mike's caseload takes its place in the innermost circle; there is a thirteenth chair, left empty.

Charles nods his head toward the crowd, and a deep murmur rises as Lara Webb works her way to the thirteenth chair.

"Focus up!" cries Charles, and silence returns. The Family is at rapt attention.

"Now we all know that Lara and Mike have been on a ban from speaking to each other," proclaims the counselor. "And no one breaks a ban, not for a House Meeting, not for anything. But Lara has asked to address The Family about what's been going on, and to address Michael in front of The Family. So she's here with our OK. But they are back on the ban when this is over. Is that clear?"

"Thank you, Charles!" the shouts echo from the walls of Kings Hall as The Family acknowledges its understanding.

"This Brother we're bringing in front of you"—Charles begins the proceedings, slouching down low in the cushions of his chair—"has done a lot of good things in this house. Mike has come a long way, and we acknowledge that. But he's been slipping, and he's lost his program. So we're here to find out why, help get him back on track. Is that clear, Family?"

"Thank you, Charles."

The counselor nods toward the escorts at the closed doors to Kings Hall, behind which Mike has been waiting.

"Go grab Michael," Charles tells them, and they swing the doors open.

With one Brother and one Sister on either side, Mike is led to the center chair, The Family waiting in silence. He walks in a militarily erect posture, then takes his seat as the escorts withdraw. Then Mike seems to sag. His head is bowed, his back curved, his elbows on knees as he faces the floor. He's wearing an old brown jacket over his paint-stained work shirt. He would seem almost asleep, except for the nervous tapping of one steel-tipped work boot against the polished wood floor.

"OK," announces Charles. "You all know the rules. Make him do some work, but let's not rat-pack him, don't gang up on the guy. But first, I'm going to let him own his own."

Mike looks up, surprised at getting the opportunity to speak first instead of defending himself from the Family's onslaught. His gaze roams over his caseload Brothers and Sisters nearby, nodding at each of them. Then he sees Lara Webb and his eyes lower quickly, again watching the floor.

"I'm giving you the chance to own your own," repeats Charles. "If you don't take it, we got people here ready to do it for you."

Mike looks up, staring only at Charles.

"I left my Head of Core pendant in Lara's laundry bag," says Mike softly. "And I left her a note with it, while we were on a ban."

Charles pauses, then adds, "You got anything more to own?"

"No, man, that's it," Mike replies, his eyes glancing for an instant at Lara.

"OK," announces Charles. "Let's start it off."

"I just talked to you last week," his caseload Sister Donna begins softly, addressing Mike. "And you said you were getting ready for satellite, and everything was going good."

Mike looks up at Donna, nodding.

"You know," she continues slowly, then stands, shouting, separating each word, "you—are—full—of—shit! You were in deep trouble with this stuff over Lara, inner trouble, and you weren't talking to nobody about it! So you weren't the goddamn perfect-program freak you made out to be! And you fucking lied to us all."

Clifford reaches out to touch Donna's shoulder and she sits back down, fuming.

"I'm really sad to see you at a House Meeting," says Cliff. "You were my role model, man, and you were my friend. But even I could see something was up with Lara, and now you're still telling us that everything was going just fine and it was like a lightning bolt or something that made you drop your pendant in her laundry basket. But see, I don't believe that it happened all of a sudden like that. So what you've been telling me and this caseload and this whole Family for all these months is, *FUCK YOU ALL*—you don't need to talk to us! Well, who the fuck are we, then? What do you think your message is to us? It's that we don't count. So do you know what our message to you is?"

Cliff waits a second for Mike to look up at him.

"It's to get the fuck out of this Family! That's my message to you, my mentor!"

A cry comes from the back of the room, "You been saying, 'Hey, Family, leave me alone!' Well, you're alone now, Mike! Deal with it."

"What'd you come to Walden for?" shouts another. "So you can slap us in the face?"

"Focus up!" cries Charles. "One at a time."

He looks over at Mike. "You still got nothing else to own?"

Mike is rigid in his chair. He turns his head to look at Lara, then speaks slowly, deliberately.

"I own having sex with Connie when I went out on dinner or movie passes with her, without permission for a clinical. I own being lonely, and having sex with my girlfriend."

Lara remains expressionless, her stare not leaving Mike's face.

"You threw your whole program away, Mike," says Maria from the front row, "to give Lara that pendant. And still, right here in this House Meeting you're giving us some bullshit about Connie! You're not talking about no feelings you have for Lara, you're still scamming this family, you are still being a junkie! And we thought you had a program."

Maria's voice quiets. "I need to get this clear," she says. "Did you and Lara play each other close while on the ban or not? You've come a long way, and to go out lying like this, it's unbelievable, Mike. Something more was going on than this pendant thing."

"Nothing was going on," Mike replies instantly. "It was an impulse of the moment. Lara just had her birthday, I was feeling good about going off to satellite and I thought I wouldn't see her for a while. It was an impulse, it didn't mean nothing."

Lara leans forward suddenly, about to speak, but a shout from a counselor in the back stops her.

"What do you do when you have an impulse, Mike?" asks Harriet, who teaches Walden's parenting classes, from which Mike had graduated. "You just act on the impulse, go right ahead?" she continues. "Have you been listening around here or you been asleep all these months? You're supposed to pull somebody over and say, hey, help me out here, I'm about to mess up! But what I'm hearing from this Family is that you didn't speak to anyone all this time about your feelings for Lara."

Harriet walks slowly around the circle, closer to where Lara is sitting with Mike's caseload.

"I know you, Mike," says Harriet softly. "And I know that you carry a lot of shame about your life, and that might keep you from opening up with The Family—"

"We all got shame in our lives," a chorus of voices interrupts, but the shouting stops instantly as Lara rises to her feet, directly in front of Mike.

"How come you didn't even tell *me*, Michael?"

She's facing Mike, her voice so quiet that only those in the front hear her words; a buzz echoes through the room as her question is repeated down the rows.

"You told me you volunteered for a ban against talking to me," continues Lara, "because everyone was suspicious of you and the women in the house. Not because you really had feelings for me."

Her hands are trembling as she speaks and she folds them carefully in front of her, interlocking her fingers.

"You didn't tell anyone in The Family what you were feeling, Mike," says Lara. "And you didn't tell me, neither. Not till you left me that pendant and love note."

Mike raises his hand to cover his eyes, then spreads his fingers over his face, watching Lara from the spaces between them.

"Mike, I just want to say," she pauses, tightening the grip of her hands in front of her, "that ever since we first met, I have really respected you, for who you are and for the tight program you've been doing here. So when you told me you thought it was safest we be on a ban, just to keep the rumors down, I really admired that you could say that, to do the ban so you could keep focused on your program."

Lara's voice is more firm now, her breathing steady. She turns slightly, to face The Family as well as Mike.

"I thought you were doing the ban as some formality thing," she says, "not because you had emotional feelings for me, not because you loved me. But after the ban started I walked around this house missing you a lot. Because I had those emotional feelings for you. Because I loved you."

Lara glances up at the ceiling of Kings Hall, as if suddenly realizing where she is. Then she stands firm upright, lowers her head, and continues, her voice strong.

"When I found your pendant in my laundry basket, and a note that said you love me— do you know what I saw, Mike? I saw Arthur Hudson's face, laying dead right there next to me. It just freaked me out, frightened me so much to see you do something so out of character, so risky to your program like sneaking me a love note. So I supported you to staff, because after all this time of you saying nothing about your feelings, you were suddenly so impulsive and careless I was sure you were losing it. And I didn't want that to happen, not when I care about you so much. So if you love me like you say, Mike, you'll stop your shame right now and start talking to The Family about what's inside you. 'Cause if you don't start talking about whatever's scaring you—next thing is, it'll scare you right back to the dope. And I don't want to hear they found you dead in some chair in a hotel room, all stiff."

Lara stops suddenly, looks about her, and quietly takes her seat. Minutes go by without a word. Then Mike speaks.

"I am scared," he says slowly, eyes darting about the room. "And I'm ashamed. I'm always ashamed, that ain't nothin' new. And man, this is going to sound like some lame excuse, but I ain't been talking to The Family about how I been feeling 'cause, I mean, I don't *know* what I been feeling, so how do I talk about it? So I been following all the rules, graduating from all the classes—"

Mike looks across the hall at his parenting teacher, Harriet.

"See that! I even graduated from parenting class," he continues. "But I ain't a good parent! And I graduated from classes to keep me off dope, but I don't know if I can keep off dope. You see how scary all that is? There's nothing real inside me, nothing I can trust. So everything's going good in the program, but I'm scared out of my mind, have been all along. How was I going to talk about that? And then I get these feelings for Lara, but my daughters love Connie to death and I'm still with Connie, and then I dump that pendant in Lara's basket so there goes my whole program and—"

"Cut the bullshit, Mike!" Maria's voice rings out. "Your program didn't stop when you slipped that pendant in Lara's basket, it stopped when you started hiding your feelings from The Family, and from yourself. Far as I can tell, you been here seven months, you just graduated to satellite—and you've had no program the whole time. You win the best acting award, Mike. But any junkie can do that."

Mike is silent, the thoroughness of his shame overwhelming.

"Michael," says Charles from his staff chair, theatrically glancing as his watch and finally returning to the traditional flow of a House Meeting. "You've got two minutes to explain why you should stay with this Family."

"I been sitting on the Chair these last three days," says Mike, his voice hoarse. "And this thought kept running through my head, to just slip out that door, get some dope, and forget about all this shit coming down on me. That'd be so easy, and I got so close to splitting I actually felt the rush of the dope in my head. But, man, I didn't do it. Something kept me in that Chair, so there must be *something* to my program. But I know I got some screws that have come loose. And my program isn't what I thought it was. Maybe it ain't nothing."

Mike looks up, as if he's staring right past the family and through the very walls of Kings Hall. Then he focuses on Lara.

"I'm ashamed of myself," he says. "I betrayed you. I betrayed The Family. I betrayed my kids. And I betrayed myself. Tell the truth? I can't think of any reason you should let me stay."

The two escorts march Mike out the door of Kings Hall, so that the Family can vote.

In a sense, Mike's signal to Lara as he walked out the door of Walden had been his first open cry for help. And to Walden's credit, they heard his plea, called him back in, dug deeply enough to uncover his obsessive emotional isolation, then accepted his return to the family. They made it clear that Mike's downfall had not been through his feelings for Lara, but rather that he'd kept himself bottled in, had not learned to talk about or confront his innermost fears. Achieving long-term sobriety, they told him, would require more profound, deeper transformations.

Yet the House Meeting, by its very style, had left him frightened, demoralized, and still very much alone.

"For addicts to see the reality of their situation," writes Gorski, "does not mean attacking the person's character and tearing down self-respect. . . . Confrontation should be used sparingly. It should be replaced with education, problem solving, and support. . . . Allowing yourself to be degraded and humiliated is not therapeutic."

The House Meeting had convinced Mike that he needed to share his deepest emotions with his Brothers, Sisters, and counselors. It had also left him, relapse warning lights flashing, too ashamed to do so.

The day after the House Meeting, back at his job, Mike hefts a thirty-foot length of copper tubing alongside the wooden wall of a partially renovated wooden building in the Mission District. He carefully measures the distance from the first-floor bathroom to the corner of the house, does a quick calculation in his head, etches several marks on the tubing, and trudges toward the electric pipe cutter set up on wooden horses at the back of the house.

"I'm happy that they kept me in The Family," he tells me when I arrive at the end of his day's work. "But I still got this weight on me, and it feels like I ain't never gonna shake that off."

Mike slips the pipe into the cutter and flips the switch.

"I busted my ass to get into that program," he says, watching sparks fly from the spinning metal blade and the pipe split in two. "And then I busted my ass for seven months in the program. But I did it all wrong. Took me all this time to figure that out."

He tosses the cut section of pipe to the ground and begins to pack up for the day.

"If I could do it all over again," says Mike, "I wouldn't have fixed the damn plumbing in the mansion, and I'd have let the heaters stay cold all winter. I'd have asked for a job in the kitchen instead of being house plumber, kept more humble. And I'd be raising my hand when I'm in trouble, when all those thoughts come into my head, when I'm lonely. I'd be raising my hand so much asking The Family for help they'd have to tie it down. And once asking for help becomes a habit, then I'd be on my way to doing that instead of dope when I feel bad. But it ain't too late, man, I can change all that now, do my program the way it should be—from here on in."

Mike carries his toolboxes and the metal tubing sections to the basement of the building, locking up for the day.

"That pipe's expensive stuff," he says, crouching in the basement and loading everything away. "And I hit the estimate of how much we'd need to fix this house dead on. This is the work I like, big construction projects to occupy my mind. So it feels good to be out here on a job again, not thinking about all that program stuff every day. I got one thing on my mind right now: twelve-foot length of pipe, vent it like it should be. That's it, man."

Mike locks the basement door behind him and squeezes alongside the alleyway crowded by scaffolding, out onto Shotwell Street.

"See, that's the problem right there," he says. "One part of me says, get back to Walden, raise my hand, get involved, confront my issues. And the other says, lay out this pipe like I'm doing here, keep it nice and simple. So I ain't got it figured out yet, I know that."

Mike wipes his greasy hands on his work pants, then checks his watch.

"I got to get back to the satellite apartment and shower," he says, "and then over to Walden. My contract for being accepted back into The Family is I got to clean the whole second floor of all dust with a little brush every evening. Then I go back to satellite at night, and I ain't allowed to leave the apartment night or day except to go to Walden, to Narcotics Anonymous meetings, or to my plumbing work. That's it. Oh, and I can't watch no TV either," Mike laughs, his thumb twitching to imitate the remote control. "And I can't make no personal phone calls, only business-related. But that's OK with me, I ain't in the mood to talk anyway. This last week just wiped me out."

He walks down Shotwell, then makes a left on 26th up to where he'll catch the bus at Mission Street.

"I should be taking the Valencia bus instead," says Mike, " 'cause this one goes right past 16th and Mission, where I used to score my dope. Relapse prevention lesson number one, right? 'No hanging out in your old sleazy places.' But I'll be OK, I'm too tired to score any dope. I just want to get my butt back to Walden right now, finish dusting the second floor, and go back to satellite to sleep."

We stand at the corner of Mission, waiting with the after-work crowd for the bus.

"Only one thing I'm still afraid of," he tells me. "Gives me butterflies just thinking about it—running into Lara. I don't think I could look her in the eye, man. And besides, we're still on the ban, can't say a word to each other, which is good 'cause I got to focus on getting back to my program, nothing else."

The bus pulls up and Mike waits until everyone else has boarded, then he swings himself in and grabs a pole for balance, standing wedged in with the crowd.

"You ain't going to believe I'm thinking this," Mike tells me, "but I mean it. The most healthiest thing Walden could do is to lift the ban between me and Lara. Way it is now, we have no way to deal with the confusion about our feelings. Man, I got to learn to be able to set boundaries in my life, and I don't learn that by no Walden-enforced ban. It's like, on the one hand they're telling me, 'Hey, deal with your inner feelings, Mike, don't go sweeping 'em under the rug.' And on the other hand they say, 'Hey, man, you can't even talk to that woman.' So how am I going to learn about being in the world again if they keep holding me back with all these weird rules? Want to know the truth? I think if they lifted the ban and I had a chance to talk with Lara, the feelings would probably just evaporate. It's like this obsession, man, and it won't go away, like she's this forbidden-fruit thing, you know? It's like dope, almost—the more forbidden it is, the more obsessed I'm getting about it."

Mike left his plumbing job too late to get to Walden for dinner, so he finishes his dusting on the mansion's second floor and then hangs out on the patio for smokes with a couple of his Brothers.

He'll be allowed to stop his nightly dusting job when he completes a 750-word essay, "Why I compromised my recovery by saying I Love You." But he hasn't started writing it yet.

"I don't mind doing the dusting for a while longer," Mike tells me. "It makes me show up at the house every evening, talk to folks, not isolate so much. I'll get to the essay eventually."

Now, past 10:00 and having missed dinner, Mike is starving. He signs the log at the front hall to leave the mansion and head back to satellite, silently passing a Sister, her head bowed, on the Chair. I walk him home, trudging the three blocks uphill to the apartment, stopping in with him at the corner mom-and-pop grocery to search out his dinner.

"Damn, I don't know what to do for food," he says. "Walden's been feeding me all this time." He wanders the aisles at the store. The stove in his apartment is caked with grease, clogging the gas jets. That eliminates the canned soup. Finally, a package of Wonder Bread in one hand, can of tuna in the other, he picks out a couple of bananas and a pack of cigarettes at the counter and pays up.

"Welcome back to the real world," he announces, and crosses the street to his apartment.

As I walk to my car I see the flickering blue light of the forbidden TV set in the window of Mike's room. Had I been one of his Brothers or Sisters, I'd have had to support him to staff; breaking any rule is a relapse warning sign.

In many ways, relapse prevention's connect-the-dots approach can seem petty. Or, it can save someone's life: You broke a rule and watched TV; you must be lonely; you've used drugs before to fight off loneliness; you're at risk of relapse. Turn off the TV and call some-one to talk about how lonely you feel.

Friday, July 31, three weeks after his House Meeting, Mike lies quietly on his bed by the window over the bus stop on Fillmore Street. He's home early from work, his back aching from a strenuous day connecting pipes in the narrow crawl space under the refurbished house. Because of his back, Mike's been excused from his evening dusting job at the man-sion. But he has promised to write his relapse prevention essay, and he puts his notebook by his side on the bed. Soon the late afternoon sun warms him into a restless haze of half-sleep. Eyes closed, he tries to focus in on the music from the boom box on the shelf next to him, playing his favorite singer, Tom Waits. He nods sleepily to the rhythm of the gravelly voice.

> always chewed tobacco
> and the bathtub gin
> he went down down down
> this boy went solid down

It's been days since Mike's been over to Walden to chat with his Brothers and Sisters. He's been too tired after work to bother doing anything but heat up some spaghetti on the now-fixed gas stove, eat quickly by himself, and sleep. Then he's up at five every morning to take the Mission Street bus to work, putting in twelve-hour days, weekends as well. Connie's been calling, wanting to see him, but Mike's told her he's too busy, still adjusting to being outside Walden, not ready to be with her yet.

When the sunlight hits his half-closed eyes, Mike wakes from his daze and looks around, trying to reorient himself. Beside him on a cork bulletin board is a picture of Connie, posed with Mike and his two preadolescent daughters at the edge of the Grand Canyon only two summers before—the last time he'd had his turn at custody. Mike opens his eyes now, tak-ing in the photo of his daughters' smiling faces, their arms around their daddy's waist, the vastness of the Grand Canyon behind them.

As the memories flood in, he suddenly slams his fist on the nearby wall.

That was the summer he'd received a check for $62,000 in payment for the accident that had damaged his back. So he'd rented a fully equipped RV, and he, Connie, and his girls headed from San Francisco toward the Grand Canyon, singing songs along the way at the beginning of their family adventure.

When they reached the outskirts of Las Vegas and pulled up in a trailer park, Connie and the girls got out to look around, go for a swim in the pool. Mike seized the moment and went to the back of the RV where he'd stashed his heroin. But the package was gone, six hundred dollars' worth of powder nowhere to be found. He was already shaking and sweaty from the daylong drive without a fix.

In the hour before the girls and Connie came back from their swim, Mike tore the trailer apart looking for his dope.

When Connie and the girls opened the RV's door, they found clothes scattered all over, drawers overturned, and Mike pale and sweaty. While he still hadn't found his heroin stash, his pack of syringes was clearly exposed in the midst of their tossed-about clothing.

Mike had convinced Connie and his daughters that he'd been off heroin for two years. His tremulous body, sweaty face, and look of panic and shame at being discovered now told them a different story.

As he lies in the bed at Walden's satellite apartment, Mike's thoughts pile up with memories of that day, the quiet, desperate tears of Connie and his daughters. But back then, even watching their tears and disappointment, he'd had only one thought: find more dope to replace what he'd lost. He needed to stop the cramps and sweating of his heroin withdrawal before the vomiting started, before he doubled over, barely able to walk.

Mike's memory blurs from there: a cab ride to the seediest part of Las Vegas; counting out four hundred dollars to two men he didn't even know; waiting in a flophouse, sweating, vomiting, while they went to find him some dope; chewing on a couple of Valiums they'd given him to pass the time, not knowing if they'd ever come back or had split with his four hundred. Finally, hours later, they brought in four grams of heroin, three for Mike, one for their efforts. Then the two men started arguing about how to divide up their gram of powder, and when a gun appeared Mike headed for the door, glad he'd escaped with his life, happy to have scored some dope.

The three grams held him for the trip to the Grand Canyon, and back to San Francisco in time for his daughters to return—earlier than planned—to their mother. Within four months, the $62,000 was gone, spent on the trip in the RV, for a used pickup truck Mike wanted for his plumbing work, and the rest for heroin and cocaine. He spent the last $400 to buy enough dope for "that final fix, six rockets so I could do the big sleep."

Mike sits up in his bed at satellite and leans forward to pull the window wide open and feel the gentle breeze on his sweat-soaked T-shirt. From the day he'd arrived at the apartment he'd been planning on calling his girls, telling them he's out of the main house at Walden, doing good, inviting them over so he could cook up a special dinner. But somehow he hasn't gotten around to calling. It's the end of July, and he hasn't seen his daughters since they visited him at Walden, on Easter Sunday in April.

"Damn," he thinks, sitting up in the heat of the small bedroom at satellite. "How could I not even call them? I just love 'em so much, and I'm fucking up with them again."

His mind is racing now. Get up; go to the phone; call them right away; tell them how sorry he is. As he stands by the bed his back stabs in pain and he sits again, looking once more at the Grand Canyon photo of his daughters on the bulletin board. Instead of seeing their smiles, he now sees only an image of their tears, the disappointment on their faces when they'd run back from the pool in the Las Vegas trailer park and, giggling and eager to tell him about their swim, had thrown open the door to the RV.

Mike stares at the floor, alone for the long weekend ahead, images and memories rushing at him from all sides. His heart is pounding, sweat dripping from his forehead, his shirt soaked and his back aching. He leans closer to the breeze coming from the window and hears the bus heading down Fillmore, still some two blocks away.

"Just a touch," he thinks suddenly, "quarter bag, that's all it would take, one tiny hit, just this once—"

He closes his eyes for a moment and already feels the high, the hot rush of heroin flooding his brain. Then he bounds from the bedroom and through the apartment doorway. Mike's shoes pound the ratty carpeting in the building's front hall and he's out the door— just in time to swing up into the Fillmore bus, on his way to 16th and Mission.

A house with 120 addicts in recovery can, in and of itself, take on the characteristics of a conscious, living being. Toss in a counseling staff of hard-core ex-addicts, and the house develops a sixth-sense intuition that is, at times, simply spooky.

On the morning of July 31, hours before Mike heads for 16th and Mission, Sylvester places a small plastic cup labeled "Michael Pagsolingan" on the front desk of the counseling office. Whichever staff member sees Mike next is to go with him to the bathroom to witness his filling of the cup with urine—a random drug test, just to be sure he's OK.

Mike drops down from the last step of the bus and glances quickly around the four corners at 16th and Mission. Within a minute, across the street, he spots a familiar stooped figure leaning against the railing of the BART station, wool cap pulled low over his forehead. Mike lifts his hand, puts the tips of two fingers to his lips, and slowly exhales, a low, soft whistle. The man looks up and Mike moves his hand from his mouth, lifting it to the sky, one finger extended for the one bag of heroin he's shopping for.

Both Mike and the man in the wool cap scan the four corners for cops, and then the man, too, holds up one finger: got one for you, get over here, quick.

The bus has pulled away, no cars are coming, and Mike steps off the curb, but then catches himself. The light is red. The man in the wool cap is waving now, get over here, man, move it!

The rush from the dope is already flashing in Mike's head; and with equal intensity, Walden's unwritten rule number three: No jaywalking. He waits.

By the time the light turns green and Mike runs across the traffic lane, the man has disappeared down Capp Street. Panting now, Mike turns the corner and spots him. They shake hands, a firm grip, and Mike has his packet of dope, the man a twenty-dollar bill.

Fifteen minutes later Mike is back at the satellite apartment, rummaging through the bathroom medicine cabinet. He finds a Q-tip and tears the cotton off the stick.

"By now, I'm like totally paranoid," he tells me later. "I feel that cotton rolling in my fingers and for the first time it really hits me—Mike, you're going to use! I got my rig set out, my needle, my Zippo, the whole religious ritual. Only this time I'm like sweating from how dirty I feel. This time, it is *not* fun."

He pulls his pants down to his ankles, sits on the toilet, cracks the bathroom door slightly open so he can hear any noise that might come from the hallway. If one of his roommates comes in, he can pretend he's just sitting on the throne.

"You're blowing it," Mike tells himself, over and over. "Throw the dope in the toilet, don't do it."

He has a spoon—from Walden's kitchen—on the edge of the sink in front of him. He bends it ever so slightly so that he can re-form it to perfect shape when he's finished; even the slightest crick in the handle of a spoon would tip off his roommates. He cuts open the tiny packet from 16th and Mission with his pocket knife, divides the heroin and cocaine mixture into four parts, puts three back in, pours the remaining quarter-balloon of powder into the spoon, adds a few drops of water, and flicks on the flame of his Zippo. Then he blows on the bubbling, melted brown powder to cool it down, and sucks it into the syringe.

Mike stabs the needle into his flesh over the deep blue vein in the crook of his arm. When a drop of blood spurts into the barrel, guaranteeing he's pierced into the vein, Mike pushes the plunger.

"It was like goin' home," he tells me later, "and mom's got your favorite dish on the stove, and you smell it, to the back of your tongue, way back. That's the rush of the dope. It's right there, and for like two, three minutes I'm floating. But it was just a quarter bag, a baby rush. So I get up and lay down in my bed, put on the Tom Waits tape again. And I'm feeling dirty, man. I'm thinking, that wasn't nothing, it wasn't worth it. Two, three minutes of this hot euphoria and then I just nod off to sleep. I'm thinking, you scumbag, you just fucked up, big time."

An hour later, the cool evening air from the open window blows over Mike's bed and he wakes up, the raspy voice of Tom Waits again drawing him into focus. His thoughts drift back to the afternoon and a chill of sadness sweeps over him. He reaches up and closes the window.

"I've been isolating again," Mike tells himself. "Haven't been to the house for days. Can't do that no more. And I'm not doing any more dope, either. Ain't worth all this worry, feeling so dirty. And it didn't do nothing for me. I'm still here, and I'm still alone."

He shakes off another chill, heads down the hall toward the apartment door, stops at the bathroom to be sure he's left no evidence behind, then walks the three blocks downhill to Walden hoping to hang out with The Family during a lazy Friday evening, catch up with his Brothers and Sisters, stop isolating.

The smell from the polished-wood floor of The Boulevard floats up to Mike as he opens the mansion's front door. He takes in a slow, deep breath, like coming home. Then he heads down The Boulevard toward the outdoor patio to see who's around, looking forward to hanging out with his Brothers and Sisters. On the way, he passes the open door of the counseling office and leans across the threshold to look in.

"Hey, John," says Mike, "you got the night shift, huh? Just thought I'd say hi."

Mike turns to continue down The Boulevard, but John calls him back.

"Good to see you, Mike," he says. "Come in for a second."

A moment later Mike is in the bathroom, John by his side as Mike fills the urine cup labeled with his name.

John initials the slip of paper signifying that he'd witnessed Mike providing the specimen, notes the date and time, and then asks, "This is a clean test, right? No dope in it?"

"Yeah, sure," says Mike, quickly calculating how long it had been since he'd shot up, figuring it was too soon for the test to be positive.

" 'Course it's a clean test," says Mike.

John notes his response on the slip of paper.

Sunday, early morning, Mike calls. I'm still half asleep.

"I got some time this morning," he says. "Thought I'd call and talk."

"Mike, you never just call to talk. What's up?"

"Aw, man, yeah, you're right. It's just that—I kind of messed up."

"Uh-oh. Where's Lara?"

"No, it's not that." He laughs. "I been over to 16th and Mission."

"Oh, no."

"But I just did a little hit, quarter bag. Don't mean nothing, I was kind of like testing myself. I hardly felt it, and it made me feel more dirty than high. So I ain't doing it again. Not ever."

"OK," I say, wide-awake now. "You going to support yourself at the house? Talk about what happened, figure out why?"

"Can't," says Mike. "They dropped a bottle on me, man, like an hour after I did the hit they had me peeing in a cup."

"You're kidding? How'd they know?"

"I got no idea! It's like they can smell it or something. John says they'd arranged the bottle for me that morning. And I hadn't even been thinking about doing dope that morning. But they dropped it on me only an hour after I fixed, so the test is going to be negative, right?"

I sigh. "Mike, how long did it take for the heroin to reach your brain?"

"I don't know, like thirty seconds."

"So how long before it reached your kidneys, got into your urine?"

There's silence on the phone. Then a long, drawn-out, "Fuuuck."

Then, moments later, "Hey, man, can you come over? I got to think this through. They're going to spot me man, I'm kicked outta here as soon as that test result comes back."

A major goal for programs and individuals who practice relapse prevention is to prevent a brief return to drug use from exploding into a full-blown, disastrous relapse. Many in the field distinguish between a limited slippage to drug use, a *lapse,* as compared to a complete and ruinous return to the devastating lifestyle of addiction, a *relapse.*

"A lapse may end quickly or lead to a relapse of varying proportions," write Marlatt and Daley in the textbook *Substance Abuse.* So when an addict has lapsed, they advise, relapse prevention should hone in tightly on preventing that initial, brief lapse from exploding into a prolonged disaster.

"Rather than looking pessimistically on a lapse as a dead-end failure," they observe, "the relapse prevention approach views each lapse as a fork in the road, one path returning to the former problem behavior (relapse) and the other continuing in the direction of positive change."

One interpretation of Mike's return to the mansion immediately after his hit of dope at satellite is that he was trying to save himself from further collapse. For those rehab counselors immersed in relapse prevention theory, Mike's lapse is a window of opportunity, a chance to grab the emotional energy of his lowest moment and use it like a boomerang to spin him back on track. To other, more traditional counselors, his lapse is simply the final warning sign of an inevitable, complete relapse.

Abstinence from drug use has long been defined as the goal of rehab and the very measurement of its success. Addicts in recovery (and many counselors) view *any* drug use as no less than a complete failure of treatment—a view that may lead to despair. "If they believe they are hopeless or that they have failed totally because they have lapsed," says relapse prevention specialist Gorski, "they will give up and not continue in their efforts to recover."

Mike's fateful trip to his dealer, in relapse prevention terms, was the most drastic of warning signs, a screaming admonition that true relapse was banging at the door—and that treatment must be intensified before it is too late.

I meet Mike at the satellite apartment on Monday morning. He's pacing the tiny bedroom, speaking softly so that he can't be overheard even by his roommate Casey, who is booming salsa refrains from disco speakers in the living room.

"I'm going to milk this situation for what I can," says Mike within moments of my arrival. "That may sound kind of scandalous, but I got to think of myself now, not Walden. It can be a week or so before that urine test comes back, and I been doing some planning. Earliest they'll have the results is like the end of this week. Then I'm spotted, kicked out with nothing but the clothes on my back."

Mike sits on the edge of the bed, his 195 pounds barely creasing the military-tight sheets and cover. Whatever rebellion against Walden Mike is feeling this morning, he's made his bed as perfectly as if he were still at the mansion and Dolores was on her way to inspect the room.

"It's not like it's written in stone that they have to spot me," says Mike, "but in the seven months I've been at Walden, every single time somebody's used dope while in satellite or in the house, and not supported himself to staff, that's what's happened—whssh, out the door."

"And if you supported yourself to Sylvester right now, if you admitted what's been up instead of waiting for the urine test to trap you—"

Mike interrupts, shaking his head.

"Aww, man," he laughs, "think strategy! Let's say I do support myself this morning, tell 'em I shot up in the bathroom, used dope on Walden property. Odds are—sixty-forty at best—they ask for my key to the apartment and show me the front door. Bye-bye Mike. I've got six bucks in my pocket, so if I support myself now and they spot me, I am one messed-up guy back out on the streets."

Mike is up and pacing again. "So here's the scam."

The scam, as Mike describes it, is that he continues to act as if nothing were wrong. He can get away with that until his urine test comes back. In the interval, he'll tell Walden he's going to open a savings account, which he's supposed to do anyway as part of his reentry process into society. (Walden, of course, keeps the ATM card.) Once he's told them he has a savings account, Mike plans to take from his Walden balance the $1,200 earned from his job that they've been holding for him, saying he's putting it right into his new bank account. Then he walks out the door with the money in his pocket.

"So, you got it?" asks Mike grandly. "I could do as the rules say and support myself this morning, tell them I did a hit of dope. And they say, 'Aww, Mike, first you screwed up on

your ban with Lara, then you just squeaked past a House Meeting, and now you're shooting heroin? You're outta here, man!' So I'm wandering the streets, six bucks in my pocket, and it gets cold at night—and what do I do? I call Connie, who knows nothing about dope fiends even though she's been living with me for how many years now? So she lets me in, and I'm like right back in the same house I was in a year ago, same relationship, same everything! So that's like relapse triggers all around me, and I get into my woe-is-me stuff and—"

Mike sits on the bed and sticks his left arm straight out, his right thumb on the plunger of an imaginary syringe.

"I tell Connie I need to go out looking for a job," he says. "She fronts me some money, and *bam!* Right up my arm!"

Mike looks up suddenly. Casey has slipped into the room and is standing in front of him, his head bouncing to the salsa rhythm from the living room, oblivious to all else. He's holding a bright pink envelope out to Mike.

"Letter for you," says Casey, "smells nice," and he boogies back out to the living room. "Just what I need," mumbles Mike, shoving Connie's letter into his pocket, unopened.

"Here I am getting booted out of Walden," he says, "and there's Connie, right there for me. Same old same old, and I know where that leads—it's not like I wasn't listening in relapse prevention classes. My sobriety's not strong enough yet to be back in that apartment with Connie."

If Mike is a veteran scammer, Connie has been the soft touch every scammer dreams of snuggling up to. Naïve to drugs, in love with Mike, she had been living with him during his heroin addiction for two years before she'd realized that his excessive sleepiness and nodding off in mid-conversation were not merely fatigue from his work as a plumber. Then, when she finally caught on that he'd been shooting heroin every day, he told her he had just quit. After that, when she'd repeatedly found syringes and needles in his coat pockets, Mike would tell her they were from when he used to do drugs, swearing up and down he was still clean. Connie, soft, sweet, good-hearted, and lovingly naïve, believed him every time.

As much as Mike loves Connie, and she him, their relationship thus far has been that of scammer and scammed, dependent and codependent. Now, Mike wisely sees that returning to Connie during this time of crisis would be about as safe as sharing a hotel room with his dealer.

Mike stands, rubbing his hand anxiously underneath his sweaty T-shirt.

"Let's get out of here," he says, "it's too damn hot. I'm skipping the plumbing job today, told 'em my back was hurting too much. I got stuff to plan out."

We walk along Hayes Street to Alamo Square, two blocks west of Walden House, to the most famous picture postcard view of San Francisco. Alamo Square's grassy park hovers over a hill graced by a string of pastel-painted Victorian houses. Skyscrapers of the San Francisco skyline and the Bay hang in the background. On this hot, sky-blue August 3,

Mike and I dodge between buses pouring forth hordes of camera-toting tourists rushing into the park for a Kodak Moment. We find an empty bench.

"I have to keep only one thing in my head," says Mike. "Don't use dope. So what's my best chance? Support myself to Walden now and risk being out on the streets today, broke and desperate? Or play my cards tight with them and scam some money to set myself up in an apartment, keep up my job, go to Narcotics Anonymous meetings at night, use the recovery tools I've learned even though I'm out of Walden? Then, when I'm OK again, got things stabilized, I can get in touch with Connie."

Mike turns to me, his expression resolute and proud. "See, my whole world's like falling apart here, and I'm thinking ahead, right?"

"Stinking thinking," I say, mimicking Sylvester's tone of voice.

Mike stares at me, his eyes showing a moment's letdown in his blustery bravado. And within seconds he's sobbing, a howling cry of despair so intense that the camera-toting tourists turn suddenly from the magnificent San Francisco view and flee.

He slams his fist on his knee. "I can't believe how bad I fucked up," Mike wails through his tears. "Damn! I know what happened ain't nobody's fault but mine, and I'm eating myself up over it. All this planning I'm doing now? It's 'cause I'm scared out of my mind. I mean, it's like I'm afraid of myself. I really see it now, there's so much shit inside me from my past that I ain't worked out yet that I scare even me. So where do I go with that if they kick me out? How do I stay off the dope if I'm alone again?"

Mike looks up, his eyes wide, wet with tears.

"Fuuuck, maybe what they say is true, I'm already a junkie again, it's too late. But I did just one hit, that's all. And I can't be doing more dope, I know that. If I go on a real run of heroin this time, I won't come back, ever. I've seen it now—I *can* blow it, I *can* relapse, I *can* die. Damn! This is the time I need help more than ever, and this is when they're going to kick me out."

Mike wipes at his face with the back of his hand, as moist from sweat as his eyes are from tears.

"What really gets me is that if I get spotted, The Family's got rules about that. If any Brother, Sister, or staff ever sees me again they got to shun me, walk by like I don't exist. Even if I'm clean and doing OK! Those are my Brothers and Sisters, man"—Mike's voice breaks—"and I'm like this lump of shit out there. Hey, step around Mike, don't get your shoes dirty."

He stands now, rising to his full six-foot-two, still crying. A few tourists have returned, staring right past him at the view. Mike turns to me and says, "Maria, Cliff, Mike Wallace, my Little Brothers, the whole damn staff—walking right by me. Man, that'd really mess up my mind. I mean, I can't take it personal, they're following Walden rules. But that's fucked up, them trying to make me feel even more dirty than I already feel. What good does that do?"

In fact, Walden has no formal policy to kick clients out of the house if they use drugs while in the program. So it is possible, even likely, that Mike is creating a self-fulfilling prophecy. Believing so intensely that Walden will throw him out when they discover his lapse to drug use is causing him to act so deviously that he has virtually guaranteed they *will* put him out the door.

Though it is true that Walden does not formulaically kick out all clients who do drugs while in rehab, it is also true that when Family members are struggling in that nether-nether land between lapse and relapse, Walden throws up the most intense obstacles to keep them from continuing in the program—punishments, haircuts, the Chair, House Meetings, work contracts, and a heaping on of potentially intolerable shame.

In this sense Walden, the premier treatment agency, has found itself once again at odds both with San Francisco's new policy of Treatment on Demand for drug users and with our nation's growing emphasis on rehabilitating hard-core addicts. "The important thing is for relapse to be contained," writes Dr. Avram Goldstein in *Addiction: From Biology to Drug Policy.* "Training in how to handle relapses is, therefore, an important part of drug addiction treatment." In San Francisco, the Treatment on Demand Planning Council writes in its *First Steps Plan:* "Programs must make the extra effort to ensure individuals are given repeated opportunities to succeed."

It might be argued that Walden does provide such repeated opportunities to succeed; the mansion is full of Walden *retreads*—those who are in the program for second, third, or even fourth tries. But almost all who have returned to Walden have done so months or years after their initial failures. Those Brothers and Sisters who suffer a lapse while in the program, and nonetheless crave a repeated opportunity to succeed, must first climb a seemingly insurmountable wall of Walden obstacles.

So Mike, after his single trip to 16th and Mission, may indeed be creating the circumstances that will guarantee his forced exit from Walden. But he also may be justifiably planning and scamming to protect himself, to minimize, on his own, the damage. If Mike is to begin the climb back to sobriety, he'll need to encounter fewer obstacles, not more. At the moment of his lapse, torturing himself at the brink of a full-blown relapse, the prospect of further degradation at the hands of Walden does not encourage him to return.

"If I were honest with them at this very moment," explains Mike, "odds are I'd be out in the streets five minutes later with just the clothes on my back. Or they'd have me on the Chair, then curse me out even more than I'm cursing myself out right now. Better off being on my own again," he says, his eyes wide in fear.

Many addicts' habits of lying, scamming, and cheating are as intense as their addiction to drugs. But it is possible that the severity of Walden's response to Mike's lapse is partially responsible for his return to old, familiar behaviors. Mike lied when they tested his urine, and never did come forward to support himself. He's planning a scam to get his savings out of Walden by lying about opening a bank account. If the rules of relapse prevention really hold true—that one moral slip leads to another and then finally to all-out relapse—Mike is well on his way.

Yet even at this moment, if Mike were to own his own to Sylvester, admit his single lapse to drug use, spend time on the Chair, expose his deepest feelings at a House Meeting and act appropriately contrite, The Family would most certainly take him back in, do the best they could for him. Some Walden clients have been able to do all of that, and they've successfully converted their lapses into years of sobriety. Many others, less strong, have been lost to the streets.

"Shit, man, it's too late for me to get back into Walden's graces," says Mike, ducking past the tourists and their cameras at Alamo Square and heading back downhill to his satellite apartment. "Only way I could have got myself back into The Family was to like walk in there with that needle still in my arm, saying, 'Hey, I'm about to screw up, help me! Pull this thing out!' After that, man, it was just too late. But I've learned a lot in the past seven months in the program, so from here on in I've gotta make it on my own."

He's sweating, breathing heavily even on the downhill walk, panic seizing his breath more than the physical exertion. He turns to me, eyes wide.

"So I'll make up whatever story I can to stay in the satellite apartment a while longer and

get myself organized. And I call that my own rehab program? Lying like that? Fuuuck. If I had any guts I'd just go in and tell 'em what happened, ask for my money and say, 'Hey, thanks for the help, you guys, but I kind of messed up at 16th and Mission on Friday, and I know how you feel about that. So I gotta go now. But thanks, really, for all you've done. I'm all right, I'll be OK now.' Then I'd go out that front door with my head held high."

Mike unlocks the iron gate that will lead him into the hallway up to the satellite apartment.

"So why don't you do just that?" I ask.

" 'Cause I don't fucking believe it," he says. "If I believed I was really OK, if I wasn't so ashamed of myself and so fucking scared, I'd damn well go up there and tell 'em the truth about what I did."

He reaches out his hand to say good-bye.

"Now that makes sense, don't it. When we're feeling OK about ourselves, we can stay at Walden. When we're not, when we fuck up and need 'em the most, we're outta there."

I grasp his hand for an extra moment, then ask, "What if your scam works? What did you do the last time you were out on your own with twelve hundred dollars in your pocket?"

Mike looks down at the ground, then lets go of my hand and opens the gate.

"Same thing I did when I was out in the street with six dollars in my pocket. I found a way to shoot up. But hey, listen, I'm doing my best not to go back on the spoon, right? And with the twelve hundred I can get a cheap hotel room to stay in for a month or two. I can keep up my job, stay busy, keep my mind off that stuff that drives me nuts. It ain't having twelve hundred dollars or six dollars that decides whether I do dope—it's me who's responsible, not the money."

Mike jogs up the ratty carpet to open the door of the first-floor apartment, then turns and says, "I got it under control, man. Really. Hey, come meet me at my job at the house on Shotwell on Wednesday, during lunch break. I'll catch you up on how things are going."

Wednesday morning, 6:30, I call Mike before he'll be leaving for work, to see what time to meet him. Casey answers the phone.

"Mike ain't here," he mumbles, and hangs up before I can get the next question out.

11:00 A.M., I knock on the back door at the house Mike's been renovating at Shotwell, where a Latino family has continued to live during the construction—parents, grandparents, babies, and all. The grandmother answers.

"That plumber?" she asks angrily. "He turned off our water to fix the pipes, then he doesn't show up today to turn it back on like he said he would. We have no water!"

"Sorry. If I find him I'll let him know," I reply, puzzled. Mike had told me how much being around this family and their babies has made him feel connected to the world outside of Walden again. Proud to be fixing up their house, he's been repairing even more than the landlord has paid him for. Now, mid-job, he's gone.

Worried, I head for my car to drive over to Walden, planning my own scam to find out if Mike has been spotted and is back on the streets. I could ask Sylvester directly, but if Walden hasn't yet found out about Mike's hit of dope on Friday I'd just be arousing the counselor's suspicions that something was up. Sylvester would see through me in seconds, and the game would be over for Mike.

I walk through the front doors of Walden and sign in at the front desk. The Sister in charge of the day's sign-in and sign-out log smiles and says, "Hey, how you doing? Good to see you," with typical Walden grace.

"I may have screwed up," I tell her, blushing my way through the scam. "I had an appointment with Mike, but can't remember whether I was supposed to meet him here at Walden, or at his job. You seen him?"

"Haven't seen Mike this morning," she says, poring over the sign-in sheet to see if his name is there, still smiling, not a hint of anything unusual in her manner.

I sign in, writing "Sylvester" in the "Person You Are Visiting" column. Then I stroll down The Boulevard, glancing quickly to my left at the clients' names chalked on the blackboard under the bold heading *Splitees,* and then under *Spotted. Mike P* is not on either list. I sigh in relief that he hasn't yet been caught in his lies and thrown out, certain that if he had been spotted he'd be out in the city, somewhere, already shooting up.

Before Sylvester might see me on The Boulevard, I saunter back up the hallway to the front door, sign out, walk past the engraved wooden placard advising that *Today Is the First Day of the Rest of Your Life,* and out into the street in front of the mansion.

"Stinking thinking," I chastise myself for my behavior, wondering where to go next in my search for Mike.

Darrell, having graduated months before from Acceptance Place, has found housing at the Salvation Army's Bridgeway apartments. Clean and sober, he's still working at the chic cafe on the first floor of the Nordstrom shopping center. In the evenings, he goes to business school, working with spreadsheets and scoring A's in Business Dynamics classes. After twenty years of doing alcohol and drugs he's now one month shy of the first anniversary of his sobriety.

Darrell, however, does not find this reassuring. Once before, in his twenties, he had gone for two solid years without drugs or alcohol. But right before his second "birthday" he'd started an explosive, lingering relapse.

I catch up with him in the crowd of downtown shoppers at the end of his shift at the cafe. There are still a few hours before he starts evening classes.

"You've just been recruited as my guide to the San Francisco street drug scene," I tell Darrell after an update about Mike. "We're on a search and rescue mission."

"To rescue him from what?" he asks. "Walden, or relapse?"

"Maybe both," I say as he gets into the car. We drive away from the bustling downtown shopping district toward the heroin market at 16th and Mission.

Before I first met Darrell at Target Cities he had blown out of Walden after five months in the program, drawn back to the streets by an offer of free beer and cocaine. Of course, relapse prevention theory would say that Darrell had relapsed long before that day.

"What kept you from going back to Walden after you relapsed?" I ask, driving past 16th and Mission, scanning the sidewalk for Mike.

"I was too ashamed to show my face at the house again," says Darrell. "I had every intention of returning, but I just couldn't go back to the Chair and a House Meeting and get humiliated back to sobriety."

"You think that's what's going on for Mike?"

"I think Mike's out here doing dope," says Darrell dismissively. He waves his hand at the crowd in the street around the BART station at 16th and Mission, most of whom are not there to catch the train.

"Mike may have felt shame for maybe a day or two after he did his first hit on Friday," says Darrell. "But if he's out here on drugs now, the only thing he's feeling is high. And all he's thinking about is how to score his next fix."

I park the car and we get out to wander the streets and alleyways of San Francisco's heroin central.

"Couldn't it be," I ask Darrell, "that Mike's first lapse scared him so much he's out looking for an apartment, maybe a new job, so that he'll be OK when he gets kicked out of Walden?"

Darrell shakes his head, pointing at the droopy-eyed addicts and hyped-up dealers all around us. I nearly trip on a sleeping body stretched out perpendicular to a storefront doorway on 16th. Darrel, barely noticing, steps over the man.

"Once you've had a taste of being high again, like Mike's had," he says, "there are triggers everywhere you turn. I mean, today at the cafe there was this old song on the radio, and suddenly I'm thinking of a cold beer and a hot hunk of a guy and some dope. So I get into that memory and I'm not some shy and lonely little gay kid afraid of his own shadow. One drink, and I am Mr. Cool!"

Darrell turns and looks back at the man we had just stepped over. "But I've also been down there," he says softly. "So I'm not going back."

We peer down the alleyway at Capp Street. It's crowded with streetwalkers, pimps, and heroin dealers. But no Mike.

"Mike's had a taste of drugs again," says Darrell, scanning the street. "And that's the only way he's ever known to turn off those thoughts that drive him nuts. The reason he came out here on Friday and copped some heroin was because something was really hurting him inside. And whatever that was on Friday, it's not gone by Wednesday. So take my word for it, he's scoring dope today, not apartment hunting."

We head uphill to Dolores Park, three blocks west. There's a public bathroom in the center of the park where junkies get water to mix with their heroin and shoot up. Scattered about the grassy hill are men and women of all ages, mostly dozing in the sun, others chatting with each other. We walk slowly across the park and glance into the bathroom. The legs stretching out from under the toilet-stall doors are all too short to be his. No Mike.

We walk back to the car; it's time for Darrell to get to school.

"I get this crazy nostalgia about my dope and drinking days," he says, staring out the window as the Mission district rolls by. "I was loose, comfortable, at ease with myself and with other people, and with my sexuality. I don't have that now that I'm sober, don't think I ever will. I'm an alcoholic, and an alcoholic doesn't think he'll *ever* feel well without alcohol. It sounds dumb, I know. I mean, look at what we saw today. But in many ways, I really miss being high."

We're at First Street, by the towering office building where Darrell takes his business classes. "Mike started with one little screwup," he says, gathering his books together. "That Lara Webb thing. And that made him feel real bad, especially with the way Walden reacts. So he gets to thinking he'll never feel good again, and he romanticizes those times when he did drugs. And then he just wants that one hit, just one. So there he is, in full relapse. I don't believe in this *It's just a lapse* stuff. I mean, you feel bad, you use dope, and it's not like in a couple of days you're going to straighten out the bad stuff you were feeling and not want the dope again."

He opens the car door and swings from his seat out to the sidewalk, then walks around to my rolled-down window, traffic whizzing around him, the evening breeze feathering his thick black hair.

"Mike's still hearing the dope in his head," says Darrell. " '*This way out, Mike, you'll feel much better.*' When he comes down from each high he'll be desperate for any way to *stop* shooting up. But Walden won't give him another chance without humiliating him first."

Darrell taps on the door and dodges oncoming cars as he crosses the street.

My next stop is the 18th Street onramp to highway 280, at the east end of the city. Or actually, *under* the freeway onramp. While Darrell is streetwise and knows most of San Francisco's drug hangouts, Darlene holds a doctorate in the drug scene. Even though her hyperactive methamphetamine crowd frowns on the seemingly useless addictions of the nodding-out heroin addicts, the meth freaks and the heroin junkies each know where the others tend to congregate—if for no other reason than to avoid each other.

Darlene's reaction to hearing about Mike and Walden is, not surprisingly, different from Darrell's.

"Go, Mike!" shouts Darlene when I tell her the news. She's lived outdoors for sixteen years, following no one's rules but her own. "So he finally got tired of being told when to wipe his ass," Darlene says, laughing. "Good for him! But damn, did he have to shoot heroin just to get out of Walden?"

Darlene ducks under the freeway ramp, closes the flap of her improvised tent, then jumps into the car.

"Mike's going to use dope or not use dope whether he's in Walden or he's out of Walden," she says, directing me down a dirt road under the freeway toward the CALTRANS railroad tracks. "So he might just as well be out of Walden," she concludes. "We gotta find him, though. If he's in the streets, I bet he doesn't even know where to find a shower or food. The guy's going to die out here with no one to tell him what to do."

Darlene squeaks out her high-pitched laugh. "If we can find Mike," she says, "I can at least help him stay alive on the streets, whether he's doing dope or not."

Then she gets serious, studying the scenes passing by the window.

"He *has* to say clean," Darlene murmurs under her breath, then turns to me. "He's been clean for what, eight, nine months? I can't even make it like eight or nine days most times."

She frowns, trying to puzzle it out. "I guess some people go right back to where they were, and you never *can* figure out why," she says quietly.

Then she cries out for me to drive straight across the railroad tracks, to a homeless encampment colonized by heroin addicts. She jumps out and asks around. No Mike. We continue our fruitless search, from homeless encampments to the parks and public bathrooms, and then to the beach and seawall at the west end of town. At dark, we give up.

It's too big a city, I think, heading home. I had even driven past Connie's house, but seeing that the lights were off and knowing she might not even be aware that Mike had disappeared, I had left without knocking on the door.

I'd looked everywhere, it seemed. But in my own frenzied thinking about the supposed depths of Mike's relapse I had missed one place: Walden's central intake center, where Mike had first interviewed to get into the program ten months before. It's in the Mission district, far from the Hayes Street mansion and The Family.

And that's where he had gone.

Hansel Cancel had been a counselor working with Mike and The Family at the mansion on Hayes Street, but then had transferred to Multi Services, Walden's office building in the Mission district. He hadn't seen Mike for two months when, on August 5, the receptionist rang Hansel's line to say that someone calling himself "Mike P" had come to see him.

It must be over a hundred degrees in the upper loft of the three floors of offices at Walden's Multi when I find Hansel the next day, but he seems not to notice the heat. His straight black hair extends in a tight braid halfway down his back. Below his bushy mustache is a nearly constant, gentle smile that crinkles his face up to his soft brown eyes in a gesture of concern and caring.

"Mike *was* here yesterday," he responds to my initial inquiry, offering me a seat near his desk. "He walked in, just like that, said he wanted to talk to me, to support himself, have an opportunity to make things right. Said he'd been out doing dope and hadn't told anybody at the house. Poor guy, he looked like he'd just come off a three-, four-day binge—scruffy, pale, sweaty."

Hansel had asked Mike why he'd come to him at Multi instead of to one of the counselors at the house.

"They ain't going to listen," Mike had replied. "They'll just jump all over me."

"OK, I'll listen," said Hansel. And he did, as Mike told him how he didn't mean to do dope, but one thing had just led to another; that if only he could have seen his daughters again he would have done OK; how he knows now that he needs people around him, positive people, people with some recovery behind them; how he has to raise his hand at the house, ask for help, open himself up.

Hansel had listened quietly, then asked a few questions, "General stuff, just to get a sense of how far this has gone."

How much heroin had Mike been using?

"Quarter of a bag, just once, still have the rest, haven't used it."

Where had he been using?

"Out in the park."

How much money had he taken from his account at Walden?

"Four hundred dollars."

Was he keeping any drug paraphernalia around, needles, syringes, so he could keep using?

"Nah, man, I'm done with that."

Hansel had nodded slowly, then asked Mike to have a seat downstairs, he'd be back with him in a minute.

It had taken only one phone call to Walden, and then a brief wait while they checked, for Hansel to find out that Mike still had a syringe and needle hidden behind a picture by his bed at satellite, that there wasn't any still-three-quarters-full balloon of heroin, and that Mike had removed six hundred dollars from his Walden account, not four hundred.

Hansel called Mike back into the office, asked him to sit down.

"When you were at Walden, you kind of lied to them, right?" asked Hansel.

"Yeah, right, right," said Mike. "That's what I came here to you for, to support myself, you know, make amends."

"And have you been lying to me also, right here in this office?" asked Hansel.

"Nah, man, what I'm telling now is the truth, honest-to-God truth."

Hansel held out his hand, palm up, and Mike quickly slapped his own palm against it, a high five.

"No, Mike," said Hansel, his arm still outstretched. "Put your apartment keys in my hand. You're spotted. Out the door."

"What the fuck? I came here ready to go back in, man, to support myself, do what I needed to do. I just poured my guts out to you!"

"You came here to keep scamming us, Mike," said Hansel softly. "So you go right back out there, get yourself cleaned up, stay off the dope. Then when you're clean and sober for a while, come back and we can talk, OK? You're spotted, man, out of here. Don't make it any harder on yourself."

Mike threw down the apartment keys and turned and ran, down the stairs and into the street below—the corner of 15th and Mission.

Allowing Mike back into the mansion with his Brothers and Sisters who are struggling to maintain their recovery would indeed have been a disastrous decision. Continuing to lie and use dope, Mike might have nodded out in a caseload meeting, stumbled along The Boulevard, shot up in the bathroom. Being around the house in that condition, he might have triggered who knows how many addicts in recovery to have intense flashbacks to their own dope days.

"We cannot have people in this house who are using drugs," Sylvester had told his caseload months before. "It's a clean and sober facility; if you are high you are jeopardizing the sobriety of every client in this house. And you put the whole program at risk because we're funded from like thirty different sources and if people are high or shooting dope in here—" He lets out a booming laugh. "Oh, no! *Bam!* Funds all dried up, ain't nobody gets treatment. So if we find you using dope, or you are high in this house, you are spotted, out that front door, no questions asked. We don't need drug orgies in this house; plenty places outside for that."

Hansel had kindly taken Mike into his office, listened carefully to his story, and then checked out its validity. When he'd learned that Mike was still lying and using, he had appropriately followed the rules and spotted him, protecting over one hundred addicts who were succeeding in their sobriety from one addict clearly out of control with his.

There *are* treatment centers designed for those very addicts. Detoxification programs are set up to help actively using addicts get off the streets and, temporarily, off drugs. And detox provides medical and social services during those days it takes to get sober and withdraw from heroin, cocaine, speed, or alcohol.

By no means is drug detox to be confused with drug rehabilitation, however; detox is no more than a place for addicts to stay alive and relatively safe during that initial dangerous and painful period of getting off drugs. Maintaining sobriety is an entirely different issue. Addicts may detox thousands of times and not gain an inch of rehab and recovery. Yet without that initial detoxification from the chemical influence of the drugs, true recovery cannot even begin.

Walden's mansion is not a detox center. Clients enter rehab programs like Walden House clean and sober, ready to work on rehabilitating their lives from the effects of their drug use. But many Brothers and Sisters working intensely on their long-term sobriety, like Mike, still head back to drugs.

"There's not a lot I can do for a person at Mike's point in the game," Sylvester tells me after I leave Hansel's office and go back to the mansion to talk with him, still not knowing where Mike is. "You see," says Sylvester, "what Mike needs now is detox and crisis intervention, real front-line trench work like what those street outreach folks do to keep addicts alive while they're using. Mike's back to the basics now—don't get yourself AIDS, don't overdose, don't get no abscesses from shooting up, remember to eat, don't get yourself thrown in jail. So he needs counselors who deal with people that are still using, and that's not me and that is not Walden House."

That all sounds fair and good. But when Walden counselors spot clients who are using drugs, they show them the door without referral to a detox center or crisis intervention counselor; without offering help or references to find a place to stay; without allowing them to gather their clothes, call friends or family; without starting them off with a box lunch, a bus token, or a referral to a shelter for that first night on their own, without any referral to a facility willing to work with them while actively using drugs, to help them survive their relapse and get clean again. Brothers or Sisters who are spotted from Walden go out with the clothes on their backs. And that is all.

Walden is a nationally recognized, respected, and often emulated drug rehab program. But when a Therapeutic Community like Walden wipes its hands of a client who has lapsed or relapsed, it's as if detox and every other form of drug treatment do not exist. And Walden forbids other Family members from talking to their relapsed Brothers or Sisters, prohibiting them even from offering advice about detox programs where they themselves had cleaned up and then headed back to rehab—as retreads, ready for another shot at it.

It's not as if the dilemma of what to do with Mike is unique, or even unusual.

"The norm is relapse," Dr. Alan Leshner, director of the National Institutes of Drug Abuse, told a gathering of addiction scientists and rehab counselors in San Francisco. "Very few people have one treatment episode and never relapse. That's a sad fact, but it is a fact. And so the norm is that people will go through treatment, they'll do pretty well, ultimately they'll relapse, they'll go through treatment again—but the interval between relapses will become longer and longer."

"For most folks," Sylvester told his caseload at Walden, "it takes more than one or two relapses before you get recovery down. So relapse can be an important part of your recovery—learning what your triggers are, why you went out, what led you back to drugs. Hell, I like to get retreads into my caseload, because they understand relapse firsthand. So relapse can be a learning experience—if you survive it."

A Walden client has few places to go when he or she is spotted: to a rarely willing family who might take them back in, to the streets, to detox, or to a harm reduction rehab program that will work with a still-using addict. Detox and harm reduction programs offer some hope of halting the relapse and helping the client back to sobriety. The streets provide the least chance that an addict will recover from the relapse—or live through it—and arrive at rehab again.

Yet when an addict at Walden is spotted for using drugs, the counselors take only one action: they open the door. That is therapeutic insanity. It is a policy that begs disaster and risks people's lives.

Five days after Hansel spotted him, Mike calls me at home.

"Aww, man, I got to talk to you face-to-face, not on the phone," he says. "Meet me at Dolores Park, noon, OK? Hey, can you buy me lunch, some cigarettes?"

As I pull up to the curb at the edge of Dolores Park, where Darrell and I, days before, had searched the public bathroom, I spot a tall figure in silhouette at the top of the hill and recognize Mike's shape, but not his walk. His face is turned down, like some professor on a university campus lost in deep thought. His head is bobbing back and forth, swaying with the rhythm of his arms as he walks uphill, his torso shifting to the left and right with each step in an unmistakable dope-fiend swagger.

I walk rapidly uphill, watching Mike as he reaches the shade of a tree, throws off his shirt and shoes, and collapses by its side. He's wearing black chinos heavily stained with mud and grass. He's somehow found himself a spiffy pair of black-leather business shoes, size twelve, now tossed to the dirt by his side. It's only about seventy degrees outside at midday, but Mike is drenched in sweat from his forehead to his bare chest.

He leans on his elbow and opens a tattered paperback book he's carrying, carefully studying the page. When the darkness of my shadow comes over him from behind he slams the book closed and jumps up.

"What the fuck?" He's stunned at first, then laughing. "Sneaking up on me like some cop! Scared the shit out of me."

"Yeah, I was going to bust you for reading a romance novel in the park, chest bared and all that. Feeling a little paranoid?"

Mike nods his head, looking around to be sure there's no one else nearby. Then he holds the book out—*Necessary Losses* by Judith Viorst. It's got an odd bulge in it, and when Mike flips through the pages a syringe and small packet of heroin and cocaine powder fall into his hand.

"I didn't think you'd come so early," he says. "I was just about to fix, so I'd be OK when you got here, not so sweaty and jumpy. I haven't done no dope since like five in the morning so I've got this little withdrawal thing going on, you know?"

Mike has a slight lisp to his speech and I notice the gap where his two lower front teeth are missing. I've forgotten about that hole in his smile; it had disappeared after Walden had sent him to a dentist to have a removable plate put in. Now, from his chapped, tobacco-stained lips, clammy skin, and jittery movements to his awkwardly altered gap-toothed smile, Mike looks exactly like the heavily addicted and very desperate man I'd first met in the sweltering room during Marillac's group at Target Cities nearly a year before. In the five days since he's been spotted, nine months of rehab seem magically to have disappeared.

Mike is constantly looking over my shoulder as he starts rattling incoherently through his story. He has brief moments of lucidity scattered among rapid-fire, paranoid descriptions. His hyper speech is interrupted only by his drawn-out *fuuuck* as a descriptive modifier, about three times in every sentence. If I listen carefully, I can make out a clear thought now and then; and a remarkable amount of pain.

"Aww, man"—he stops the flow, staring at me—"I ain't making no sense like this, I'm like cramping and withdrawing and my mind ain't going nowhere. I got to do this, OK?"

He sits down at the top of the hill in clear view of the entire park, pulls his Zippo out of his pocket, and begins pouring powder from the tiny balloon of heroin and cocaine into a thin, polished metal ashtray.

"Right here?" I ask, looking around at picnickers and kids playing downhill from us on the grassy slopes of the park.

"Best place in the world, man," Mike replies as the white powder begins to bubble up brown in the ashtray over the flame of his Zippo.

"If there's a cop around, I got the high ground," says Mike. "So I'll see him coming way before he spots me."

Mike puts on his shoes and shirt, thinking he'll look like the average Joe in the park should one of the police who circle every fifteen minutes or so on bicycles spot him.

Then he drops a small piece of cotton from a cigarette filter into the ashtray of bubbling brown liquid and sucks the fluid through the cotton and into his syringe. He takes a final look downhill, scanning the park, and within seconds has impaled a vein, seen the flash of blood, pumped the heroin and cocaine speedball into his arm, and tucked the empty balloon and syringe back into *Necessary Losses*. He closes the book, stretches flat on his back so his face extends past the shade of the tree and into the sun, and closes his eyes.

For the first time, I can see the full title of the book. *Necessary Losses: The Loves, Illusions, Dependencies and Impossible Expectations That All of Us Have to Give Up in Order to Grow.* Mike may have lost the teeth that Walden had provided, but he's managed to keep some of its library with him. I open the paperback to where the syringe marks his page, the middle of Chapter Ten: "Childhood's End."

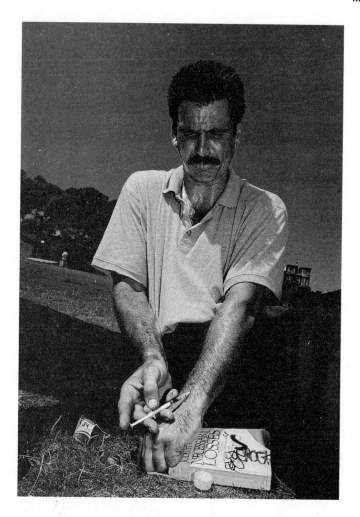

"Look around you and count the faces," Sylvester had instructed as Mike had gathered with his caseload early during his stay at Walden. "When you reach ten, pick one of you, because only one in ten will stay clean."

It's a ratio every addict and counselor seems to know, yet none can say what it's based on. "It comes from facts," insists Sylvester.

Dolores, the house director, is only slightly less certain. "I think they just picked one in ten," she says. "But that is, in fact, what it is!"

Yet Therapeutic Communities often boast of another fact: that three of every four of their *graduates* stay clean and sober. "In residential Therapeutic Communities," writes rehab researcher Dr. George De Leon, "success rates (no illicit drugs and no crime) for clients who complete two years of treatment are seventy-five percent."

Dr. De Leon also notes, "Dropout is the rule. Most substance abusers do not complete the planned duration of treatment." His research has shown that "the ten-month retention rates [in programs] are ten to fifteen percent"—bringing us back to Dolores's and Sylvester's "one in ten."

If you follow a group of one hundred addicts from the day they enter a Therapeutic Community, only ten to fifteen will complete the program and, of those, seven to ten will maintain long-term sobriety.

From these studies another research finding of major significance to the entire field of drug rehabilitation emerges: *The singular and most crucial determinant as to whether addicts entering rehab will eventually maintain sobriety is how long they are retained in the rehab programs.*

"The longer an individual stays in the Therapeutic Community," concluded the National Institutes of Health after reviewing the research, "the greater the likelihood that elimination or substantial reduction of drug-related behaviors will be achieved and sustained."

The message, then, to addicts trying to maintain sobriety, and to the programs charged with helping them to do so, is straightforward: Stick it out with each other. If you make it together for two years, according to De Leon's statistics, you'll achieve a 75 percent chance of continued sobriety. Work together for one year, and 50 percent will maintain sobriety after they leave rehab. But if a client splits the program—*or if the program spots the client*—before that one year is up, the rate of continued sobriety falls drastically.

It has always been obvious that addicts who want to remain clean and sober should not split their programs. But it should now be equally obvious that rehab programs should not be kicking addicts out so readily.

For those addicts in recovery who have relapsed to active drug use—who should and must be removed from physical proximity to The Family—every effort should be made to provide them with detox and program services elsewhere to help control the relapse, and aid their return to The Family.

"You have to be literally implacable," Dr. Stephen Hyman of the National Institutes of Mental Health advises the rehab programs, citing the research evidence. "You must never give up with an addicted person. You have to come back at him again and again and again . . ."

Or, as one Therapeutic Community counselor in a relapse prevention seminar in San Francisco commented: "People are not born walking. We need to put a lot of pillows on the floor so that when they do fall, they're not going to get badly hurt. And then we help them get up and try again. When my clients relapse, I can't cut them off at the neck! I may be the only resource they have. I tell them, relapse is not a shame, relapse is not dying. We want you back in treatment, but in the meantime these are the places you can go for help."

The place where Mike went for help after he was spotted by Hansel was only one block from Walden's Multi offices at 15th and Mission. He was alone, cut off by Walden's rules from even speaking to anyone from The Family. But at 16th and Mission, Mike found many old friends.

Forbidden from returning to Walden's satellite apartment even to pick up his clothes, Mike spent his first night out after nine months in Walden at a bar where he knew his cousin Jeff hung out, waiting to see if he might arrive and help him.

When Jeff didn't show, Mike went home with a man from the bar who wanted to pay him for sex. Mike planned to take the man's money and get out before the sex part, he says, but got too high and nodded off, not waking up until the man's hand was down his pants. He spent the rest of the week fighting off flashbacks of being raped when he was a child, and shooting up heroin and cocaine speedballs. Finally, after a few days, he called me to meet him in Dolores Park.

As the needle pierces a vein in Mike's arm and he pushes the plunger on the syringe, his frown of concentration eases to a hint of a smile. Then he folds the syringe into the paperback book, slowly murmurs, "Nice, nice," and leans back in the grass, his face in the sun. "Yeah, that guy got me some good stuff." His voice is barely a whisper as he nods off.

Ten minutes later his eyes slowly open.

"Hey," he calls out. "I guess I'm in full-blown relapse now, huh? The big R! You know what, man? I wish I wouldn't ever have been to Walden House. Because I know too much now. See, what am I doing getting fuckin' loaded in the park? I got to be a moron to be doing this, man, must be insane or something. Damn!"

Still lying on his back, Mike slams his hand on the ground. Silent tears streak the sweaty grime on his face and he closes his eyes tightly again.

Moments later he sits up, looks about him, then vigorously shakes his head and rubs his callused hands over his face and through his hair. He stares at the scattering of people flat out on the grass in the park, a few going in and out of the public rest room to get a spoonful of water.

"I'm starving, man," he says, suddenly standing. "Hey, buy me some lunch, some cigarettes?"

Without a moment's pause Mike is running downhill across the grass of Dolores Park, racing away.

After lunch in an outdoor cafe in the Mission district, Mike, now somber and quiet, tells me he has some business to attend to. But he'll phone soon, he adds, check in to let me know how he's doing. I watch him walk down Mission toward 16th, disappearing into the warm glow of the mid-August sun.

I don't hear from Mike again until January 5, 1999, although I search high and low, both alone and with Darlene or Darrell as guides. But on January 5, Mike calls to announce his recent marriage to Connie, and the upcoming birth of their child, due in four months.

I congratulate him, and we pass some time in small talk, catching up. Then I ask, "And the heroin?"

"Aww, man, I'm clean!" he says. "Had my last hit on New Year's Eve."

He waits out my silence.

"Yeah, I know, I know," Mike sighs, "that's less than a week ago. I wish I'd have stopped sooner, man, I swear I do. I kept trying, and I'd make it a couple of weeks clean, staying with Connie and back at plumbing work. But then I'd be back on the spoon again. Since I seen you last, I been trying to clean up on my own, you know, using the tools I learned at Walden. But it's been on and off, on and off, like a roller coaster—one day I'm getting high, the next I'm getting clean, next I'm looking for drugs, next I want to kill myself, and then the next I'm getting off the dope again. On the spoon, off the spoon. Been driving me crazy."

"Does Connie know?"

"Nah, damn, she'd kill me, with the baby coming and all? Hey, man, I didn't know where to go to for help, who to call, so I just kept trying on my own."

Mike is quiet for a moment.

"That's some lame excuse, huh, that I didn't have no help? I know that. It's my own responsibility, I ain't denying it. I'm off the needle again, though, got the baby to think about now. I can't be doing drugs no more. So I'm back in recovery, man, and that feels real good. But, damn, it's taken like a lifetime since they spotted me."

"The hardest thing to get down in relapse prevention," Hansel had told me the day after Mike had been spotted at Multi, "is to understand what your own particular triggers are. Being able to put yourself out there emotionally, to open up so wide that you can let out what you fear the most and get help with it. Mike just never got there."

Awaiting his new baby with Connie, Mike tells me that the responsibilities of fatherhood will finally motivate him to a sustained sobriety. "I've been able to stop for short times," he says, "now I just got to stop, period." But for a man still filled with tremendous self-contempt for the way he's treated the two daughters he already has, and a man whose memories of his own childhood still haunt his dreams, having a baby may be both a wondrous blessing for Mike and a worrisome trigger.

"After you get clean, that's when you've got to be careful," Hansel had said. "You don't know what's in store for you, don't know what's ahead 'cause you haven't been there without drugs before."

Sylvester would certainly agree. "I relapsed six times," he tells me after we talk about Mike's soon-to-be fatherhood, sitting in the counselors' office just off The Boulevard in the mansion. "I went through *seven* programs," says Sylvester. "And I'm a Vietnam vet and an ex-convict. I mean, I have been there! So I know what Mike's going through, I know the shame he feels. Guy hates himself. I know that 'cause I hated myself, too. But when I reached the end of my line, I saw it. And I didn't want to die. So I changed."

"Good evening, Family," the voice booms out from the mansion's loudspeakers. "All Family members are to report immediately to Kings Hall for a House Meeting. That word was *immediately*. Thank you, Family."

Sylvester sighs, rises from his chair in the counseling office, and heads toward the stairs to Kings Hall. Hand on the smoothly polished wood banister, he turns and quickly sums up.

"See, I honestly don't think Mike's ready yet," he says. "He's out there again, doing OK, so he's sure he's got it down this time. But look up there," Sylvester tilts his eyes toward the top of the stairs. "What do you think I'm going to find at that House Meeting? Another junkie who thought he could do it on his own, didn't raise his hand to get help. And that's about where I see Mike now. The guy's *got* to have issues popping off like firecrackers in his head, with that new baby coming and all. I mean, shame and guilt and remorse is an automatic part of being a dope fiend. And there's a whole lot of that stuff Mike still hasn't worked on. But do you see his hand up? You see him asking for help?"

Sylvester trots up the stairs, catching up to the Brothers and Sisters, their heads bowed in solemn procession as they head for the House Meeting.

"Know what I hope?" says Sylvester just before he goes through the door and into Kings Hall. "I hope I see Mike back here one day. I mean that. It's better than the alternatives."

The hope for Mike, then, is that if he does again relapse, he would ask for help instead of trying to stop on his own. And that there would be programs that would open their arms to him, rather than shut their doors.

But neither the programs nor Mike is to find out whether such an open-arms policy in response to his relapse might help him back to sobriety. When Mike does relapse again, just before his daughter Michaela is born, no doors close him out. Instead, a large set of doors locks him in, with a loud, metallic clang.

PART II: WE DEMAND YOUR TREATMENT

GLENDA AND CRYSTAL: YEAR ONE
MIKE, DARLENE, AND DARRELL: YEAR TWO

INTRODUCTION TO PART II: COERCED TREATMENT

When San Francisco's spanking-new Treatment on Demand system was inaugurated with great fanfare in the dawning days of 1997, the director of the federal Center for Substance Abuse Treatment, Dr. David Mactas, proclaimed, "San Francisco is right on target. . . . We're all invested in the success of this program." Since our national drug policy makers had also recently embarked on their own glacially slow but iceberg-powerful shift toward rehab, all eyes in Washington were turned westward to watch San Francisco. The *Christian Science Monitor* announced that "[San Francisco's] experiment may provide the nation's clearest test of whether expanded treatment can help eradicate the drug problem." San Francisco itself boasted that Treatment on Demand was such an "innovative development" that "the city that knows how" was once again bursting forth as "a leader in social and health policy, with many other cities, counties, states and federal agencies" waiting to follow suit. In a cautious challenge to San Francisco's characteristically proud swagger, the national newsletter for rehab policy decision makers, *Alcoholism and Drug Abuse Weekly,* ran the banner headline: TREATMENT ON DEMAND: CAN SAN FRANCISCO WALK THE WALK?

Two years later, a walk through the swarming drug scene shows a virtually unchanged vista. The city's bold resolution to provide rehab to "all individuals who are ready and willing to enter treatment," it appears, has played out to zero effect on the streets.

On the grassy slopes of Dolores Park, overlooking the white adobe walls of the city's historic Old Mission Dolores, the worn-out bodies of Mike and dozens of other addicts still dot the green hills, shooting heroin mixed with water from the public bathroom. It's a daily ceremony at the precise geographical site where, on June, 29, 1776, Fathers Francisco Palou and Benito Cambón dipped their hands into The Lake of Our Lady of Sorrows for water to celebrate mass, thereby marking the official birth date of the city of *San Francisco de Asís*. The expansive Mission Dolores, rising up from that first baptismal site, was anointed the symbol of the city's future.

Today, when the addicts in Dolores Park complete their own liquid ritual, they stand and gaze out over the Old Mission itself. Then many cross the street to the Golden Gate Lutheran Church where, at 12:15, they crowd into a Narcotics Anonymous meeting, followed by a hot, free lunch. A large segment of the participants then embark on a six-block walk to 16th and Mission—where the demand for drugs overwhelmingly eclipses any demand for treatment.

Twenty-two blocks due east from there, just short of the blue waters of the Bay, you can peek under the freeway onramps or tilt your gaze up to the "Opera Boxes" in the concrete walls that buttress Highway 280. There, you'll still find Darlene and hordes of other speed freaks peering out from their rough-hewn habitats. The best that San Francisco has been able to offer up in rehab hasn't even touched the city's methamphetamine encampments.

Across town in the Tenderloin district, where the crack smokers and alcoholics congregate, Darrell leaves his tiny room in Salvation Army housing each morning to head for work, and then to business school. Whispered voices touting, "Bennies, base, nose candy; you need it, I got it," still flutter relentlessly through the air as he walks by—a buzz identical to that when he'd first arrived at a homeless shelter in the Tenderloin a year before, struggling to get sober.

As 1999 dawned, the *San Francisco Chronicle* complained in an editorial that the city was spending $46 million a year on substance abuse treatment programs, and should be witnessing a more impressive result. "Even the humane and tolerant city of St. Francis," decried the *Chronicle*, "is losing patience with rowdy, out-of-control public drunks and dopers who trash the landscape and violate public decency. Taxpayers deserve a return on that investment . . ."

Yet no one had ever claimed, or realistically anticipated, that Treatment on Demand alone—treating addicts who *ask* for help—would wipe the streets of San Francisco clean of the detritus of addiction. Forty-five thousand citizens in the city are deemed by the Department of Public Health to have "major health, social, economic and legal problems" brought on by drug and alcohol use, to the extent that they are in need of treatment. Only 12,000 of them, the health department reports, receive "at least one treatment episode annually." The other 33,000 addicts and alcoholics in need of rehab are either on waiting lists (some 10,000), or don't want treatment at all. And even among the favored few who *have* received their "one treatment episode annually," the outcome has been some unknown mixture of Mike's disaster, Darrell's triumph, or Darlene's frantic but fruitless search for help.

The most sophisticated and advanced attempt ever in this country to reach addicts who *want* rehab is doing no more than aid those best-behaved and easiest to treat. The more intensely addicted, who show up for rehab but then relapse, are dumped in frustration back on the streets. And those even more direly addicted—who tend to do society the most damage—don't volunteer for treatment in the first place.

For that treatment-resistant group the city launched another approach, to *force* them into treatment. When I first heard of this absurdity I didn't believe it even warranted a closer look. Strong-arming unwilling addicts into rehab seemed not only unpalatable, but from what I had already seen in the programs with *motivated* addicts, logically unlikely to succeed.

But then I saw what happened to Glenda Janis, who, on June 12, 1998, was literally kidnapped from the streets by a city rehab worker and dragged into treatment. I had never known a more pitiful, disheveled, near-death, long-term street alcoholic than Glenda. After being carted off to a program, she came out three months later—cleaned up, sober, and healthy.

Glenda's seemingly miraculous return from the near-dead teased me just enough to look more deeply into this seemingly doomed policy. Given the limited successes of Treatment on Demand, I was now to witness "We Demand Your Treatment"—coerced rehab.

I headed to San Francisco's Drug Court to watch Judge Newton Lam propel arrested addicts to rehab and distribute them to programs (Walden House included) throughout the city. Those addicts bounced in and out of rehab, like the others I had known, but with one momentous difference: no matter where they were, the court stuck with them.

What I learned from Glenda—and then from Crystal Holmes and others sentenced to programs through Drug Court—convinced me that in coerced treatment rests the elusive secret to effective rehab. That secret, however, lies not only in coercing addicts into programs, but in coercing the programs to do rehab right.

With the power of the court looming over them, both the addicts *and* the programs behave better. And that can make rehab work.

11: THE DEATH PREVENTION TEAM

GLENDA JANIS

The winter wrath of El Niño relentlessly assaults the city of San Francisco nonstop through the spring of 1998. On May 13, a rare tornado touches down directly to the east; another appears immediately to the south; the city is drowning in rain, while snowstorms swirl about the state's ski resorts. Columnist Steve Rubenstein writes, "A lot of people are starting to take it personally, and the rest are still skiing."

In downtown's Hallidie Plaza, where San Francisco's street alcoholics congregate, the drenching downpours have left Glenda Janis's slow-healing leg wounds so constantly moist that the city's Death Prevention Team has come out to a bench in front of the Bank of America building to pick swarming maggots from the holes in her flesh.

"That day in May was when I first met Glenda," says Francine Buckner, a twenty-eight-year-old AmeriCorps worker who was out with the Death Prevention Team. "I was trying to distract Glenda from the pain while they worked on her wounds," she recalls, describing the anguished grimaces on the ancient, wizened face of the street alcoholic, who is thirty-seven.

"Glenda told me she's from the Pine Ridge Reservation in South Dakota," says Francine, "so I asked what she missed most about home. She said it was the Indian fry bread, and singing with her people. Then she started crying and, oh, man, I was totally overwhelmed. We started hugging each other, for a really long time. But we had to stop so they could work on her legs."

The flesh on Glenda's legs had been torn open a year earlier when, drunk at one o'clock in the morning, she had fallen trying to get into a flophouse hotel room, from the outside window, three stories high. After the paramedics scooped her up from the pavement, the hospital fastened her broken bones together with steel rods and reshaped her fractured face. Glenda made it out from physical therapy and back to her bench in Hallidie Plaza just in time for the winter rains of 1998—her twenty-first year on the streets.

Five years before that, her body withered from malnutrition, her skin yellow from liver failure, the barely conscious Indian woman had been admitted to the city's hospice for the dying—and became the only patient to walk out alive.

While it appears that Glenda, like some nine-lived cat, possesses an innate talent for fending off death, the city's street outreach Death Prevention Team nonetheless places her, in May of 1998, at the top of its list of street addicts and alcoholics most likely to die.

So when Francine, the following month, hears that a slot has opened up in a residential treatment program for Indians, she will kidnap Glenda and cart her off to rehab.

In the cramped office that serves as base camp for the city's six-member Death Prevention Team, Tony Patchell reads out loud to me from a poster-sized *List of the Deceased* taped on the wall above his desk. It's an inventory of thirty-six people he's had contact with in the past year who still had died on the streets. Tony carefully pronounces each name, and then, slowly, the cause of death. "Suicide. Homicide. Overdose. Vomiting blood. Burned to death. Hit by car. Fell and hit her head. Alcohol. Exposure and hypothermia. Dead for weeks, coroner couldn't tell the cause. Boyfriend killed her."

"That fucker," mumbles Tony, who had met the boyfriend in his street rounds. In the eight years that he's been a homeless outreach worker, 184 of the clients Tony has worked with have died. He hasn't tracked so compulsively the number he has saved.

On an early morning toward the end of May, Tony dons his wool beret, loads his backpack with antiseptic hand lotion, toothbrushes, personal hygiene kits, Vitamin C, and Power Bars, and heads from his office near City Hall to check on Glenda and dozens of others he and the Death Prevention Team have declared to be at risk of dying on the streets. He walks east on Eddy Street through the crack-dealing sectors of the seedy Tenderloin district, directly into Hallidie Plaza, downtown. Hallidie frames the ragged border between San Francisco's drug-infested Tenderloin and its money-laden downtown shopping mecca. The western half of the concrete, one-block square plaza is home to the most gaunt and cadaverous of the city's street alcoholics; the eastern portion plays gracious host to tourists who swarm around the Powell Street cable car turnabout, their shopping bags heavy from Nordstrom, just across the street.

Tony finds Glenda at her permanent spot, third bench along the walkway by the Bank of America's stately white-columned Hallidie Plaza branch.

"How're you doing, Half Pint?" he says, using her precisely appropriate street nickname, squatting on his haunches to be level with her. Glenda is stretched out on the bench, to all of her five-foot length.

"Not so good," she tells him, her voice raspy. "Going through d.t.'s."

"Oh, sweetie, that's really awful," says Tony, in the same breath noting the rank odor of urine emanating from her wet clothes. Glenda can barely walk with a walker, which Tony provides for her when he can get one. But walkers and wheelchairs are high-ticket sale items on the streets, so Glenda's walkers are stolen as quickly as Tony can replace them.

"Remember Bill?" he asks. "The guy who worked on your legs, right here at the bench? Here's a medical note from him, explaining why you missed your last welfare appointment, so they won't cut you off. And so you won't lose your room at the Mission Hotel."

Francine gets credit for the coup of finding Glenda a room at the Mission Hotel, paid for by her welfare checks. So on most evenings now, Glenda pulls herself along the wall of the Bank of America building, over to a bus stop, and makes it indoors. But she's lonely at the Mission Hotel, and every day she struggles back to her bench and her street buddies at Hallidie. Glenda is perpetually drunk, her clothes drenched with urine, her eyes increasingly yellow from liver failure, her leg wounds eternally infected (although finally cleaned of maggots). Before Francine found her a room at the Mission Hotel, Glenda had spent each night curled up on her bench under piles of newspaper. Without the Mission Hotel, says Tony, Glenda would not have survived the winter; with it, she barely has.

But after San Francisco's wintry weather storms right on through May, June glides in with shimmeringly intense sunlight. Glenda, drying out, appears briefly to come back to life.

As I ride the escalator from the underground Powell Street BART station to street level at Hallidie Plaza on a clear, warm day that first week of June, I hear an eerie three-part harmony of a Janis Joplin refrain, backed up by the distinct thrum of Indian drumming echoing across the plaza from a band of street musicians.

Busted flat in Baton Rouge, waiting for the train . . .

The lead vocal, raspy like Joplin herself, but holding the melody, is Glenda.

I step from the escalator and spot her elfin form amid the Indian drummers playing for the tourists at the cable car turnabout. Glenda's scarred, swollen face is turned to the sun, her eyes are closed, and her head bobs rhythmically to the drums as her soulful voice floats the Joplin tune crisply over the din of the crowd. The tough, weather-beaten leather skin of her extended hand faces palm upward, and her fingers close quickly when an occasional coin is deposited by a passing tourist. Except for that brief clenching of her hand, Glenda is lost, eyes closed and head held high, in a daydream of hot sun, harmonized singing, and rhythmic drumming.

The song ends with a pounding of the drums and Glenda opens her eyes, laughing when she sees me next to her.

"Hey, you're the guy who's always out here taking pictures with the outreach people," she cries out, her voice now strangely pathetic in its high-pitched hoarseness. Glenda doesn't miss a beat, turning to introduce me to the woman she'd been leaning against while singing.

"This is Cynthia," she says, "my Lakota buddy. We been together nine years. And we met right here by my bench!"

Glenda is giggling now, hugging her Lakota friend to her. She chats away while Cynthia lifts Glenda's tiny body into a shopping cart, wheeling Glenda from where the band is playing at the escalator over to her bench by the Bank of America building. There, Cynthia unceremoniously unloads her.

"I was sitting here singing up a storm nine years ago, just like today," Glenda tells me, settling in at her bench and pointing to Cynthia. "And I seen this Indian woman walk by. So I yelled out, 'Lakota winyan henica he?' Which means, 'Are you a Lakota woman?' Cynthia turned to me like she'd seen a ghost. Then she says, 'Han!' which means yes. And I said, 'Leci hiyu na Lakoliya wounglakin kte'—'Get on over here so we can talk Lakota to each other!' We've been best buddies ever since. And we never even knew each other on the reservation."

Cynthia, as large a woman as Glenda is small, excuses herself to head back toward the drumming, and Glenda turns to me with an impish smile. She unabashedly pulls a bottle of vodka from under her coat, taking a long swig.

"I'm not going to hide nothing," she says. "I've been drinking like this since I was sixteen, and I'll be drinking like this when I'm sixty. Tony and Francine, they're real nice and they want me to spend more time indoors, at that hotel place they got me. But I been at this bench since 1983, got all my friends out here. So I'm not going nowhere else now. Especially to some rehab program, like Francine wants me to."

Glenda holds her hands up high into the sun for me to see. The joints of her fingers are scarred and twisted from her injuries; her skin appears as much composed of layers of dirt as it does of flesh.

"Before my accident I was doing Indian beadwork," she says, "selling what I could on the street. It's hard to do that now, 'cause my hands got all busted up. So I need my friends out here. They sit with me, watch out for me. And they keep me company."

Glenda points to Dave Stewart, who has braced himself in his wheelchair against the wall of the Bank of America building for seven straight years. "They've tried to arrest me for holding up the bank," Dave jokes in his rare sober moments. But at this moment, he's screaming incoherently at two men who are dodging in and out, trying to grab at the bottle of vodka they know he keeps tucked under the foam seat of his wheelchair. Spittle flies from Dave's mouth as he shrieks at them, waving his arms wildly to fend off the men.

Glenda's gaze moves from Dave and she glances around at the bodies strewn about the west side of Hallidie Plaza, hordes of street denizens who've poured themselves into the open and sunny town square to dry out from the winter rains. They had passed around some brown-bagged bottles, and then passed out against the walls of the bank.

"Guess I got nobody to talk to today," says Glenda, turning her attention back to me, and unraveling the story of how she had come to San Francisco from the Pine Ridge Reservation in South Dakota. After hearing her out I realize why, in spite of the caring ministrations of Tony and Francine, it is impossible to think of Glenda ever leaving her bench.

The Indian reservation at Pine Ridge, South Dakota, can be described by a series of numbers: Unemployment runs at 85 percent and the average annual income of the residents sits at $3,400, distinguishing it as the poorest county in the entire United States. The 24,000 Sioux who live at Pine Ridge are forbidden by tribal police from buying liquor on the reservation, but two miles from the Pine Ridge border, in the town of Whiteclay, Nebraska, population twenty-two, four liquor stores sell some four million cans of beer annually. Interstate Highway 407 between Pine Ridge and Whiteclay is easy to find—it's littered with beer cans, broken liquor bottles, wrecked cars, and the memories of shattered lives.

The numbers that describe these tight connections between poverty, alcohol, and the Pine Ridge Indian Reservation today are derived from national trends that date back hundreds of years: On November 12, 1766, the British colonial trading house of Baynton, Wharton and Morgan, in Philadelphia, listed in its inventory 1,236 gallons of rum to trade with Indians at Fort Chartre. One partner, George Morgan, had already delivered 8,000 gallons of distilled spirits to use in bargaining with the Indians in Illinois country. In Detroit in 1767, the commissary of Indian affairs tracked 24,000 gallons of rum imported to trade for Indian fur pelts. In the southeast alone, during three months of 1776, Indians were sold 30,000 gallons of rum.

"The poor Indians," wrote Edmund Atkin, a superintendent for Indian affairs at the time, "are unable to resist the Bait; and when Drunk are easily cheated. After parting with the fruit of three or four Months Toil, they find themselves at home, without the means of buying the necessary Clothing for themselves or their Families." According to Peter C. Mancall, a historian at the University of Kansas, most of the liquor transported to the Colonies was paid for by the British Crown "to maintain or create alliances in the western-most regions of the empire." In the 1700s, notes Mancall, "the alcohol trade became perhaps the most insidious aspect of European colonialism in North America." Mancall concludes, "Wherever the liquor trade flourished, poverty seemingly followed in its wake."

In August of 1998, U.S. Housing Secretary Andrew Cuomo visited the Pine Ridge Reservation, announcing that it was "a metaphor for poverty." "We didn't get into this situation in a couple of weeks," noted Secretary Cuomo, "and we're not going to get out of it in a couple of weeks."

In San Francisco, on June 12 of that same year, Glenda Janis, a thirty-seven-year-old em-igrant from the Pine Ridge Indian Reservation who has been continuously drunk for twenty-one years, is coerced by Francine into a twelve-week rehab program—in the hope that when she emerges she will stop drinking.

"I remember every Christmas on the reservation until I was eight years old," Glenda tells me, sitting on her bench, her voice gritty and hoarse as she reaches for her lap where she's secured a brown-bagged bottle. Glenda carefully unscrews the lid and tilts the bottle up, her head raised to the hot sun illuminating the plaza.

"My dad burned cedar logs every Christmas," she says. "I can smell that cedar like it's in the air right now. We'd sing Christmas carols, and I was already the best singer from the powwows we had at the community house."

"*Feeling good was good enough for me,*" Glenda sings out suddenly, her croaky voice transformed magically again to a melodic tenor. She grins, holding her hand out to a pass-ing phalanx of tourists, who ignore her. Then she pulls the bottle to her lips again, and care-fully screws the top back on before she tucks it into her pants.

"I *love* to sing," she tells me. "I'd get together with my cousins and my sister on the reser-vation, and I'd put on these cat-eye glasses and I'd be jamming!"

Glenda holds her hand out a moment more, palm up to the passing tourists, then shrugs, chewing for a moment on her chapped and scarred lower lip before she goes on.

"When I was eight, my sister told my mom things about my dad that weren't true, like he tried to rape her. And that caused a riot in the family, everyone fighting. We were just chil-dren, so there wasn't much we could do but watch and be crying. Then my mom opened up her purse and took out two candy bars. She cut them in pieces and gave us each a little bit and wiped our tears. Then she left, and we didn't see her no more."

Glenda's father worked construction, and at first he tried to stay with his children. "He was the best daddy anybody could have," she says. "But when his drinking got too heavy he got mean, and beat and kicked us. So he went to live alone, turned us over to our aunt. And she gave all us five kids away to foster care, when I was twelve, just coming of age."

There's a flurry of activity alongside Glenda on the bench as two withered women, ciga-rettes dangling from their lips, join her and start unpacking makeup, hair brushes, and nail polish from a Nordstrom shopping bag.

"This is Debbie and Vicki," she introduces them. "I got lots of street buddies."

"You just go right on talking, honey," says Debbie, and she pulls a long, sharp pair of scissors from the Nordstrom bag, then stands on the bench, bracing one leg on the back to balance herself over Glenda's tiny body, scissors ready.

"You're kind of a mess, Half Pint," Debbie tells her, "so we brought some stuff to fix you up."

I watch the bizarre scene unfold as Glenda continues her story while Debbie and Vicki—"We went to cosmetics school before the booze got to us"—busy themselves with what may be the world's most challenging makeover.

"I was a pretty quiet kid in the foster homes on the reservation," says Glenda, nodding her head as Debbie gently combs through her deep black hair. "I didn't do much more singing after my daddy left, and I never did learn to really love anybody."

"I'm so sorry, honey," says Debbie as Glenda suddenly grimaces and pulls her head away. "It's just that we got to get the lice out before we can cut and feather your hair."

"I'm trying to tell my story!" croaks Glenda. "So try not to distract me. OK?"

Debbie reaches her thin arm out, placing her cigarette in Glenda's mouth so she can take a drag. "It's OK, baby," says the hairdresser, "we got most of the nits now, you just go right on talking while we work. " The tiny woman obligingly tilts her head back to the ministrations of Debbie and Vicki.

When Glenda was sixteen, her mother suddenly arrived at the reservation, eight years after she had left.

"All my brothers and sisters were scattered in different foster homes," says Glenda. "But I happened to be at my aunt's house that night, and I was laying on the floor reading the yellow pages of the phone book when the door opened. I looked up, and there's my mom! Then I looked away, pretending to keep reading. And she says, 'How're you doing, my little girl?' But I kept on reading."

Debbie backs away from the bench, inspecting Glenda's now neatly trimmed and feathered hair. She picks up her makeup kit, but then puts it back down.

"Honey, we can't do your makeup while you're crying," she tells Glenda. "We'll come back later, OK?" The Hallidie cosmeticians move on along the benches, to their next mission.

"My mom asked my aunt, 'Where are my children?' " continues Glenda, wiping at her eyes. "And Auntie was so ashamed to tell her she'd put us all in foster care. I was the only one nearby. Then my mom says to me, 'I'm moving to Denver. Will you come?' "

Glenda's hand brushes from her wet eyes to the new bangs dangling onto her forehead. "What did they do to me?" she rasps, laughing, running her fingers through her freshly fluffed hair.

"Hey, Debbie!" she calls over to the next bench and lofts her bottle to the air, offering up a toast.

"So that's almost the end of the story," Glenda tells me, taking another swig before recapping the bottle. "I said, 'Yeah, Mommy, I'll go with you.' So we went to Denver, and we fell in love with each other again."

The waiflike woman's scarred, dirt-encrusted cheeks crinkle upward in a smile, and a hoarse, charmingly childlike chortle flutters from her lips. "My mom was giggly," says

Glenda, "always laughing, visiting, talking with everybody who came by. I'm a lot like her, you know. We'd sing together, and she *loved* the blues. She didn't get violent when she drank, and that's like me, too. I just sit here, and drink and drink and drink."

"Why?" I ask.

Glenda stares, then her cheeks crinkle up again and her high-pitched laugh soars across Hallidie Plaza. "To get drunk. What else?"

Glenda's eyes glaze over and her voice goes flat as her story returns to Denver, and her mother.

"One day my mom says, 'Stay home with me today, Glenda. Keep me company. My stomach is hurting so bad I think I'm going to die.' My mom was all yellow from drinking too much, but I didn't think she was that sick. I said, 'Mommy, don't say that! You're forty-three, you're not going to die.' Then she says, 'Turn off the TV, I want to hear Dorothy Moore doing Misty Blue.' So we're humming along to the music together.

"Ohhhh baby I should forget you, Heaven knows I've tried . . .

"Then, all of a sudden, my mom jumps up and runs to the bathroom. I'm right behind her, and she slams the door and it hits me in the face. So I'm standing there crying, 'Mommy, you hurt me, you hurt me.' But she didn't say nothing, so I push open the door and I see blood all over the place, and my mom's on the floor in it."

When Glenda screamed, a neighbor ran in. She saw the scene in the bathroom and dialed the hospital.

"The ambulance got there, but my mom was unconscious," says Glenda, now hugging her arms to her chest, rocking back and forth on her bench. "They carried her out of the bathroom, but they wouldn't take me in the ambulance with her. So I ran all the way to the hospital, and that was a two-mile run. When I got there, my mom was dead. They say it was a stomach hemorrhage, from her drinking. I was sixteen, and it was just nine months after my mom came back to me."

Glenda hasn't noticed that Debbie has returned to the bench with her makeup kit, sitting silently by her side. As Glenda ends her story, the tall, thin woman stretches out an arm and encircles her, cradling the tiny, crying woman against her own gaunt torso.

"Aww, Half Pint," she hums like a lullaby, "why do you have to keep telling that story? It was such a long time ago, honey, such a long time."

The two women rock together on the bench, then Glenda lays her head in Debbie's lap. "You've got other memories besides that one," croons Debbie, "must be some good ones in there. Tell me some good memories."

Glenda does have other memories. Five years after her mother died, Glenda at twenty-one had her own daughter, the first of two taken away by child protective services because she was drinking so heavily she couldn't care for them. Glenda can recite every detail of the day in court when the social worker, admiring her three-month-old Dierdre, lifted the baby from Glenda's arms, and never gave her back. Then there are the years in the streets; and her crippling three-story fall, followed by the maggot-ridden infections of her legs. Those nightmarish memories, says Glenda, keep her drinking. And her drinking, says the street outreach Death Prevention Team, leads Glenda to repeated disasters, from which new nightmarish memories are made. Glenda has traveled from catastrophe, to drinking, to disaster—all merging into a single heartbreaking image within her, an image drowned in alcohol, without beginning, or end.

Near dusk in Hallidie Plaza, Larry Hamilton, a tall, soft-spoken Death Prevention worker whose tight cornrow braids poke out from under his black beret, finds Glenda at her bench, still cradled in Debbie's arms.

"Please, Half Pint," cajoles Larry, literally on his knees beside her. "We've got the van right here, let's take you on back to the Mission Hotel. Hot shower waiting, get you into some clean clothes."

Larry curves his neck to bring his face near Glenda's. Her yellow eyes stare blankly back at him.

"I'll take a bus to the hotel later," she says, and Larry leans in even closer to make out her words, now thoroughly slurred by drink.

"Hey!" shouts Debbie angrily, extricating herself from cushioning Glenda's head. "Listen to what the man says, Half Pint! You're not doing good. You need to get off the streets!"

"I'll go later," murmurs Glenda, struggling to push herself upright on the bench.

"Liar!" shouts Debbie, her eyes wide and glaring. "Tell him why you won't go! They won't give you no booze there, so you're going to stay out here all night and mooch off the rest of us. Tell the man the truth!"

Larry stands and turns to calm Debbie.

"I know the truth," he says softly.

Then he squats again to say good-bye to Glenda, his laminated Health Department ID card dangling like a cross on a gold chain from his neck. An official seal overlays his photo, and written in bold letters below: "Death Prevention."

"Let's pick her up and carry her to your van," Debbie tells Larry. "Haul her off to detox."

"I'm tempted," he replies, peering down at Glenda.

The street outreach worker silently scans the scene around him. Tourists and shoppers are out in droves, striding past the benches on their way back and forth from Nordstrom. Larry's gaze moves from Glenda, to the tourists, to the waiting health department van.

"It wouldn't be the first time I've done it," he tells Debbie with a sigh, and a sly smile. "But Glenda would kick up a hell of a fuss, and with all these people 'round here watching, I can't just be grabbing folks off the streets."

THE HALLIDIE MAKEOVER TEAM

The most liberal city in the country has become so fed up with the scourge of addiction that its major newspaper cries out in an editorial that the worst of the addicts and alcoholics should be given "a choice of jail or rehab." The editors of the *San Francisco Chronicle,* frustrated by the lack of results from voluntary programs supported by Treatment on Demand, argue that "forcing the worst cases into rehabilitation is a kindness that could help transform wasted lives while cleaning the streets."

But it is far from certain that dragging unwilling addicts and alcoholics into rehab can in any way turn their lives around.

"You can coerce people for a time, but it won't take long before coercion stops working if they themselves aren't ready to be off drugs," says Dr. Marsha Rosenbaum, a sociologist, director of the Lindesmith Center in San Francisco, and researcher for the National Institute on Drug Abuse. "I've done a lot of work in drug treatment," says Dr. Rosenbaum, "and what I've found is, in terms of getting off and staying off drugs—people have to be ready. That part is absolutely simple."

Dr. Rosenbaum's logic seems infallible, insisting that addicts who are not themselves motivated toward sobriety will continue to use drugs. Other researchers have concluded, however, that forced treatment not only works in overcoming addictions, but works as well as, or better than, voluntary treatment. "When you follow them up five years later, coerced clients, in every well-designed study, do better than voluntary clients," says Dr. M. Douglas Anglin, who directs UCLA's Drug Abuse Research Center. Yet Dr. Anglin agrees that "the role of internal motivation and treatment engagement must not be overlooked. . . . In the end, it is the client who decides upon the outcome."

Can the scientists have it both ways? Addicts must be internally motivated if they are to succeed at rehab, *and* unmotivated addicts coerced into rehab will succeed. The researchers claim to make sense of this seeming contradiction. Drug abusers who are not motivated to sober up, yet who are forced into rehab programs—soon become motivated. "You'll get a lot of complaining in the first thirty to sixty days," says Dr. Anglin of addicts dragged into treatment. "Then things will settle down, if the program is good."

John Erickson, assistant director of substance abuse programs for the California Department of Corrections, holds a similar point of view. "They may go in involuntarily," he says, "but, we see it all the time, as their participation goes on, their attitudes change."

The Department of Corrections is not the only powerful force dragging addicts to rehab. Wives, husbands, children, and other family members have propelled addicted loved ones to rehab with the ultimatum, "Get clean, or get out." Employers have shown addicts and alcoholics the door to rehab, as an alternative to an exit from their job. District attorneys have offered rehab deals in exchange for prosecutorial leniency. Judges have sentenced addicts to rehab, holding over them the threat of jail should they not stay clean and sober. Child abuse authorities have removed children from the homes of addicts, offering to return them only when the parents complete drug treatment. And San Francisco's kindly but streetwise Death Prevention Team has at times, in desperation, hauled unwilling addicts off the streets and into treatment.

The conspiracy had started months before the kidnapping.

"I thought Friendship House would be a good place for Glenda," says Francine, "because it's a Native American program, and because it's good. But there was this huge wait for beds, and she had to have an intake interview before they'd even put her on the waiting list. The chances of Glenda making it over there for an interview were like zero. So the whole thing seemed hopeless. If you're as severely addicted as Glenda, you can't meet the requirements for rehab."

Francine herself, now twenty-eight, had been homeless as a child with her family in Seattle, which she distinguishes from the times she was homeless after age fifteen, on her own. She finally wrestled some stability into her life, moved off the streets, trained as a health worker, managed to get AmeriCorps to pay her to do street outreach work, and then latched on to Tony and San Francisco's Death Prevention Team. Like Tony, Larry, and the other street workers, Francine has few qualms about stretching the rules.

"I borrowed a cell phone," she says, "and took it out to Hallidie Plaza, found Glenda, and dialed up the number for the intake worker at Friendship House. I persuaded him to do her interview right then and there. So here's Half Pint, drunk on her bench with all these tourists walking by, doing a program intake interview on a cell phone!"

By some miracle, and a lot of cajoling by Francine, the street conference call works. Glenda is placed on the Friendship House waiting list. And she promptly forgets she's ever done the interview.

A month later, on June 12, Francine gets word that a slot has opened up at Friendship

House. The Death Prevention Team van has already headed out for the day, so using her own money Francine flags down a cab and directs the driver to Hallidie Plaza—only to find that Glenda is not on her bench. It doesn't take long, though, to spot her on Eddy Street, dragging herself along a wall on the way to a liquor store. Glenda has fifty-two cents in her pocket, and she's begging passersby for spare change "for a sandwich."

"That cabdriver takes one look at Glenda," Francine recalls the scene, "and she's got this urine-soaked blanket wrapped around her tiny body, she smells horrible, and she just *won't* get into the cab. So the driver wants to split, Glenda is screaming at me to leave her alone, and I'm like, damn, I don't know how this is going to work! They'll only hold the bed for her at Friendship House for so long."

By this time, Glenda's yelling has attracted a crowd—including one of Glenda's trusted street friends. "Give me your change," he tells her, "I'll put in some of mine and we'll share a bottle."

Glenda calms down for a moment, hands the man her fifty-two cents, and he helps her sit on the edge of the seat of the cab, telling her he'll come back with the booze. As soon as she hits the seat, though, the man lifts her inside, slams the door closed and slaps the hood of the car, signaling the cabbie to take off.

Glenda, screaming in protest and banging on the window of the cab to get her fifty-two cents back, is on her way to rehab.

"I'm not ready to be sober," she yells at Francine. "I'm shaking so bad, you got to get me a drink! You let him steal my money—you owe me a beer!"

"You can ask the guys at Friendship House for a beer," says Francine to Glenda, later telling me, laughing: "I guess I'm sort of morally absolved of tricking her, because it was true. She *could* ask them at Friendship House for a beer."

Glenda's kidnapping was either the most egregious violation of her civil liberties, or the most clever intervention to save her life. "I wasn't about to let her die in the middle of Hallidie Plaza," says Francine. "It's all about pragmatism out there; you do what works, not what the rule books say."

Pragmatism is the code word for the Death Prevention Team. Tony Patchell hands each rookie street worker a list of rules he's written, gently titled, "Suggestions for More Effective Street Outreach."

Rule #1: When you go into a strange room & you're invited to sit down, always say Excuse me, I don't mean any disrespect, but do you mind if I check for needles?

And on down the list, a potpourri of folk wisdom that melds street pragmatism, professionalism, and self-protection into a compassion shaped by expediency.

Do not physically intervene into a lover's quarrel; together, they will kick the shit out of you.

If someone hugs you, or is clinging to you, take the opportunity to check them out for lice and scabies.

Make eye contact. If the person does not like eye contact, stop making it.

If it's wet, and if it's not yours, don't touch it.

Be prepared to meet people more intelligent & perceptive than you.

Don't feel bad if you get fooled.

Don't call the cops unless you absolutely have to; know when that is.

Finally, revealing Tony's leanings toward Buddhism:

Accept small victories. If you feel you must save the human race, do it one person at a time.

"Our program is designed to work with the folks other programs cannot or will not work with," says Tony. "We are the bottom line."

Tony, who prefers to call himself coordinator rather than boss of the Death Prevention Team, perfectly describes how he came to this line of work. "In a way, it's simple," he says. "There's a terrible amount of suffering; I'm involved in it. I don't have to look for connection, it slaps me in the face every minute."

San Francisco's Death Prevention Team was created when a newspaper died. Every year since 1985, reporters for a "street sheet" called the *Tenderloin Times* had marched to the coroner's office around Christmas to calculate, and publish, the number of homeless who had died that year. And every year, the numbers went up. In 1994 the *Tenderloin Times*, like the street denizens its reporters wrote about, went broke and met its demise.

The newspaper's annual death survey had been the city's only tabulation of deaths of the homeless. So when the street tabloid folded, San Francisco's health department took up the Christmas survey. It was so appalled by what it found (the average age of death on the streets was forty-one, with 44 percent succumbing to lethal drug combinations) that, just after Christmas of 1996, the health department created the Death Prevention Team. As a result, Tony, Larry, and their colleagues embarked on the business of saving lives—sometimes by unorthodox means.

Glenda's first days in rehab are as turbulent as her ride over in the cab. Immediately declared too physically ill for the program, the tiny woman is shipped straight off to the city's drug and alcohol detox unit. Workers there take one look at her, and without further ado call an ambulance to take her directly to the emergency room at San Francisco General

Hospital. From there, infected, jaundiced, disoriented, and nearly seizing from alcohol withdrawal, she is admitted to the ward. Stunned by her whirlwind tour of the city's health facilities, Glenda finally arrives at Friendship House three days after Francine had scooped her off the streets.

Two weeks later, Evelyn Wade, her counselor, lets me in to see her.

It takes me a moment to adjust to Evelyn, a fifty-eight-year-old Indian woman whose twenty-seven years as a drug and alcohol rehab counselor have added nothing but kindness to her soul. Her deep brown eyes sit in doelike contrast to the long, gray hair that cascades down her back. Her soft and remarkably expressive face is framed by dangling turquoise earrings. But it is Evelyn's manner of speaking that is most noticeable, especially when compared to the rapid-fire street talk of every drug counselor I had previously met. Evelyn listens intently, then pauses at length before uttering a reply. A characteristic mid-phrase *mmm-hmmm* rolls her every expression into a liltingly musical rhythm, followed by a pause as her brown eyes fix on yours to see if you've grasped her meaning.

"Glenda is here with her people again, *mmm-hmmm*," says Evelyn as we wait for the new Friendship House client to come from her room. The rehab counselor leans forward to see a photograph I had taken of Glenda, leaning on her walker a few weeks before in Hallidie Plaza, barely holding her balance.

"She'll seem much different than when you last saw her," Evelyn tells me. "Glenda walks with a wooden cane now, *mmm-hmmm*. Sometimes even without it."

At that moment, Glenda, grinning from ear to ear, strides down the hallway, cane dangling from her elbow. But when she reaches me and throws herself into a long hug, I see that the miracle is far from complete. Glenda, thirty-seven years old and standing next to her fifty-eight-year-old counselor, looks like the older of the two. While this is the first time I've seen her sober, not reeking of alcohol and urine, not stumbling when she walks, she is still a wizened ghost of a woman, with yellow eyes and leathery skin, her face and arms disfigured by scars from her multiple injuries and the surgical patching together of her broken parts. Glenda is far from the picture of health; but she's upright, and she's alive.

She escorts me to the front of Friendship House, to a long table in the dining room overlooking Julian Street, only three blocks up from 16th and Mission. The room is a narrow, wood-paneled alcove adjacent to the kitchen, and Glenda pulls up a chair by the front window while another woman, wearing an apron, sets a plate of Indian fry bread in front of us, next to a filled, plastic Honey Bear. From directly below the window comes a pounding, rhythmic noise and I glance out to see three tall Indian men in their twenties, bouncing a basketball on the sidewalk.

"I was sure shocked a couple of weeks ago to know I was on my way to getting sober," says Glenda, pouring honey on the fry bread and slowly, ecstatically munching while she talks. "I sure didn't wake up that morning thinking I'd be going to rehab," she laughs. "Once Francine got me into that cab, though, I knew I wasn't strong enough to get out; but

I didn't think I was strong enough to stop drinking either. I don't even remember those three days in the hospital, but then I got here and the first thing I noticed was that the food was so great! And the people are so loving and warm with me. And they're sober."

Glenda pushes a piece of fry bread my way, then looks wistfully out the window. "But mostly," she says softly, "I have Evelyn. Yeah, me and Evelyn talk real good to each other." I'm not surprised to hear Glenda follow her sentence by humming, slowly, *mmm-hmmm.*

"Evelyn tells me," she continues suddenly with a laugh, " 'Glenda, you're a strong, wise lady.' She says all *kinds* of things about me that make me feel really good. And I'm in the healing process, doing it the old Indian way. Praying, and smudging." She waves the twisted fingers of one hand near her face, showing me how the clients waft smoke from burning sage toward their faces in the healing rituals. "It's like going to church," she says, "only we do ours differently, like it's been done for centuries."

There's a shout of voices from just below the open window, and the pounding of the basketball on the sidewalk beats out a quick, staccato rhythm.

"Evelyn has me writing about that, too," says Glenda, leaning back from the window and opening a lined student notebook she'd been carrying, selecting an entry.

"My brother Glenn was the shortest on the reservation, but he was the best basketball player," she reads slowly, one finger tracing the words she's written in the journal Evelyn has asked her to keep. "Glenn was real small, but he ran real fast and he could score over and over. I would sit and watch while everybody cheered my little brother." Glenda's voice is still hoarse, but there's a floating lightness to it, the tone I had heard when she was singing in the streets.

"Glenn got a big old trophy for his basketball playing, with a red and white ribbon on it," she recites from the journal, and the rhythmic bouncing from the pavement below seems to play to the cadence of her reading.

"But my brother Glenn took a lot of pills one night," she reads on. "He went to sleep and never woke up. And my other brother, he was partying around with some friends on the reservation and got real drunk. He lay down on the ground, and he froze to death. So that leaves me just one brother. It makes me real sad."

Glenda holds her finger to mark the spot in her journal, sobbing quietly, until a cry from the street below draws her attention to the window.

"Hey, Glenda! Come to the park. We need a cheerleader."

She leans her head out. "I can't walk that far. Bring me that wheelchair."

Evelyn is suddenly at her side, hand perched on Glenda's shoulder.

"No more wheelchairs," she says. "You walked to the park with a cane yesterday, *mmm-hmmm.* Take your time, you'll get there again today."

At the sidelines of the basketball court at Mission High School, five blocks uphill from Friendship House, Glenda sits on a bench, catching her breath as she leans against her cane. On the court, young Indians from the rehab program, men and women together, pass the

ball and charge from basket to basket. The ends of their long, black braids are tied together to keep them from flying about. Their T-shirts are drenched with sweat.

"Hey, Glenda," shouts one of the women breathlessly. "Watch me put Billie on his ass!" She runs straight into Billie, then flings the ball at the basket, missing by a yard. Glenda grabs her cane, pushes herself up from the bench, and throws her free arm high above her head, shouting, "Go, Carrie, go!" Then she squats suddenly, coiled for a cheerleader's jump to the sky, and falls, laughing, to the ground. She holds out one hand and a player swings out from the field, grabs hold, and lifts Glenda back up to her bench, barely breaking stride before he's back on the court.

"When I first got to this program," Glenda tells me, her head wagging from side to side as the game moves back and forth, "I was so lonely for my friends at Hallidie. And for my bench. And for something to drink. So I tried to sneak out, but the door was locked. Then the next night I got to thinking—hey, this is pretty nice in this warm bed. And I woke up in the morning, all these people around me, and the smell in the kitchen from the fry bread. It was so beautiful I cried happy tears. I've been crying sad tears for such a long time, and there's these happy tears all of a sudden, like I'd forgotten how to do that. It's just affection, that's what I live for now, the family I got here. We all give each other that."

A roar rises up from the court as two players collide and bounce off each other, one flying straight at Glenda but catching his balance just in time to pluck the tiny woman off the bench and spin her about in his arms, until she's giggling so hard she can barely breathe, tears of laughter wetting her face like the sweat on his.

Then he's back on the court with the others. They're passing and faking, shooting long and running in for smooth layups, dribbling the ball behind their backs before charging for the basket or passing to a friend closer to the hoop. As the game froths with intensity, a crowd gathers to watch. None might possibly guess that the court is filled with men and women who've spent more time shooting heroin than hoops, more of their lives lying in the streets in drunken stupors than in running layups.

And when the ball swishes through the net, Glenda jumps from her seat, shouting at the top of her lungs, at times so loud that the action on the field stops momentarily and the players shout back, "Go, Glenda!" That night she writes in her journal how much she misses her brother Glenn, and wishes that he, too, had made it from Pine Ridge to the basketball game in San Francisco.

Evelyn's office is up a narrow flight of stairs from the main house, in a quiet one-window room far from the noise and hubbub of the kitchen and dormitory below.

"Does it make any difference that Glenda was forced to come here?" I ask.

She watches me carefully before answering, reaching out to her desk and picking up a long feather, rolling her thumb and index finger against the soft edges.

"I don't know how Glenda came here," she replies slowly. "It's not a question I would ask."

She says no more, her brown eyes focused intensely on mine. I break from her gaze, looking about the small room. Above Evelyn's desk hangs a plaque, inscribed in elegant calligraphy:

Indian Alcoholism Commission of California
Certificate of Substance Abuse Counselor

She follows my gaze.

"I've heard all about those claims, that an addict has to be ready or treatment won't work," she says, a smile playing on her lips. "And I can say only one thing. Maybe Glenda wasn't ready to stop drinking when she came here. But she was tired, and she was sick, *mmm-hmmm*, and somewhere she knew she didn't want to die. I wonder at all these questions you ask. Glenda is here. We work with what we are given."

Evelyn extends her hand, pointing the feather at a small calendar on her desk.

"Ninety days, that's our funding for each client," she says softly. "Ninety days, and Glenda is still barely learning to have compassion for herself."

She folds her hands in her lap, gently encasing the feather.

"In the talking circle we pass around the eagle feather," explains the counselor. "In the traditional way, we tell our stories; we travel to our memories, way back to childhood, to learn why we drink. We call it the Red Road to Recovery—our way of healing from the effects of the drugs and alcohol, going back to our own culture. But we have three months, and Glenda needs to deal with her abandonment, with her resentment, with her anger, with her abuse by so many people over so many years. And mostly, with her abuse of herself, *mmm-hmmm*. She has to do all of that, so she can move ahead again. When Glenda came here, she peed all over herself, she was dirty, and she was sick. Now she remembers that, and all the years before that, as her story. And she sees that she wants to stay the way she is, here, now—in her new story."

Evelyn points to the notepad I've been writing on.

"I know Glenda has told you that her story is finally coming to a closed circle," she says, "here, with her people." Evelyn shakes her head. "But Glenda is wrong. That's not the true story. Her story *doesn't* end here because after ninety days we have nowhere else to send her. We get three months—after Glenda's thirty-seven years, first at Pine Ridge and then living on the streets; years that have made her look like she's sixty, *mmm-hmmm*. So we really need help to find her somewhere better after she leaves here, somewhere where she can become thirty-seven again, to live her new story."

"Where?" I ask.

Evelyn shrugs, pointing to the certificate on her wall. "I'm a drug and alcohol counselor," she says, "not a housing specialist. I rely on other people for those answers."

"Who?"

"I don't know," says Evelyn. "There's really no one who helps us like that. We ask around, and we take what we get."

She rises from her chair, there are clients waiting.

"You came asking about how Glenda got here," says Evelyn, opening the door for me. "All your questions about whether Glenda was forced to the program, or came on her own." She smiles. "Or maybe an eagle dropped her down our chimney, *mmm-hmmm*? So write down your answer: She's here, and that's a good thing. What's important is not whether she was forced into this program, but that when she leaves there may be no place for her to go—except maybe back to where her old story is. Glenda can only change so much in three months, and we'll do what we can for her. But after that, we don't have much help out there."

The government's massive studies on the effectiveness of drug rehab can be rattled off as lyrical acronyms: DARP, TOPS, DATOS, and the most recent, more tongue-twisting NTIES. Each study evaluated different populations of addicts, at different times, undergoing different methods of rehab. Yet the unvarying conclusion of each and every one was that the minimal effective treatment time hovers at around three months.

"Participation for less than ninety days is of limited or no effectiveness," summarizes the National Institutes of Health in its book, *Principles of Drug Addiction Treatment*.

While beneficial effects of treatment begin to show up at about three months' time, researchers for the *Archives of General Psychiatry* who reviewed the government studies concluded that "better outcomes for patients with medium- to high-level problems were dependent on longer treatment stays."

Glenda probably breaks the scale of the "medium- to high-level problem" classification, given the drinking and disasters she has squeezed into her thirty-seven years on this earth. Yet in a one-size-fits-all approach to addiction treatment, Glenda was funded for three months of rehab: the minimum.

The government knows this is wrong. "Individuals progress through drug addiction treatment at various speeds," notes the National Institutes of Health, "so there is no predetermined length of treatment." Still, predetermining length of treatment is exactly what every federal and local rehab funding agency does, every single day, for every addict in treatment; in Glenda's case, deciding on a ninety-day limit.

UCLA's Dr. Anglin has his own manner of evaluating the rationale behind such rehab time restraints for clients like Glenda. "Brief interventions for the dysfunctionally dependent and lifetime poor," says Dr. Anglin, "are like pissing upwind."

Still, watching Glenda's miraculously rapid improvements within weeks of having arrived, kicking and screaming, at Friendship House, it seems clear that ninety days *is* long enough to bring about some remarkable changes. While longer times in intensive rehab would be lovely, ninety days can mean something—if tied to significant aid and follow-up when the clients, three months after walking into the programs, again head out into the world.

At noon on September 10, graduation day for Glenda and four other clients at Friendship House, thirty people crowd into the dining room above Julian Street and stand by their chairs, heads bowed, silent. Beams of sunlight crisscross the room, and the linen blouses of the women and vest-covered T-shirts of the men become clammy.

Five young men seated in a circle lift their palms to the air, and a drug rehab counselor pours water on their creased, callused flesh. They place their wet hands on the skin of a round drum between them, stroking the stretched hide in circular movements, testing its tension as it absorbs the water. During the ten minutes that they caress and prepare the drum skin, no one in the stiflingly hot room seems even to breathe. Finally, one drummer nods and all hands withdraw. A split second later, five padded sticks descend and the first heartbeat from the taut hide pounds through the room. Before the second beat hits, the haunting chant of thirty voices in raw, high-pitched harmony saturates the hot air.

Waiting for the graduation ceremony all morning, Glenda has been irritably on edge. Her joints are inflamed from her never-healed injuries, the pain worsened by walking with a cane instead of her walker or wheelchair. At first, as the drum starts pounding and the voices of the addicts and counselors rise in haunting song around her, Glenda's lips move silently along with the chant. But soon her head lifts high and her gravelly voice joins in. Then, as if a flock of birds had turned all at once, every head rotates toward the tiny woman as she finds her wind and her strong tenor cuts like a knife through the thick heat and pinched, nasal harmonies.

Glenda's body, barely holding its balance on her cane, sways to the rhythm of the song. She appears as if in a trance, hypnotized by the music, by the smell of burning sage, by the

EVELYN AND GLENDA

brilliant beam of sunlight striking her closed eyes as the room itself pulsates with sound from every breath. Finally, abrupt silence, as if their bodies had emptied.

"Three months ago, I didn't even want to be here," the soft voice of Roy Long, the first of the day's graduates to speak, breaks the silence. "But I was given a choice by my parole officer," Roy continues, "either come here, or go to prison."

There's a collective nodding of heads toward the stick-thin man, whose dark flesh has been scarred by needles and abscesses.

"So I came to the program, but you all know my heart wasn't here with you. And you waited me out, a real long wait. And then, I don't know what happened, but I've got to say that it's only been three months and my heart's been pulled wide open by you all. And I'm grateful for that. Not just because you kept me out of jail, but because what I've learned here has given me back my family."

The man stops, his head turned down as if he might hide the break in his voice. Then the sigh of a deep breath rushes into him, and a single drumbeat urges him on.

"My mom was so sick of the way I was treating her, she threw me out of our house. And Donna, my girlfriend, she was sick of me, too. And our little boy, even he was sick of me. So Donna took him away, and told me to come back when I could deal with people."

Roy holds out a hand and his counselor, standing next to him, takes it tightly in his own.

"So when I leave you all today," says Roy, "I've got Donna, and my mom, and my son back to support me again. Thank you all for pushing me so hard while I was here, so I'm a whole enough person that I can be with them."

Roy laughs nervously, staring at the floor and then back up at the crowd around him. "It was real scary shit to walk through that door three months ago," he says, trying to smile. "But this program saved my life. So that's my heart beating with those drums. I love you all."

The room explodes with noise as tradition gives way to whistles and catcalls, thumping of backs, pounding on the tables, and a foot-stomping thunder that drowns out the drums.

Until Evelyn holds up her hand.

"You know I don't use many words," begins the rehab counselor. "But I want to talk about our next graduate, because I have worked with hundreds of clients over so many, many years, and this one has touched my heart. In just ninety days, Glenda has learned so much. And today she walks out that door into her new story. And she walks on her own, no more walker. She's just a little thing," smiles Evelyn, "but I'm going to miss her so much."

All eyes turn toward Glenda.

"I never really had a mom," she says, smiling at Evelyn even through her tears, "until I met you." And that is all she says.

Three more graduates make their speeches; the clients at Friendship House and their guests polish off mounds of Indian fry bread smothered with chili and melted cheese; the graduates blow out the candles on their graduation cake. Then the drums pound again, at first slowly but soon picking up the rhythm as the addicts and their counselors take up a final, piercing chant.

Glenda rocks so hard with the rhythm that her cane slides out from under her and she begins to fall. Without a missed musical beat, two clients' hands reach from each side and slide under her arms, and then link across her back. And as the three sway together, others hook arms with them, until an unbroken circle has formed around Glenda's fallen cane.

Once again the tiny woman's voice flies above the crowd, and I remember Hallidie Plaza on that day in June, only three months before.

Busted flat in Baton Rouge . . . Glenda's hand was out, begging a few quarters toward her next bottle of vodka.

At the end of the ceremony, exhausted, Glenda folds all of her clothes into one pillowcase, dons a new, bright-orange basketball windbreaker, two sizes too large, and heads toward the door.

"Bye, Little Dude," says Roy, bounding down the stairs to where his girlfriend and son are waiting. "I'll see you here in a couple of days," he shouts back to her, reminding Glenda of their twice-weekly commitment to check in at Friendship House.

After searching long and hard, the best Evelyn has been able to find for Glenda's after-program care is a room in the Salvation Army's clean and sober housing. The support there includes mandatory attendance at a weekly meeting, and a straightforward rule: If you drink or use drugs, you lose your room.

Three months after Francine had thrown her into the cab, a rejuvenated and optimistic Glenda heads from Friendship House to her new room with the Salvation Army. In the Tenderloin. Three blocks from Hallidie Plaza.

Although the Death Prevention Team had referred Glenda to Friendship House in the first place, nobody in the rehab program thinks to tell Francine, Tony, or Larry that she's out of the program, or where she is now housed.

"God*damn*!" says Tony, when he hears, eleven days later, what's happened. "After Glenda had all this support, and support, and support," he pounds his hand on his desk in frustration, "to send her right back where she was picked up in the first place! And not even tell us she's there?"

As if some unseen, ironic hand is guiding her new story, on September 10, 1998, still wearing her white silk graduation blouse, Glenda checks in at the Salvation Army's housing on Turk Street, and is assigned to room 227. I help carry her pillowcase filled with clothes up the stairs to the second floor, past the communal kitchen, and then along the dingy hallway to her room just beyond the shared bathroom. Then I excuse myself for a moment, bound up the stairs, and navigate precisely the same path on the third floor. At room 327, directly above Glenda's, I knock on the door. But Darrell is not at home.

It's been eight months since Darrell graduated from his three-month program at Acceptance Place and was referred for "aftercare," as Glenda has just been, to a room at the Salvation Army's clean and sober housing. Today, as Glenda moves into a room directly below his, Darrell is only sixteen days shy of receiving his one-year medallion from Alcoholics Anonymous, having finally added actual sobriety to his numerous other recovery skills. Early each morning, he leaves his tiny quarters at the Salvation Army and scurries past the crack dealers on Eddy Street, walks determinedly by the alcoholics in the western end of Hallidie Plaza, then crosses Market Street to his morning job in the Nordstrom building. After evening classes, he hustles back to his Salvation Army room at 10:30 each night, to sleep and then start the day again early the next morning. On the weekends, he's at an Alcoholics Anonymous meeting called First Place.

"Most people fresh out of programs and fresh into their sobriety," Darrell had told me when he'd graduated from Acceptance Place eight months before, "need a lot more structure than what you get just by living at the Salvation Army. But my parents were good about the work ethic and all that stuff. I grew up that way, so I'll be able to build my own daily structure, even with such little after-program support."

Glenda's experience with her family on the Pine Ridge Reservation in South Dakota had been as different as could be from Darrell's middle-class upbringing with his family (white, working, and alive) in Vermont. So while Glenda and Darrell had both become incorrigible alcoholics, it should be simple enough to predict that their requirements from rehab would diverge.

But on September 10, 1998, the only apparent difference in their planned rehab paths seems to be that Glenda is assigned to room 227 at Salvation Army housing in the Tenderloin, while Darrell is in 327. The deck of recovery has been stacked against both of them, but Darrell seems strong enough, for now, to be beating the odds. Glenda, however, is the more optimistic of the two.

"I see flowers brighter than I ever did," she'd told me during the drive from Friendship House to the Salvation Army. She had leaned out the open window, admiring the scenery. "Even the colors of the cars are more pretty now than when I was drunk," exclaimed Glenda. "Because, when you're drunk, you're not looking at cars. You're not looking at anything. I never want to be back in that darkness again, so I'm sober from now on. Forever."

Glenda's confidence, three months into her sobriety, contrasts starkly with Darrell's as he approaches a full year without drink or drugs. "The hard part isn't sobriety," he says, "it's me! The same thing happens every time I get sober—I've got to go through all these feelings of not wanting to get close to people, like I'm afraid of them, or afraid of myself. It's so much easier when I'm drinking. So everything *you* see about me that looks so good on the outside now, *I* see as still painful and uncomfortable on the inside." Darrell, who can recite chapter and verse of Alcoholics Anonymous, maintains that it's "the healthy fear of relapse that keeps me from drinking." At the same time he laments, "Sometimes I get so frightened about relapse, I think that's what will make me drink again."

I leave a note on Darrell's door telling him he has a new neighbor just below him in the building, and head back down to help Glenda unpack. On the way over from Friendship House, she had stopped at a Goodwill and two other thrift stores, picking out an odd assortment of items she said she would need to set up house. Now, in the tiny room with an old porcelain sink and a single window opening onto a narrow air shaft, she sets about unpacking: six wooden napkin rings; a full set of measuring spoons for cooking; an onion slicer; two long, sharp kitchen knives with which she jokingly makes stabbing motions about the room.

"That takes care of my kitchen needs," says Glenda, tossing the empty paper bag into the corner and starting on her pillowcase full of clothes, and a photo album she'd received as a graduation gift. Sitting on her bed below the open window, she slides snapshots of the friends she'd made at Friendship House into the acetate sheets of the album.

"You know, I can be a role model for my old friends at Hallidie," says Glenda, "teach 'em some of the stuff I learned from my recovery. Just because I'm through drinking, doesn't mean those people out there aren't my friends no more. I'm not going to forget where I came from just because I'm sober now."

Glenda finishes tucking photos into her album, then slides one of Evelyn on the front cover and, like a proud schoolgirl, clutches the album to her chest, her smile beaming into the room.

"You know what Evelyn said about me touching her heart?" she says. "Well, that goes for me, too—she really touched my heart."

The frail woman gingerly places her album on the cracked wood dresser at her bedside. Then she eases herself up from the bed and opens the door to a closet by the sink in the corner of the room. She reaches out and grips the bars of her walker in the gnarled fingers of one scarred hand, then rolls the walker into the closet and closes the door.

"Won't be needing it no more," declares Glenda. "I'm just three blocks from Hallidie. I can walk there easy now."

She moves back to the bed, proudly surveying her new room, then overturns the pillowcase of clothes and begins meticulously folding them into a pile on the mattress.

"Once I'm done with this, I'll be able to go outside," she says. "Going to find me a quiet spot with a cool breeze in my face, just like at my old bench. Maybe find a newspaper on one of the benches to read. That's what it was like out there." She holds her hand up, fingers pinched together. "I'd have this much of a cigarette I'd find, and then a newspaper. And I'd sit on my bench, do some reading, take a drag on that cigarette, have the sun in my face."

"And you'd drink until you were unconscious," I add.

"No more," says Glenda. "I got too much love in my life to go back to that now."

She folds her last blouse into the neat pile of clothes, then strains to lift her twisted body from the bed, pulls at the handle on a dresser drawer, and tucks the clothes carefully in. Then she picks up her new, reflective-orange basketball windbreaker, slowly contorts her body to get her arms through the sleeves, and limps across the room to open the door to the hallway, ready to go out.

"I got to go down there, see my old friends," says Glenda, "try to talk them into going into programs. I'm not going to let them die out there on those benches."

Two days after Glenda's move to the Salvation Army, my phone rings late at night, Darrell calling after he's come home from school.

"I met Glenda," he says, excited. "And she is so sweet, she's like a little Kewpie doll! I was walking on Turk toward the Salvation Army, and this really small Indian woman was walking by. So I took a chance, because I remembered how you'd described her. I said, 'Are you Glenda?' And her face lit all up, and I told her I was your friend. She was so cute, all smiles, and she gave me a big hug."

I laugh, remembering the gruesome condition that both Darrell and Glenda had been in when I'd first met them; and now, the tall, bushy-haired Darrell is racing back to his room from business school and running into the tiny, sober Glenda as she walks to her own room for the night.

"Glad you two got to meet," I tell Darrell. "It's so strange you've both wound up at the same place."

"I know!" he says. "But you didn't tell me she's still drinking."

"What?"

"I'm sorry, it's been a rough day, I could have done that better. I thought you knew."

"Are you sure?"

Darrell sighs.

"She was either very, very tired, or very, very drunk," he says. "But remember who you're talking to. I can usually tell the difference. And she was with two other guys I recognized from Hallidie. If she wasn't drunk, they sure were."

The next evening, Chris, the clerk at the front desk at Salvation Army housing, greets me with a smile.

"You here to see Darrell?" he asks.

"Not this time," I reply, plunking down my ID, required from every visitor. "I'm looking for Glenda. Room 227."

"No need to go up there," says Chris, flipping through some papers on his desk. "She's gone."

"Gone where?"

"She's not here, I assure you," he says. "And she has her right to confidentiality, so I simply cannot tell you why."

He looks around the lobby to be sure no one else is around.

"We've locked the door to Glenda's room, so that she can't get back in," he tells me, nearly whispering. "I know, it's sad, but there are rules, and she'd been drinking. She has three weeks to contact Lewis and make an appointment to come get her things. We're holding them in storage."

It's 8:00 P.M. and, as usual after the sun sets in San Francisco, the temperature has dropped quickly and a drizzly fog has blown in. I leave the Salvation Army and walk the three blocks to Hallidie. The plaza is eerily quiet, sounds muted by the mist. No more than a dozen people are out at the end of the shopping day. The police have recently started clearing the homeless from the plaza at night, so even Dave, who holds up the Bank of America building, has found another spot until sunrise.

The last of the tourists are gathered at the cable car turnabout, and from just up the block comes the rhythm of a street blues band—a tinny, battery-amplified guitar, a drummer, a bass player, and two vocalists. About ten tourists have gathered around them, swaying to the music as they wait for the cable car to rumble by and take them away. I barely glance at the group, but then notice a streak of bright orange against the brick wall of the building, Glenda's shiny windbreaker reflecting the glimmer from a streetlamp.

Her eyes are closed, and she's leaning on an old, wooden crutch braced under one arm. Glenda's other hand is stretched in front of her, palm up, toward the tourists. She's crooning the blues with the two singers in the band.

The thrill is gone, babe, the thriiiiil is gone—

Glenda reaches to the floor for a thin glass bottle and barely stops singing while the liquid oozes down her throat. Then she swipes the sleeve of her coat against her mouth, and lifts the bottle again.

I'm leaning against the wall by her side now, surprised at how quickly Glenda has regained the odor of the streets. An overpowering, concentrated stench like mildewed socks radiates from her like a heater. As the song winds down and the men in the band hold a hat toward the tourists, I touch Glenda's shoulder. Her eyes open and she twists about to face me.

"Oh, no!" she moans, half smiling through her drunken haze. "I really messed up, huh?" The words drool out, and she swabs her sleeve against her mouth as if to wipe the slur from her speech. "I took me a drink," she says, "couple days ago, 'cause it was so sad to see my old friends on the benches. But that drink made me even sadder, and I was so ashamed, thinking of Evelyn and them at the program. So I went back to the Salvation Army place, feeling real bad, and they threw me out! Couldn't even take my clothes and shoes, told me I had to make some appointment for that."

Glenda looks down at her feet, almost losing her precarious, drunken balance. "I had to borrow these sorry-ass shoes," she laughs, regaining her equilibrium, "so I got all these blisters on my feet now. I got this far, but can't walk no more. So I'll stay here, singing like I always do. Wait for the sun to shine and get me warm again."

Glenda reaches down for her bottle, but the crutch she's been balancing on slides and she falls to the pavement, staring straight up at the sky. She immediately recovers her intent, searches about on the ground, finds the bottle, and takes a long swig, emptying it. Moments later, Glenda lays her head on her arm, tucks her body in closer to the wall of the building, and closes her eyes, asleep.

The guitar player closest to her puts his instrument down, and as the band starts up its next song he pulls over one of the shopping carts used to carry their instruments. Without

a word, the man bends over and scoops Glenda's tiny body into his arms, then eases her limp form into the shopping cart.

"I'll be right back," he says to the other musicians, who haven't missed a beat.

The man wheels the shopping wagon down Powell, through Hallidie Plaza, across Market Street, past the Nordstrom building, and along 5th to Howard. There, in a corner by the wall of the M&M Bar, he lifts a barely conscious Glenda from the cart and sets her down on some blankets, in what has become her new bedroom.

"Let me see if I've got this straight," says Tony, as he and Larry pull up their chairs to look at the photographs I've laid out on a table in the cluttered office of the Death Prevention Team at San Francisco's Department of Public Health.

"Four months ago," he says, "Glenda was drinking heavily at Hallidie, but was housed at the Mission Hotel. Then, we go through all this damned effort, and now she's drinking heavily, and she's homeless? So is that what we bust our asses for out there?" Tony asks incredulously. "To take housed alcoholics, and make them into homeless alcoholics?"

He stares at the photograph.

"God*damn*!" he explodes, and then lowers his head into his hands, crying.

Larry, whose voice is so soft you have to strain to hear him when he's out working the streets, looks up from the photo. "She was in a program," he says, "so there was no rush. All they had to do was find a place for Glenda that wouldn't kick her out if she started drinking again. They knew she might drink once she left program, you got to anticipate that. Rule number one: Don't lose their housing, people die on the streets. They could have used the Senator Hotel, the Isabel, the Ambassador, the Arlington—" His voice trails off.

"We started working with Glenda over a year ago," says Tony, shaking his head as if to clear out his bottled-up frustration and fling it across the room. "Everybody in this damn city is chasing each other's tails! Who in the hell thought to put Glenda in zero-tolerance housing three blocks from Hallidie Plaza? If she'd have been placed anywhere but there and got into trouble, we'd still have something to work with. She'd be housed, have some fresh recovery experience under her belt, even if she is drinking again. That's progress, something to work with. But now, she's worse off than when she started."

Tony and Larry pack up their gear to head out for the day's work. They'll start off this particular morning chasing down a rumor they'd heard about a woman living in a van under the freeway who'd fallen and hit her head days ago, and hasn't been out of the van since.

Tony shoulders his backpack and he and Larry wait for the creaky back-hall elevator that will take them to ground level, where they'll meet the Mobile Assistance Patrol van and head into the streets.

"Sometimes I feel like we're not helping a goddamn soul out there," says Tony, leaning against the wall. "And when we do make some headway, like with Glenda, somebody else screws it up."

"It's that first week out of program, that's the toughest," adds Larry. "They're trying to feel out where they're at in the world again. So, sure, they might start drinking. That's the time to really work with them, move in real tight, not throw 'em back into the streets. Friendship House is a good program and all that, but they basically finished up with Glenda and put her out there with a slippery banana peel in front of her."

"What would work better?" I ask. "Evelyn told me, 'I'm a drug and alcohol counselor, not a housing specialist.'"

Tony sucks in a deep breath, as if warming up for an aria.

"Our job is to do death prevention," he begins. "If we can get somebody off the streets and into a really strong container like Friendship House, we expect the program to pick up the ball and carry it from there. But they do their program thing, no more. And it's not their fault, because they're as stuck for help out here as we are. Friendship House chalked Glenda up as a success because she made it for three months and left clean and sober. So their program's statistics are looking real good. And our numbers look good because we got her off the streets and into a program. And the mayor gets to point out statistics about all this great stuff happening in San Francisco. But hell, I'll bet if you checked the city's records, the last note for Glenda would be 'Completed Program Successfully.' After that, nobody's watching, nobody's providing follow-up care like they should be, nobody hears anything more about her. And the next note you're going to find in the city's records for Glenda, couple of years down the line, is a report from the morgue, 'Found dead on the streets.' What happened in between 'Completed Program Successfully' and 'Found dead on the streets'? Nothing. That's the problem. But every program got to write her down as a success story. Keep up the good work, everybody's happy! And where is she in the system now? Back full circle to us, the damn street outreach workers, to try to get her stabilized again. And if we don't, then everything anybody's done was a waste of time, and a waste of money, and a waste of Glenda's life."

Tony finishes his rant and strides into the elevator, closing the ancient iron gate and pushing the button for the ground floor. Out on the street, he and Larry climb into the Mobile Assistance Patrol van, and Tony leans out the window to say good-bye.

"Thanks for the follow-up on Glenda," the death prevention worker tells me, signaling to the driver to head out. "We'll hit Hallidie today, see if we can find her. We don't quit so easy."

The van starts rolling, and Tony shouts out a final comment. "Hey, did you hear we got Dave off the wall at the Bank of America and into a room at the Senator Hotel?" He laughs. "That's our motto: One down, fifteen thousand to go."

———

No one in this country argues more vociferously that addicts and alcoholics should be coerced into treatment than does Dr. Sally Satel, a Washington, D.C., psychiatrist who wrote a 1998 op-ed article in the *Wall Street Journal* entitled, "For Addicts, Force Is the Best Medicine."

"The correct treatment for drug addiction," says Dr. Satel, who does not beat around the bush, "is coercion. It is the prescription of choice. You have to realize that so many addicts are so ambivalent about giving up their drugs, so afraid of living life unfiltered by drugs, that they won't go to therapy unless they're pretty much forced to."

Dr. Satel's enthusiasm waxes strong. "As a clinician," says the associate scholar at the Ethics and Public Policy Center, "I'm often relieved when an addict gets arrested. If that's the way to get them into my treatment program, great!"

For those drug treatment professionals who still believe that addicts must be motivated before they can be helped (or that civil liberties apply even to people addicted to drugs), Dr. Satel still has a kind word. She calls those rehab workers "misguided, but well meaning."

Dr. Satel is not waving the banner of some radical rehab fringe. At the American Society of Addiction Medicine's annual conference in 1998, Dr. Normal S. Miller, associate professor of psychiatry and neurology at the University of Illinois, Chicago, declared, "Coerced treatment is effective in a broad array of populations and it should be adopted as policy." And John T. Carnevale, director of Programs, Budget, Research, and Evaluation at the White House Office of National Drug Control Policy, notes that his agency "embraces the idea of using coerced treatment; it gets people into treatment."

Without "coercive strategies" as a "key component" of our national drug control policy, claims Dr. Satel, "we will lose the best chance we have for treating addicts in ways that significantly improve their lives and that of society. Without formal coercive mechanisms, the treatment system would not attract many of the most dysfunctional addicts."

Yet if Glenda is any example, "attracting" those most dysfunctional addicts into rehab can be a colossal waste of time and money—especially when people more motivated, and thus more likely to succeed, are waiting anxiously in line for the same, scarce treatment slots.

Did Glenda's rapid return to street intoxication and homelessness really indicate that forcing dysfunctional addicts into treatment does not work? Or was her failure more indicative of the fact that forcing addicts into a dysfunctional treatment system is not likely to rehabilitate them? Had the treatment system been more cohesive, a linked structure of comprehensive services that had continued past three months of care, might Glenda's kidnapping have actually succeeded in turning her life around?

The social experiment that might answer such a question cannot be performed, not in a society of rights, liberties, and rules. In spite of Dr. Satel's wishes, our ability to abduct addicts is limited. And in cases like Glenda's, where we do take intoxicated hostages, we rarely deliver them to our best treatment centers for prolonged rehab, or continue to supply them with appropriate follow-up services, all of which would be necessary to learn if forcing addicts into rehab can actually work.

Tony, Larry, and Francine could only dream of achieving tightly supervised rehabilitation with Glenda, not merely to coerce her into a program but to watch her and monitor her progress while she is there; and then to pick her up when she comes out, and keep working with her; and then do everything possible to be sure her treatment and access to services continues for a full year, or two, or until she is stabilized and likely to make it on her own. The Death Prevention Team doesn't have the manpower, funds, or persuasiveness to pull off such rehab feats.

Glenda's initial, remarkable turnaround at Friendship House provided a tantalizing, teasing hint that coercion might be one effective tool in repairing some of the devastations of drug addictions. But as soon as she offered us a glimmer of hope, we pulled back all services and quit the experiment. Glenda was simply not enough of a plague on our society to warrant prolonged, vigilant tracking. As offensive an appearance as she presented to our senses, Glenda's major transgression had been to misuse a bench at Hallidie Plaza (although she'd run up some impressively costly hospital bills with each catastrophic use of one of her nine lives). Had Glenda, let's say, repeatedly helped herself to costly jewelry from Nordstrom to trade on the streets for booze or drugs; or if her outstretched hand had picked the pockets of passing tourists while she sang her Joplin tunes; or had she committed any of a number of even more serious criminal infractions instead of simply offending our sensibilities—we would surely have provided her with more than three months of watchful supervision.

Glenda's story would have played out to a better ending had she committed crimes serious enough to send her to Drug Court, where they back up coercion with prolonged, comprehensive assistance, and intensive care.

JUDGE NEWTON LAM

In September of 1998, after Mike relapsed and Walden had shown him the door, he moved in with Connie and they conceived a child. Elated by this fresh start in life, Mike began anew his relentless but now solitary drive to stay clean. Between that September and Connie's due date the following May, he would consistently hold out for weeks without heroin. Then, in panic, he'd head to his dealer at 16th and Mission, finger in the air, "Need one, just one."

Mike was still overwhelmed by shame over his rehab fiasco at Walden, too humiliated to ask The Family to take him back in, then endure a House Meeting of attack therapy. So he brazenly tried to barrel his way, alone, through his daymares and nightmares of the white room, and feelings of failure with his two daughters. Mike bounced between psychological torment when off dope, and torturous self-hatred when on dope. He worked sixty-hour weeks at a new plumbing job, saving money so he and Connie might leave their city apartment for a more spacious suburban home when the new baby arrived. But frequently, after he'd kiss Connie good-bye in the morning, he'd stop off at 16th and Mission on his way to work.

Two blocks away, at 18th and Mission that same early September of 1998, Crystal Holmes was dealing crack cocaine in ever-increasing quantities to support her own heavy habit. While Mike was wallowing in guilt over his relentless addiction, Crystal was floating high on her pride as the savvy street drug dealer and crack cocaine queen of the Mission. After a 1992 arrest, a judge had sentenced her to an addiction diversion program. She'd never shown up, kept dealing drugs, and hadn't been caught since.

If any addict in San Francisco was ripe for a push toward rehab that September of 1998, it was Mike. And if any addict seemed the least likely to benefit from *any* attempt at rehab, Crystal headed the pack. Mike craved getting clean before the arrival of his and Connie's new baby, while Crystal became more brazen and proud with every street deal that put cash in her pocket and crack in her pipe.

Later that month, Mike was still stopping off at 16th and Mission, while Crystal Holmes stood in Drug Court in an orange jail jumpsuit facing Judge Newton Lam, who released her to rehab.

Much of what Crystal Holmes tells me about herself is true. Much is not.

She married too young, she explains when we first meet, to a computer engineer who graduated from M.I.T. in Washington, D.C.

"I thought M.I.T. is in Cambridge," I say. "You know, *Massachusetts* Institute of Technology?"

"Well, he went to the one in Washington!" insists Crystal, not missing a beat.

What *is* certain about Crystal Holmes is that the sheer volume of her rapid-fire bullshit and bravado is immediately seen by the court as no more than a flimsy cover-up for some as yet unknown plague that tears at this thirty-five-year-old mother of three from the inside. Crystal's gut is fretfully churning even as she exudes a bold and perfectly enacted self-confidence that rarely fools anyone.

"That's Cuban turf," announces Crystal as we drive along Mission Street, past the corner of 18th, on her way home from an appearance in Drug Court. "Anybody else sells dope there without the Cubans' nod first"—she laughs—"*they'll* call the cops on you! But I get along OK with them."

"OK enough to have been arrested on that corner," I note.

"It wasn't them that got me arrested!" exclaims Crystal indignantly. "It was my own damn fault. I let my guard down. And I'll tell you one thing, the last thing I was looking for that day was some rehab program. I was looking for dope! Hell, before that undercover pulled me in, I never even knew there was this Drug Court thing. And I ain't too happy to know about it now!"

With that, Crystal launches into her rapid-fire don't-interrupt-me narrative style that makes listening to her so entertaining, and so frustrating.

"See, I started that day—it was September 9, never forget it—by running into crazy little Cuban Andre. He was always getting his ass whupped because he owes people money, so he wanted to hang with me because this girl Kim was going to kick his ass. See, Kim won't bother him if he's with me because—you might not believe it looking at me now, all cleaned up and all that, but on the streets I'm called Stephie, not Crystal. And Stephie is ruthless! Somebody gives me a hard time, I'll put a crack pipe in their mouth because I know they want drugs, and soon as that pipe's in their mouth I hit 'em in the stomach and cut off their air. Then I tell 'em, 'Next time you fuck with me, I'll kill you.' So they don't fuck with me out here." Crystal lets out a high-pitched cackle. "You only know Crystal," she tells me, "you never met Stephie. And Stephie is *crazy.*"

I add *Stephie* to my mental list of Crystal Holmes's aliases. When I'd first met her in Drug Court, Judge Lam was still calling her Karla Holmes, the name she'd used when she was arrested. But even after she had finally told the court her true name (she didn't want to give the real Karla Holmes, Crystal's very straight-and-narrow sister, a criminal record), it took a while before the staff stopped referring to her as Karla and got used to Crystal.

"So I'm with Cuban Andre all day," Crystal continues as we drive along Mission Street, "and I know I should be going home to get Tony's meal ready before his shift driving a MUNI bus, because that damn man don't even know how to cook for himself! You'd think *he* was the one on dope, not me, and he doesn't touch no drugs. But just as I'm thinking about going home, I see this girl Patricia who I used to run with. And right behind her is this guy, and he's saying out loud, 'Who's got a twamp?' "

"A twamp?" I interrupt.

"Damn," says Crystal, frustrated that I had disrupted her flow. "A twamp, a two-oh, and no, I do *not* know how to spell it! It means drop a fat two-oh on me, a twenty of crack. So there's this guy behind Patricia, saying out loud, 'Who's got a twamp?' He's a white man, and there's all these Cubans selling right there. And I *know* somebody's holdin' a dime that we can pass off to this white guy as a twenty, then use the money to get some more dope. Quick and easy, I'm thinking. So I look to the Cubans to see who's going to be the connection to this guy who wants a twamp. And I get the nod from them, and one guy spits on the ground, means he's got a dime of crack wrapped in plastic in his mouth. So I give the nod to Patricia, and she goes and gives that Cuban guy a hug and a kiss, and now she's got the dime in her mouth. See, we take the risk off the Cubans, so they'll cut us in. So I walk up to the white guy and say, 'You got the cash?' He says, 'Yeah,' and I say, 'Hold your money, I'm going to get me a cigarette.' I walk by him and over to Patricia, give her a hug, and now I got the dope in my mouth. I go to the white guy and cough in my hand and hold out a cigarette for him. So he passes the twenty to my hand and I slip the dime of dope into his. But the guy don't look at his hand right away."

Crystal pauses to suck in a breath between words, shaking her head.

"Damn!" she says. "Man, a crack fiend don't look at you, he looks at his hand, where the dope is. But this white guy, he's looking around him, he's looking at me, he's looking at everything but his dope. Damn, I'm thinking—he's a cop!"

We've reached the outer Mission, the corner of 30th where Crystal lives with Tony in the tiniest of walkup flats. Somehow, in spite of the recommendation of Drug Court's intake evaluator, Crystal has convinced Judge Lam not to send her to intensive residential rehab, but to let her continue living with Tony and show up on her own for outpatient treatment every day.

I stop the car at the corner where San Jose Avenue, 30th Street, and Mission angle into one another at a triangular intersection where buses, trolleys, delivery trucks, and cars simultaneously accelerate with a deafening roar that bounces off a peeling gray stucco corner building. On the third floor, Tony is waiting for Crystal in their one-room apartment down the hallway from the squalid bathroom shared by all the tenants. I don't know it yet, but Tony is getting angrier by the minute because Crystal has been away the whole day, at rehab program and court. As Tony will carefully point out when I finally do meet him weeks later, "I don't allow you or anyone with the drug programs to even phone Crystal here. It's bad enough she's away from the house all this time, I won't have her bringing that rehab shit home."

"I got to go," says Crystal, bundling into her arms the groceries she's bought for her and Tony on the way home. But first she quickly wraps up her story.

"So that white guy was looking over his shoulder," she says, "and then he turns and walks away. And I just *know* that twenty in my right-hand pocket is a police-marked twenty! I turn to Patricia and say, 'Get the fuck out of here, quick, I just sold to a cop.' And I'm pissed off now, walking real fast 'cause I see this white car driving down the block and I recognize the driver, this undercover we call Bizarro. Before he can get close enough to see me, I reach into my left pocket and dump my money out. But, damn! I dumped my own money instead of the marked money in my right pocket, got mixed up. So when Bizarro pulls up to check me out, he finds the marked twenty on me. And suddenly there's undercovers all over the place, and I'm on my way to jail! That's the first time since '92 that I got caught. And I never did show up for my '92 sentence. So now I'm thinking, shit, they're going to find my record and I'm going to jail for a *long* time. But I didn't know nothing about Drug Court then. I got out in thirty-four days."

Almost nothing shocks Crystal, or even ruffles her carefully composed facade. "When I see a situation coming down," she says, "I know just what to do with it. That's who I am, always been that way." But after Crystal's third week in jail following her arrest by the undercover cop, when they bring her to take a look at Drug Court and talk to Judge Newton Lam, she retreats in confusion. She simply cannot figure out what is going on with this Drug Court stuff. So how can she scam her way through it?

"Damn! I am so pissed off!" declares Judge Newton Lam from the front of the packed courtroom, his black judicial robe flying about him as he slams his open palm against the top of the polished-wood judge's bench, hovering high at the front of the very formal court.

Standing at a podium ten feet in front of Judge Lam, Brian Walker, a twenty-year-old heroin addict, drug dealer, and car stereo thief, is looking at his feet, tapping the toes of his high-topped Nikes on the polished wood floor of the court.

From the side of the courtroom, dressed in an orange jail jumpsuit, sitting with the other prisoners under the watchful guard of a uniformed sheriff's deputy, Crystal is suddenly paying attention. She's never seen a judge lose his cool or use such language in a courtroom before. But that doesn't faze her; Crystal has long ago learned how to charm her way through other people's anger. Soon, though, her stare at this oddly behaving judge turns from confidence to uncertainty as the court scene becomes even more bizarre.

"I have cried with you here, Brian," says Judge Lam, now leaning forward in his tall leather chair, his voice almost cracking as he implores, "Brian, please, look up at me."

Brian slowly raises his head toward the bench.

"I am lost, man," Judge Lam tells him softly, the entire court watching. "I am so sad that we've come to this point, that we are about to take you out of Drug Court and send your case back to criminal court. I had such high hopes for you, and I am hurt to my heart."

"But I ain't been doing no drugs," Brian interrupts. "You've seen my tests, they're all negative. What else you want me to do?"

"I want you to want *your future* as much as I want it for you!" exclaims the judge. "How many weeks have I sat here now waiting for you to show me you've started that high school equivalency course? You've been out there, hanging out with your same old friends, and I don't care if you're testing negative for drugs! You've left the drugs behind, but you haven't left the drug lifestyle behind. And that will bring you back to drugs, sure as shootin'. And if you blow out of Drug Court, you're facing time in state prison. Goddamn, Brian, you're twenty years old. What the hell are you doing? We're giving you a chance, and you're blowing it."

Judge Lam looks down from his bench toward Marianne Barrett, the district attorney in charge of prosecuting Brian's case through Drug Court. She quickly closes his thick court record in front of her, assuming that, as per her earlier agreement with Judge Lam, he'll now send Brian's case on to criminal court because the young man hasn't followed through with Drug Court's requirements of him.

Judge Lam's sigh, loudly projected, echoes from the wood-paneled walls of the courtroom, reaching the orange-clad prisoners in the gallery on the right, and back to the rear gallery where addicts he'd released to rehab programs weeks and months before have returned to report in to the judge.

"All right, Brian," says Judge Lam, carefully penciling a mark in the file in front of him. "I'm going to see you back in this court next Wednesday, and you're going to bring documentation that you've started high school equivalency classes." Judge Lam looks quickly down at the district attorney, who is staring at him in wide-eyed astonishment, shaking her head at his sudden change of heart.

"Brian," says the judge, "I know you think you're a big man out there in the streets. But I'll tell you something, if you don't follow your dreams, you are nobody. And you have *told* me, time and again, that your dream is to get off those streets. So you keep that appointment at the school, you follow through on your plans, and I'll see you back in court next week."

Without so much as a pause, Judge Lam calls the next case.

"Line fifty-two. Deanna Booth."

A young woman in a business suit quickly leaves her seat in the rear court gallery and approaches the bench, grinning.

"Deanna, you're looking *good!*" declares the judge, matching her smile. "I am so glad to see you here. The first time we met, you were in jail clothes, shoulders hunched over like a tore-up junkie. Now, you carry yourself with pride."

Judge Lam turns in his seat, facing the inmates in the side gallery, Crystal among them. He stretches the palm of his hand out toward the orange-dressed side of the court, and then swings it in an arch to the rear gallery of addicts in rehab programs, and then back to Deanna, grandly presenting her to the entire courtroom.

"Seeing you today, Deanna," says the judge, "makes me so happy. And it's more than your new clothes. I've read the reports from your program, and they say you're doing great."

Judge Lam holds up a sheet of white paper from Deanna's file. "Look at this! A long line of negative drug tests, marching right up to the sky! Deanna, keep up the good work. I'll see you back here in a month. Meanwhile, start graduation planning with your case manager."

"Thank you, Judge Lam," says Deanna, smiling softly as she turns from the podium to head back to her seat, where she's required to remain until the end of the court day, observing each case.

"No, Deanna, we thank you," says Judge Lam. "It's our pleasure."

Back in her jail cell after watching the entire day's Drug Court transactions, Crystal is puzzling over what she's seen, and about the court's offer to move her drug-sales charge from criminal court to Drug Court. But as she leans back in her bunk and tries to figure it all out, Crystal has no idea that she's been intentionally set up.

"The Drug Court is theater," says Judge Jeffrey Tauber, Director of the National Drug Court Institute, explaining why inmates like Crystal—not yet accepted into Drug Court— are brought from their cells to watch the proceedings.

Dr. Sally Satel, who has studied the dynamics of Drug Courts across the country, makes similar court-as-theater comparisons. "Drug court is fertile ground for the unfolding of psychological drama," says Dr. Satel, noting that Drug Court judges are as much responsible for "therapeutic impact" as they are for judicial authority, and become most effective "by engaging the Drug Court 'audience.' "

"The Drug Court judge's role is unconventional," adds Dr. Satel. "The depth of involvement with the defendant is unprecedented."

Such unprecedented behavior, performed by Judge Lam in front of his captive audience, seems so bizarre to Crystal that, as she tells me later, "It was a hard choice between jail time, or Drug Court and treatment time. It was like the blind lady with that scale of justice. Which is going to weigh more on me?"

Back in his chambers at the end of the court day, Judge Lam describes to me his carefully calculated blend of real emotion and courtroom theatrics that had led to his initial outburst with Brian, followed by his fatherly, open-court heart-to-heart.

"Brian *needs* to be agonizing over his life," explains the judge. "So I had to show him, and everybody watching in the courtroom, what agonizing really looks like, what it feels like. I mean, there are choices about how I can present myself to someone like Brian: Anger? Well, that was just to get his attention. But if that were all I had done, he'd be saying to himself, 'I'm not going to take that shit from nobody!' He'd just cop an attitude, stick out his lower lip, and I've lost him. Instead, I agonize over him in open court, in front of all his street friends and program friends. And nobody has a set response to a judge, up on the bench in court, agonizing over them. It's so unfamiliar, it sets the whole place off guard. So they've got to come up with a new way of dealing with it. Sure, it's theater—and I've got the best seat in the house."

Judge Lam smiles, taking off his black judicial robe to relax in his chambers.

"It's no good if we graduate people from Drug Court just because they've stopped using drugs—and then they're back in a year because we failed to make fundamental changes in how they see themselves, who they are in the world. Behind Brian's tough show, like just about everyone in that court, he really doesn't believe much in himself. But I *know* he has the potential. So I try to find the right tone, whatever it takes to get him motivated. Sometimes that wins them over." Judge Lam laughs, shaking his head. "And sometimes," he says, "I'm sure it just confuses them."

"I've never seen no courtroom like that," Crystal tells me after she finally decides to move her case to Drug Court, where Judge Lam will release her from jail and then supervise her journey through rehab. "This ain't no courtroom where the lawyers chat up the judge and you don't get to say nothing," says Crystal, "and then he bangs the gavel and tells you where you're going to go, and for how long. 'OK, six months, next case.' So I got to figure out what to *do* with a judge who's yelling at you, then crying, talking about his heart being broken! What is that? I mean, I watched this graduation at the end of the court day, and the damn judge got up from his bench, long black robes and all, and he's hugging the defendant! See, I got to think this one over, because that's a year or two they're asking me to spend in Drug Court. And I'm not one to be following all their rules and be this Goody Two-shoes for a couple of years just so I can get a hug from the judge! I'm thinking, how do I play this so it's best for Crystal?"

The day after Crystal has her first look at Drug Court in action, she figures out her plan. "I'm thinking, look, they got me in jail," she says, "nothing I can do with that. So I see this Drug Court stuff, and they *want* me to get out of jail, take classes, get a diploma, job training, whatever! And if you do it for a year and don't do no drugs, they drop all the charges against you. So I'm in this jail cell thinking about the Drug Court thing, and I realize, Crystal, they're holding out their hands with free gifts! Fine, sign me up! Because I am a chameleon, I can fake my way through any program. I'll take 'em for what they got."

Crystal laughs and figures out a way, as usual, to convince herself and everyone else that she's doing what Crystal wants, not what the court has ordered. "I always did want to go back to school," she says.

"What's really interesting about this particular court drama," notes Dr. Renée Emunah, a professor of drama therapy who observed Judge Lam in court, "is that the characters—judges, lawyers, addicts—are all really good actors. But in *this* courtroom setting, the defendants, all of them addicts, don't only watch, they've got to interact and play their roles. And they're acting in front of the judge, and in front of their drug counselors, and their case managers who are in court, and in front of a whole bunch of addicts who know all the same scams. So this has to be their top show, the master performance! And I see where it can go—they put on a really good act, time after time for a whole year, trying to convince the court that they're making it. And like all actors putting on a good show, it gets more and more authentic to them. So after a while they'll internalize the role, and they really are making it. I don't think it automatically happens, but there's a great potential the way it's set up so that the defendant has to do his best acting job. And the best of theater becomes so convincing, it becomes real."

Janet Reno, who became Attorney General of the United States in 1993, was the state's prosecuting attorney in Florida's Miami-Dade County in 1989 when the drug crisis so overwhelmed the courts and jails that she searched urgently for a new strategy to deal with crime-committing addicts.

Judge Gerald T. Wetherington, then chief judge for the county, recalls the desperation of the times. "It became very clear in the latter part of the 1980s," says Judge Wetherington, "that the drug problem in Dade County had become epidemic, and our efforts to deal with it . . . were fragmented."

Dade County was not alone. According to a U.S. Department of Justice report, court dockets in the late 1980s became so "overloaded with drug cases and drug-involved offenders" that resources to deal with dangerous felons had become seriously jeopardized. And merely expanding court and jail resources to deal with the influx of addicted criminals seemed to offer little hope. "Incarceration in and of itself does little to break the cycle of illegal drug use and crime," notes the Department of Justice report.

In 1989, at the height of the crack cocaine epidemic, the courts and jails in virtually every city across the country were drowning in a sea of addicts. In Florida, Janet Reno teamed up with Chief Judge Wetherington to try a bold, possibly foolhardy experiment in criminal and social policy. In Miami's Eleventh Circuit, they asked Judge Herbert Klein to start moving nonviolent addicted lawbreakers out of criminal court and into a separately run

Drug Court that would place them in community-based rehab, where the judge would supervise the addicts' treatment.

For Janet Reno, a prosecuting attorney holding an elective office in 1989, spearheading a special court to *help* arrested addicts seemed an odd and risky move. The public was clamoring to put more criminals behind bars, not find ways to let them out. And at the time, the best of studies were showing decidedly low success rates with rehab for any addicts, let alone those who arrive in handcuffs.

Janet Reno and two Dade County judges staked their jobs and public reputations on being able to take thousands of addicts like Crystal Holmes out of jail and keep them clean, sober, and crime-free.

5:00 A.M., October 13, the sheriff's deputy shakes Crystal awake in her bunk to tell her she's being *dressed out* of jail. Head to the holding tank, instructs the deputy, strip off your orange jail sweat suit, take the plastic property bag that's got the clothes you were wearing when you were arrested. Get dressed, then you're out of jail.

The sheriff handcuffs Crystal to her jail friend, Connie Davis, and the three walk down the rear security hallways that connect the county jail to the court building. At the end of the walk through twisting corridors, they reach the holding cell behind Judge Newton Lam's courtroom.

"So the sheriff turns us over to the court bailiff in Judge Lam's holding tank," recalls Crystal. "And as soon as the bailiff takes off the handcuffs, Connie and me start jumping up and down and screaming, 'We're going home!'"

It takes ten minutes for the bailiff to calm the two down so she can open the door of the holding tank, to let them in to see the judge.

"Glad to see you, you're looking good!" says Judge Lam, glancing up from the paperwork on his desk. His mornings are devoted to business, signing papers, dressing out inmates who've been transferred from criminal court to Drug Court, meeting with the rehab team to discuss the progress of the clients who'll be arriving from programs all around the city for that afternoon's formal court session.

Crystal hardly notices that the judge is extending his arm, holding out a sheet of paper for her. Instead, she's facing the back of the court, smiling and waving, thrilled that Tony has come to get her, and anxious to be with him after thirty-four days in jail.

But Ron Thomas, her rehab case manager, taps Crystal on the shoulder, gives her the paper from Judge Lam, and holds out a pen so she can sign it.

"The judge is releasing you to us, in rehab," he tells Crystal, "not to your boyfriend. Try to remember that?"

She stares up at Ron, a tall man in a double-breasted suit whose soft smile and calm manner don't disguise the fact that he knows jail and drug treatment from both sides of the fence.

"But Tony's waiting for me!" protests Crystal as Ron leads her past the visitors' gallery, out the courtroom door, down the elevator, and into the street where, in a concrete bunker of a building only one block from the court, she begins rehab.

In October of 1998, when Crystal is dressed out of jail by Judge Lam, he sends her to a Target Cities pre-placement group to learn the rudiments of rehab while waiting for a program slot to open up. The counselor in charge of the group, in a corner room at the Sheriff's Department a block from the court, is Marillac Mayorga, the same woman who had run Mike, Darrell, and Darlene's group in September of 1997.

"My name's Kenneth, and I'm a heroin addict," Crystal hears the first *sign-in* for the day, after her case manager has led her straight from Judge Lam's courtroom, right past Tony, to a seat in Marillac's pre-placement group.

"Hi, Kenneth!" the assembled addicts chant, and then fall to silence as Crystal, with a great flurry of movement, settles into her chair. She cautiously checks out the scene, fourteen men and women in a semicircle of seats, facing one another.

"Kenneth"—Marillac moves to the blackboard at the front of the room to get him back on focus. She points to the first question he's supposed to answer in his daily group check-in: *Why are you here?*

Kenneth stands abruptly at his seat, stretches to his full six-foot-three football player's bulk, and turns from Marillac to face the others. "I'm here"—his voice booms emphatically—"because that Judge Lam made me come here!"

The group breaks up in laughter and catcalls, and Marillac stands quietly at the front, waiting until the noise dies down.

"Mr. Kenneth," she says softly, "if I remember correctly, you are here because you chose drug treatment instead of prison time."

"You mean I'm not forced to be here?" Kenneth responds, his eyebrows raised in fake surprise. "Then I'm outta here!" And he mocks a gangster strut toward the door, but stops quickly and, his grin exposing the four broken teeth that are all he has, returns to his seat.

"Thank you, Mr. Kenneth," says Marillac. "I see that you've made the choice to stay with us another day."

"No, I'm serious, Marillac," says Kenneth, shaking his head. "I'd never go to no program unless some white man tells me to. I can clean up on my own when I'm ready."

"Well, then, I guess you must be ready," says Marillac, "because you show up here every morning, and when you're not being such a clown you've got a lot of good things to say."

"It's like a job," replies Kenneth. "I come on time every day, I do my job. It ain't like you *want* to go to work. You just do it."

"This isn't a job," says Marillac. "This is your life."

"Right," says Kenneth, "my life, that's why I'm here. But I also got this itch on the back of my head." His hand flies up and he furiously scratches at his scalp.

"What itch?" wonders Marillac.

"The Judge Lam itch!" Kenneth laughs. "I come here 'cause it's the only way I can scratch it off."

The counselor waits for the group's laughter to quiet down again, then says with a smile of her own, "You know, Mr. Kenneth, it doesn't matter what itch you came here to scratch off. As long as you come *here* to do it, instead of scratching it with a needle out there."

Marillac turns her attention to Crystal, and asks her to sign in.

"My name is Crystal," she says, sitting straight up in her chair, "and they say I'm a dope fiend."

"*They* say?" asks Marillac. "What do *you* say?"

"I say I'm here because being in jail would have been a waste of my time. So I heard you're going to give me job training, groups, counseling, school, and all that. And whatever you got, I'm going to take it."

"Very good, Crystal," says Marillac, nodding. "You go to the head of the class."

"I don't want no head of the class," Crystal says, frowning. "I want my ass out of this chair and back home to my man! I been in jail over a month!"

"You'll be on your way as soon as today's group is finished," says Marillac. "But at eight tomorrow morning, I hope you'll be right back in that seat."

"It's not like I got a choice," says Crystal. "I'll be back."

I linger behind with Marillac after Kenneth, Crystal, and the rest of Judge Lam's wards of the court have scattered from the building.

"I was surprised," I tell Marillac, "at the way you ran that group. I thought you'd be a tougher and stricter counselor with the Drug Court clients here than you were with Mike and the others in your voluntary group a year ago."

Marillac shakes her head. "It's just the opposite." She smiles. "I have to be more relaxed with them here. The fact that they're mandated to be in rehab doesn't make their treatment easier, it makes it harder. They have to show up, but then I have to win them over to wanting to change their lives. If I act tough, all I get is an addict who's pissed off at another authority figure. So I've got to grab at what good they have inside them, and they have to see me grabbing it, bringing it out—accepting them."

In an odd turnabout, coerced rehab in the criminal justice system often winds up being more compassionate than are many voluntary rehab programs.

From the moment Crystal entered Drug Court, not a single counselor who evaluated her thought she should be placed in an outpatient rehab program: going home to Tony every night, showing up on her own to group every day. The severity of Crystal's addiction and the craziness of her life led everyone to conclude she would need live-in, intensive treatment in a residential program like Walden House. And once the rehab staff got to know Tony— as they quickly did—the need to tuck Crystal away in a residential setting became even more apparent.

Yet had the counselors and Judge Lam merely used the power of the law to send Crystal, kicking, screaming, and scamming, to a residential program, they'd have lost her before she set foot in the door.

"We *know* Crystal needs residential treatment," Colin Eaton, clinical coordinator of rehab services for Drug Court, tells me. "And we *know* she needs to be away from Tony. But it won't do any good just to force her into residential right away. So we'll let Crystal get herself in trouble with an outpatient program or two. The way she's living, she'll relapse, big time. Hell, she'll probably relapse a bunch of times before catching on that she needs more intensive treatment than she's getting. So we'll just let the game play itself out, take our time. Crystal's going to take us for a rough ride. But we'll stick with her, because we can't just tell her what she needs—she's got to buy into it herself."

It doesn't take long for Crystal to play out her predicted role. Thirteen days after she's released from jail, she hits a weekend run of crack cocaine that makes Mike's heroin relapse when he was at Walden's satellite housing seem in comparison like a sip of beer.

When that weekend ends and Crystal's urine test comes back positive for cocaine, the court's response to her relapse is stunningly different from the reaction Mike had received from Walden. Instead of throwing Crystal out of rehab because she's relapsed, Judge Lam uses the relapse to pull Crystal even further in.

Here's how Crystal tells me her relapse came down:

> I wasn't even thinking about using dope when I left Marillac's group on Friday. This thing happened real sudden, took me by surprise.
>
> Everything was going good; I'm taking on the responsibilities that God sent my way. I'm even thinking about telling my mother about me being in recovery—and she doesn't know I been to jail! I told her I just been away for a while.
>
> My mom lives on a ranch, and she takes care of my three kids, but she'd dropped 'em off with my sister here in the city for the weekend. I hadn't seen 'em for almost two months and I was planning on seeing them that night. But my sister called me at Tony's, says the kids are tired and she's going to put 'em to bed early, why don't I see them another day? So now I'm tripping, because how could she tell me I can't come see

my own kids? Then I figure, yeah, I know, I'm an addict and I gave up that right; that's what the child protectives told me. It's nothing new, so I wasn't really tripping out about it.

I start making Tony's dinner, but then he calls from work and he's missing his calendar, wants me to find it and read him his schedule. Then he gets all pissed at me because of the way I'm reading it, so I hang up the damn phone on him. But I'm calm in my anger, I ain't at no point of frustration where I'm thinking about doing dope. I just need a little break, get out for some fresh air.

So I walk down to the Safeway and come out with a bag of cookies and ice cream. It's like a perfect night, smells real fresh, and I'm walking real slow. I'm thinking how good I feel 'cause I accomplished something this week, got to every treatment group, making progress. I'll be getting my life back with my kids, getting ahead again, get them to start me back in school like they promised.

But I get to the corner and all of a sudden I hear, "Stephie," real loud, you know, my street name. And it's Georgie, pulling up in his car. He says, "Hey, you looking good!" And I'm going, "Georgie! What's up?" And then I'm bobbing and jiving to the music in his car, real cool, rocking the bass coming from his amp.

So Georgie says, "Hey, Steph, I need your help. Hold this for me, I'll pick it up later, you take your cut." And damn, he drops this package in my grocery bag and takes off. And I know what's in that package! So I'm standing on the corner, looking stupid, and all I'm thinking is I got to get this dope out of the Safeway bag!

I am tripping out! So I go into a phone booth and stuff the dope down the front of my pants into my underwear. I'm thinking, I'm going to make some junkie real happy, walk down to 16th and Mission and give this dope to somebody, because I am in recovery. So I'm walking down Mission with a Safeway bag of ice cream and cookies, and a couple grams of crack cocaine stuffed in my underwear. Then I'm thinking, why do I want to give free dope to some dope fiend? I'm fine, I don't really do drugs no more, so I'll just have a little taste of the stuff first. I am serious! I said that to myself, and I had $135 worth of dope in my panties! So that was Friday night, and I didn't make it back home 'till Sunday afternoon, sold some dope, made some money, found my old drug buddy Michael and got a hotel room and some more dope, had me a real good time. But I made it to Marillac's group on Monday. Kind of stumbled in, but I got there.

"Crystal's been doing just fine in Marillac's group," rehab coordinator Colin Eaton tells Judge Lam at the next day's morning gathering in the judge's chambers. Each morning, the judge holds a meeting with the clients' rehab case managers, the court's probation officers and police investigators, and the district attorney and public defender for the Drug Court.

"Crystal's been at group every day," continues Colin, reading from Marillac's report. "She's participating, she's energetic, and she seems to want to advance in the program."

The Drug Court team has pulled their chairs around the judge's desk to discuss each case that will appear in the formal court session that afternoon. Now, they jot down notes in their files on Crystal Holmes and then, assuming they're moving on to the next case, close their copies of her folder.

"*However,*" Colin gets their attention with a sly, jocular tone, "our young lady ran into a little problem over the weekend." The group lets out a collective groan and, knowing Colin's teasing style, each makes a grand gesture to reach for Crystal's file again, waiting for the news.

"She hit a heavy crack cocaine run all weekend," says Colin, "didn't even show up at home. So we have to deal with her relapse. And, her enraged boyfriend is bitching at her, and at us. But the good news is—Crystal came to group on Monday morning and told us she'd been using crack again, even before her pee test came back positive."

"Sure," says Marianne Barrett, the Drug Court district attorney who prosecutes the cases. She turns to Judge Lam. "Crystal's shoving it in our face and saying, 'Hey, I'm doing dope, what're you going to do about it?' " Marianne thumbs quickly through Crystal's file. "Look," she shows the judge, "she's got a '92 case she skipped out on; and now she's going on drug runs while in Drug Court. She's begging to be sent back to criminal court, and we should take her up on it."

"Or," adds Jami Tillotson, Crystal's public defender, "she's saying, 'Hey, I messed up, I know it, but I came right back in and admitted what I did, I still want to try—"

"OK," says Judge Lam, cutting the discussion short while his gaze Ping-Pongs between the prosecuting and defense attorneys. "I'll give Crystal the usual relapse speech in court, get a feel for where she's at. It's her first relapse—"

"Within two weeks of getting here!" interrupts Marianne. "That's no relapse. You've got to *stop using* drugs before you can have a relapse. She's just out there doing dope like she's always been doing. We haven't even touched her."

Judge Lam raises his eyebrows and, as he often manages to do, sighs and smiles at the same time. He looks over at Colin to scope out the opinion of his clinical rehab manager, then closes Crystal's file and opens the next one, saying, "I'll give Crystal my relapse speech in court, we'll see how it goes," and moves on to the next case.

At 3:00 that afternoon, the rear gallery of the courtroom buzzes with the noise of clients waiting to report to the judge. The right gallery fills with orange-clad inmates. A hum of gossip and greetings flies about the high-ceilinged room, ceasing suddenly as the bailiff cries out, "All rise! The Honorable Newton Lam, presiding." A wooden door at the front left of the courtroom swings open and Judge Lam enters and ascends to the bench.

Facing the judge's bench at the front of the court are two long desks, on each side of a tall wooden podium. The district attorney and public defender have spread their files on the left desk and now take their seats. To the right are the rehab case managers, led by Colin, and the court's probation officers. In a small gallery at the left-front corner of the courtroom, memorizing the features of every client's face, are Fred Ponomarenko and Dave Kamita—two narcotics police officers, neither in uniform.

Crystal, in the rear gallery, waits while Judge Lam hears some dozen cases before he glances down at the court calendar and calls out, "Line one-oh-four—Karla Holmes." She makes her way to the podium, front and center in court.

"It's *Crystal* Holmes," she tells the judge. "I thought we changed it from Karla?"

"OK, how're you doing, Ms. Holmes?" asks Judge Lam.

"I've been doing OK," replies Crystal. And then, seeing his raised eyebrows, she adds, smiling, "I mean, I'm doing OK right now."

Judge Lam nods down to Colin, who begins his public report.

"Crystal has been doing excellent work in her pre-placement group, Your Honor," announces Colin. "However, she ran into a little problem with some crack cocaine over the weekend. So I have explained that she may face some consequences today."

"Thank you, Mr. Eaton," says Judge Lam, and then he places his black-robed arms in front of him, leans forward, and stares at Crystal, waiting. She says nothing, but locks eyes with the judge.

"Ms. Holmes," Judge Lam starts out, his voice carrying to every corner of the courtroom, "I want to congratulate you."

The judge pauses, but Crystal continues to stare at him, poker-faced. The addicts in the audience lean forward in their seats, fascinated.

"I'm congratulating you, Ms. Holmes," continues the judge, swinging into his relapse speech, "because even though you relapsed, you are here. So you are still focused on your recovery, and not on the relapse. And that is exactly what we like to see in this court."

Judge Lam has captured Crystal's attention, a look of confusion taking over. Once again, she simply cannot figure out what kind of show to put on for this judge. She waits him out, attuned to his every word.

"Don't get me wrong, Ms. Holmes," says the judge. "It's not that we encourage relapses. It would have been better if you had prevented it. But that's what you're in court and rehab to learn—so that the next time you get to the point of a relapse, you'll recognize it and know how to stop it. A relapse can take you all the way to the bottom again, but you didn't go there with this one. So I congratulate you, for minimizing the effect of this relapse and being back in court today. I am disappointed that you relapsed, but I am elated that you handled it well."

Crystal has recovered her role.

"Thank you, Judge Lam," she says, in her most sincere voice. "Like you said, I really am trying my hardest."

"Well, we're going to help you try harder," replies the judge. "I'm assigning you to do a ninety-ninety—that's ninety Narcotics Anonymous meetings in ninety days, in addition to your regular daily group. And I want you to bring this court a record of every one of those meetings. Between your daily groups here, and the ninety-ninety at N.A., I'm presuming you'll gain a better idea of what brings you to these relapses—so that next time you see one coming, you'll head it off instead of jumping into it. Thank you for being here today, Ms. Holmes. I'll see you back in one week. Good luck to you. And keep up the good work!"

The probation officer at the right side of the podium hands Crystal a slip of paper with her new assignment on it, and the clearly written date of her next court appearance. Then, wide-eyed but smiling, she heads back to her seat in the rear gallery.

At the end of the court session, I ask Colin if, given Crystal's intense level of resistance and manipulation, the consequences she had just received for a weekend crack cocaine binge might have been too mild.

"Of course they were." Colin laughs. "But we haven't lost her yet, have we?"

The rehab case manager packs up the huge pile of files he carries to court each day, preparing to head back to his office in the sheriff's department down the block.

"We want to send Crystal out from Marillac's group to day treatment at the Iris Center for women," Colin tells me. "She needs more intensive rehab, around her problems with drugs *and* her problems with men. I mean, Crystal is still Crystal! It wouldn't have done us any good to come down much harder on her today, risk her running from rehab before we've had a chance to really work with her. She's learned that she's having some difficulty staying clean out there, so we've got a reason for sending her over to the Iris Center now. We'll let them do their thing, see how she responds."

As Colin has noted, Crystal is still Crystal. She immediately bounces out of the Iris Center; she gets so caught up in lies to Tony that he reports to the court, in panic, that she's been kidnapped; she storms out of court one day in such an angry tirade that the Drug Court plainclothes narcotics police officers scour the city looking for her, hoping to head off trouble, they say, before it happens. When they find her, she laughs at all the fuss. "I just needed to take a walk," she says. And on that day, her urine does test negative for cocaine.

Yet for every trick Crystal throws at the court, Judge Lam and the rehab team come back at her with a surprise, albeit the same one each time: they simply stick to her like glue.

"Look, addicts are addicted to drugs, and that means they'll relapse," observes Colin. "That's why they're here. And they don't change overnight just because we're watching them. So they relapse, and we pick 'em up wherever we find them, dust them off, figure out what went wrong, and take it from there. Drug Court works," he concludes, "because we hang in there with them."

———

Drug addiction is a potentially treatable illness, and a fundamental principle of treating *any* illness is that if the patient's symptoms become worse, the level of treatment increases.

Imagine any physician screaming at a diabetic patient, "You ate a piece of chocolate cake? You're out of here!" Or think of accidentally running into your cardiologist at the local pizzeria, just as you finish a slice of double-pepperoni with extra cheese. Not knowing she had witnessed that final bite, you sheepishly tell the doctor you're there retrieving take-out for your kids. "Not only are you loading your body with fat," shouts the cardiologist, in full public view, "but now you're lying to me! Don't show up at the door of my office again!"

In the world of medicine, such behavior is called abandonment, and would warrant an investigation by the local medical board (if not a visit from a malpractice lawyer).

Yet in the world of drug addiction treatment, no counselor batted an eye when, as Michael Pagsolingan's illness worsened, he was subjected to public ridicule at Walden and then his rehab was canceled. How many of us have listened with a sad but agreeing nod when a colleague or friend has whispered, "Jonathan's started drinking again, so they had to kick him out of the program"?

But when Judge Lam, faced with Crystal's accelerating drug use, encourages her to do better and, instead of throwing her back to criminal court, offers her an increased intensity of treatment—the public and much of the rehab world is scandalized because he's "coddling" the junkie, not punishing her severely enough, letting her manipulate him. In fact, it is so unusual to see someone *not* kick an addict out of rehab for using drugs that Judge Lam uses it to achieve an element of surprise, to throw the Drug Court client off balance.

As I drive Crystal to the Iris Center for her first day of rehab there, she tells me she's decided not to do the ninety-ninety—ninety N.A. meetings in ninety days—that Judge Lam has ordered her to attend.

"I have told Colin," she exclaims, "and I have told Marillac, and I have told anybody who'll listen to me, that I am not going to do something just because they want me to! I do things that's going to benefit *me*, Crystal. So I'm doing a ninety-sixty, no ninety-ninety."

"Ninety-sixty?" I ask.

"Yes! Ninety meetings in sixty days! Get the damn thing over with and get that judge out of my hair! I'll do it my way."

We've pulled up in front of the converted storefront that houses the Iris Center—an intensive outpatient rehab group for women only, at 15th and Valencia Streets. Crystal opens the car door and suddenly cries out, "Oh, my God! Wait right here for me!"

She slams the door closed and runs to the building, her head quickly darting in all directions as she checks out the street scene around her. I watch through the glass front door at the Iris Center as she leans immediately across the desk, says a few quick words to the receptionist, and then runs from the desk and flings the door open, trying to get out so quickly that the door slams into her face. Holding her nose, checking for blood, she darts out of the building and throws herself back into my car.

"Drive!" cries Crystal, slouching down in her seat. "Damn, my nose hurts."

"Not until you tell me what the hell is going on," I reply, my foot firmly on the brake.

"Just drive the car!" insists Crystal. "Goddamn! Colin didn't tell me the Iris Center was right across the street from the Pink Palace." Her eyes drift toward the block of pink-painted low-income housing projects across the street.

"Apartment 318," says Crystal, "is Georgie. Apartment 220, that's another of my dealers. Apartment 183, that's where I smoke it up after I score. I know every crackhead in that building, half of them's my old boyfriends, the other half's my business associates. Now the damn Drug Court wants me to take a bus to this block every day for rehab? They crazy!"

I start driving away from the Pink Palace. "What did you tell the receptionist at the Iris Center?" I ask. "They're supposed to be reporting to the court if you're there or not."

"I told her just what I told you," says Crystal. "I cannot walk by the Pink Palace every day, 'cause if I get within a block of that place there's a hundred people crying out, 'Hey, Stephie! What's up?' I come here every day, I'll be right back on the dope. Receptionist says, 'Good thinking! I'll call the court and tell them our program is not for you.' "

I drop Crystal off to talk to Colin, and he sends her back into Marillac's pre-placement group.

"What do you think?" Colin asks me when Crystal's out of earshot. "Is she scamming us?"

"I don't know," I reply. "If she is, that was an impressive performance."

Colin sighs. "OK," he says, "no Iris Center. I'll tell the judge. She's back in Marillac's group until we can figure out what else to do with her."

I head in to join Marillac's session, just as Crystal is reciting her group sign-in.

"My name is Crystal, and I'm a dope fiend."

"Hi, Crystal."

She looks up at the board. *Why are you here?*

"I am here," says Crystal, sitting primly upright in her chair, "to work on the biological, social, psychological, and spiritual issues around my addiction."

After a stunned moment of silence, the entire group of addicts in court-mandated recovery breaks into boisterous applause. Crystal stands, laughing, and takes a bow.

As Christmas and New Year's of 1998 approach, three months after her start in Drug Court, Crystal hits her third relapse. This time, she disappears entirely from the watchful eyes of the court. Judge Lam issues a warrant for her arrest, and sends the narcotics police and warrant officers out to search the Mission district and bring her in.

At the same time, Mike is doing his best to avoid the Mission as he winds down from his wedding with Connie and prepares for the arrival of their baby the following May.

"I'm doing good, man," Mike tells me when I pick him up at work to drive him back to the apartment he and Connie are renting.

It's been months since the hot summer day when I'd watched a broken-down Mike shoot heroin in Dolores Park. Now, he looks great. There's an easiness to Mike's mood as he gives me a big hug and apologizes for having disappeared for so long.

"I've been sticking with this new plumbing job," he tells me, "getting my life back together with Connie. Don't drink none, don't even do marijuana. And I'm working hard every day, got some extra money coming in. I just do a hit of heroin every now and then, that's about it drug-wise."

We drive west through San Francisco's outer Sunset District to just a few blocks short of the beach along the Pacific Ocean, pulling up at a row of small condominium-style apartments. Mike opens the door to his house and I am greeted by a scene of working-class domestic bliss: Connie, visibly pregnant, still in a dress and sport jacket from her insurance-adjuster job downtown, greets her tall, handsome man in his grease-covered overalls with a warm hug and a kiss; they talk for a moment about their days' work; Mike pets and feeds the cat; then the two sit on the couch in front of a 27-inch TV embedded in the shelves of an entertainment center facing the couch, while Connie sorts and folds the wash.

It's a small apartment, but they've figured that with their combined incomes of $3,700 a month they'll be able to move up to buying a house away from the city soon enough— provided that Connie shops a bit less (they have over $7,000 in credit card debt), and Mike cuts back on his heroin purchases, for which, unfortunately, he must pay cash. Connie has no idea that her husband is still spending money on drugs.

"I wish I could be honest with her about it," Mike had told me on the way over to their apartment, "but she'd kick me out in a flash. What good would that do? I'll be off the dope before the baby comes, so it's best she doesn't know right now."

The phone rings and Mike answers. It's Connie's younger sister, Geraldine, who not only works at the same company as Connie but also lives in an apartment at the same complex as the newlyweds. Mike hands the phone to Connie, makes a silly face to me, and whispers, "It's my sister-in-law. She doesn't like me too much. Thinks I'm a bad influence on Connie."

He taps his wife on the shoulder to interrupt Connie and his sister-in-law's conversation. "Hey, babe? OK if me and Lonny go out for a little drive?" Connie nods and Mike ushers me to the door.

"Let's drive out to the ocean," he says. "Get a chance to talk."

The Great Highway runs parallel to the beach at the west end of San Francisco, fading from touristed seaside to isolated sandy stretches as we head south. Mike tells me to pull over at a small, remote parking area that hangs over a deserted, rocky beach, where a large sign announces NO PARKING AFTER DARK. He directs me to a pitch-black corner, hidden from the view of the highway, then rolls down the window, and the noise of the waves and smell of the ocean flood in as he lights up a cigarette.

"This is where a bunch of us come to shoot up after we score at night," says Mike, taking a drag on the cigarette, blowing smoke out the window, and leaning his head out to suck in the sea breeze. "It's a nice safe place right here," he says. "Cops can't see you at all."

"Right," I reply. "A dark corner in a hidden parking lot, the roar of the ocean to overcome all sounds, invisible from the road, and loaded with desperate junkies. I think your idea of safe may be different than mine."

"Just keep the engine running and the doors locked." Mike laughs, turning his head to look out the rear window. "I'll keep checking around to be sure nobody comes up to toss us out of the car and steal it. I'm on top of it. Trust me."

He leans back for a moment, taking a long draw on his cigarette, and then turns and says, softly, "Man, I'm sorry. I let Walden down. I let Connie down. I let me down. I been too ashamed to see you until now. But Walden did me a lot of good, man, so don't go blaming them. What's happening with me is my own damn fault, not theirs."

"I knew they had *some* effect on you," I tell Mike. "Last time I saw you, you were still doing dope, but you wouldn't jaywalk to go get it."

"Fuuuck." He lets out a low laugh. "That was crazy, huh? But since then I keep making it like a month, maybe six weeks in a row staying clean before I hit the needle again. That's compared to me doing dope three, four times a day before I started treatment. I mean, I ain't proud, but it's something."

"What makes you start up again after you reach six weeks?" I ask.

"Man," sighs Mike. "If I could tell you that—" His voice trails off and he looks out over the ocean, now dimly lit by a quarter moon breaking briefly through the clouds. Then he shakes his head and rocks forward.

"I don't know, man, everything's going good, and I get to four, maybe six weeks clean. And then suddenly I'm feeling real scared, and I don't even know what about. Like Christmas just came, right? And my ex-wife is keeping me from being in touch with my girls. I mean I couldn't even give them no presents. So that freaked me out, what kind of father am I, huh? I should be giving 'em presents, seeing 'em open the presents, sharing Christmas together, the whole thing. So I start beating myself up for what I done to my girls their whole lives. And then I get all these visions in my head, and it's like torture, man. So I start feeling sorry for myself, but try to tell myself, it's OK, I got a good wife now, another kid coming along, it's going to be OK. But it ain't working just saying that over and over in my head. And shit, I ain't making no excuses, but I get to this point where, fuck, it's like this light goes on inside me that says, man, a fix of dope would be *good* right now. Ain't no way I can feel worse being a junkie than I'm feeling not being a junkie! You know, self-medication stuff. I feel better, even if it's just for a few moments. But then I sink down again."

"Would you have used that expression, 'self-medication,' " I ask, "before your Walden days?"

"Never even heard of it before Walden," replies Mike. "I mean, I know what I'm doing, and why, because of what I learned at Walden. I'm on my pity pot, feeling sorry for myself, trying to medicate my feelings with dope. And I know that's a fucking lame excuse. But listen, man, I've had a taste now of what life can really be, here with Connie, the baby coming and all, and I'm going for it. I am doing everything I can to get there, and I know it means no more dope, no matter what. I want to give this kid a fair shake, you know? I want to be a part of this baby's life. I *got* to be part of it. I'm off the dope, completely, by the time the kid comes. I swear it."

The roar of the waves from the darkness outside the car almost drowns out the sound of Mike's sobbing, and we've both forgotten where we are, let our guard down, when a harsh beam of light suddenly probes at our faces through my window. Then there's an abrupt pounding on the roof to get our attention from Mike's side. The engine is running and I grip the wheel, ready to hit the gas, but Mike reaches across to grab my hand.

"It's OK, officer," he says, leaning out his open window. "We're just sitting here, having a chat."

The light that had blinded me moves from my face and around to the front of the car, checking the license plate while a second officer heads back to the patrol car. I whisper to Mike, "You carrying any dope on you?"

He stares at me, his eyes wide, then gently pats his shirt and pants pockets. He lets out a sigh of relief. "No dope, no syringes. I'm clean."

The police officer's flashlight beams again into the car, into Mike's eyes, back to me, then searching the backseat before he says, calmly, "No parking allowed here at night. I don't care if you're having a talk or what you're doing." The light clicks off and the officer moves back into the darkness, the brilliant beam coming on again a moment later as he searches through the line of bushes that marks the edge of the beach.

"There's probably a dozen guys scattered in those bushes, shooting up," says Mike. "Damn! Could have been me in there."

I slowly turn the steering wheel, ease my foot on the gas, and start back to his and Connie's apartment. Mike slouches in his seat, and I beat him to his line. "Fuuuck," I say slowly.

Back on 44th Avenue, I follow Mike's gaze to the apartment, where Connie is waiting for him.

"You lived with Connie before I met you, before all this rehab stuff," I said. "If I had walked into your house then, what would I have seen that was different?"

Mike responds instantly. "No, man, you don't get it!" He laughs. "It's what you *wouldn't* have seen. Those VCRs we got? Gone! The TV? Gone! Connie would come home and she'd say, 'What happened to the TV and VCR?' And I'd say, 'Damn, somebody must have broke into the house when we were out, took 'em!' "

"You sold them for dope?"

"Hell, yeah! That house was stripped bare, damn thieves coming in all the time."

Mike is suddenly serious.

"But you know what else you wouldn't have seen back then that you see now?" he asks. "Me saying to Connie, over and over, every chance I get—'I love you, honey. I'm going to be here for you and that baby 'cause you're both more important to me and I love you more than anything in this whole, wide world.' "

Mike opens the car door to head back into his home, but then leans over to give me a long, warm embrace. "You get it, man?" he asks. "If you had known me a couple of years ago, you wouldn't have seen no hope. And that's what I got now. All this hope for my future."

Crystal is bubbling over with glee in anticipation of seeing her children for Christmas. On December 11, already awaiting the upcoming holiday, she tells me, "I got to get Colin to excuse me from giving pee samples here during Christmastime, 'cause my mom wants to take me up to the ranch for the week, to be with my kids."

Since the time she had fled from the Iris Center, nearly breaking her nose on the way out, Crystal has been showing up every day at Marillac's group. And she has indeed been attending, as she had threatened, more than one N.A. meeting every day; she's on schedule to finish her assigned ninety meetings, in sixty days. Colin and the entire rehab team and Judge Lam have been pleasantly surprised, although cautiously optimistic, about her progress. So during a morning team meeting they decide to give Crystal permission to spend Christmas week out of town at her mother's ranch, with her children and family.

At 3:00, ten days before Christmas, I wait in the rear gallery of the courtroom to watch Crystal's appearance before Judge Lam. Everyone is milling about, waiting for the bailiff to announce, "All rise," when there's a sudden, heavy tap on my shoulder. I spin around to see Tony, neatly dressed in his MUNI bus driver's uniform.

"Do you know where she is?" he shouts, and all heads in the courtroom turn our way.

"I presume she's coming here," I say.

"No she's not," replies Tony. "She's gone. She left the house on Friday night to pick up dinner. Four days ago. Never came back."

Tony's words are spewing out in ragged bursts of anger.

"I haven't seen her," he exclaims. "Her sisters haven't heard a word from her, neither has her mother. I've checked."

I look down quickly and see Tony's clenched fists, and then up to his wide-eyed stare.

"So *you* tell me where she is," he spits out. "*You* know."

"Can we go out to the hallway?" I ask. "They're about to start the court session."

Tony follows me out the thick double doors of the courtroom and, standing now in the long hallway, I see that he is near tears.

"I called the morgue," he says, his voice cracking. "I called the jail, I called the hospitals—I used every one of the aliases she uses. Nothing. I'm going downstairs now to file a missing persons report."

"I'll check with the Drug Court probation officers and the counselors," I tell Tony. "I'm really sorry."

He stares down at the floor for a moment, then looks up. "Here's my phone number," he says. "If you hear anything, call me." He strides toward the elevator, heading to file a missing persons report on Crystal with the police.

"Line seventy, Crystal Holmes," announces Judge Lam, halfway through the day's court calendar. He waits, and then repeats the announcement insistently, looking about the courtroom. "Line seventy. Crystal Holmes."

Judge Lam stares at the rear door, as if Crystal might somehow, miraculously materialize.

"OK," he declares after a moment, jotting a mark in her file. "I'm issuing a warrant for Crystal Holmes. No bail if she's picked up." Fred Ponomarenko and Dave Kamita, the plainclothes narcotics police officers in the small left gallery of the courtroom make a note of the warrant, and Judge Lam moves on to the next case on the calendar.

"I don't know anything," says Colin, holding his palms up as soon as I approach him at the end of the court session. Jami Tillotson, Crystal's public defender, has come over toward Colin with the same questioning look.

"I haven't heard a thing," says Jami. "It's weird. I mean, she's street smart, and she knows that if she's in trouble she can call me, and that she *has* to come to court. This feels like more than her usual relapse stuff. It worries me."

"We have no idea where she's at," says Colin. "And in this courtroom, with these clients, that's not so unusual. We'll just have to wait it out."

"Tony's downstairs filing a missing persons report," I tell them.

Colin stares for a moment, and then smiles as he turns to pack up the day's files.

"Tony," he says, "is probably why Crystal has disappeared. That man is a time bomb, so maybe she's just diving for cover. But wherever she is, if and when she shows up again, she's going to have to come up with one good story for the judge not to throw her butt in jail."

————

In the week before Crystal shows up again, everyone has a theory about what's happened, and the rumors fly high.

Connie Davis, her friend from jail: "I heard Crystal's old boyfriend just got out of prison. She's with him."

Marillac: "Crystal and Tony planned it all out, so she can escape from the court. That's why he's putting on this big show of concern. Tony knows where she is."

Colin: "Crystal lies, so whatever she winds up telling us about where she's been, that's not it."

Kenneth, from Marillac's group: "I checked with some people over at the Pink Palace and they say they seen her there, all stoned out. But they was all stoned out, too, so who knows what they saw."

Jami: "I don't do the rumor game. We'll know soon enough where she's at. If she shows, I'll try to keep her out of jail and persuade the judge to send her straight to a residential program. I think she'll be ready to buy in this time."

At 8:00 A.M. on December 23, eight days after Crystal disappeared, she walks calmly into Marillac's morning group and takes her usual seat.

She looks like a cat just dragged in from the rain. Usually meticulously dressed, Crystal is now wearing a blue-denim shirt over a white T-shirt, each untucked and hanging loosely over a pair of dirty blue jeans. Her head is crowned by a tattered baseball cap, the hat's front bill shadowing her face, her hair sticking out from the corners. The forlorn look on her face would convince anyone she had just climbed out of her deathbed.

"Crystal," says Marillac, "you're in the sheriff's department and you're not allowed to wear a hat. They have to be able to see your face."

"No way," says Crystal, lifting her hand to her mouth to block a hacking, choking cough. "My hair's all messed up and I ain't showing it to nobody." She twists the cap around backwards on her head so her face is better exposed.

"That's better," says Marillac. "But I have one question for you."

"What's that?" Crystal looks up, her lips pursed, waiting.

Marillac hovers over her. "My question is," she says, straight-faced, "do you know how happy we are to see you?"

The counselor breaks into a grin, and then bends down to give Crystal a hug.

"Thank you," says Crystal, a smile barely easing onto her lips. "I'm happy to be here. Sort of."

And then she's off and running. "See, it all turns out for the better because I was supposed to have been up with my kids by now, but I got kidnapped by this guy named Pops, so I got to explain to Judge Lam today what's been up, where I been at. But this gives me some more time to go shopping for my kids' presents today. Tony's going to take me shopping right after court, 'cause I still got my kids' Santa Claus list, and I can't wait to see the look on their faces when they see me come up to the ranch with their presents. But then, you know me, I could talk forever if you don't stop me—so we better move on. Oh, yeah, I forgot," she looks at the sign-in board. "My name's Crystal and I'm a dope addict. I'm here because," she pauses, "because it's better than being out there."

Marillac stares for a moment, letting Crystal's chatter dodge any discussion about the reasons she had disappeared, or where she's been.

By 3:00, Crystal has finished talking to Colin, and he has reported her story to Judge Lam, who adds her case to that afternoon's list of formal court appearances. She and I are sitting in the back gallery, with the other addicts to be seen in open court that day, waiting for the judge to enter.

"I don't know why everybody's so surprised that I disappeared," Crystal tells me. "I *told* Marillac I was going to relapse."

"What? I thought you said you disappeared from court because you were kidnapped?"

"Damn, I thought you been paying attention!" says Crystal. "I relapsed first. Just for a day, though. *Then* I was kidnapped. I ain't going to lie about it." She reaches into her backpack and pulls out a sheet of paper, a writing assignment about "How do I feel" that she had handed in to Marillac just days before she had disappeared.

I feel like a little girl caught up in a world of misunderstood layers trying to fit in this world so it will open up to me with full arms. But I feel uncomfortable and misplaced. I was more successful in my old world. People their liked me, they excepted me. I didn't have to worrie about a lot of things there. Life was better there. So why am I here? Today I have money, food, clothees, am OK. But fucked up mentally. I am letting everyone tell me were I should be and were I am going and how I should feel. I don't feel good about anything right now actually I'm crying inside, breaken down emotionally, to scream feels good to shout even better. The situation to use dope is at its full scale. Lord Help me not to blow it. My nights are longer my days longer. If I don't find myself soon I'll fuck it all up.

"All rise," announces the bailiff. "Judge Newton Lam, presiding." When he calls Crystal's name and she faces him at the podium, there is no debate about kidnapping, lying, or truthfulness. Without further ado, Crystal nods vigorously in assent to the court's plan that, as soon as a bed opens up at A Woman's Place—an intensive residential rehabilitation program—she will go there, and stay put.

The introductory pamphlet to A Woman's Place, *Beginning My Plan of Action,* refers the client to page sixty of the *Big Book of Alcoholics Anonymous:* "Each person is like an actor who wants to run the whole show; is forever trying to arrange the lights, the ballet, the scenery and the rest of the players in his own way. . . . Is he not, even in his best moments, a producer of confusion?"

A Woman's Place could not have picked a better passage to describe the commotion that ensues the moment Crystal leaves Judge Lam's courtroom that day, when she, Tony, two narcotics officers, and the court all try to run the show their way—even though Crystal had, just moments before, *agreed* to start rehab at A Woman's Place.

Tony stops Crystal and me as soon as we step through the courtroom doors and into the hallway.

"We need a conference, the three of us," he says, blocking the way.

I look at Crystal, who is glaring at Tony, her arms crossed against her chest.

"Go ahead," she tells him, "have your damn conference."

The stream of addicts exiting the court flows around the three of us.

Tony turns to me. "I need to tell you what's really up with her," he begins, "because I love Crystal, I really do. But she's taking me down with her, and I don't know how to stop it. I swear, I thought she was dead when she disappeared like that. But now I know where she was gone to, and I'm going to tell you—"

"What the hell are you doing?" exclaims Crystal, staring at Tony as if he were an alien being.

"I'm spilling the beans, that's what!" he shouts at her, and I look desperately down the hallway, anxious for any excuse to get out from between them.

"Ain't nothing you can tell anybody in this court that they don't already know," exclaims Crystal. "I done told 'em!" With that Crystal starts giggling, shaking her head back and forth as she looks up and down the empty hall.

"Don't be laughing," says Tony. "This is not some joke."

"I'm laughing because I'm nervous," she shouts. "You know that's what I do when I get nervous! Your whole attitude scares me. You scare the shit out of me, Tony!"

Just then the courtroom doors open and Fred Ponomarenko, the court's plainclothes narcotics cop, heads into the hallway, in time to hear Crystal shout, "Fuck you, Tony!" and see her race down the stairs, to the streets.

"Is she OK?" Fred asks Tony.

"No, she's not OK," he replies, and I can hear Tony suck in a deep breath. "She's going out there to use dope," he tells the narcotics cop, "and that's what she's been doing behind all your backs all this time!"

"I thought you backed up her story about being kidnapped?" asks Fred.

"Bunch of bullshit," replies Tony. "She came home three days ago, and she's been using dope ever since, and letting other people abuse her body. I'm going to go get her." And Tony, too, turns and runs down the stairs.

"Aww, damn," says Fred, turning to me and looking down at his watch: 5:15. "Let me drop this stuff in my office." He sighs. "Looks like we got some street work to do. Meet me in front of the courthouse."

By the time I hit Bryant Street, directly in front of the stately, columned courthouse, Tony is a block up, pacing back and forth in front of his car.

"I don't want to put Crystal out of the house and into the streets," he tells me when I catch up to him, "but that's just what I'm going to do." He turns and slams his hand against the hood of the car, then resumes pacing. "Damn! I did this scene ten years ago, with a woman who I loved, but I didn't know she was into drugs. We had a baby, and then she split, and now I've got to support them both. It's ten years later and I've finally got a stable job and I've pulled my own ass up again. I am *not* letting Crystal pull me down with her."

Fred, with his partner, Sergeant Dave Kamita, walks up alongside us.

"She's not here at the car," Tony tells them. "She was supposed to meet me here. So she's out there doing dope, and who knows what else."

He reaches out suddenly to shake the hands of the two plainclothes narcotics officers and says, without a hint of irony, "You both have a happy holiday, best wishes to your families." Then Tony gets into his car and drives away.

"Here we go," Fred tells Dave, and they head for the police parking lot, filled with identical white, unmarked cars. The two pile into the front seats, Fred driving, with me in the back behind the metal grating. They pull out to scour the streets for Crystal.

"Technically, we can't do anything even if we do find her," Fred turns to tell me as they drive onto Bryant Street from the parking lot. "I mean, she showed up in court today, she hasn't done anything to get arrested, and all we seen after court is that she had a fight with her boyfriend. By all the rules, she's still with the program."

"So why," I wonder out loud, "are two narcotics officers and a reporter, in an unmarked police car, at six at night, out in the streets searching for Crystal?"

Dave turns to face me. "It's just to let her know we're around," he says. "You know, that we're watching out for her."

"I'm sure she'll find that very reassuring," I offer. "And what happens if you do find her?"

"I'll just pull the car over," replies Fred, "and say, 'Hey, Crystal, what you doing out here in this neighborhood? What you got in mind?' You know, just let her know we're thinking about her."

As the hunt for Crystal continues, Fred and Dave chat, in a friendly and caring way, about their assumption that, wherever Crystal is, she's up to no good. There is no presumption of innocence—we're in a cop car, not a courtroom. Since Crystal always plays her role lavishly as the scamming junkie, Fred and Dave respond with their own superb performance as streetwise, suspicious narcs.

Fred guides the plain white car up Mission Street, driving slowly in the right lane as he and Dave scan the scene. At 15th, he makes a slow right turn, goes up a block to Valencia, and pulls up by the street crowd in front of the Pink Palace. Nobody seems to notice the white car, but within two minutes every single person on the block has drifted away. We're parked at the sidewalk, alone.

"They kind of recognize the car by now," says Fred, pulling out from the curb to continue the search. "We're out here cruising every day, looking for any of the forty or so addicts Judge Lam's put warrants on because they've split from Drug Court."

"How many do you find?" I ask.

"Dave and me get about two a month," says Fred. "The rest that get caught are picked up by other cops, for various infractions. They fingerprint them, find they're Drug Court refugees, and bring 'em in. So Dave and me are really out here just to maintain a street presence."

They give up on their cruise through the Mission and head toward the Tenderloin. "I got this itch that says she's in the Tenderloin, streetwalking," says Fred. "She'll hit a quick high and then be out of money, so she's gonna have to turn a trick or two to get some cash, keep the dope run rolling."

"I think she'll find a John *first*," says Dave, "and *then* cop the drugs. That's my gut feeling."

"I don't remember anything on Crystal's rap sheet about prostitution," I comment, and the two turn to stare.

"Sorry," I say. "Silly of me."

We cruise down Eddy Street, past rows of desperate-looking women in tight pants and tiny halters, all of whom turn their faces away when they see our car. There's no sign of Crystal, but when we swing past Hallidie Plaza I do see that Glenda is out on her bench, curled up for the night. I'm tempted to ask Fred and Dave to stop and see if they can find her a shelter bed before the evening rains start—but that's not their mission.

"You know," says Fred, turning the car toward 6th and Market, another crack cocaine hot spot, "I've told Crystal, I'm a cop, but I ain't no liberal cop. So if you mess up, I'll come find you. But I also told Crystal, like me and Dave tell them all, we're part of Drug Court now, so even if we are cops, we're your friends if you're doing good."

Dave pulls out his cell phone and dials Tony's number as they continue their cruise.

"Tony? It's Sergeant Kamita," he says. "Where's Crystal usually hang out when she's doing dope? Does she have money with her? Just twenty bucks? Yeah, that's gone by now, we're sure of that. Listen, if she comes in, you give us a call. And keep this conversation just between you and me, OK?" He snaps the phone neatly shut.

After two hours, they quit the search, Fred getting out at the BART station to head for his home in the suburbs, Dave dropping me back at the front of the courthouse where we'd started.

"Maybe Crystal will show up at Marillac's group in the morning," I suggest, getting out and thanking him for the ride.

"If she does"—Dave laughs amicably—"you give me a buzz, OK? I like surprises."

When Dave pulls out, I go into the court building to dial my home phone machine and check messages. The first is from Crystal, giggling.

"Hey, Lonny, I was right there at the apartment when Sergeant Kamita called Tony, looking for me! What they doing out there, chasing around like that? I was just pissed at Tony and walked home instead of riding with him. I'll see you in group tomorrow morning, they may have a bed ready for me at that Woman's Place program. I sure hope so. You know what? I'm getting tired of being out here running around like I been doing. This last week nearly killed me. Time to get myself inside and into that program. See ya tomorrow! Oh, and say hi to those cops for me, OK?"

The movement toward Drug Courts pushing rehab—instead of criminal courts doling out prison sentences—has come to resemble a populist uprising composed of the strangest of bedfellows. Hard-core, hard-on-crime conservative narcotics prosecutors have joined with liberal, reform-minded judges, police and probation officers, district attorneys, public defenders, and addicts' advocates—all of whom promulgate an approach to addiction that appears, from every which way you examine it, to be soft on crime.

Such an unwieldy and politically unpalatable strategy in the war on drugs is perpetually at risk of being shut down by prison-building politicians responding to cries of *lock-'em-up* from the voters. The Drug Court programs would have disappeared long ago if not for two facts. One, they work. Two, the professionals who work in the Drug Courts have formed alliances as powerful as their jail-oriented opponents.

On December 10, 1998, just before Crystal took off on her pre-Christmas holiday drug run (aka her kidnapping), Judge Lam and the entire San Francisco Drug Court team travel to the state capital for a meeting of the California Association of Drug Court professionals. In the ornate ballrooms of the Doubletree Hotel, men and women in dark business suits mingle with others in relaxed sportswear, Black Muslim caps, and African dashikis. Then they all file into a chandeliered banquet hall to sit at elaborately set tables and dine, waiting for opening remarks from the Honorable Darrell Stevens. Judge Stevens, a rural Butte County superior court judge, lists among his ardent community supporters such known radical organizations as the Chamber of Commerce and Lions Club. As the main course is served by formally attired waiters, the dignified supervising judge for the Butte County Drug Courts ascends the podium, adjusts the microphone, and in the best of revolutionary traditions raises a tightly clenched fist in the air, proclaiming to a boisterous outcry from the audience, "We cannot be stopped! The momentum is here!" A sea of clenched revolutionary fists rises in the air to join him, then returns to the chicken cordon bleu.

As prosecuting attorney Helen Harberts describes these conferences: "Try to think of hanging around a campfire singing 'Kum Ba Yah,' with handcuffs."

Since the first experiment in Dade County, Florida, in 1989, 455 Drug Courts have been established across the country, with 287 more in development. Yet the concept of treating criminal-offending addicts in community-based rehab instead of prisons is still seen by mainstream law-enforcement and the judiciary as a fringe, radical movement, known disparagingly in the halls of the criminal justice system as *Hug Courts.*

"Any thug-huggers out there?" jokes the Honorable Jeffrey Tauber, president of the National Association of Drug Court Professionals, addressing the audience of four hundred court judges, attorneys, cops, and rehab workers now starting dessert. But then Judge Tauber, and every speaker after him, gets down to business, describing study after study that have shown that Drug Courts, in spite of their hug-a-thug reputation, have been more effective at keeping addicts off drugs and away from committing crimes than anything else the criminal justice system has ever thrown at them.

The U.S. Department of Justice calculates that "close to 100,000 drug dependent offenders have entered drug court programs . . . and over seventy percent are either still enrolled or have graduated—more than double the rate of traditional treatment program retention rates." For those addicts who have graduated from rehab under the supervision of Drug Court, the rates of repeated criminal offenses have been an astonishingly low 2 to 20 percent.

More important, says the federal Drug Courts Program Office, "Unlike traditional treatment programs, becoming 'clean and sober' is only the first step toward Drug Court graduation. Almost all Drug Courts require participants to obtain a General Equivalency Diploma, maintain employment, be current in all financial obligations, including drug court fees and child support payments . . . , and to have a sponsor in the community. Many programs also require participants to perform community service hours—to give back to the community that is supporting them through the Drug Court program."

Slowly, the word about Drug Court successes has spread, pulling in even the most hard-on-crime conservatives to fight the lonely battle of Drug Court revolutionaries.

In a conference room to the side of the banquet hall, Helen Harberts, also from rural Butte County, addresses a Drug Court discussion group.

"I used to be a hell-on-wheels narcotics prosecutor," says Harberts, in a gruff voice that seems to substantiate her claim. "And I will tell you—it did not work! In ten years as a criminal prosecutor, I saw five addicts who came back clean and stayed that way. I get five every month at Drug Court now. So let me put it this way: My name is Helen, and I'm a Drug Court addict."

I ask her after the session why, if Drug Courts are so effective, they are so little used? Looking at national arrests for drug possession alone, there are 800,000 addicts brought to the criminal courts annually; and there are hundreds of thousands of others arrested for nonviolent property crimes each year, offenses committed solely to feed addictions. Yet in ten years, only 100,000 addicted criminals have been sent through Drug Courts instead of to prisons.

Harberts would like to see all addicted nonviolent criminals file through Drug Courts rather than jail cells—which return addicts years later to the same drugs and crimes they'd been arrested for in the first place. But she knows this is a far-off dream.

"It's going to take a while to filter down," explains the prosecuting attorney. "Drug Court people talk treatment, we talk cop, we talk court, we know legal, we know drugs, and we know therapy. So who else should be dealing with addicts but us? But prosecuting attorneys and politicians see Drug Courts as all warm and fuzzy, so they back off. How often can you tell lawyers, district attorneys, and public defenders, 'Sit down and be quiet, let your clients talk'? They're not *good* at that. So we're fighting an uphill battle for recognition."

In that battle the Drug Court revolutionaries are bombarded by the heavy artillery of opinion polls, showing that citizens are crying out for prisons, not rehab. In 1998, 84 percent of polled Americans wanted to see tougher criminal penalties for drug users. When citizens were offered nineteen options for reducing the effects of illegal drugs on our society, their top three choices were: severe drug penalties; anti-drug education; more funding for police. Only 19 percent supported increased treatment for addicts.*

Harberts fights those opinion polls with her own hard data: "We've got an eleven percent recidivism rate at our Drug Court," she says, "and I never, never would have believed it." Then she returns, jokingly, to the hug-a-thug theme. "I can understand where the public doubt is coming from," she tells me. "You should have seen me the first time I was in court and saw the judge and D.A. hugging a new graduate. I thought, those judges and lawyers ought to go get themselves some real jobs. I mean, my eyes were bulging out of my head!"

Harberts, who looks as if she could stare down the coldest murderer, and has, shrugs. "You should see me now," she tells me. "I'm at those Drug Court graduations and a graduate comes over to me with his arms outstretched, and"—she scrunches up her face into the tightest of grimaces—"I'm whispering to myself, it's OK, I can do it, take a deep breath, it'll be all right—" Harberts throws open her arms, spread wide, ready to hug a thug, and then falls back, laughing.

"OK, now that we're through with *that*," she emphasizes, "let me tell you what Drug Court *is* about. It's about public safety. Drug Court is the community, and the community is us, because we all have children and relatives who are dying from this plague. So we are results oriented. We have to show our community that what we do works, that it improves public safety, and that we are on the same page with them. So our Drug Court joins up with the rehab programs, the hospitals, the police, probation, the business community. Hell, you got a job opening? Hire somebody from our program—we *know* when they're clean, and we *know* when they're using. Hire anybody who's not in Drug Court and, I'm serious, you

---

*In November 2000, California reversed this trend and voted to send non-violent addicts to treatment. See Political Update at the end of the book.

don't know what they've been putting in their bodies on the way to work! We guarantee our workers, and they keep their jobs."

Then Harberts delivers the most straightforward answer as to why she insists there should be more Drug Courts. "Eighty-nine percent of our graduates are still clean," she says. "You want public safety? Look at those numbers."

Therapeutic Communities, without Drug Court, also boast success rates for *graduates* of 75 percent. But in Therapeutic Communities, nine of ten drop out long before graduation. When Drug Court is supervising rehab, a full 70 percent are retained in treatment—an overall success rate that leaves non–Drug Court programs in the dust.

Listening to Harberts and the other Drug Court converts, it all sounds too simple to be true. And it is.

Crystal, as she had told Judge Lam she would, did enter the residential rehab program at A Woman's Place. She stayed for ninety days, and became their star rehab pupil. Then, just before her graduation, she went out on a one-day pass with Tony—and disappeared. Fred and Dave, armed with a warrant for Crystal's arrest issued by Judge Lam, climbed into their white, unmarked car and searched high and low for her. But she had vanished into thin, crack-cocaine-filled air.

Six months later, on September 14, 1999, a police officer in the Mission, looking for a robbery suspect, stops a small black woman for questioning. She's not the thief he is looking for, but the cop plugs her fingerprints into his computer. He comes up with Judge Lam's warrant for Crystal Holmes, and throws her in jail.

The sheriff's deputy leads me into the tiny jail interview room, then disappears to get Crystal. Down the hall, I hear the repeated clanging of metal doors as they bring her through the security gates to the interview room.

"I'm glad to see you," I say when the deputy brings her in. "It's been a long time."

"Yeah." Crystal laughs. "I'll bet everybody's glad to see me. Judge Lam's probably having a party right now!"

In fact, Judge Lam is not having a party. Judge Julie Tang is. She has taken Newton Lam's position as Drug Court judge, and during the time I am interviewing Crystal in jail, Judge Tang is organizing the morning team meeting with Colin, the D.A., public defender, rehab case managers, probation officers, and narcotics police. I scurry from my interview with Crystal, down the back corridors from the jail to the courthouse, and into Judge Tang's chambers in time for the meeting.

"Let's start the day off with the good and bad news," Colin tells Judge Tang. "The good news is that they've picked up Crystal Holmes. And the bad news—is that they've picked up Crystal Holmes!" Colin shakes his head, laughing, and tries to explain Crystal to Judge Tang, who has never met her.

"It took us months, and a whole bunch of relapses, to get Crystal tucked into A Woman's Place, and we thought we had her settled down just fine," says Colin. "She was doing real good for a few months and then, *poof,* gone! That was six months ago. We have no idea where she's been since then, what she's been up to, or even how or why she's back again. All we know so far is that some cop found her, and she's on our court calendar today. So we either throw her case back to criminal court, or we stick with her."

Judge Tang barely bats an eye, quickly overriding the objection of the D.A., who insists that Crystal's case bounce immediately back to criminal court. "It seems that she's scheduled in Drug Court this afternoon," says the judge, "so let's hear what she has to say."

At 2:00, the sheriff marches Crystal along with the other orange-clad inmates to the gallery at the right side of Judge Tang's courtroom. Crystal knows that this time there will be no surprises, she has pushed the court way too far with her last, prolonged disappearing act. She is certain she's come to Judge Tang today to do no more than the paperwork that will remove her from Drug Court and send her case back to criminal court.

"Line seventy-six," calls out Judge Tang, "Crystal Holmes."

The deputy nods to Crystal and she leaves the orange-clad zone and steps up to the podium, front and center in the courtroom.

"How're you doing, Ms. Holmes?" asks Judge Tang.

"Fine, thank you," says Crystal, meeting the judge's eye.

"I hear you left our program," says Judge Tang, watching Crystal carefully. "And now you're back with us again?"

"I guess so," says Crystal, nodding. "Just for today."

"I would like you to write me a letter, Ms. Holmes," says the judge, "saying why you left the program, what's been happening while you were gone, and why you want to be back in Drug Court. Maybe this court is not the place for you. But maybe it is."

Judge Tang makes a note in Crystal's file, and then closes it. "Let's keep you in jail for thirty days while you write that letter and have a chance to think about things," she tells Crystal. "Then we'll talk some more."

Crystal, once again, is stunned to silence. She stands motionless at the podium until Jami Tillotson, the public defender sitting quietly at her side, pulls gently on the sleeve of her orange jumpsuit.

"Oh, right," says Crystal, as if recovering from a trance. "Thank you, Your Honor," she mumbles, then looks up, getting her bearings. "Thank you very much." She takes a seat in the right gallery of the courtroom to watch the rest of the day's proceedings.

"What's the plan, Crystal?" I ask her the next day, back in the tiny interview room at jail.

"The plan," she replies quietly, all her bluster gone, "is for me to comply with the rules and regulations of Drug Court in order to not go to prison and do more time. I mean, have you seen this jail? This is my last chance at Drug Court, they ain't going to give me no more."

Six months later, I join Crystal and the Walden Family at a morning meeting in Kings Hall. After her thirty days in jail, she'd been referred by the Drug Court team to long-term residential rehab, and Walden had accepted her. Now, as the morning meeting winds down, the entire Family links arms in a circle around the perimeter of the mansion's polished ballroom and chants the Walden creed.

W is for who you are
A is for ask yourself
L is for learn to listen
D is for demanding of yourself
E is for eagerness
N is for now is your life

When the chant ends, Crystal, her hair pulled back in a somewhat matronly bun, puts her arms around the waists of two newly arrived Little Sisters, and they head out to walk The Boulevard. Crystal is now a Big Sister, and she instructs them in the ways of Walden.

"Everything here is a test of your ability to stay off drugs," she says. "If they keep you in a meeting for two hours, if they tell you to sit with your legs straight, if they give you a *pull-up* or a *learning experience* to recite in front of the whole Family—it's a test and a lesson about not doing dope. If you can't do this Walden stuff every day, then you don't have the strength to get out of here and resist your old dope habits."

I stay to the end of the Walden day, filled with *one-to-ones,* anger management classes, relapse prevention groups, caseload meetings, and Family gatherings. Then Crystal gets

CRYSTAL, BY THE ENTRANCE TO WALDEN HOUSE

permission from her counselor to take a break, and we head across the street to the Fillmore Grind for a cup of coffee. Crystal stops diligently at the curb for the red light, waiting for the green before she will cross.

"Nice to see you're still hanging in at Walden," I say as we reach the opposite curb. "I'm surprised."

She turns suddenly, perfectly performing a theatrical mime of stunned amazement.

"I told you when I got here I was going to stay!" protests Crystal. "Why didn't you believe me?"

"Because," I say, imitating her own look of simulated shock, "you've been bullshitting me and the court since the first day we met you."

Crystal doesn't miss a beat.

"Of course I was bullshitting you all!" she says, laughing. "I didn't *know* you or the court then. So why tell you the truth?"

"Understood," I say. "And now?"

"Well," says Crystal, taking an odd pause to think through an answer while opening the door and going into the cafe. "The damn Drug Court stuck with me all this time," she tells me finally. "And I got to say, I respect them for that. So I guess it's time I stick with them all, too. Besides, damn it"—she laughs—"I'm still waiting for Drug Court to come through with that education and job training stuff they told me I'd get. I got to stick around for that. I've come too far not to get something in exchange for all this time I've put in."

"What is it you really want to get out of all this?" I ask.

"The truth?" asks Crystal.

I shrug my shoulders. "If you can."

She goes up to the counter and orders a coffee, again pausing to ponder before she replies.

"I need to figure out how to stay off the streets," she says finally. "And I do need help with that. 'Cause it's a kick-ass lifestyle out there, but it's all I know."

We move to a table by the window, with a view of the Walden mansion across the street.

"See," says Crystal, sipping at her coffee, "truth is I wasn't no big-shot Stephie out there. I was a pawn of the drug dealers. Because when you need drugs like I did, you become either a victim or a stalker. I was both. We were eating each other alive to get our dope, and it was killing me. That's what finally brought me in here for good. I just wore out. I mean, I once thought it was a real cool trip out there, but I've come to see that I can't have that and also have me a real life. I'm just glad the damn Drug Court was dumb enough to hang with me long enough till I figured that out. So I'm here. And Walden's a weird trip, I'll tell you that. But I'm staying."

Crystal and I linger on the mansion's Boulevard, *running stories* with The Family. I shake off a disquieting déjà vu of my months here with Mike, a year before. Crystal is at precisely the same phase in her recovery as Mike was—except that she never *asked* to be at Walden.

During her year in the program, both her parents die, and Crystal is often at the edge of blowing out to find her dealer. She is repeatedly accused of having romantic ties with one of her program Brothers. I check the list of *splittees* for her name each time I walk through the front door. But unlike Mike's run through rehab, Crystal's yearlong stormy voyage through Walden is tightly supervised by the Drug Court team.

"When things get any deeper at Walden than 'Don't do dope,' " she tells me, halfway through the program, "they don't know how to deal with it. But I talked to the judge and my Drug Court case manager, and they're insisting I have a therapist at Walden, 'cause I need some real help with this depression stuff or I'll be back on the crack pipe."

At the request of the court, Walden arranges weekly individual psychotherapy for Crystal, and her therapist meets frequently with Walden's drug rehab counselors. Crystal's depression slowly lifts.

When Mike was at Walden, the one therapist there was so overwhelmed with work she forgot to refer him for treatment of his flashbacks of childhood sexual abuse. With no one else advocating for him in the program, individual skilled therapy for Mike ended right there. Crystal's experience is different. "The judge has me checking in every two weeks," she tells me, "to see how it's going at Walden and in therapy, find out what else I might need."

Walden's staff is required to communicate directly with Crystal's Drug Court case manager about her progress toward lasting sobriety—and about the program's plans to help her get there. This reporting system provides Crystal with independent checks on her rehab program that were absent for Mike.

"You're not lost yet," I told Mike when he'd relapsed and been kicked out of Walden. "There are a hundred thirty-five other drug programs in this city."

"Fucking right there are," he sobbed. "And I just got kicked out of the best of them. But I'm going to pick myself up again. So who do I talk to? Where do I go?"

No one outside of Walden was overseeing Mike's path through rehab. When the program abandoned him without a referral to a detox program or case manager, he headed to 16th and Mission instead.

Had Crystal relapsed while at Walden, the counselors could not have ejected her to the streets, but would have had to send her to the Drug Court case manager, to find out what happened and to help Crystal plan a path back to sobriety.

Close and consistent supervision of clients in rehab accounts, in large part, for the success of our Drug Courts, an accomplishment now noted at the highest levels of government.

Drug czar General Barry McCaffrey, never one for understatement, has called Drug Courts "one of the most monumental changes in social justice in this country since World War Two."

"The results have been remarkable," announced President Clinton in his weekly radio address to the nation on July 11, 1998. "In some cities Drug Court participants have recidivism, or repeater rates, as low as four percent."

Drug Courts provide not only coerced treatment but *coordinated* treatment, bringing the myriad aspects of rehab together under the watchful eyes of a single agency. While McCaffrey told Congress as far back as 1996 that Drug Courts can "effectively coerce offenders into treatment," he also emphasized that ultimate success will be gained by "closely supervised, court-ordered rehabilitation."

The lessons in rehab from the Drug Courts apply not merely to addicts who have been arrested, but to every addict and each drug program across our nation: Guiding, coordinating, and organizing our rehab programs is as crucial as coercing or motivating the addicts to stay clean.

It doesn't take the power of the courts to supervise the drug treatment system. The city of San Francisco, and all other cities trying to provide effective treatment to addicts who want it, can and must oversee the programs. By sticking with the addicts, and watching the programs, Drug Courts have shown how rehab can work.

NOVEMBER 14, 2000 CRYSTAL GRADUATES FROM DRUG COURT

Two months before Connie is due to give birth, she and Mike, at their apartment near the beach, prepare to head out for an evening Lamaze class.

I have never seen either of them looking better. Connie is radiantly pregnant, leaning against Mike as he greets me at the door with a glowing smile and a warm embrace. He's fresh from a shower, clean shaven, still barefoot, in jeans and T-shirt. As Mike raises his hands to slick back his still-wet hair my eyes reflexively scan the skin of his arms: no needle marks.

Mike moves quickly across the room, clicks off the sports news on the TV in the entertainment center in front of the couch, and then bends suddenly and swings about to face me, holding a large box over his head in a triumphant pose as if he had just won the Olympic Gold Medal in the box-lifting event.

"Hey, babe," he says to Connie, "come help me. I'm dying to see how it looks set up here in the living room."

He puts the box down and as Connie bends to her knees beside him he kisses her cheek and the two uncrate a baby-blue bassinet and drape the top in a frilly, pink-flowered trim. "Boy or girl," Mike tells me, "we got all the bases covered!"

Arms around each other's waist, the proud parents-to-be stand back and beam at the bassinet.

"Damn," notes Mike suddenly, "we're late for Lamaze!" The three of us pile out of the apartment and into Connie's black Honda Civic hatchback. It's March 23, 1999, and it is impossible to guess as we barrel down the highway toward Lamaze class that, four days later, I'll be searching for this same black Honda Civic all around the Mission district, praying to find Mike before the police do.

"Hey, Lonny," says Mike as he eases the car onto the highway entrance ramp and heads south toward the hospital where the class is, "I got this freaky phone call a couple of weeks ago. Some guy, doesn't even say his name, tells me he's with my ex-wife, going to marry her. Then he says, 'And I'm adopting your girls, so you can forget about being with them again.' Then there's this silence, and all I say is, 'Who are you?' And he hangs up the phone."

"We don't even know if it was real," adds Connie. "We think maybe Mike's ex-wife heard that we got married and I'm pregnant, so she's jealous and trying to piss him off. See, Mike's got visitation rights with his girls, but it's been a year now since his ex-wife's let him see them. She won't even tell us where they are."

"Then, a week after that guy calls," continues Mike, "my ex-wife phones all of a sudden, says I got to increase child support from $200 to $1,200 a month or I can't see the girls no more. And I could hear Jessica in the background, screaming at her mom that she wants to talk to her dad. That really tore into my gut, man, I can't begin to tell you."

Connie and Mike traced the telephone number and found the address the calls had come from.

"You know what?" says Mike as we drive into the parking lot at the hospital. "If I was the old me, just a couple of years back, I would have drove over there in a minute and punched out whoever that guy is who's keeping me from seeing my girls."

"What kept you back this time?" I ask.

Mike laughs and turns toward me in his seat before we get out to head to Lamaze.

"*And then what?*" he sings out, reciting the mantra he'd learned at Walden. "And *then*— I'd be in big-time trouble, my girls would see their daddy beating up some other guy, and then I'd say, 'Fuck it!' and head for a needle. But, man, when I put down that phone after hearing my kid calling for me in the background, I was really shook up. So I sat and talked it out with Connie, had like a Walden *one-to-one* with her about how I was feeling. And she helped me calm down. So we're going to find a lawyer. I'm really missing my girls, man, but I can't be doing stupid stuff on my own no more. I got my girls and this new baby to think about. Me and Connie, we're going to work it out."

Mike's mood instantly brightens in the Lamaze class as he, Connie, and the other couples learn breathing exercises, pass around a baby doll, practice changing diapers. Mike, laughing about being a plumber, points out the advantages and disadvantages he sees in the various styles of breast pumps on the front table of the classroom. This tall, joking, wholesomely good-looking man has such a warm and easy manner that the entire class seems to take his cue and relax. At the end of the class, the last of the series, the two nurses say goodbye to the students. "We've worked with hundreds of couples," says one to Mike and Connie, "and we've got our instincts fine-tuned. You guys will do just fine. But remember, take really deep breaths, OK?"

Back at their apartment, Connie finishes arranging the new bassinet while Mike slips out to the front patio for a cigarette. "No smoking in the house when the baby comes," he tells me, "so I'm starting the rule now."

"And heroin?" I ask.

"Nah, that's gone, too," says Mike. "You know why I'm so sure about that?" He takes a long draw on his cigarette.

"I *know* I'm going to be OK with the dope," he says, and then laughs. "I mean, without the dope. I know that because a year ago if this stuff had happened with my girls, I would have been awake all night, pissed off, not sleeping, memories flying all over the place, sweating and freaked out. And the next morning I'd have gone right out to 16th and Mission to calm it down."

"And last night?" I ask. "How did you sleep?"

"Damn! Hardly at all," Mike grins. "See, Connie gets these headaches, so last night I put her head in my lap and stayed awake for hours, massaging her scalp. And I talked to her about how scared I am. You know, my girls, the new baby coming. Then, like at four in the morning or something, I was still massaging Connie's head and we fell asleep. And this morning I didn't hit the Mission. So something's different for me now, I can feel it. I mean, I'm bummed out about what's happening with my girls, and that usually puts me into a nosedive, big-time crash. But I got to take it easy, do it right this time. I just got to. So that's what I'm doing."

"I'm glad," I tell him. "And what's happened to that dream of the white room that used to wake you up so often?"

Mike stares. "Gone," he says quietly. Then he repeats, with surprising vehemence. "Gone. I ain't letting that white room into my head no more. Never."

He tosses his cigarette to the floor and grinds it out with his shoe, then purses his lips and a long sigh escapes into the breeze of the night.

"There ain't no more of that dream," says Mike determinedly, "because instead I got to dream about this baby coming up, and about Connie, and this house, and my girls. That's my whole life, man. If I let that other dream in, all the rest goes down the tubes."

The phone call from Connie comes early Saturday morning, four days after the Lamaze class.

"Mike left a message on my voice mail at work yesterday." Connie is speaking so softly into the phone I can barely hear her. "He said the car wouldn't start, so he couldn't pick me up at work. I haven't heard from him since."

I listen intently, trying to be sure I'm understanding every word. Her voice is so hushed, I realize, to smother even the remotest possibility that what she's telling me has actually happened.

"I've called all the hospital emergency rooms," whispers Connie. "And I called the police to see if there was an accident, or if my car got towed. Nothing. That was at five this morning. Can you think of anything else I should do? Anybody else to call?"

"Let me be sure I'm tracking this," I tell her. "On Thursday, Mike was supposed to come to my house. But he called, said he couldn't make it, the car was broken. Now it's Saturday morning—"

"On Thursday?" she interrupts. "My sister's apartment, right here next to ours, got broken into on Thursday. And when Mike picked me up at work that night, the car was working fine, he didn't say anything about missing an appointment with you. He went out checking the pawnshops for the stuff that was stolen from Geraldine's apartment."

"Like what?" I ask.

"Almost nothing," says Connie. "A couple of checks, and this signed 49ers football she has. Somebody broke the window of her apartment and took them."

"Did he seem high on Thursday night?"

"No!" says Connie instantly. And then, "I mean, he's been tired and falling right to sleep, every night since we saw you for Lamaze. You know that when he's upset he can't hardly sleep, so I've been thinking, that's good, he's doing OK."

I flash back on the stories Mike had told me. For years, after shooting up with heroin, he had nodded off while in mid-conversation with Connie. She'd always thought it was fatigue from his plumbing work. Connie is not the best judge of whether or not Mike is stoned.

"He *was* kind of upset on Thursday," she tells me now on the phone. "Because he and Geraldine never get along, so he was afraid she'd accuse him of breaking into her apartment. I think that's why he split, he got scared."

"I'm so sorry, Connie," I say. "Listen, I'm meeting Darrell today. We'll head out to the Mission and look around for Mike. What's the license number on your Honda?"

"Of *course* it was Mike who broke into the apartment," says Darrell as we cruise Mission Street, our eyes peeled for the black Honda Civic. "I can't believe you're even thinking it wasn't him. Like he heard about it and got scared that they'd accuse him, and *then* he took off. Right. Mike's on a dope run, big time."

I sit quietly for a moment, then turn right on 19th and drive to Mission Dolores Park, where I had watched Mike shoot up in the hot August sun after he'd split from Walden. Darrell and I had been out looking for him that time, as well. We leave my car and walk uphill to the bathroom where the junkies in the park get water for their rigs.

"This time," I tell Darrell, "I *really* don't get it. You should have seen him and Connie setting up that bassinet, and at Lamaze class—they were just glowing. The guy's got everything going for him and—"

"That's exactly it!" interrupts Darrell. "That's when we do our worst, when things are at their best."

He peeks through the door of the park's bathroom. No Mike.

"People in recovery," says Darrell, "get this idea in their head—get clean, get your life together, and everything'll be hunky-dory. And then we do it! We get clean. We get a job, a relationship, a baby, whatever. And everything is *not* hunky-dory, and that scares the shit out of us."

"So you do whatever you can to destroy everything you've achieved?" I ask, incredulous.

"Of course," says Darrell. "Because we never believed we deserved it in the first place."

We've hiked to the top of the hill, the high ground where Mike used to shoot up knowing he could see the police before they would spot him. From here, we can scan the parked cars on two sides of the park for a black Honda Civic hatchback. And one block away, we spot one.

"I know just what's going on for Mike," says Darrell as we trudge down the hill toward Connie's car. "Look—I've just been accepted to be a drug counselor at Acceptance Place. It's the kind of job I've wanted all my life. I should be ecstatic, but I've never felt shittier. I can't trust these good things that are happening to me because I've never had the experience, never stayed sober long enough to find out what Darrell is like as a sober, upstanding citizen. I mean, it's totally new territory, this 'you're doing OK' place. And I promise you, Mike's never known that place either. All we've ever heard, from ourselves and everyone else, is that we're the scum of the earth and we'll never amount to anything. So even if you find Mike stoned out in Connie's car now, he's going to be in more familiar turf than the Mike you saw at that Lamaze class. And he's going to want to stay right there. And then what do you do?"

I glance in frustration at Darrell.

"And then I pick his ass up and get him some help."

"Sorry," says Darrell quietly. "I didn't mean that you give up. I was just trying to explain—Mike's not going to be in any mood for help from anyone. Why do you think he's out here in the Mission instead of at home with Connie? He's more comfortable hating himself out here than he was hating himself as the supposed husband and father back there. So I'm just saying, you've got to be ready for it—he won't want to come back with you."

I pull out the crumpled paper where I'd scrawled the license number Connie had given me. No match.

It's near dark now, and I ask Darrell if he'll drive with me out to Connie and Mike's apartment, see if she has any news.

Connie is sitting on the couch next to the new bassinet. Her shoulders are wrapped in a quilted blanket, legs tucked under her. She's staring at the TV, but had turned the sound off long before we'd arrived.

There's been no news from or about Mike, she tells Darrell and me. She's been home alone all day except for a visit from a policeman who came out to take down the details for a missing persons report. Lying next to Connie on the couch is her open checkbook.

"I found two missing," she says softly. "So I called our account line and the checks were cashed. Seventeen dollars on Wednesday, thirty on Thursday—the day before Mike disappeared. So I think he's been getting high again, and then he really freaked out when he heard that Geraldine's apartment got robbed. Mike gets paranoid when he's high."

"It must be torture staying here and waiting by yourself," I say. "At least your mom's coming to stay with you tomorrow. Will you go to work on Monday?"

Connie nods. "The last time Mike disappeared like this, he called me at work four days later. Just out of the blue. And then he came home again." Her eyes well over in tears, but she says no more.

As soon as we hit the car, Darrell lets out a whoosh of air and exclaims, "That is *scary!* Seeing that sadness in Connie's eyes and face, next to that bassinet. My God, she's about to explode. But she's sitting on that couch, all pregnant and wrapped in a quilt—looks like the Madonna or something."

"After all these years of watching her man do the same thing to her over and over again," I reply, "she's still sitting there, waiting for a fairy tale to come true. I think Connie's as addicted to Mike as he is to drugs. If anything, her addiction is more intense, and harder to explain."

"Yeah, but she's a survivor," observes Darrell. "And Mike's on a death trip. I don't know what his issues are, don't even think he knows, but Mike is handsome, he's funny, he's smart, he's got a beautiful wife, a baby coming—and there's something deep inside that's scaring him so much he'd rather be dead."

Mike lasts on the streets for five days before he gets arrested, caught by a security guard stealing a boxed set of Frank Sinatra CDs from Tower Records on Columbus Street. After taking him away in handcuffs, the police call Connie to come get her car. On the passenger seat, she finds a notebook that Mike had been writing in. Scrawled on the front page is a list:

Please let me die
overdose
drown
violently
the Golden Gate Bridge
saving another by sacrifice
in the streets
in a fire
starvation
freezing
Please don't let me breathe

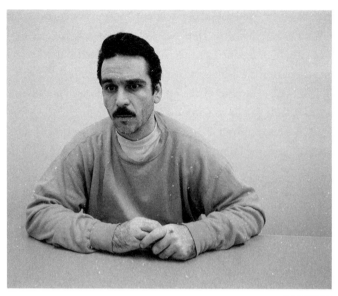

COUNTY JAIL

"I can certainly encourage that Mike be brought into the Drug Court program," Jami Tillotson, the Drug Court public defender, tells me. "But it depends on the details. The shoplifting charge from Tower Records is OK for Drug Court, as long as he did it to feed his addiction. But the residential burglary? That's going to be up to the D.A. They come down hard on you if you break into a private house. I can make an argument that it was his sister-in-law's place, so it's not like he was out there randomly breaking into people's homes, scaring the populace and all that. And from what you tell me, there's no question that these were addiction-motivated crimes. So whatever his drug use is about, he needs treatment, the long, intensive kind that we do in Drug Court. I'll try what I can, but tell Mike I can't promise him anything. The D.A. has the final decision about sending his case to criminal court or Drug Court."

Then Jami smiles. "Maybe the judge can have some influence," she says. "There are always surprises around here."

It takes four days from the time Mike is arrested until I can get into the jail to see him. During that time Mike has, without consulting a lawyer, confessed to everything.

The sheriff's deputy guides me through three *slam gates* in the long corridors that lead to the cells, each closing behind us with the resounding, metallic clang of incarceration. Walking toward me from the other end of the final corridor, under the guard of another deputy, Mike is so hunched over I barely recognize his form.

We both know the rules: To prevent the handing off of drugs, razor blades, or other contraband, interviewers and prisoners cannot physically touch each other, in any way.

The deputies open and bang closed the last gate between us, and Mike stands next to me as the officers, one on each side, escort us to the interview room. We're shoulder to shoulder, almost touching, and I suddenly feel fingers encircling my wrist and look up to see Mike, staring straight forward, watching the deputies out of the corners of his eyes to be sure they can't see this contact. His hand closes around my wrist, squeezing tighter, and then tighter again, almost bruising my arm in its vise-like grip. I stare straight ahead and can barely make out Mike's words, hoarsened by his flowing tears. It's a low, rhythmic chant. "Thanks. Thanks, man, thanks. Thanks for coming."

The deputies bring us to the small, glass-windowed interview room and guide Mike to an aluminum chair opposite the table from mine. Then they step outside and close the door. I wait silently, until Mike's sobbing eases to the point where he can speak. But as his first words come out, he loses it again and lowers his head onto his crossed arms on the table, to muffle in the orange sleeves of his sweatshirt the wail of pain that has been waiting days, weeks, years to be set free.

"If you had your way," I ask Connie on the phone after my visit with Mike, "would you want to send him through Drug Court and rehab—or does he finally need to understand the consequences of his actions and do prison time?"

"He's the father of this baby that's in me!" replies Connie. "I want him to get help. But he can't be back here with me until that happens. So I want him to cool off in jail for a while, realize what he's done—and then go out to treatment. But my sister's opinion is that Mike's already had his chance at rehab with Walden House, and that didn't work. So she's pressing charges, full out. She wants Mike put away for as long as possible."

I make plans to meet Connie the next morning, Saturday, at the jail when prisoners are allowed family visitors for twenty minutes.

"I'll see if Geraldine will come," says Connie. "She doesn't know anything about rehab. Maybe you can talk to her while I'm in seeing Mike."

In the hallway on the sixth floor of the county jail building at 8:00 A.M. a sheriff's deputy with his pants tucked into combat boots and black leather gloves protecting his hands sets up a table and orders the fifty or so people milling about to form an orderly line. Women, with babies now crying in their arms after an hour's wait in a hall with no bathroom access, calm their children as best they can and rush to the front of the line. Elderly men and women waiting to visit their imprisoned sons and daughters move quietly behind the women carrying babies. Filing in after them, as if in some preordained pecking order, are young men with slicked hair and tattoos who've come to visit recently arrested friends, followed by teenage-appearing women with puffed hair and thick makeup waiting for a chance to visit their boyfriends behind bars.

In the corner by the elevator, I wait with Geraldine while Connie, so pregnant that no one questions her presence at the front of the line with the women carrying babies, signs the jail log to see her husband. Or at least to talk with him on a telephone in a small booth with a thick glass barrier that separates the inmates from their visitors.

Geraldine opens the conversation while we wait for Connie to return. "If I could put Mike in jail forever, I would. I want him out of my life and out of my sister's life. Permanently. If the court could guarantee that, I'd sign on the dotted line right now. He has hurt this family so badly."

Then, through her tears, Geraldine apologizes, telling me she knows there is another side to Mike's story and she's willing to listen. So I try to explain to Connie's younger sister the complexities of rehab, the requirement for repetition, the realities of relapse, the need for true psychiatric care as well as drug rehabilitation, and the remarkable track record Drug Court has been achieving with addicts like Mike. But as I watch the sorrowful look of hopelessness on her face I grasp her point of view, even while trying to promote my own.

"Look at how many people he has affected," says Geraldine. "Michael has stolen from Connie, from me, from his own father to get drugs! He's just about abandoned his daughters to his addiction. Then he disappears into some drug haze just before Connie's about to give birth! He has tortured this entire family, and he has had chance after chance after chance to get better. Michael is only one person, and if I can put him away forever there are dozens of us out here who will have better lives."

I can't help but nod in agreement. When, I wonder, is it time to admit defeat at the hands of the addiction demon, to cut our losses, stop banging our heads against the manipulations, scams, and thievery, acknowledge that we've done the best we can—and slam closed the jailhouse doors?

"It may indeed be time to give up on Mike," I tell Geraldine. "But I wonder if what you say is true. Has he really had chance after chance to get better? Or has Mike merely had one run through a single, poorly performing rehab program?"

Geraldine listens patiently as I describe what I know of Mike's rehab to date: A visit years ago with a psychiatrist, who correctly diagnosed post-traumatic stress disorder brought on by his repeated rapes as a child, but who refused to treat Mike's psychological distress unless he stopped using heroin; a trip through Target Cities' pretreatment groups, preparing him for rehab while he waited months for a bed to open at Walden House, and nearly died from an overdose; ten months at Walden, which taught him every detail about how to modify his behaviors under the watchful eyes of The Family, but offered virtually no psychiatric care, then kicked him out after his first relapse.

If Mike's case could be moved to Drug Court, I explain, he would finally receive, under close supervision, the rehab he has never had. And seven times out of ten, it works.

"On Monday," I tell Connie's sister, "I'll be at a meeting with the district attorney and public defender for Drug Court. I'd like to talk to them about Mike. But from everything

I've heard, the chances of getting his case transferred to Drug Court from criminal court are much better if you, the crime victim, ask the D.A. to send Mike to court-run treatment instead of to the state penitentiary."

To her credit, Geraldine listens carefully.

"I'll think about it," she says finally. "No promises."

In February of 2000, the U.S. Department of Health Services, after years of study, issued a report stating that drug rehabilitation programs across the country had not been dealing adequately with the deeper psychological agonies that make it so difficult for addicts in rehab to remain clean and sober. In response, the department issued a "Treatment Improvement Protocol," calling for addicts in rehab to receive intensive therapy for the underlying psychological disorders that so often drive them to relapse. Purely behavioral therapies for addictions, the department concluded, are not enough.

Two-thirds of those in substance abuse programs, the Treatment Improvement Protocol points out, have been physically, sexually, or emotionally abused during childhood. For those addicts, drug use is not merely a behavioral abnormality but also a response to overwhelming emotional trauma. Without specific treatment for their past and present psychological distress, they will invariably return to drug use.

"It is critically important that professionals who treat substance abuse in adults recognize the signs of prior childhood neglect and abuse," emphasizes Dr. Nelba Chavez, of the Substance Abuse and Mental Health Services Administration. "We must focus on treating those adults."

Dr. H. Westley Clark, director of the federal Center for Substance Abuse Treatment, concurs: "Understanding and treating the root causes of clients' symptoms will greatly increase the effectiveness of substance abuse treatment."

Benefits of in-depth psychological care, according to the Treatment Improvement Protocol, will include "Decreasing the probability of relapse. Many substance abusers consume substances to self-medicate post-traumatic stress symptoms related to childhood physical or sexual abuse or other trauma. . . . Clients receiving more specialized services . . . are more likely to stay in recovery."

The specific recommendations put forth in the Treatment Improvement Protocol sound, almost eerily, as if they'd been written with Michael Pagsolingan in mind:

Clients with childhood abuse histories have been found to have more severe substance abuse disorders, to have started using at younger ages, and to use substances for reasons that differ from other clients. They are also more likely to have attempted suicide, to have PTSD, and to have personality or relationship problems that make them hesitant to accept help, which also makes them more vulnerable to relapse. . . . People who were severely sexually or physically abused as children often develop PTSD, and this disorder increases their risk of relapse because it engenders intrusive memories and attempts to avoid those memories through self-medication. . . . Adult clients with a history of childhood abuse and neglect . . . may feel permanently damaged and hopeless, and may experience shame . . . be hostile, self-destructive, and impulsive. . . . Because an abuse history and a diagnosis of PTSD increase the risk of relapse, it is advisable to address these issues at some point during the course of substance abuse treatment . . . before they can achieve sobriety. For some, it is during sobriety when they begin to experience symptoms of PTSD (such as flashbacks and nightmares) or recall memories of long-forgotten or repressed experiences of past abuse. As these uncomfortable and sometimes debilitating symptoms and memories emerge, many individuals return to using substances in an attempt to suppress their problems and manage their emotional pain.

In spite of the report, Geraldine, the public at large, and most legislators understandably still look at repeatedly relapsing addicts like Mike as concrete evidence that intense addictions are not treatable, that continued drug use and its associated crimes are inevitable, and that our overflowing jails are a sorrowful but best response to the horrifying realities of addiction. Mike, and hundreds of thousands like him, they believe, have had their chances at rehab, and failed.

Mike waits in a cell on the sixth floor of the county jail while the district attorney's office prepares its strongest case to put him behind bars for the longest time possible. Geraldine, a month after Mike is arrested, goes back to the hospital where Mike and Connie had attended Lamaze classes together, and coaches her sister through the birth of Michaela, seven pounds nine ounces, twenty and one-half inches with, as Connie notes, "feet as big as her daddy's."

"Hey, Lonny, can you do me a favor?" Mike asks me by phone from the jail on the day his daughter is born. "Can you go over there, and hold the baby for me?"

Post-traumatic stress disorder from childhood abuse is only one of dozens of psychological ailments that, if left untreated by specifically trained therapists, invariably lead to repeated relapses to drug use in spite of the best of efforts on the part of drug and alcohol counselors in rehab programs. Finding cases in our jails comparable to Mike's is as effortless as locating the haystack around the proverbial needle.

Months after Mike is incarcerated, James Henderson, also garbed in an orange sweat suit, joins him in the county jail. They are already close friends, since they had been Walden House Brothers a year before—both in Sylvester's caseload. Like Mike, James relapsed soon after moving to satellite housing, and was forbidden to enter Walden again without *regaining graces*—coming back for an in-your-face screaming match with 120 addicts in The Family.

James, now fifty, has been addicted to drugs since he was thirteen. Unlike Mike, he had never been sexually abused as a child. But it would not take a brilliant psychiatrist to realize that James's intense, seemingly untreatable passion for drugs is driven by a need to cover up emotional pain brought on by his early-life agonies.

At thirteen, James sat alone in a room with his drunken father and slowly coaxed a gun out of the man's hand. His father had been aiming the pistol at his own head. When James was fourteen his father, in a drunken haze, slammed the car he was driving into a tree. James's mother was in the passenger seat, and neither parent survived. By sixteen, James had taken on his father's profession, traveling from bar to bar hustling pool. He often received his winnings (and he always won, his dad had taught him well) in cocaine, heroin, and alcohol.

Dig only slightly deeper into James's psychological history, and you find that he hated the image of his own "fat body" so much that, beginning at age ten and continuing for years after, he purged himself by vomiting after every meal. James is five feet, eleven inches tall, and when he got down to 117 pounds he still hated himself for being too fat. Add a dozen or so suicide attempts over the ensuing years, and any amateur therapist might conclude that James's intense bouts of depression extended far beyond the mere sadness brought on by his undoubtedly difficult life, that he was using drugs for reasons other than having fun, and that he would continue to relapse unless an experienced therapist helped him deal with the traumas of his youth and the darkest depressions that have continued to plague James throughout his adult life.

In the early seventies, James Henderson entered a Synanon-style rehab program, thinking his major problem was his addiction to drugs. "I stayed for a year," he says, "shaved my head, carried signs around saying what a shithead junkie I was. You know, behavior modification to the max, not a hint of treatment for any psychological stuff. Two months after I finished the program, I was back on heroin."

The next twenty years form a continuous blur. "I didn't give a damn anymore," recalls James. "I was overdosing so much that if I showed up at my friends' house they knew they'd be calling an ambulance by the end of the night. That's when my criminal activity started, too. Let's just say I was involved in crime and I was incarcerated. That took care of the seventies and eighties."

In 1994, at age forty-seven, James was out of jail, homeless, weakened by a hepatitis virus he'd contracted from a shared needle, and recovering from multiple surgeries for abscesses all over his body. "It was the end of the line," he says. "My physical condition was so bad I was physically unable to shoot drugs. So I thought I'd give rehab one more shot."

James hit Walden House, in desperation, in 1994. "I stayed at Walden for a year," he says, "did the behavior-mod thing again. And I guess it felt good to have all those people around me, because I was clean that whole time. But when I got out of program, I didn't have a clue about what to do with all this emotional pain I still had. I started doing dope again."

That same, precise pattern repeated in 1998, when James again went through Walden's rehab, this time in Mike's caseload. He stayed clean while at the mansion with The Family, and once again relapsed soon after he moved out to satellite housing.

To get money for his drugs, James stole telephones, radios, CD players, and VCRs from electronics stores. He was soon arrested and thrown in the county jail. His story, like Mike's, might have ended right there, as yet another addict who's had his chance at rehab, time after time, and failed. But James's unwitting strategy had been much wiser than Mike's: he stole electronic equipment from stores instead of a football and two checks from his sister-in-law's apartment. Commercial burglaries committed by addicts are eligible for Drug Court. Residential burglaries are not.

Judge Lam (and later Judge Tang) took James Henderson's case on. And James took the Drug Court team for a roller-coaster ride that made even Crystal Holmes's journey through rehab seem smooth in comparison. The Drug Court team could not figure out, for the first year or so, why this intelligent, articulate, talented, and motivated man simply could not stay off the needle no matter what the court tried to do with him. But if the Drug Court team does one thing well, it is to keep trying.

On July 23, 1999, Judge Tang, at her wit's end, threw James in jail, where he was re-united with his old friend from Walden, Mike Pagsolingan. But on October 13, James said good-bye to Mike and was sent by Drug Court back to a Walden program—this time to Walden Intensive Treatment Services, a program specifically designed to offer addicts with deeper mental and emotional problems intense psychological therapy in addition to behavior modification for their addictions. At Walden Intensive Treatment Services James attended daily individual and group therapy sessions, a psychiatrist carefully and continuously raised his dosage of antidepressant medications, and a treatment team arranged for him to receive long-term psychiatric care. When James was emotionally more stable, he transferred to Connor House, a halfway house run by the city's mental health services. Connor House and Drug Court continued to supervise his care, case-managing James's route through city services so that he received continued intensive psychotherapy and anti-depressant medications.

Finally able to stay off drugs, James reflects on his arduous, decades-long path to sobriety.

"For years I thought all my depression and mental craziness stuff was just due to my addiction to drugs," James tells me. "You know why I thought that? Because every program I'd been in told me it was true! So I thought I was just a regular old drug addict. Now you know what I think? That there aren't a whole lot of regular old drug addicts in those programs. Most of us have had problems like what I've had. I'm not making excuses, but there are reasons we're drug addicts, and until we get help figuring out those reasons and dealing with them there's not a chance in hell we'll stop doing drugs. I'm fifty years old now, and this is the first time I'm really getting to see it. Recovery does work, if you get the right kind of treatment."

If James is correct and the majority of addicts are not just "regular old drug addicts," then it will take some major restructuring of the rehab system to catch up to that reality. Walden, a program admired across the country as an exemplary model of rehab, has 227 Therapeutic Community behavior modification treatment slots with The Family at two separate mansions. Walden's Intensive Treatment Services for in-depth psychological care has fourteen slots, of which eight are reserved for HIV-positive clients. That leaves merely six of 241 total Walden rehab openings available to addicts like Mike or James who require skilled therapy for their emotional problems if they are ever to stay off drugs, and out of our jails. But the fed's Treatment Improvement Protocol states that two out of three addicts, not six of 241, need such advanced psychological care. Walden, in 1999, increased the number of licensed therapists for the 120 Family members in the mansion at 890 Hayes Street. From one, to two.

"Basically, I don't think the drug rehab counselors even knew what to do with a therapist here at Walden," says Lubov Smith, the newly hired psychotherapist at 890 Hayes. "It took some very forceful persuasion to make sure the counselors knew why we were here and that, yes, they needed to refer their clients to us"—Lubov Smith takes in a deep breath, and then blurts out in frustration—"and that the counselors cannot have public screaming sessions to humiliate *any* of my severely depressed clients in front of the entire Family! I mean, these are depressed and suicidal clients! You don't get them off drugs by shouting at them in Kings Hall."

At Walden's Intensive Treatment Services, I ask Dave Seymour, James Henderson's therapist, whether the drug rehab counselors at other Walden facilities, such as the mansion at 890, are becoming more aware of the importance of treating addicts' deeper emotional problems.

Dave nods his head, and then laughs.

"Yes, they're more aware, but they're going down kicking and screaming. The higher-ups and the old-timers who still make up the bulk of drug rehab counselors don't like this new emphasis on psychological therapy, because they can't keep up that old in-your-face treatment that's been in place from the beginning, since Synanon days. Slowly, by necessity, we're heading away from that and toward more emotional, therapeutic work, like I get to do here. But the bottom line is that there's still an attitude among rehab counselors that their clients are dope fiends, and if they can't stick with the Walden structure while in The Family, then they are out of there. So what's happened is that most of the clients who have mental health issues have been driven out of Walden. We're doing a lot of retraining with the counselors, but there's still a significant resistance and a lack of understanding. Change comes slowly."

"If you were to walk The Boulevard at the mansion at 890 Hayes right now," I ask Dave, "how many addicts would you find who need more intensive psychological therapy, not just behavior modification, to have a real chance at sobriety?"

Surprisingly, Dave doesn't pause to gauge his response.

"Some thirty percent at all the Walden facilities have major mental illnesses," he says right off the bat. "And probably eighty percent have real problems of living that will require a therapist's help if they're going to be able to stay off drugs."

"And here at Intensive Treatment Services," I note, "you have six slots for non-HIV clients."

Dave smiles gently, nodding at the irony.

"Moving drug rehab programs from addiction into mental health issues," he says, "has created a lot of anxiety for the staff. They're not ready for it, and they're not trained for it. James was one of the lucky ones. He got sent over here by Drug Court because they recognized he didn't need to be in jail, he needed medications and a therapist. So I've been privileged to get to work with James. But there are hundreds, even thousands like him in the county jail right now who will never get the chance James had."

On February 25, 2000, the month the federal government released its Treatment Improvement Protocol insisting that addicts receive more intense therapeutic care, drug czar General Barry McAffrey traveled to Bogotá, Colombia. It was his second trip in six months to reassure the Colombian government of his plans to provide $1.6 billion in U.S. funds to combat our "huge drug emergency" by increasing military aid to chase after Colombian cocaine growers. That same year, McCaffrey's planned funding for expanding Drug Courts in cities and towns across the entire United States was $34 million.

On the Monday after Mike's arrest, I arrived early at the courthouse in San Francisco in hopes of a chance to talk with the Drug Court district attorney about Mike before the team meeting began.

Judge Tang had decided to hold that day's conference in the formal courtroom rather than in her chambers. Jami Tillotson, the public defender, Colin Eaton and the rehab case managers, the probation officers and narcotics police, Fred and Dave, all milled about casually in the courtroom waiting for Judge Tang. Last to arrive was Marianne Barrett, from the district attorney's office.

As Marianne hurriedly unpacked her files of cases for the day, she saw me waiting and greeted me with a smile.

"You still chasing our clients all around town?" she asked.

"I am," I replied. "But I've got a new case to ask you about."

Marianne listened carefully, nodding her head with a concerned look as I summarized Mike's history of childhood abuse, his nightmares of the white room that he'd tried, for years, to drown out with heroin, his experience at Walden, and his final collapse to drug use just as his wife was about to give birth.

"Sounds like one of our boys," said Marianne. "What's his crime? Let's see if we can get him in here."

"He broke into his sister-in-law's house," I replied. "Stole a football and a couple of checks to get money for his dope."

I watched Marianne's face undergo a sudden, complete transformation, from soft compassion to a rigid frown.

"Drug Court admission criteria do *not* include residential burglaries," she said quickly, "and the D.A.'s office will fight to keep your guy out of this court. Our position will be that he doesn't belong in Drug Court, and we've got legal precedent on our side and won't give an inch of wiggle room. Just read the Drug Court eligibility rules. Residential burgs are not on the list of crimes accepted by Drug Court because we will not have addicts out there terrorizing the community."

"There is no justification for limiting Drug Court programs to the least serious offenders," says Judge Jeffrey Tauber. "The people who are excluded from drug courts right now are often the people who need the level of supervision, drug testing, and control that drug courts provide."

Judge Tauber, who started a Drug Court in Oakland, California, was so impressed by the results he obtained with addicted criminals that he joined the nationwide movement to expand Drug Courts. He is now director of the National Drug Court Institute.

"Despite the overwhelming prevalence of substance abuse," says Judge Tauber, "only about three percent of drug-using offenders participate in Drug Court programs. Clearly, Drug Courts must reach a broader population if they are to have a substantial impact on our communities."

Vernon Grigg, chief narcotics prosecutor at the San Francisco District Attorney's office, is also an ardent supporter of Drug Court. Grigg admits, however, that getting addicts into the Drug Court rehab system has been an uphill battle with his own staff of prosecutors. "We make seven to eight thousand narcotics arrests every week," says Grigg, "and yet there are only one hundred seventy addicts in Drug Court."

Grigg has his own theory about his department's resistance to the Drug Court revolution. "Prosecutors don't get into this business to be social workers," he says. "They're here because they like to win cases—to put people in jail. So it requires a real effort to teach them to say to themselves, 'What will work best for this particular individual?' "

Two months after Mike was arrested, San Francisco Drug Court's public defender Jami Tillotson won a major battle to expand the list of crimes for which addicts with "a serious underlying substance abuse problem" can be moved from criminal court to Drug Court. The newly released inventory of offenses included drug possession, possession with the intent to sell, auto burglary, commercial burglary, felony petty theft, forgery, and passing bad checks. Jami argued forcefully that the Drug Court judge should also be given the discretion to accept selected addicts who had committed residential burglaries to feed their drug habits. The D.A.'s office fought her tooth and nail, and won. When the final list of crimes eligible for Drug Court was released, all addicts who had committed residential burglaries had been excluded—including Michael Pagsolingan.

Not only did the district attorney's office exclude Mike from Drug Court, they dug back to 1977, when he was seventeen years old and had joined some friends in stealing rings and a gold chain from another kid. Mike was eighteen by the time he was tried on that charge, and pled guilty as an adult—his first felony. Mike's record also showed an offense in 1992. He was drunk, having an argument with a friend, and kicked in a window of his friend's house. The police charged him with attempted burglary—felony number two—and he served eight months of county time at the Elmwood Farm in San Jose, then completed three years of probation without a further offense.

The 49ers football and the checks he stole from Geraldine, then, made felony number three for Michael Pagsolingan.

In April of 1994, the California legislature—in response to the kidnap and murder of twelve-year-old Polly Klaas by a repeated felon—passed a "Three strikes and you're out" law, to put away repeat criminal offenders by mandating a twenty-five-year-to-life sentence for anyone who has committed a third felony. On January 11, 2000, the San Francisco District Attorney's office told Michael Pagsolingan's lawyer that they would prosecute Mike as a three-strikes offender, giving him twenty-five years to life—unless he accepted a plea bargain of eight years in the state penitentiary.

Mike turned down the offer. Instead, he asked to serve a year in the county jail, followed by two years of court-supervised residential drug rehab, followed by five years of probation and drug testing during which any violation would put him immediately back behind bars. The district attorney refused Mike's plan, reiterating the offer of eight years in the state penitentiary.

Michael Pagsolingan stayed in jail, awaiting trial. Two possible outcomes remained: He might win at trial and go free, with no court-enforced rehab. Or he might lose at trial, and serve twenty-five years to life in the state penitentiary as a three-strikes offender.

"I'm going to keep hammering away and try to get Mike into Drug Court," public defender Jami Tillotson insists. "The other choices are crazy."

By January 1999, a year and four months since Darlene first arrived at the city's Central Intake Unit asking for help, she has been tossed about in a cyclonic quest for rehab: referred to and then immediately kicked out of three drug treatment programs; flung through a futile search for a case manager in the mental health system; referred by the city's mental health counselors to the substance abuse counselors; referred back to mental health again in circles that have spun me dizzy just watching.

As 1998 rolls into '99, Darlene abandons the maelstrom of her rehab search and, in the winter wrath of El Niño, beats a hasty retreat back to her tent at the Opera Boxes overlooking Highway 280. There she regresses into a methamphetamine mania that makes her so crazy she often barely recognizes me when I come to visit.

San Francisco had lured Darlene to its drug rehab Central Intake Unit in September of 1997 with flyers spread to every windy street corner announcing the city's new *Treatment on Demand* promise of rehab. "I never did get into no program," declares Darlene one winter day as she huddles in her tent against the rain, "because they say I'm uncontrollable, although I still haven't figured out what parts of me they want to control. They say they want me to tell them what's on my mind, then when I do, they tell me I got to leave. So I got thrown out of STOP, Genesis, Walden, even Target Cities. But I don't say nothing bad about Target Cities because that's Kathy's home and she really did try—but no program would have me."

Darlene frowns, trying to puzzle it all through.

"I know I'm weird and strange and odd and all that stuff," she tells me. "But I'm not *that* weird that in two years nobody can find one place to help me."

Wondering if Darlene's path through rehab has been a rare example of what happens to the most-difficult-to-treat addicts, or if her experiences are shared by the thousands of seemingly intransigent hallucinatory drug users, I meet with Dr. Pablo Stewart, the psychiatrist who specializes in treating mentally ill substance abusers. By the end of our conversation, the first time I've attempted to pull together a concise summation of all that has happened to Darlene, Dr. Stewart and I are so stunned by Darlene's story that we abandon any veneer of professional distance—and decide to intervene on her behalf.

"Awww, no!" exclaims the psychiatrist as I wind up the account of Darlene's search for the Wizard behind door number 17 at Westside Mental Health Clinic, telling him how Kathy had referred her there from Target Cities to find her case manager, but they had sent Darlene right back. "We're just trying to get your care organized properly," they had told her.

I scan through my notes from that day, reading to Dr. Stewart Darlene's reply to the mental health workers: "It's Kathy what first sent me here in the first place!" she had told them. "Why are you sending me backwards in time when I'm right here now, like in the present and the future?"

"Out of the mouths of babes!" Dr. Stewart laughs. "Both the substance abuse *and* mental health programs had Darlene right in their hands, time after time," he exclaims. "And each time they sent her away."

"And how common is that?" I ask. "Or is this some weird conspiracy that fell, happenstance, on Darlene?"

Dr. Stewart hesitates, frowning for just a moment.

"Some people in this city would protect their hides and go off the record with a journalist at this point," he tells me. "I won't. What you have just described occurs in every organization in this city I have ever worked with. Counselors and administrators find excuses *not* to provide services to folks like Darlene. Look, I'll be as kind as I can be here. There are legitimate reasons why health workers feel uncomfortable with mentally ill patients who are also doing drugs. But that does not justify denying them treatment slots. People like Darlene are the high-end addicts, the ones that do our society and themselves the most damage. So they're the ones we have got to get engaged in the treatment system, and we've failed miserably at doing that. Which means that the patients who need treatment the most get it the least."

Dr. Stewart picks up one of the photographs of Darlene that I had laid out on the table while telling her story.

"The way Darlene's been bounced around is the rule, not the exception," says the psychiatrist. "We split her into two parts, and that's when we lost her. We found every excuse to avoid the hard work by repeatedly telling her she's walked in the wrong door. In the end, that's left her nowhere."

"But what's the final answer?" I wonder, pointing to a photograph of Darlene standing near the freeway, screaming incoherently at a truck passing by.

Dr. Stewart stares at me, and then smiles.

"Are you willing to do some work to find out?" he asks. "What if you and me have a try at seeing what happens if Darlene gets a real chance at rehab? Nothing special, just another shot at it, but at a place where she won't get chased away. I may be risking making a public fool of myself, and of my beloved Haight Ashbury Clinic—but can you get Darlene to show up at the clinic, just like any other client, this Wednesday?"

I convince Darlene to try just one more program, telling her there's a rehab door that, just possibly, is sliding open for her. On Wednesday, she arrives, warily, at the Haight Ashbury Clinic for an intake evaluation.

The next day, Dr. Stewart nearly quits his job over what happens.

The Haight Ashbury Free Clinic was born of necessity in 1967, when thousands of flower children arrived in San Francisco for an LSD- and marijuana-laden Summer of Love that, depending on your point of view, revolutionized or ruined the country. The hippie communes of the neighborhood have long since been replaced by bed and breakfast inns, and today more customers stroll to Ben and Jerry's Homemade Ice Cream than to head shops in search of reefer paper. The Haight's flourishing street culture has undergone its own changes since 1967—tie-dye to tattoos, flower-power posters to facial piercings, and weed and psychedelics to heroin, methamphetamine, and crack cocaine. The Summer of Love is long gone, but the drug detox and rehab business is still hopping as Darlene walks up the front steps of the three-story renovated Victorian that houses the Haight Ashbury Free Clinic's Outpatient Substance Abuse Services.

Darlene strides to the reception counter in the first-floor waiting room lined by ancient, soft-cushioned couches. The wall is decorated with a sign painted in psychedelic colors:

Magical Mystery Tour
No Dealing
No Holding Drugs
No Using Drugs
No Alcohol
No Pets
ANY OF THESE CAN CLOSE THE CLINIC.
WE LOVE YOU.

Her wild tufts of hair poking out from an Alien Invader beanie, Darlene leans across the reception counter, arms covered in the loose, torn sleeves of an old gray sweater. A thin young woman wearing a tight leather halter top looks up and greets her.

"My name is Cindy," she says. "Can I help you?"

"I doubt it," replies Darlene. "I wouldn't mind having your vest, though—not that it would look the same on me like it looks on you!"

She lets out a cackle so loud that even the heroin nodders on the couches glance up.

Cindy laughs. "Tell me why you came?"

"I'm supposed to get off drugs."

"First visit?"

"You ever seen me here before?"

"No."

"Then why ask if it's my first visit? I'm not here to waste your time, don't go wasting mine. Next question?"

Cindy takes in a deep breath and, her smile now a bit more forced, hands Darlene a clipboard with an intake form to fill out.

Darlene moves to a corner of the room where, talking to herself, she runs quickly down the checklist on the form, making marks almost at random. Then she walks back to the counter and again leans forward. Cindy is facing the other way.

"Yo, Cindy!" Darlene cries out to the young woman's back. "I'm done."

The receptionist turns suddenly. "You're *really* going to be done if you shout at me like that one more time." She takes the clipboard from Darlene, glancing at her responses.

"You checked off yes *and* no for this question," says Cindy, thrusting the clipboard back across the counter. "We need yes *or* no."

"Which question?" asks Darlene, ignoring the clipboard.

Cindy looks down. "It *says,*" she reads in a loud voice, and the heroin nodders again look up, " 'Do you have suicidal thoughts?' "

Darlene glances at the clipboard, then at Cindy. "Can't you read what I wrote on the damn form?"

"I can read, but maybe you can't!" Cindy shoots back, not realizing she's come close to the truth for Darlene. "The form says pick yes *or* pick no, not both!"

Darlene looks around the room, where everyone is now watching her. Then she leans forward on the counter, sucks in a breath, narrows her eyes, and plants an intense stare on Cindy. The young woman backs up.

"I checked yes *and* no," Darlene grumbles, and then her voice matches the energy of her stare, "because I *meant* yes and no. And you don't have no right to cop an attitude and get in my face about it!"

Cindy slams the clipboard on the counter.

"Take this to the second floor," she snaps. "And you'd better calm down when you get there. You're seeing the psychiatrist today."

Darlene's first meeting with Dr. Stewart is surprisingly straightforward.

"How can I help you?" he asks, leaning back in the seat at his desk.

Darlene has selected an overstuffed, cushioned chair in the corner by the window, as far as she can be from him. She pushes herself deeply into the cushions, shoving her weight down so she's as low as possible, and then cranes her neck up to watch Dr. Stewart. He's six feet tall, wire thin, wearing tight blue jeans, pointed cowboy boots, and a faded sweatshirt. This contradiction of styles is topped off by a mustache that quivers over his trademark, constantly quizzical smile.

"What's your name again?" asks Darlene.

"Dr. Pablo Stewart."

"Well, which is it? Doctor, or Pablo, or Stewart?"

"It's whatever you want it to be," he says, rocking back in his chair, his smile and jokingly raised eyebrows not disguising in the least how closely he's watching Darlene.

"It's Pablo, then," she tells him. "And why do people come here to see you?"

"Most of the time, it's because they want help with drug problems."

Darlene lets forth one of her cackles and leans forward to stare Pablo down.

"But let's just say some person doesn't *want* to be off drugs? You can talk at them until your eyes turn blue, and they'll just tell you to *fuck off.*" She spits out the last two words at a near shout.

Pablo nods his head.

"Darlene, I rarely talk at anyone until my eyes turn blue," he says. "So this *person* you're talking about who doesn't want to be off drugs? I would guess that in some teeny, tiny way—" He holds his hand up for her to see, his face grimacing as he squeezes his thumb and index finger as tightly together as he can. "Just possibly, that *person* who you're speaking about may have the teeniest of desires to be doing less drugs, maybe to be a little less freaked out by what happens when that person does too much, say, methamphetamine."

Darlene laughs, joining him in the game. She scrunches up her face and squeezes her fingers together, the two facing off in an odd competition at demonstrating smallness.

"Well, what if that person only has"—Darlene puts on her squeaky little girl's voice—"the teeniest, teeeeniest, tiniest wanting to be off drugs?"

"Then," says Pablo, standing and offering Darlene his hand, "I would think that such a person would do very well in this clinic. And it would be my pleasure to invite that person to come back next week to see me again."

Darlene ignores his hand, rising at his signal that their session is over.

"That's it?" she asks.

"No," says Pablo. "I want to thank you for coming today, I'm glad you took the time. And I hope to see you again next week."

"And what do we do then?" asks Darlene.

"You'll tell me that," he replies. "From what I understand, you hear voices when you're doing speed—"

"Not voices. Noises," interrupts Darlene.

"Noises?"

"I can't tell you no more, so don't ask me no more. Some things I'm just not allowed to talk about."

"Well, maybe, just maybe, I can help you out with those noises. Next week?"

"It's hard to come here from my house," says Darlene. "And I don't come on time, hardly ever. One program threw me out the first day just for that."

"I'm here from ten until three," replies Pablo. "Around one o'clock it gets a little crowded, so you might have to wait a bit longer, but just show up anytime between ten and three and I'll be glad to see you."

Darlene mumbles something inaudible under her breath.

"Darlene," says Pablo, "I don't throw anybody out just for being late. You come when you can, OK?"

"I'll think about it," she replies, and walks out the door.

She charges down the stairs back to the first floor, her unlaced combat boots pounding the steps as she flees.

"Well, that was useless," Darlene tells me.

"Completely useless," I say. "Will you come back next Wednesday?"

She jumps from the last step to the landing outside the first-floor waiting room, glancing with a frown at Cindy behind the counter, and then turns to look at me.

"It wasn't so bad," she says softly. "I'll come back."

On Haight Street, Darlene dives quickly into a comic-book store, pulling me along. She searches the racks, then grabs one comic and holds the cover out for me to see. It's a busy, medieval scene. Dark, ominous castles are surrounded by wooden carts filled with dozens of blood-soaked, nearly naked women's bodies. Men in armor, holding swords, gawk at their exposed, bloodied flesh. I look at Darlene, puzzled.

"Shrinks always want to know about the noises in my head," she says, pointing to the comic-book cover. "That's a picture of my noises. It's the place I don't want to go no more. You can tell Pablo that."

She shivers, takes the comic book from me, and pulls me by the hand out the door.

"Can we go get a burrito?" asks Darlene, taking my elbow in her hand as we walk down the street. "I didn't eat since yesterday."

The next morning I'm on my way to a Drug Court team meeting and run into Pablo. It's his consulting day for the court. He takes me quickly into a small side room while the Drug Court rehab team gathers outside.

"Were you in the first-floor reception room at the clinic when Darlene checked in with Cindy?" he asks, and I nod. "What was your take on it?"

"It was nothing," I say. "The usual overworked and irritated staff member, made worse by an irritating Darlene. Why?"

"Because Darlene's been thrown out!" exclaims Pablo. "Look, let's sit down, professional-like, because I've been thinking about doing some very unprofessional things to some people at that clinic. And I'm a shrink, I don't think too good unless I've got a chair under my butt."

He finds us some chairs and leans forward, his usual sardonic smile obliterated.

"I went crazy today," he tells me. "I have *never* yelled at a person in that clinic, I have never stomped out of there in disgust. And today I did. We have this rule, that if any staff member feels physically threatened by a client then that client is eighty-sixed—that means out the door, permanently forbidden from ever coming back."

Cindy, it appears, had told her supervisor that Darlene had frightened her with a sudden aggressive movement across the reception counter. The supervisor went to the clinic director, and the director met with Pablo and recited the rule about threatening behavior. Then the director told Pablo he could no longer work with Darlene.

Pablo and I look at each other incredulously, then he breaks out laughing.

"She lasted one day!" he exclaims. "Or we lasted one day with her. Damn! I'm sure that Darlene *did* act out downstairs. That is what psychotic methamphetamine users do—they act unreasonably! Otherwise, we wouldn't need to treat them. So right there, one floor down from my office, the receptionists are screening out the dope fiends that need my help the most. Darlene only made it upstairs to see me because you and I had already talked about her, so I'd left explicit instructions at the front desk for her to be sent up after the intake. Had she just walked in like any other patient she'd have been thrown out by Cindy right then and there. And I never would have known she'd even come in. How many have we turned away like that? Nobody knows!"

Pablo gets up and starts pacing the small room.

"I've been in denial!" he says, his eyebrows furrowed in mock amazement. "I mean, I've been teaching about this dual diagnosis stuff all around the country for years, and I've had no idea what's going on just one floor below my own office. But my eyes are wide open now, and I am pissed! This isn't about Darlene, it's what she represents to the system—the untreatable, the undesirable, the uncooperative, the unmentionable. So we cast her out of our vision, saying she'll interfere with our work!"

Pablo checks his watch. The Drug Court team is waiting for him.

"Look," he tells me, opening the door of the small room. "We're going to have a staff meeting at the Haight Clinic about Darlene next Wednesday. The director told me that she has the right to come and speak up for herself, explain why she should be allowed in the clinic."

"I can't ask her to do that," I tell him immediately. "Yesterday, Darlene got the barest hint from you of finally being wanted, and she's willing to come back. But if I tell her she has to face your entire staff and fight her way into treatment, she'll just prove their point. She will walk into that room, shout 'Kiss my big black ass!' and slam the door on her way out. Then they'll say, 'See, we told you she's untreatable.' "

"I already told the director that Darlene is *not* coming to face a staff meeting," replies Pablo, "because a meeting like that would ruin any trust I'm trying to develop with her."

Then Pablo smiles, and puts his hand on my shoulder. "So I told them that you're coming instead. If you tell them what you saw in the waiting room, and what you know about Darlene and how she's been chased all around our fair city this past year, then maybe, just maybe, they'll decide to keep her in. But if they won't override their decision to eighty-six Darlene, then my job's going to be on the line. Because I'm not going to accept any action that keeps her out."

I've arranged to pick up Darlene by her house at the Opera Boxes at eleven on the morning of the staff meeting, and give her a ride to the clinic. Pablo and I have decided to break the rules and, for now, not tell her what's going on, only that we have a short clinic business meeting to attend while she waits. If all goes well and Darlene is accepted back into treatment, she will simply see Pablo that day as planned. But if the staff decides to keep her out, we'll tell Darlene what happened. And then I'll take her back home.

At eleven, I pull up to where Darlene usually waits for me, by the DANGER! DO NOT ENTER sign on the padlocked gate. She's not there. Wiser from prior experiences, I try to open the padlock, knowing it's been hacksawed through. But it's a sparkling new, heavily bolted lock.

Once again, I climb over the coiled barbed wire at the top of the gate, this time careful not to rip the seat of my pants. And this time I'm not worried about William's reaction to my being there: he's long ago been arrested on a parole violation. Darlene is a single woman, alone in her cave by the freeway.

I scramble up the steep slope some thirty feet to the fourth cave in the ten-foot-high retaining wall. Darlene's tent is gone. From the detritus of human habitation strewn around me, it looks as if a tornado suddenly struck, lifting the tent and everything in it, ripping it to shreds, and throwing it all back to earth with demonic force. The only intact object I can see is a bright yellow sign tacked to a nearby tree: 24-HOUR WARNING TO VACATE. ALL ILLE-

GALLY PLACED OBJECTS AND RESIDENCES WILL BE REMOVED. CALIFORNIA DEPARTMENT OF TRANSPORTATION.

I pick up a pair of boots, a soaking-wet teddy bear, and a tattered children's book, *The Snuggle Bunny,* and carry them down the path toward the gate. I don't need to rush to the Haight Clinic, I think, as I trudge back toward my car. The last time Darlene was bulldozed out of her home, she had disappeared in a hallucinatory haze. Wherever Darlene is now, I tell myself, Dr. Pablo Stewart and the Haight Clinic will be the last thing on her mind.

I climb back to the top of the gate and nearly lose my balance when I hear a sudden shout from the street just below.

"Lift your ass up or you'll cut your pants again!" cries Darlene, laughing as I try to untangle her damn teddy bear from the barbed wire.

"Thank you for bringing teddy," she says when I hit the ground. "And sorry I'm late. Can we go now?"

I give her a big hug. "Your house!" I say. "And then you weren't here. I got worried."

Darlene takes her *Snuggle Bunny* book from me, then does a swift pirouette.

"I didn't want to be all muddy for my appointment with Pablo," she says. "So I got me a shower at Martin de Porres, found some clean clothes in their free box."

She laughs. "What do you think Pablo would say if I showed up leaking mud all over his office?"

"He'd probably say, 'Glad you're here, Darlene. Thanks for coming.' But you know what? When I saw your house all torn to shreds in the mud back there, I was sure you would just disappear—back to China Basin someplace. I certainly didn't think you'd be here to go see Pablo."

Darlene frowns as we get into my car. "Remember how you told me that after all those other programs turned me down, these visits with Pablo might be like a second chance? That I needed to learn to trust people a little bit more?"

"I remember," I say, turning to face her, my key still not in the ignition.

"Well," says Darlene, "so how come you keep thinking I'm going to blow it? Maybe *you* need to trust me a little more, too. Can we start the car now? It's a far way from here to the clinic."

As I drive, Darlene flips through the pages of her *Snuggle Bunny* book.

"See, there's this snuggle bunny," she tells me, returning to her little girl's voice. "And he gets to roll around in this meadow *aaaall* day long. But then he gets lonely out there, and that makes me sad."

She flips to the back of the book and, haltingly, picks out each word, her finger moving along the page. "After a while," reads Darlene, "the Snuggle Bunny wishes he could snuggle against someone who would snuggle back."

———

Fourteen staff members of the Haight Ashbury Free Clinic gather in a circle of chairs in a third-floor meeting room to discuss whether Darlene should be forbidden from returning.

When I enter the room, the tension is palpable. Pablo had told me that *the Darlene question* has nearly split the staff in two. "I know she didn't intend to be a lightning rod that illuminates all these issues," he'd explained. "But Darlene sure as heck has become just that. She's lit up a whole bunch of questions about our attitudes toward the very clients we're supposed to be serving. And those questions have extended way beyond Darlene. Everybody's pretty on edge about it. You wouldn't believe the personal dirt that's rising to the top as we dig deeper into what everybody's reaction to this is about. Eerie stuff."

Darryl Inaba, the clinic's director, sees me enter the room, points to an empty chair, and invites me to join them.

"Our eighty-six policy protects our workers from violence," he begins, addressing the entire group. "If a staff member feels threatened by a client, he or she initiates the eighty-six process and that client is not eligible for services here. Ever. And that's what our intake worker has done with Darlene. To appeal such a decision, the client can come to this meeting and present his or her case."

The director explains that I am there to speak in Darlene's behalf.

"A physical threat is a personal judgment," says a tall, well-dressed woman, the supervisor for the intake workers. "There is no way we should be second-guessing the perceptions of the intake worker who was there at the time. And none of my workers should have to put up with such disrespect as Darlene was showing. We don't come here to be abused by our clients!"

Pablo, surprisingly, just about loses it before he begins.

"You *do* come here to be abused by our clients!" he exclaims, wide-eyed. The entire group stares at him.

"Look," continues Pablo, "I'm sorry to start right in like that, but let's hit reality here, huh? We deal with some very disturbed individuals. How can you expect to work with disturbed and mentally ill clients and not have to take some disrespect? Being disrespected comes with the job. So you learn to calm the clients down, not go at 'em head to head and accelerate things until we've got to throw them out. Darlene has been kicked around this city so much, of course she fights back. Then we say, aww, hell, this woman has a bad attitude, doesn't give us no respect, so we kick her out. What is that?"

Ignoring Pablo's outburst, the supervisor for the intake workers turns to me.

"May I ask you a basic question about Darlene?" she says. "I mean, is she interested in getting off drugs, or is she just unhappy with her life and needs help from some treatment center? I'm asking, because we are a drug program, not a mental health clinic."

The question stuns me. This was the last place in the city where I would expect her to be split down the middle: Is she mentally ill, or does she abuse drugs?

"Darlene shoots speed," I say slowly, feeling my way along. "And she hallucinates, gets hyper, and can be extremely obnoxious. But I just walked along the same Haight Street that you all walk along to get to work every day, and it's pretty freaky out there. The drug users who are having problems, the ones that need your help the most, are the ones who get hyped up, in your face, hallucinatory, and obnoxious. Sure, Darlene gets crazy at times, maybe because of speed, maybe because of what her life is like, maybe she was just born that way—probably all three. But if you exclude Darlene from your services because she acts crazy, then only the nicest of the folks I saw out on Haight Street this morning will get through your door. I don't know, is that your goal?"

My comment goes unanswered as Pablo speaks up. Then, as if they were a bickering family at Christmas dinner, all hell breaks loose at the meeting.

"The patients aren't the obstacle to care here, you are!" says Pablo, the chief of psychiatry, addressing the physician who heads the clinic's medical section. "If you could do it, you'd have a clinic without patients."

"Pablo, I'll be damned if I'm going to sit here and listen to that from you!" the medical director fumes back at the psychiatrist.

"How about we cut out both of your jobs," mutters a pharmacy worker next to me, "and use the money to get the medications we need."

"OK, OK," interrupts the clinic director. "One person at a time!"

The group falls to silence, glancing at the floor, ashamed at their outbursts.

"This one provocative patient," says Pablo softly, "has provoked our entire clinic. Amazing."

"This one provocative patient," I add, "seems to have provoked every clinic she's ever hit in San Francisco. Each program finds seemingly good reasons not to treat her, and each program acts crazy in response to Darlene's own craziness. So then she cops an even more defiant attitude when she hits the next program. But if I might try to explain Darlene's point of view, maybe you all can be the first people not to throw her out."

"Let's hear what he has to say," says the clinic director. "I think we've reached the point in this meeting where we can understand that any of us, even if we think we're reasonable people, can be provoked to outbursts of anger."

"Am I really crazy?" Darlene asks Pablo at their session that afternoon, after Pablo had been advised that Darlene could remain at the clinic. She has again scrunched down into the corner chair, unaware of the preceding struggle. "I mean"—she stares at Pablo—"just because I get all these noises in my head when I'm doing meth, that doesn't mean I'm crazy, does it? I mean, it's a mind-altering drug, right? So is my mind altered, like by the meth, or am I crazy?"

"That's a great question," replies Pablo. "But I need to know what you mean by crazy before I answer it. Please understand, I'm not trying to avoid your question. I just want to be sure I know what you're asking. Can you tell me what happens when you do speed, or when you're off speed, that makes you think you're crazy?"

Darlene giggles, bouncing forward in her seat. "I haven't been *off* speed enough for like fifteen years now to know what happens! If I get off speed, some new Darlene's going to come along right behind me and bite me in the ass! And I don't even want to know that chick."

"Why not?"

"Because if that chick is crazy, then that means Darlene is crazy, even without doing speed." She stops suddenly, at the edge of tears. "And that would be really sad."

Pablo raises his eyebrows and, inquiringly, extends his hands with palms upward, his fingers stretched toward Darlene. She stares.

"That," says Pablo, "is psychiatrist talk for, 'And—tell me more—' " He mimes the gesture again, and Darlene wipes at her tears and giggles.

"You were saying," notes Pablo, "that if you're really crazy, it would be really sad."

"Because," says Darlene, "I've fought against that my whole life, all these people telling me I'm a nutcase. And I've tried so hard to make that not true."

Pablo waits her out.

"It's your turn," says Darlene. "Am I a nutcase, like somebody *waaay* out there? Or do I just do too much dope?"

Pablo sighs. "I think that using speed brings on some of the problems you have, Darlene. And because you're still using speed it confuses the picture about what you're like if you're not using speed. So, I don't know."

He sees her look of disappointment.

"Hey, Darlene," Pablo says, smiling, "I'm a pretty good shrink, trust me on that one. But I'm not going to be able to answer that very good question you have—unless I get to see you off speed for a while. So I'm going to strongly encourage you to start decreasing your speed use, see what that does to these noises you have in your head. Can you tell me some more about the noises?"

"No," says Darlene quickly. "I don't tell nobody about my noises, especially no shrinks."

"Why?"

"Because whenever I tell anyone, they say I'm crazy. And I'm not."

"I can understand that," says Pablo. "But over time, if you can cut down on your speed use, would you feel comfortable enough to tell me if your noises are getting better?"

"I haven't done no speed for two weeks, and the noises are the same."

Pablo stands up from his seat, and Darlene matches his movement.

"I know what that means," she says, putting on a prim English accent. "Thank you for coming, Darlene. I'll see you next week. Now, get out."

"I can't hide a thing from you," says Pablo, laughing and opening the door. "But let me end with a couple of quick thoughts. First, those two weeks you've been off speed, after some fifteen years on it—that's not enough time to let us know what your brain is like off speed. It can take months, sometimes years for your brain to get back to what it was before. The second thing is that sometimes my patients don't exactly tell me the truth about how much drugs they're using. So I *know* you haven't used any speed for two weeks, but I'd like to strongly encourage you not to use speed, even when you're not using speed."

Darlene is out the door, calling back to Pablo, "It was two days, not two weeks. See you next Wednesday."

"So, did I pass his test?" Darlene asks me as she skips down Haight Street after her session with Pablo.

"It seemed like you were the one testing him," I reply. "Did he pass?"

"Oh, he's doing OK, so far," she says thoughtfully. "It'll take a while for me to know."

I drive to the Mission, and pull up next to the parking lot behind the S.P.C.A. After CALTRANS had destroyed her housing at the Opera Boxes, Darlene, for the first time in years, is living openly on the streets. We get out of my car by the two shopping carts where she's storing her clothes and sleeping bag. At night, she stretches a plastic tarp between the two carts, makes sure there are enough homeless friends camped out around her so that she's safe, and gets a few hours of sleep before the police roust all the homeless on the block at about six in the morning.

"I ain't used to this homeless shit," she says, pulling out her damp, crumpled clothes from the shopping cart and starting a neatly folded pile on the sidewalk. "I've been living in my mansions at China Basin and the Opera Boxes all this time, and now this. It freaks me out."

She reaches into her shopping cart to pull out yet another pile of wet clothing.

"This sucks, it really does," says Darlene. "I got to find a new place to stay every damn day! And all these people out here, I got no privacy. And if I'm trying to stop doing dope, look at this block—people freaking on speed all around me! You know what? I got so much noise from all this other stuff in my life right now, if I do any more speed I may just lose it. I'll be *waaaay* up there, and you wouldn't be able to find me again. I mean, even *I* wouldn't be able to find me again! So I ain't doing it for Pablo, but this may be a good time for me to chill out on the speed, maybe switch to a little marijuana, a beer at night to mellow me out. I got so much noise in my head right now, I can't even sleep no more."

"Which noises are keeping you awake?" I ask.

"The screaming ones," she answers. "People hollering for help. And when they're in my head I can't just ignore them. I put my Walkman on, real loud, and that kind of helps drown it out, like part of it anyway."

"Darlene, how come you won't tell Pablo any of that?"

"I only just met the man!" She turns, staring at me with wide eyes. "And if I tell him any of what I just told you he's going to want to put me on crazy-people's pills."

"How do you know?"

" 'Cause he's a shrink. I'm not new at this game, you know. But I've been on those pills before, and I'm not doing it again. I came to that clinic to get off drugs, not be put on 'em."

Darlene misses her next two appointments with Pablo, simply doesn't show up. And I can't find her anywhere I look in the city. My phone rings during the third week she's been missing, at the crack of dawn, a Wednesday morning.

"Can you come get me?" says Darlene, as usual with no other introduction.

"Get you where?" I ask, half asleep. "And for what?"

"Don't play with me!" she says. "It's Wednesday, so the *for what* is to see Pablo. And the *where* is the Homeless Women's Shelter, on Fifteenth."

I'm wide-awake now.

"Darlene James? In a homeless shelter? Building, roof, beds?"

"Just come get me, OK?"

In the car driving from the shelter to the Haight, I can coax only a few details from her.

"I'm in the shelter because I got tired of being hit!" she says finally. "William's out of jail, and I ain't telling you no more except that he doesn't know I'm at the shelter and that's just fine with me."

We trudge up the stairs of the Haight Clinic to the second floor. Darlene, hating the crowds in the waiting room, plants herself on the top step, where Pablo will spot her as he passes by, bringing patients back to his office.

"I'm probably kicked out, anyway," she tells me. "They do that if you stop showing up like I did."

Darlene is scheduled for therapy only once per week, as an outpatient. Pablo knows he's pushing his luck even asking for that. Having lived on the streets, with her own schedule and rules, for sixteen years, Darlene takes poorly to structure. More frequent therapy appointments, or even an attempt at residential treatment, would lead quickly to failure. Pablo is deliberately unhurried with Darlene's rehab.

The psychiatrist walks through with a patient, sees Darlene, and stops to offer her a grand, silent curtsy, then continues on. Three patients later, he calls her in.

"I'm glad to see you," says Pablo, with a verifiable grin as she scurries to her seat in the corner.

"I thought you were going to kick me out," she tells him. "But it's not like I quit, I just needed a vacation."

"I can understand that," he replies. "Glad you came back."

"You mean it wasn't wrong to just skip out a few weeks?"

"Let's put it this way, Darlene," says Pablo, leaning forward toward her stare. "Missing a few weeks with me isn't the best idea for your recovery. But missing a few weeks and then never showing up at all—well, then I'd *really miss you.*"

She looks down, embarrassed.

Pablo waves to get Darlene's attention, then puts on his comical, raised-eyebrows look, hands outstretched, waiting.

She sits bolt-upright in her chair and announces, "I need you to put me on some of those pills for people with voices."

She glances over at Pablo, and then breaks into an hysterical cackle.

"Look at you!" she cries out. "Don't get so excited, baby! What'd I just do, tell you some shrink's wet dream?"

He doubles over with laughter. "I guess I'm a sorry excuse for a psychiatrist," says Pablo. "I'm supposed to keep a neutral expression on my face, no matter what."

"Yeah, you should!" laughs Darlene. "But I like you better 'cause you don't."

"OK, I was surprised you asked for pills," says Pablo. "And you read it right through me. The first time I mentioned medications to you, you said, 'I ain't going to take no government pills!' I wasn't even going to bring it up again, for a long time. So, what's up?"

"I can't tell you all the details, except that I was like living on the streets and really stressing out about that, and then my old man got out of jail and we had some problems. So now I'm in this shelter with like 250 people around me all the time, and I just don't live that way! I'm doing less speed, I really am, but I still got all these thoughts in my head, like the pieces of my mind are coming back together again and one half of my mind is talking to the other half. And I'm like caught in the middle? So I can't sleep no more, all that chatter going on."

"Darlene," says Pablo, "you keep looking over your shoulder while you're talking to me. Is that the noise you've told me about?"

"Wasn't me who talked about my noise, because I *can't* tell you about it. But I need you to give me something to quiet things down so I can get some rest at night. It can't be no pills that turns me into no zomboid, though, like those other pills I been put on did. But if you won't give me nothing because I won't tell you about my noises, then that's fine, too! I can use my Walkman, but I've got the Walkman on so much I can't even think no more."

"The Walkman drowns out the noise?" asks Pablo.

Darlene nods silently.

"Well, the Walkman seems like a good ride compared to what the other noises must be like," he says. "But let me get you some pills; they may be just a little bit better than the Walkman."

Pablo disappears for a moment to the pharmacy, returning with some tablets of Zyprexa, one of the newer antipsychotic medications. He holds out the first pill for her to take.

"Darlene," says Pablo, "I can't even imagine how stressful it must be for you—first out on the streets not knowing where you're going to sleep at night, then whatever came down between you and your old man. And now in a shelter with 250 women. All that on top of what you've been doing for so many years. So I want you to know, I'm not giving you these pills because I think they're the answer to everything. They're not going to get you housing, or a job, not even food to eat. But they might chill those noises enough so you can take care of things. And if you try these pills, I'd also like you to be doing less speed. Then maybe we can work together on those other worries you've got."

"Thank you, Pablo," says Darlene softly. "How come nobody else ever knows what you just said? They never see that part of my life that's so hard." For the first time since he'd walked into the room with the pills, she looks at Pablo's face instead of his hand.

"I want to thank you for hanging in there, Darlene," he says, sitting back in his chair. "And for coming back. I know that's hard."

Pablo watches Darlene shiver, and then take the pill in her mouth, lift the glass of water, and swallow it down. Then he stands.

Darlene chokes on the water, laughing.

"And now," she mocks his deep voice, "get out!"

"You skipped the first parts," says Pablo, and they recite their now-shared ritual in chorus, laughing.

"Thank you for coming. See you next week. *Now,* get out."

So much of what happens to Darlene over the year after she began working with Pablo would have happened anyway. Bulldozed from the Opera Boxes, she moves to the streets. Beaten by William, she retreats to a shelter. Hating the shelter, she seeks out Tony and the Homeless Death Prevention Team to find city-subsidized housing and, incredibly, after sixteen years on the streets, moves indoors to a hotel room. Through it all, Darlene continues to use speed, but every month a bit less. And then, hardly at all.

In September of 1997, when I first searched for Darlene, I had to crawl through a hole in the fence of a windy postindustrial-waste zone, then traverse a scene of scattered needles and wasted bodies until I spotted her patched-together tent.

Today, when I want to find Darlene, I phone her at the Windsor Hotel. If she's there, I hear an abrupt, "Hey, babe, what's up?" If she's not, I leave a message on Darlene's answering machine; she calls back that night.

When I visit her at the Windsor, I am to this day still amazed by a compulsively neat, gently feminine side of Darlene I had completely missed while she'd been living on the streets. She's put up lace curtains, found a patchwork quilt for her bed, organized dozens of Walkman cassette tapes into precise piles, found a fashionable wooden dresser into which she's neatly folded her finally dry clothing.

Darlene's steady progression upward after sixteen years as a homeless speed freak seems, on the surface, to have as much to do with the flow of her life's circumstances as it does with Pablo's drug rehab counseling. She often misses her appointments with him, sometimes takes her pills, frequently becomes angry, and rarely follows his suggestions without twisting them about to fit her own unique way of doing things.

And yet, always, even after a month's absence, she comes back.

"I'm staying off the speed," Darlene starts out at the beginning of most of their sessions.

"Well," replies Pablo, playing his role, "allow me to encourage you to stay off the speed even when you are off the speed. Because whatever is going on, the speed's making you feel worse."

Darlene laughs and recites her lines. "Yeah, I guess I'm still doing a little speed, sometimes."

Then they get down to business.

"You ever seen the movie *The Fly*?" she asks him one day, a year into rehab. "The new one, where towards the end this lady has a baby, and it's a baby *fly!* It comes out like a mangled mess, and there's all this screaming. Well, remember how I didn't want to talk about my noises? That's because when I was *really* using speed heavy, my noises were just like that movie. So, am I crazy?"

"What's the noise like now, when you're doing less speed?" asks Pablo.

"Quieter," says Darlene. "I mean, it's a part of me, always has been. But it's much, much quieter, so I can mostly ignore it now. But I can't tell you it's gone."

Pablo smiles. "Thank you for telling me what the noises were like," he says. "And you know how to make them go away even more?"

"I know," says Darlene. "Stop the speed. I really am trying!"

Three weeks later she shows up at her appointment completely disoriented.

"What's up?" he says, watching as she sinks into her chair and stares blankly ahead.

For the first time I can remember in over a year, Darlene holds one hand to her ear, tapping her fingers in the chattering movement that she and I had long ago worked out as her symbol for when she's hearing other people talking.

"It's like me talking to you, and you talking to me," she explains to Pablo. "Only it happens all at the same time, and also you're talking to Lonny and he's talking to you, and I hear all of you talking to each other at once inside my head. So I just try to ignore the sounds that are *in* my head, and listen to the sounds that are outside of my head. But that's hard."

"What's your speed use been like lately?" he asks.

"I won't lie to you no more," she tells Pablo. "Every day, maybe a couple of times a day, for about a week now. Guess I got to stop again, huh?"

Darlene gets up from her chair, still seeming dazed. Then she looks at Pablo, as if trying to understand some puzzle.

"Thank you for bearing with me today," she says. "I mean that."

"It's been my pleasure, Darlene," replies Pablo, not disguising his concern. "You've felt better before. I'm sure you can get there again."

Two weeks later, Darlene comes to her appointment bubbling over like an excited child.

"I went to the street fair yesterday," she tells Pablo. "I was dancing up a storm, and I look down and right at my feet is this packet of pure crystal meth. I mean, we're not talking the cheap street stuff. This was the best in town, real ice, baby, like the rich folks use!"

"Darlene," says Pablo. "I think I've got the message. Maybe you should stop the story there?"

"No!" Darlene laughs and barrels along. "So I am looking at this meth, and it is looking at me. And remember, you are talking to someone who usually injects that stuff right into her neck vein!"

"I remember," replies Pablo, his head lowered as he stares fixedly at Darlene over his eyeglasses.

"So I threw it away," she says.

"Got a witness?"

Darlene giggles. "My roommate from the shelter. She was with me the whole time, I swear to God! I'm thinking, OK, if I'm not going to shoot it, I can at least make me some money. So I'm looking around for someone to make the sale to, and then I'm thinking, Darlene, look at what this stuff did to your brain. You want to do that to somebody else? So I get my roommate to come with me, because even I can't believe what I'm about to do. We find a bathroom and I open the packet and watch that powder sail down the drain. It almost made me cry. I mean, that's sixty dollars I just flushed down the toilet! But then I thought about it—maybe that's sixty brain cells I didn't kill on somebody else. I mean, think of how many of my own brain cells have died on me. So, I'm kind of feeling good about what I did, even though I do miss the money."

Pablo sits staring thoughtfully at Darlene, and then smiles.

"Darlene," he says. "You are just too cool."

Two steps forward, one step back. Over the year, Darlene repeatedly does well, and then slides back into her hazes of speed-induced hallucinations, only to crawl out again and amaze Pablo with her lucidity and insight. With time, though, Darlene's setbacks are outnumbered by her leaps forward.

By the end of 1999, Darlene is so much better that anyone who had met her when she'd first joined Darrell, Mike, and me at the Target Cities group in September of 1997 would not recognize her.

And that is just what happens.

On November 5, 1999, Darlene is accepted into Walden's Intensive Treatment Services—to one of the six slots offering full psychiatric care and drug rehab. On November 15, she *buddies* Paul, another resident, to an interview at the program across town called Acceptance Place.

By that November, Darrell, with more than two years of sobriety under his belt, is a full-time counselor at Acceptance Place. He's also still taking night courses in business school. Darrell, if anything, might be accused of doing too well.

"I take this sobriety stuff so seriously now," he complains, "I've gotten to be a bore! I need to loosen up again, learn to have fun. But first, I have to finish school."

On the day that Darlene buddies Paul for an interview at Acceptance Place, I get a call from Darrell right after he gets home.

"You will *never* guess who I saw today!" he squeaks into the telephone like an excited kid. "I walked into our living room at Acceptance Place to meet this guy who I was supposed to take back to the office for an interview. Standing right next to him is this woman, and she looks kind of familiar. There's all these people around us so at first I hardly notice, but then I look again and I'm staring at her, and she's staring back at me.

"Then I whisper to myself. 'Darlene?' I mean, she looks so different! Last time I saw Darlene I was passing by this soup-kitchen line, like a year ago, and she was all smelly and babbling away to herself, as always. So I just made a loop around her, I didn't even want to say hi.

"So me and this woman in the living room are staring at each other. And then, I am so embarrassed, the two of us just went crazy, in front of everybody. I mean, we are hugging and jumping up and down like little children!

" 'Oh, my God!' I'm yelling. 'Darlene, you look so beautiful!'

"And we keep hugging and jumping up and down and everybody thinks we're crazy because we've got tears flying all over the place and we're screaming at the top of our lungs, 'We made it! We made it!'

"But then we got real quiet and we did this big, long hug. We just could not stop bawling. And I cried all the way home on the bus today. I hadn't realized how amazing it is. I mean, look at the possibilities of what could have happened! But it's true. We made it."

"I've got all this stuff in my head that I've never had before," Darlene tells Pablo at their session that week. "Real scary stuff."

"Like what?"

"Like I've started to have dreams when I'm sleeping, and it's been so long since I've had any dreams. Last night, I had this really weird dream that I was walking around a big warehouse with a syringe in my hand. There was this radiator keeping the place warm, all these pipes all over, and I go to get water from a pipe so I can shoot up. But this horrible bumblebee comes right beside me and I'm too afraid to get the water. So then I go to shoot up anyway, but instead of a needle on the syringe there's this caterpillar."

Darlene stops, and Pablo watches her shake off a shiver.

"So now I got this syringe with a caterpillar on it where the needle should be," she continues. "And I look and there's no brown dope, it's empty. I'm standing there holding this empty rig with a caterpillar on it and no needle! And that is so freaky I wake up, scared out of my mind."

Pablo hands Darlene a tissue to wipe at her tears.

"Well?" he says, raising his eyebrows and extending his hands.

"I don't *know* what it means, that's your job!" she laughs through the tears. "All I know is that the dream scared the hell out of me. Hell, just having a dream was scary, it's been so long."

"Dreams come when you're in the deepest part of sleep," Pablo tells her. "So when you were doing a lot of speed, your mind couldn't rest well enough to have dreams. Sometimes it takes a year or more after you stop speed to start dreaming once more. So it's good that you're dreaming again, Darlene, after all these years. You'll start getting to the stuff that's been locked away all this time."

She stares, wide-eyed. "What if I don't want to know the stuff that's been locked away? Do I *have* to have these dreams? Will they get worse?"

Pablo smiles. "I'm not sure there's any way you can stop them. Dreams just happen. But let me reassure you. I promise, we'll work through whatever comes up."

Darlene does not look reassured.

"This wasn't no ordinary dream," she tells him. "It was like, I'm asleep and then, *bam!* It's my brain talking to me again, and I don't want to hear it. That's a sickness, huh? To wake up hearing your brain talking to you? It's like, this time I'm *really* losing my mind."

"No. I promise, Darlene," says Pablo, leaning close to be sure he has her attention. "You're not losing your mind. You've just found it again."

When I began this book, the question *Does treatment work?* formed the tiniest seed of an inquiry. It soon blossomed into a prickly rose. The closer I moved in to smell the flower of rehab, the more sharply I felt the thorns.

It is tempting to synthesize an answer by writing an update on how Darlene, Mike, Darrell, and the others have fared since the final chapter. But the successes or failures of drug treatment cannot be gauged by a book's-end listing of how the characters are doing. Rehab is an ongoing process, not a moment in time.

This is not to say that I've come to no conclusions. A number of truths about rehab and addicts were hammered into me while I worked on this book. Those conclusions, either by seemingly endless repetition or blatantly obvious *truth,* reach beyond moment or person.

Relapse: *When an addict in rehab gets worse and heads back to drugs, the programs must increase treatment, not withdraw it.*

Relapse to drug use, I had thought, means that both addict and rehab have failed. I was wrong. I know now that relapse is one of many ways in which an addict learns to stay off drugs. "Don't get me wrong, Ms. Holmes," Judge Lam told Crystal. "It's not that we encourage relapses. It would have been better if you had prevented it. But that's what you're in rehab to learn."

If addicts already knew how to keep from relapsing, they wouldn't need treatment in the first place. Yet people who come to rehab asking for help with their compulsive drug use still get thrown out of treatment for using drugs. For two years I watched a variety of programs send dozens of clients back to the streets because they had relapsed. There are no acceptable excuses for such a practice.

Detox: *Each and every rehab program must be required to have a formal, structured association with a drug detox center where it can send relapsed clients.*

"They'll contaminate the whole house," say many in the rehab programs about addicts who've returned to drugs. "We can't have them here." I agree. But there is nothing to keep programs from referring relapsed clients to detox centers, instead of kicking them out into the streets. We must require that every program be formally linked to a detox center that will work with the addicts to help them get clean again and, it is hoped, back to rehab. The rehab programs, too, must *encourage* their relapsed clients to return for more treatment.

Humiliation: *Abuses and humiliation in the name of therapy must cease. Cities must establish an ombudsman to monitor the rehab programs, and addicts must be allowed to access the ombudsman without repercussions.*

Relapsed Walden House Brothers or Sisters who want to come back into treatment are first confronted by an in-your-face screaming match at a House Meeting that debases them. The programs argue that this is a way to teach addicts that there are consequences to their actions, or that humiliation forces the addicts to look more deeply into their emotions and behaviors. The fact is, humiliation most commonly leads to addicts being humiliated, and little else.

While rehab organizations across the country now claim that less aggressive treatment has replaced the older Synanon-style "emotional surgery without anesthetic," my investigations following addicts through multiple programs over the past two years show that attack therapy is still commonplace.

There are many proven and effective ways to dole out consequences that will let addicts in treatment know, without thoroughly debasing them, when they have erred. Shaming and degradation induce no human being to come back for more.

Stick and stay and *keep coming back* are the most potent tools for the drug treatment industry. If there is a single consistent finding that has come out of rehab research it is that the longer clients can be maintained in the programs the more likely they are to emerge clean and sober, and stay that way. Kicking addicts out of programs because of relapses, or heaping abuse on them while they are in the programs, keeps them from coming back.

Psychological counseling: *All rehab counselors must be trained to recognize and treat the multitude of addicts who also have psychological disorders, and refer them to appropriately intensive additional care when needed.*

There is no benefit to our spending rehab funds to treat dually diagnosed addicts unless we have dually trained counselors. At least 40 percent of the people so devastated by drugs that they hit rehab have a psychological disturbance, with depression and post-traumatic stress disorder heading the list. These dually diagnosed addicts uniformly receive inadequate care. "Many addiction counselors have had little or no training in diagnosing and treating mental disorders," reports the fed's Substance Abuse and Mental Health Services Administration. In addition, "Mental health professionals . . . have received little or no training about addictive disorders." Yet an astounding ten million citizens annually have drug disorders combined with psychological disturbances and "Their needs have not been addressed by the majority of mental health and substance abuse treatment programs."

I am certain of one thing: When an addict, no matter how together he or she seems (think of Mike), works vigorously to get into rehab, persists in the program with clear and sincere intentions of overcoming addiction, and yet still repeatedly relapses to drug use—there is invariably an additional psychological disturbance underlying that failure to stay clean. Recurrent relapses are caused by psychological dysfunction, not mere lack of willpower. Until proven otherwise, a recurrently relapsing addict should be assumed to have an underlying psychological disorder. Every willing addict who repeatedly relapses in spite of actively participating in rehab must be evaluated and treated by mental health professionals trained and experienced in both addiction and psychiatric care. Addicts who have relapsed again and again will continue to do so until their mental and emotional disturbances are dealt with by competent professionals.

> Case management: *Cities must establish a comprehensive case management system to guide addicts through the maze of programs and services. The case managers should not work for any particular rehab program, but rather represent and advocate for the addicts in the overall system.*

Imagine that Glenda had been provided with a case manager to supervise her care after she'd graduated from Friendship House. She could have been referred to appropriate housing, provided with daily outpatient rehab, encouraged to keep in contact even when she'd resumed drinking—given a chance to head back toward sobriety. Had she been fortunate enough to have been arrested and sent to Drug Court, she would have received those services. There is no reason any city cannot establish an identical case management system, outside of the courts. Cities that do not set up such a system should not receive a penny of federal funding.

On April 21, 2000, Glenda's friends gathered around the benches in Hallidie Plaza for her memorial service. She had continued drinking until her liver failed, and she died.

Could a good case manager in an organized rehab system have prevented Glenda's death from alcoholism at age thirty-eight? Glenda never had the opportunity to find out.

When Mike left Walden, that program should have been required to notify his case manager (had he had one), who would have picked up from there. Instead of being ostracized, Mike would have been offered counseling and support, referred to detox, and then, quite possibly, back to Walden or another rehab program.

Oversight: *Government agencies that provide funds to the programs must assure that addicts are receiving comprehensive and effective treatment.*

In San Francisco alone, 135 drug treatment programs are run by forty independent organizations, which rely on government funding. San Francisco budgeted $49 million for drug abuse services in 1999, money that came from city, state, and federal sources. The government must assure that those millions of dollars are buying appropriate services.

According to Michael Siever, co-chair of San Francisco's Treatment on Demand Planning Council, "The Department of Public Health does not have the data to tell us what's going on." Or in Baltimore, another city attempting to provide rehab to all addicts who need it: "The money is well spent only if the city's treatment programs produce results," reported the *Baltimore Sun.* "Currently, there is no way to tell. . . . Forty-four treatment contractors run their programs largely as they choose."

Every drug rehab program in the country must currently be licensed to operate and demonstrate its treatment capabilities and adequacy of care for the addicts. Yet with 135 such government-certified programs in San Francisco, Darlene bounced repeatedly from mental health to substance abuse services, until Dr. Pablo Stewart intervened; Mike was kicked out of Walden for using drugs and offered no resources to pick himself up and move on again; Darrell graduated from a three-month program and received no further support to maintain his sobriety; Glenda was tossed back to the streets after emerging clean and sober from her program. Crystal, with thorough and comprehensive oversight from Drug Court, repetitively relapsed, resisted treatment, and then finally achieved long-lasting sobriety.

These are anecdotes about a few addicts, whose stories are repeated hundreds of thousands of times across the country each year. It is time for all city governments and innumerable state and federal agencies to maintain a true vigilance over the rehab programs, and cut off funding to those programs that do not meet specific standards of care. It is no longer adequate for the fed's Center for Substance Abuse Treatment to issue yet another "Treatment Improvement Protocol" (they have now put out thirty-six) without assuring, by funding-tied penalties and enforcement, that the programs actually enact and follow the carefully delineated and crucially needed treatment improvements.

Before investing a single additional dollar in drug treatment, or establishing one more rehab bed for an addict in need, our government must first establish rigorous oversight of the programs, along with independent case management for the addicts. With hundreds of thousands of addicts ricocheting through rehab every year, city and state health departments must tightly monitor and regulate the programs.

Funding priorities: *Federal funds and efforts must be shifted from drug interdiction abroad to drug rehab at home.*

For fiscal year 2001, our Office of National Drug Control Policy has budgeted $17.7 billion to bring our drug problem under control. But only 19 percent of those dollars are aimed at treating addicts. While $50 million is set aside to support Drug Courts, $420 million will be spent to construct new prisons, $1.3 billion to fight the drug war in Colombia. These treatment budgetary shortcomings are exacerbated by our lack of attentiveness to the details necessary for successful rehab: The National Drug Control Strategy's 282-page Fiscal Year 2000 Budget Summary uses the term "case management" only four times, "relapse prevention" just once. But "helicopter" shows up fifteen times, as in, "These helicopters will augment 18 UH-1Ns already in Colombia . . ."

A 1994 RAND study, prepared under the auspices of the White House Office of National Drug Control Policy (and the United States Army), examined cocaine consumption in the United States. Here's how much money is needed to gain every 1 percent reduction in addicts' cocaine use: $34 million on rehab for drug addicts in the United States; or, $246 million for police to enforce drug laws in the United States; or, $366 million at the border to prevent the drugs from coming in the country; or, $783 million spent in the countries that produce the drugs. Every dollar spent on drug rehab at home, concluded the study, yields the same effect as twenty-three dollars spent abroad.

It's not difficult to read these numbers and be certain that increasing drug treatment dollars from 19 percent of the total drug budget to, say, 50 percent would have the overall effect of substantially decreasing drug abuse at home, which, when all is said and done, is the goal of our national drug policy. Looking at cocaine use alone, according to the RAND study, reallocating 25 percent of money spent abroad to money spent at home "would include a one-third reduction in annual cocaine consumption."

"The struggle against illegal drugs is not a war," claims drug czar General Barry McCaffrey. "Addicted individuals are to be helped," he explains, "not defeated." Yet the vast majority of our anti-drug dollars are still spent on battles abroad rather than on treatment at home.

Does rehab work for those who are most disastrously addicted? I still don't know. In the two years of this investigation I rarely saw rehab done well enough to learn if it might work.

What we today call drug rehab does not provide consistent and coherent help to the majority of addicts who come seeking it. It may well be that the nature of the beast of addiction makes effective treatment of addicts a pie-in-the-sky dream, even with the best that rehab could offer. Or it may be that the frustratingly unimpressive treatment results we see today with those most intensely addicted are merely what happens in a rehab system that is as ill as the addicts themselves.

Can rehab work? After two years of ricocheting through rehab with these addicts, I believe the answer is a resounding *Yes*.

Rehab *can* work—in a cohesive, coordinated system that links drug programs to mental health services, and joins both together to provide addicts with lifelong care and case managers who stick with them through thick and thin.

I present this conclusion not as an act of faith but as a reality backed up by the struggles and dreams of Mike, Darlene, Darrell, Crystal, Glenda, and all those whose lives have been overrun by tragic events *and* the tragedies of drug addiction.

On March 24, 2000, three years after beginning drug rehab, Mike stood in an orange jail jumpsuit, head bowed, in the Superior Court of the state of California, at the bench of Judge Kevin V. Ryan, for sentencing. He faced twenty-five years to life in the state penitentiary, but the district attorney had finally agreed to a plea bargain.

"The prosecution wants the defendant to plead guilty and be sentenced to eight years in state prison," announced the black-robed judge from the high bench at the front of the court. "It is alleged that the defendant, who has a substance abuse problem, entered the home of his sister-in-law, stole some of her material property, and tried to cash one of her checks in the amount of $118, and was unsuccessful."

Mike, silent, leaned forward over his clasped hands at the defense table, chewed on his lower lip, and then looked up as the judge ruffled the papers in front of him.

"Pursuant to Penal Code section 1385(a), the Court has considered specifically the nature and circumstances of this present felony or felonies, the nature and circumstances of his prior conviction, the history of drug addiction, the lack of history of violence, and the interests of society in general."

Then Judge Ryan slowly read Mike's sentence, item by item:

Eight years in the state penitentiary. That sentence to be suspended, and instead the defendant will spend one year in the county jail, which time he has already served.

The defendant is to be released from jail immediately, to a two-year residential drug rehab program in San Francisco, which he is ordered by the court to successfully complete.

The defendant will remain on probation for five years, during which time any drug use or violation of the law will return him to this court, to fulfill the eight-year penitentiary sentence that has been suspended.

"The Court does believe," announced the judge in a clear, loud voice, "that there is a prospect that this defendant can rehabilitate himself."

The next day, Mike was released to rehab. I wish him Godspeed, and pray that he receives the help he needs.

Lonny Shavelson
Berkeley, California
October 2000

In the first year of the new century, California and New York initiated revolutionary plans for drug rehab. California voters overwhelmingly passed Proposition 36, the Substance Abuse and Crime Prevention Act, "to divert from incarceration into community-based substance abuse treatment programs non-violent defendants . . . charged with simple drug possession or drug use offenses." As of July 2001, some 36,000 additional addicts in California will head to rehab each year, under court order. Likewise, in New York, Chief Judge Judith S. Kaye ordered systemic changes in the courts so that nearly all non-violent drug addicts will be sent to rehab instead of prison. The policy, which will propel some 10,000 arrested addicts annually to treatment, is to be in full effect by 2003.

The backers of Proposition 36 plan a cross-country campaign, with Michigan and Ohio next on the list for citizen initiatives modeled on the one just passed in California. This national paradigm shift from jails toward rehab is the inevitable result of public frustration with years of incarcerating hundreds of thousands of addicts while seeing little improvement in out nation's crisis of drug addiction.

But as this book has shown, good intentions do not assure quality rehab. If Proposition 36 and the New York judicial mandate for treatment are to succeed, the officials putting the plans into action must establish detailed oversight of the treatment programs, provide for improved training and formal certification of rehab counselors, make skilled care readily available for addicts who have additional mental health problems, and aid recovering addicts in job training and housing procurement.

With the implementation of Proposition 36 in California, strict oversight and quality control of the rehab programs will be as important as tightly monitoring the addicts sent to those programs. Unfortunately, a RAND study found that Proposition 36 ". . . does not specify procedures for ensuring the quality of the treatment provided." On a national level, the Center for Substance Abuse Treatment announced (in the same month that Proposition 36 passed) that we still do not have "commonly accepted standards for what constitutes effective substance abuse treatment in the United States." Establishing such standards, and enforcing them, is essential to the success of the new push to rehab both in New York and in California.

Along with not supervising the programs, Proposition 36 fails to monitor the addicts. Frequent drug testing is a crucial component of any rehab program, both to rapidly discover relapses and as a deterrent to drug use. But no Proposition 36 money, says the statute, can be spent on drug testing, with the rationale that every dollar is needed for treatment. This limitation must immediately be changed by the California legislature, which is responsible for implementing the new proposition. As Drug Courts across the country have shown, a swift response to relapse is crucial to keeping addicts on track toward sobriety. A majority of those in rehab will, at some point in time, relapse. Without adequate drug testing, those relapses will be missed until users are again lost in their addictions.

The rehab methods employed by our Drug Courts provide an ideal model for successful drug treatment. Yet during the campaign for Proposition 36 an intense animosity evolved between California's Drug Court judges and the proposition advocates. Dave Fratello, who managed the Proposition 36 campaign, claimed that if Drug Courts were expanded, "the money would go to judges, staff, administrative costs, and monitoring expenses, with little left to pay for actual treatment services . . . Propostion 36 makes it a priority to invest in treatment programs, rather than Drug Courts . . ." Drug Court Judge Ronald P. Kreber fired back that Proposition 36 would be a "death knell" for the Drug Courts. "Under the initiative," said Judge Kleber, "a defendant would have no incentive to accept the authority of the Drug Court. The personality of the addict is lacking in self-discipline, and most would opt for a program that has little or no sanctions." Judge Steven V. Manley, president of the California Association of Drug Court Professionals, pointed out that Drug Courts work because of mandatory testing, immediate sanctions for drug use, frequent appearances in front of the same judge, and close supervision of rehab. "This proposition will cripple and gut the heart of an effective treatment program," said Manley. "Treatment standing alone does not work."

Now that the campaign is over and millions of dollars are to be allocated, wisdom dictates that prior battles be set aside and funds go to rehab systems with the best track records: those established by the Drug Courts. Drug Courts need the funds, and Proposition 36 advocates need the experience and leadership of the Drug Court judges and case managers to guide an additional 36,000 arrested addicts successfully through rehab every year.

In regard to the Drug Courts, California would do well to follow the example of New York. New York's Commission on Drugs and the Courts tracked the results of a number of pilot Drug Treatment Court programs, then made detailed policy recommendations. This contrasts greatly with the indistinct plans for treatment in California.

In New York's new system, Drug Courts will provide "supervision and monitoring of addicted offenders by judges and others throughout the treatment process, continued drug testing and strict systems of sanctions and rewards to motivate defendants to succeed in treatment." California's Proposition 36 offers no more guidance than, "As a condition of probation the court shall require participation in and completion of an appropriate drug treatment program."

Recognizing that drug rehab involves lifestyle changes as well as stopping drug use, the

New York system will coordinate "education, job training, basic health care, or housing assistance. . . . Drug Court case managers and judges will track the progress being made in these areas as well." California's Proposition 36 states only that the court *may* impose requirements such as vocational training. And instead of regular visits with a judge, an arrested addict in a rehab program in California will be monitored only by quarterly reports to the addict's probation officer.

The California proposition limits rehab to one year; New York provides for more than one year if needed. In California, an arrested addict graduates from rehab when there is "reasonable cause to believe that the defendant will not abuse controlled substances in the future." In New York, the addict "must satisfy other requirements likely to encourage a drug-free lifestyle, such as having a job or obtaining a G.E.D. or vocational degree."

In New York's pilot Drug Treatment Court study, only 14 percent of the offenders who participated were arrested again. The re-arrest rate for addicts who did not participate in the special courts was 35 percent.

New York's comprehensive treatment plans have a fighting chance at success, while California's vaguely elaborated system will merely push dysfunctional addicts through poorly functioning rehab programs. But California could emulate its eastern cousin with ease: there are 109 Drug Courts in California with detailed and proven rehab practices, and outstanding success rates. The majority of the $120 million in annual Proposition 36 funds should go to expanding this Drug Court system.

"Now the battle is going to be over implementation," says drug policy reform expert Ethan Nadelmann. "This $120 million [a year] could do a lot of good, or it could be frittered away."

I began the research for this book in 1997, soon after San Francisco announced its new Treatment on Demand plan to offer rehab to all willing drug addicts.

My first contact was with Dr. Larry Meredith, then head of the city's Department of Substance Abuse Services. He referred me to Target Cities Central Intake Unit, where addicts first showed up seeking treatment. At each daily Target Cities meeting I explained my intentions, advising the addicts and counselors that nothing said or done would be published without their consent. Almost uniformly, they graciously allowed me to use any material I found relevant.

From the Target Cities groups, I selected Darlene James, Michael Pagsolingan, and Darrell McAuley to follow as closely as possible when they went to the programs. Later, I met Glenda Janis while observing the street outreach efforts of the Death Prevention Team, and Crystal Holmes through my work at Drug Court. For each of these subjects, I obtained a signed "Release of Confidentiality" that allowed me to use information about them from observations and interviews, and also to receive information about their progress in the programs from counselors and others involved in their care. These confidentiality releases have an "escape clause" stating that at any time the clients (on their own or by recommendation from their counselors) could leave the project if for any reason their participation became detrimental to their recovery. This escape clause was never invoked by any participant.

When I decided to investigate the San Francisco Drug Court, I first met with coordinator Cynthia Caporizzo and Public Defender Jamie Tillotson, who introduced me to Judge Newton Lam and later to Judge Julie Tang. With the agreement of all concerned I was invited to sit in on meetings in the judge's chambers, during which I took detailed notes. By means of a San Francisco Police Department press pass (through the auspices of my photo agency, Impact Visuals), I was able to enter the jail to conduct interviews and photograph there. I obtained media releases signed by the attending sheriffs and by the inmates for all jail interviews.

The information and stories that form the bulk of this book were recorded by on-scene notes of events, and through hundreds of taped interviews with addicts, counselors, heads of programs, administrators, and policy makers.

For the photographs of individuals, I obtained signed model releases. When I photographed in places where groups of people were present, I advised those who wished not to be photographed to move to another side of the room, or to wave me off if I was pointing the camera their way. When at all possible, I also obtained signed model releases from those who are visible in an identifiable way in the background of the images.

All significant characters, with rare exceptions, are referred to by their real names, with their full consent and understanding of the risks that public exposure might bring to them. All felt that the value of having their stories told far exceeded their own personal risks in being exposed as addicts in recovery. Some whom I interviewed requested that I not use their names, and I have given them pseudonyms. However, for every individual in counseling or a public position I used real names. I did not have the chance to review the possible implications—good and bad—of exposure in this book to several minor characters, and have used pseudonyms for them.

Real People, Real Names

W. Jumbé Allen
Dolores Alvarez
Bruce
Francine Buckner
Hansel Cancel
Cliff
Cynthia
Debbie and Vicki
Colin Eaton
Larry Hamilton
James Henderson
Henrietta the Hippo
Crystal Holmes
Darlene James
Glenda Janis
Kenneth

Judge Newton Lam
Steve Maddox
Marillac Mayorga
Marlin Mayorga
Darrell McAuley
Dr. Larry Meredith
Michelle (Michael
    Pagsolingan's sister)
Kathy Meyers
Connie Pagsolingan
    (formerly Connie
    Slattery)
Michael Pagsolingan
Sylvester Palmer
Tony Patchell

Paul (Chapter 5, the house
    meeting)
Charles Perky
Red
Connie Slattery (later
    Connie Pagsolingan)
Geraldine Slattery
Dr. Pablo Stewart
Dave Stewart
Ron Thomas
Tony
Evelyn Wade
Michael Wallace
William

Real People, Changed Names

Alice
Andrew
Billie
Cindy
Deanna Booth
Brian
Carrie

Chris
Darcy
Donna
Gloria
Gomez
Arthur Hudson
Roy Long

Maria
Samantha Matthews
Patricia
Terence
Lara Webb